RETHINKING
THE FALSE CONFESSION
PHENOMENON

A Law Enforcement Perspective

Bradford J. Beyer, Ph.D.

DEFIANCE PRESS
& PUBLISHING

Rethinking the False Confession Phenomenon

Copyright © 2023 by Bradford J. Beyer, Ph.D.
(Defiance Press & Publishing, LLC)

Printed in the United States of America

10 9 8 7 6 5 4 3 2 1

All rights reserved. No part of this publication may be reproduced, distributed, or transmitted in any form or by any means, including photocopying, recording, or other electronic or mechanical methods, without the prior written permission of the publisher, except in the case of brief quotations embodied in critical reviews and certain other noncommercial uses permitted by copyright law.

This book is a work of non-fiction. The author has made every effort to ensure that the accuracy of the information in this book was correct at the time of the publication. Neither the author nor the publisher nor any other person(s) associated with this book may be held liable for any damages that may result from any of the ideas made by the author in this book.

DEFIANCE PRESS
& PUBLISHING

ISBN-13: 978-1-959677-42-0 (Paperback)
ISBN-13: 978-1-959677-41-3 (eBook)

Published by Defiance Press & Publishing, LLC

Bulk orders of this book may be obtained by contacting Defiance Press & Publishing, LLC. www.defiancepress.com.

Public Relations Dept. – Defiance Press & Publishing, LLC
281-581-9300
pr@defiancepress.com

Defiance Press & Publishing, LLC
281-581-9300
info@defiancepress.com

Table of Contents

INTRODUCTION

CHAPTER 1: Confessions vs. False Confessions: Understanding the Differences and Motivations for Each...1

CHAPTER 2: False Confession Risk Factors: Understanding the Unique Traits of the Subject...29

CHAPTER 3: Insights from Interrogative Specialists: Bringing Balance to the Research...47

CHAPTER 4: Rethinking the Innocence Project Statistics...........................63

CHAPTER 5: Examining the Perspectives of Academia, Expert Witnesses, and Advocates..99

CHAPTER 6: Reexamining the Frequency of False Confessions.................113

CHAPTER 7: Does Law Enforcement Actually Trick Subjects Into Waiving Their Rights?...129

CHAPTER 8: Reconsidering Law Enforcement's Ability to Identify Deception..141

CHAPTER 9: How Long Are Subjects Kept in the Interrogation Room?....155

CHAPTER 10: How Far Will Law Enforcement Officers Really Go to Get a Confession?...167

CHAPTER 11: Why Do Criminal Subjects Truthfully Confess?.................185

CHAPTER 12: Can Any One Particular Interrogative Technique Cause a False Confession?...241

CHAPTER 13: Reconsidering the Reid Technique's Impact on False Confessions..259

CHAPTER 14: Re-Evaluating the Effects of False Evidence on False Confessions..273

CHAPTER 15: Is Law Enforcement Capable of Differentiating Between True and False Confessions?..307

CHAPTER 16: Reassessing the Impact of Confessions on Criminal Subjects 325

CHAPTER 17: Would Law Enforcement Officers Truthfully Disclose Their False Confession Experiences? 343

CHAPTER 18: Is the University Laboratory a Good Place to Test the False Confession Phenomenon? 349

CHAPTER 19: Examining the Motivations of Academic Researchers, Expert Witnesses, and Advocates 369

CHAPTER 20: The Problems Facing Academic Researchers, Expert Witnesses, and Advocates 387

CHAPTER 21: Final Thoughts..399

REFERENCES 409

This book is written in honor of my parents who have always taught me to be a good person and to not make waves. While I will always be indebted to them for their efforts at instilling in me the first tenet, I have never really agreed with them on the second.

*Question with boldness even the existence of a God;
because, if there be one, he must more approve of the
homage of reason, than that of blind-folded fear.*

– Thomas Jefferson

*Fortunately, some are born with spiritual immune systems
that sooner or later give rejection to the illusory worldview
grafted upon them from birth through social conditioning. They
begin sensing that something is amiss, and start looking for
answers. Inner knowledge and anomalous outer experiences
show them a side of reality others are oblivious to, and so
begins their journey of awakening. Each step of the journey
is made by following the heart instead of following the crowd
and by choosing knowledge over the veils of ignorance.*

– Henri Bergson

Only dead fish go with the flow.

– Anonymous

INTRODUCTION

As I begin this text, I am well into my twenty-sixth year of service within the United States Government. The last twenty-two years have been spent as a Special Agent working within the Department of Justice, fifteenth years as a certified polygraph examiner, and five years as a Crisis Negotiator. As a result of my service, training, and professional responsibilities, I have become skilled, like many of my professional law enforcement counterparts, in speaking with a wide array of individuals, to include those who have violated the law. My passion about speaking to criminal subjects and those in crisis began relatively early on in my career.

My first assignment as a Special Agent was in a small office in the Northeast. Shortly after my first year, I received a telephone call from a local bank security specialist who informed me that one of the bank's Teller Supervisors had come up $10,000 short in reconciling her till. As no one else had access to these funds, the bank had reason to believe that this young lady had stolen the money. At that point my training agent and I visited the woman's home and asked to speak with her regarding the money that had gone missing. The woman was in her early twenties and spoke with a thick foreign accent as she had previously immigrated to the United States. While sitting at her kitchen table, we began asking general background questions and learned that she was married and had recently given birth to the couple's first child.

Upon questioning her about the money that had gone missing from her till, the young woman readily advised that as the Teller Supervisor, no other person would have had access to the money. Still, she vehemently denied taking the money. When asked where the money could have gone if she was the only one who had access to it, the woman offered that she had no explanation as to where the money went. When asked directly if she had taken the money, the woman again denied taking any portion of the missing money. In short, she agreed that the money was missing; she confirmed that she was the only one who had access to the money; she could offer no explanation for where it could have gone, and she was positive that she had not taken the money. At this time I asked her a question that would ultimately change the trajectory of my professional career, "Would you be willing to take a polygraph test?" Having had no experience with the polygraph technique up to that point, this question was born from the combination of the woman's illogical lack of an explanation for the missing money and my uncertainty as to where else to go in my line of questioning. The woman then agreed to submit to a polygraph examination, and I advised her that I would make arrangements and get back in touch with her.

Upon returning to my office, I immediately identified our division's polygraph examiner, looked up his number, and called him. I introduced myself and explained the situation to him. I had concerns about asking for polygraph assistance in this matter as I was a new agent in the division; I had no familiarity with the polygraph or the process for requesting a test, and the recognized loss to the bank was only $10,000, a paltry sum for a federal investigation. Yet, the examiner readily agreed to make the two-hour trip to my office to administer the young teller a polygraph examination. Schedules were coordinated with both the examiner and the teller and a polygraph date was set.

On the day of the examination, I met the teller and her husband in our lobby and introduced her to the polygraph examiner. I then exited the room and took a position outside the door so that I could observe the security camera monitor mounted outside of the room and attempt to listen through the door. As a new agent I had no experience with the polygraph technique, and I was anxious to pick up any insights that this unorthodox observation method was able to offer. Although I could not hear much through the door, I was able to grasp the overall progress of the examination several hours later when I heard the examiner loudly and rhetorically ask the teller, "You know what the problem is with your whole damn generation? You're just like that son of a bitch." Looking to the security monitor, I was able to observe that the examiner was pointing to the photograph of President Clinton hanging in the interview room.

It did not take a ton of experience at that point to realize that the polygraph examiner had reached his limit, and he soon exited the interview room. He then advised me that the teller had thoroughly failed the polygraph examination and that he was absolutely certain that she had taken the money. However, his interrogation (or what many polygraph examiners refer to as 'post-test' questioning) consisted of an incessant loop of the following inquiries:

Examiner:	The money was in your till that morning?
Teller:	Yes.
Examiner:	Now the money is missing from your till?
Teller:	Yes.
Examiner:	No one else had access to that money?
Teller:	Yes.
Examiner:	No one else could have taken that money?
Teller:	Yes.
Examiner:	So, you took the money?
Teller:	No.

Having reached his maximum level of frustration, the examiner asked if I would like to come in the room and try speaking with the teller. I readily agreed and followed the examiner into the room. I was not sure how I would be able to help as I was a new agent with little interview and interrogative experience. Still, I took a seat next to the teller as the polygraph examiner took a seat behind the desk. In the woman's presence, the examiner reviewed for me the results of the polygraph examination and the teller's inability to explain where the missing money had gone. Feeling for this woman's predicament, I moved closer to her and began explaining that I understood why she had taken the money. My explanation sounded something like this: "I know that you are a new mother. I also know that diapers and formula are very expensive. While I know that you would much rather be home with your baby, you are forced to work to provide for your young family." I then decided to cast blame on the bank for putting her in such dire straits by saying something similar to: "Although what you did was wrong, the bank also has some responsibility in this. If they actually paid you for what you are worth as a Teller Supervisor, you would not have to steal to provide for your child." I then offered that her motivation to take this money really had more to do with the failures of the bank than it did with her. Lastly, I added that any person who would claim that they wouldn't steal a loaf of bread to feed their family is either a liar or has simply never been that hungry.

As I talked softly and reassuringly to her, I began to feel that a sense of rapport was developing between us. My suspicion was dramatically confirmed when she lifted her head, looked into my face, and motioning toward the examiner asked me, "Why are you so nice and he is such an asshole?" Fighting the urge to smile, I responded that this matter was my case and I cared more about the outcome than the examiner.

The discussion continued in this manner for a little while longer until the idea had been floated to bring the woman's husband into the room. Upon being escorted into the room, the examiner and I explained to him the situation, and he sat on the floor as I continued to speak with his wife. As I reiterated my previous points, the teller's husband began to sob and began begging his wife to be honest with me. It became readily apparent that this young teller was in control of the spousal relationship. Shortly thereafter, the teller bowed her head and began praying in her native language. She then looked up at me and confessed to taking the money. She explained that she had stolen the money for the exact reasons that I had given and that she was simply trying to provide for her family.

At this time, the examiner asked me to escort the husband back to the lobby as he collected a written statement from the teller. While in the lobby, the husband expressed his concerns over what was going to happen to his wife, and I promised that I would work with him and his wife to resolve this matter in the best way that I could. Shortly thereafter, the examiner brought the teller back into the lobby and both the teller and her husband thanked and hugged me as they exited our office, and I promised to contact them in the next couple of days. After their departure, the examiner complimented me on my interviewing style and asked if I had ever considered joining the polygraph program.

I am confident that this story is not unique to me. Many in law enforcement, especially those who specialize in interviewing, interrogation, crisis negotiation, and polygraph, likely have a similar story. They have come to realize that they have a gift of relating to others and have correctly identified that they have a knack for getting others to open up to them at their darkest times. For countless numbers of us, this is not just the way we make a living, but an actual calling.

Unfortunately, the interrogation profession has been maligned repeatedly and consistently over the last few decades. Moreover, there is a profound anti-law enforcement bias in the United States at the time that this book is being written. It is therefore not surprising that the incessant attack on law enforcement has also made its way to our nation's interrogation rooms. This attack on law enforcement interrogators and the manner in which they question criminal subjects has been strengthened by the work of academics, defense attorneys, the media, and wrongful conviction advocacy groups, such as the Innocence Project. All of these entities have focused their sights on the invaluable law enforcement technique of criminal interrogation, and their preferred weapon of choice is the false confession phenomenon. The ubiquity of this unidirectional war can be readily identified by browsing Netflix.

Programs like *Making a Murderer, The Confession Tapes, The Innocent Man, When They See Us, The Innocence Files,* and *Amanda Knox*. Such productions lend credence to the belief that people are not only wrongfully convicted on a routine basis, but far too often their convictions stem from their own false confessions.

Hollywood, advocacy groups, and academic researchers have helped to foster the belief that people routinely confess to crimes they did not actually commit. Statistics have been carelessly thrown around to not only support this conclusion, but to elevate it to a point of undisputed fact. Academic research projects purportedly prove the ease in which this phenomenon occurs. Even a cursory review of the academic literature quickly reveals the underlying premise that law enforcement interrogators—as well as their twisted and manipulative 'tactics'—are responsible for pushing innocents into falsely accepting responsibility for criminal wrongdoing. Unfortunately, law enforcement officers have either been unwilling or incapable of fighting back against the inherent bias evidenced by defense attorneys, wrongful conviction advocacy groups, and academics. As a result, academic researchers have largely controlled the dialogue surrounding the false confession phenomenon. The outcome of this one-sided discussion has been the rise of the false confession expert witness who is repeatedly called upon, and handsomely paid, to question the methodologies of law enforcement interrogators and the confessions they elicit. For those prosecutors and law enforcement officers who have not yet experienced the arguments and conclusions of the false confession expert witness, just wait. Your time is coming.

My first experience with a false confession expert witness occurred six years into my tenure as a federal law enforcement polygraph examiner. I was called upon to conduct a polygraph examination of a young Native American father whose 3-month-old daughter died while in his care. The father agreed to be examined by means of the polygraph regarding any involvement that he may have had in his daughter's death. He was then transported to my office for the test. Prior to the examination, he explained to me that he had propped the child up on the bed with her bottle before stepping outside to smoke a cigarette. After approximately fifteen minutes, he got a strange feeling that something was wrong. He then entered the bedroom and found his daughter face down on the floor with a condom lodged in her throat.

The father vehemently maintained that he did not cause his daughter's death. He explained that he and his wife had sex that morning before she left for work. Afterward, he threw his condom in the bedroom trash can. The father then theorized that his puppy must have pulled the condom out of the trash can and left it on the floor. The father further suggested that his 3-month-old daughter must have rolled off the bed, landed on the floor, retrieved the condom, placed it in her mouth and suffocated. Based on this story, it was not a surprise to any involved that the father failed the polygraph examination.

After the examination, I informed the father that he had failed the examination. We began discussing what really happened to his daughter and the role that he played in her death. Only a few memorable statements came out of this line of questioning. For example, the father noted that while it is "possible" that he may have killed his daughter, he did not recall doing so. In addition, he stated that while he is certain that he did not kill his daughter willfully, there was a "fifty-fifty chance" that he may have killed his daughter while he was possessed as an unknown person may have placed evil spirits in his home as a means of stealing his land. Some reading these statements may assume that the subject was mentally ill, or even delusional. In reality, the subject did not appear mentally ill, and his mental health was never questioned. Instead, the subject and I ended up discussing various Native American beliefs as he was Native American, and I had a roommate in the U.S. Army who was from the Cherokee Tribe in New Mexico. The subject also referenced the Native American lore of "skin walking" and the horror movie *Insidious* as a means of explaining how the death of his daughter may have been the result of supernatural events.

Shortly after, the subject asked to speak with an attorney and be driven home. These requests thereby ended the interrogation. As many of my professional counterparts would likely concur, I did not consider any of the subject's statements to be a confession. In actuality, I felt as if I had done a poor job of getting a clearly guilty subject to admit his wrongdoing. However, some months later I learned that the subject had been charged with killing his daughter and, rather than pleading guilty, was planning to take the matter to trial. I also learned that a well-known false confession researcher and expert witness would be testifying on behalf of the subject. More specifically, I was informed that this expert witness was seeking to educate the jury about the false confession phenomenon. The expert was also planning to allege that I had utilized coercive interrogative techniques that have been shown to lead to false confessions. Lastly, the expert planned to inform the jury that the subject had dispositional risk factors that would make him ripe for a false confession.

What was particularly noteworthy to me in this situation was the fact that neither the polygraph examination, nor the post-test interrogation, were recorded. Still, this expert witness was more than willing to walk into the courtroom and offer testimony about what I had done in the interrogation room. This greatly angered me. An expert witness for the defense was ready to criticize the way in which I do my job despite having no direct evidence on which to base his claims. I was also disheartened by the question posed to me by the Assistant United States Attorney (AUSA) charged with prosecuting this case. In anticipation of the upcoming motions, and the potential testimony of this expert witness, the AUSA asked me if I had any familiarity with the false confession phenomenon. Sadly, I had to report that I had little to no knowledge about this subject. At this point, I feverishly began digesting information about false confessions.

By the end of the ensuing legal battle, the expert witness was not permitted to testify in this case due to the lack of scientific basis for his anticipated testimony. The subject was sentenced to two life sentences for his crimes. While both decisions were correct, I was left with a drive to learn more about false confessions. My interest in this topic eventually led me to a Ph.D. in Psychology and a subsequent dissertation relating to false confessions and how federal law enforcement polygraph examiners interrogate criminal subjects. I have since concluded that there exists an academic bias against law enforcement interrogators and the techniques they use to question criminal subjects. This bias, which is based on inherently flawed research, has led to countless law enforcement officers being attacked on the stand and incessant efforts to suppress legally-obtained confessions.

To date, the vast majority of research has been conducted within the academic setting by individuals who have little to no experience in actually interviewing or interrogating criminal subjects. Yet these are the same individuals referred to by our legal system as 'expert witnesses.' Moreover, law enforcement officers, who have spent a lifetime interviewing and interrogating criminal subjects to the betterment of our communities, have been portrayed as torturers, con artists, and single-minded automatons who value confessions over truth, and will do anything to accomplish that goal. As such, this book has been written to bring a much-needed balance to the existing false confession research.

In this text, I will provide readers with an extensive outline of what academics, through their research efforts, claim about the false confession phenomenon and the likely causes behind false confessions. Through this outline, it will become readily apparent how academic researchers perceive law enforcement officers and their interrogative methods. I will also discuss my own original research into false confessions from the viewpoint of state and federal interrogative specialists as well as the most effective methods they use to question criminal subjects. Lastly, I will identify and discuss various false assumptions that are routinely made by academics, expert witnesses, and wrongful conviction advocates about the false confession phenomenon. In fair warning, the information provided in this book will ruffle many academic feathers. It is a marked departure from what many *think* they know about criminal interrogation and confessions. It may be inherently uncomfortable for those who have made a handsome living maligning the methods and reputations of honorable law enforcement officers to learn that they have gotten it wrong for all of these years. In short, while some may disagree with what is presented in this book, an open and honest discussion about false confessions from the viewpoint of real-world law enforcement interrogators is long overdue.

CHAPTER 1

Confessions vs. False Confessions:
Understanding the Differences and Motivations for Each

This book has been written to help law enforcement officers, prosecutors, judges, jurors, and others within the legal process to more fully understand the false confession phenomenon. More specifically, this information is being provided from the unique viewpoint of a criminal interrogator. In many respects, this work will be a significant departure from what many in academia have typically proclaimed in their journal articles or during their expert witness testimony. However, this book was also designed to educate laypersons about the process of criminal interrogation and the counterintuitive decision of some innocent citizens to falsely confess to crimes they did not actually commit. It is therefore important to first understand the differences between truthful confessions and false confessions as well as their underlying motivations.

Admissions

Throughout the false confession research, the concepts of confessions and admissions are often thrown together. However, it is important to understand the difference between these two types of criminal disclosures. In the field of criminal interrogation, it is possible for a criminal subject to admit to actions that may be suggestive of guilt, but fall short of an actual confession.

1

Gudjonsson (2010) identified that an admission does not involve a subject accepting responsibility for the crime under investigation and/or providing a detailed narrative account of their actions. An example of an admission may include such things as the subject admitting that they were only present at the time of the offense; they were merely responsible for obtaining the weapon used for the offense, or that they simply have direct knowledge of who actually committed the offense. While this type of information may potentially benefit police in their investigation of the crime, it is not an actual acceptance of responsibility for the crime. As explained by Gudjonsson, admissions do not amount to a proper confession. Unfortunately, it is often difficult within the false confession research to distinguish between admissions and confessions: Different studies may employ different operational definitions for these terms and researchers frequently fail to make a distinction between these concepts (Gudjonsson, 2010). In short, the inability or refusal to differentiate between these terms can be equated to the lumping together of 'known cases' and 'presumptive cases' into the umbrella category of 'COVID-19 cases' during the coronavirus pandemic. As will be discussed later, the merging of admissions and confession into a single category may cause the overall number of confessions, both true and false, to appear higher than they actually are.

Confessions

According to 18 U.S.C. § 3501 and criminal law scholars, a confession is defined as an admission of guilt to a criminal act, or a statement that proves to be self-incriminating (Joselow, 2019). More broadly speaking, Drizin and Leo (2004) define a confession as "any statements which tend to incriminate a suspect or a defendant in a crime" (p. 892). Kassin and Gudjonsson (2004) more narrowly define a confession as "a detailed written or oral statement in which a person admits to having committed some transgression, often acknowledging guilt for a crime" (p. 35). These various definitions have one key factor in common—the admission of wrongdoing. However, confessions are not relegated to the realm of criminal justice. In fact, the concept of confession has been found to be important in three specific areas of human interaction: religion, psychotherapy, and the criminal justice system (Kassin & Gudjonsson, 2004). Within the first two contexts, confession can often be considered a form of spiritual or psycho-emotional cleansing. For instance, a confession occurring within a place of religious worship or before God is often associated with the cleansing of souls. As a Lutheran, I grew up reciting the "Brief Order for Confession and Forgiveness" each Sunday in the Lutheran Book of Worship (1978) in which the congregation in unison stated:

> We confess that we are in bondage to sin and cannot free our-
> selves. We have sinned against you in thought, word, and deed,
> by what we have done and by what we have left undone. We
> have not loved you with our whole heart; we have not loved our
> neighbors as ourselves. For the sake of your Son, Jesus Christ,
> have mercy on us. Forgive us, renew us, and lead us, so that we
> may delight in your will and walk in your ways, to the glory of
> your holy name. Amen (p. 77).

This public statement of wrongdoing was followed by our Pastor explaining that God had mercifully given His Son to die for us and, for His sake, God has forgiven all of our sins. The Lutheran religion is not alone in this act of confession and forgiveness.

Within the context of psychotherapy, confession is often associated with the patient's healing and therapeutic release of painful experiences and/or poor behaviors (Kassin & Gudjonsson, 2004). For example, Nichols and Zax (1977) explained that the emotional "letting go," or catharsis, associated with the expressing of denied emotions or issues is an important therapeutic device for relieving emotional suffering. Similarly, Pennebaker (1989) noted that—from a psychological perspective—confession can actually help to decrease rates of disease, ruminations, and various other psychological difficulties. In short, the fields of religion and psychology believe that confession ultimately benefits the confessor. The same is not widely held when it comes to the criminal justice system however.

Within the criminal justice system, a confession rendered by a criminal subject is often construed as nothing more than a damning form of evidence that will likely be used against the subject in future criminal proceedings. Unlike religion and psychotherapy, it is frequently suggested that because criminal confessions can be used to prosecute the subject, confessions are not in the best interest of the defendant (Bernhard & Miller, 2018; Leo, 2017; Redlich, Kulish, & Steadman, 2011). Some even argue that confessions actually offer zero benefit to the confessor (Schatz, 2018). For this reason, the criminal confession and the anticipated repercussions associated with such admissions of guilt, stand in stark contrast to religious and psychotherapeutic admissions of wrongdoing. As will be discussed later, this belief that a confession in the criminal justice context only harms the confessor is but one of a long list of biases held by many false confession researchers.

The Power of the Confession and Its Legal Impact

In addition to the legal repercussions, the sheer evidentiary power associated with a criminal subject's admission of guilt places the criminal confession in a unique category. Confessions have been identified as a profoundly powerful form of evidence (Frenda, Berkowitz, Loftus, & Fenn, 2016) and have historically stood as somewhat of a 'gold standard' in proving a criminal defendant's guilt (Kassin, 2012; Lackey, 2020; Perillo & Kassin, 2011). Any law enforcement officer or criminal interrogator who has walked into the prosecutor's office with a signed statement of guilt from the subject can attest to the power of such a document. In fact, the criminal confession has been found to be so strong that Meissner and Kassin (2002) have described it as a prosecutorial weapon of such power that it can impact not only the outcome of a specific criminal case, but the criminal justice system as a whole. Joselow (2019) cited various other academic researchers who have characterized confessions "as the "most damaging type of evidence," a "prosecutor's most potent weapon," and so convincing that juries will commonly convict without any additional evidence of guilt" (p. 641). It has also been suggested that the strength of the subject's confession will actually overshadow other

4

forms of evidence, including DNA evidence (Waxman, 2020).

Despite what some may consider to be the unfair level of consideration afforded to confession evidence, confessions greatly benefit the criminal justice system in two important ways: a) armed with a confession, prosecutors are significantly more likely to obtain a criminal conviction; and b) being that the criminal subject has already confessed to their crime, victims and witnesses are less likely to be called upon to offer testimony during court proceedings (Kebbell, Hurren, & Roberts, 2006). Costanzo (as cited by Russano et al., 2005), also noted that confessions benefit the entire criminal justice process by encouraging those who have rendered a confession to plead guilty, thereby streamlining the legal process and alleviating the pressures associated with an overtaxed criminal justice system. For these reasons, it is not difficult to see why confessions are so strongly pursued by law enforcement officers and why they are so highly valued by prosecutors.

As noted by Conti (1999), as far back as the 17th Century, confessions were treated as a conviction; physical torture was routinely employed to obtain confessions from criminal subjects; and all confessions, regardless of the manner in which they were extracted, were admitted as evidence before the court. The importance of confession evidence stems from the fact that confession evidence is extremely difficult to defend against at trial, and juries are more likely to return a guilty verdict when confession evidence exists (Leo & Davis, 2010). In essence, "confessions are often as good as convictions" (Wilford & Wells, 2018, p. 159). An argument could therefore be made that the war against law enforcement interrogations stems from the very confessions they elicit. Simply put, defense attorneys have a difficult time defending their clients after they have already admitted their wrongdoing to police in the form of a handwritten statement or recorded confession. As such, their only option is to attack the officers that obtained the confession and/or the interrogative methods they employed.

Even law enforcement officers can surely empathize with the underlying apprehension a defense attorney must feel when they are assigned a criminal case, only to find that the subject has already confessed to police. Right from the outset, this realization greatly decreases the options available to the defense attorney. Simply put, "confessions are damning to a defense" (Wilford & Wells, 2018, p. 159). The starkness of this realization can be seen in the words of Ofshe and Leo (as cited by Trocino, 2016), "defense lawyers are prone to succumb to a notion of hopelessness when facing a client who confessed" (p. 91). Similarly, Schatz (2018) cited the court in *People v. Cahill* noting that the "confession operates as a kind of evidentiary bombshell which shatters the defense" (p. 649). In light of these positions, the defense really has no other option but to attack the voluntariness of the confession. This is why the defense attorney immediately and routinely questions the law enforcement officer on the stand about how long the defendant was in the interrogation room, how small the interrogation room was, whether the defendant was free to leave, whether the officer's gun was showing during the interrogation, whether the officer yelled at the defendant, et cetera. Because of the confession, the defense lawyer has no viable alternative to defend their client other than to make it appear as if the interrogator had coerced an innocent subject into falsely confessing. As I will discuss in reviewing the false confession research, the conclusions reached by academic researchers offer defense attorneys the ability to attack *every* confession, not just the one currently before the court.

Interviews vs. Interrogations

If a confession is to be used against a criminal subject at trial, the confession must be freely and voluntarily given (Kassin, 2008; Kassin et al., 2010; Redlich, 2004; Woody & Forrest, 2009). To more fully understand the extent to which a person's admission of guilt was voluntary, it becomes necessary to understand the manner in which confessions are obtained. The questioning of criminal subjects during a law enforcement investigation can be broken down into two main categories: interviews and interrogations. John Reid and Associates (2016), one of the premier firms dedicated to interview and interrogation instruction, defined an interview as a relatively informal question and answer session with an individual related to a criminal matter. This can include victims and witnesses as well as subjects. The questioning during an interview is non-accusatory and gauged at gathering information from the individual, while simultaneously assessing the interview subject's level of credibility (Kassin, 2008; Newring & O'Donohue, 2008). During an interview, the subject is generally asked to provide their version of events with little prompting from the investigator (Moston & Stephenson, 1992).

Unlike an interview, an interrogation is typically a more formalized and accusatory manner of questioning in which the investigator attempts to elicit truthful information relating to the criminal matter being investigated once the subject has been identified as deceptive (Kassin et al., 2007). In academic research, an interrogation is routinely highlighted as a "guilt-presumptive" process (Gudjonsson, Sigurdsson, Sigurdardottir, Steinthorsson, & Sigurdardottir, 2014; Joselow, 2019; Kassin, 2005; Leo, 2007). In other words, law enforcement officers go into an interrogation believing that the subject is guilty. While this is frequently presented as being indicative of the officer's bias, in reality it is a logical and critical antecedent as there would be no reason to interrogate a person who is believed to have no involvement in the criminal matter under investigation. What would be the ultimate goal of such questioning? Why would a law enforcement officer waste their time asking a person if they committed the crime if they don't believe the person actually committed the crime? From a medical perspective, wouldn't it be necessary for the doctor to believe that the patient's arm is broken before ordering an x-ray? Does the medical literature breathlessly refer to the x-ray process as "fracture-presumptive"? So yes, the interrogator must believe that the subject is guilty of the crime being investigated. An interrogation therefore involves an investigator's attempts to persuade the subject to provide accurate and truthful information relating to their involvement in the criminal act (John Reid & Associates, 2016).

Academic researchers, expert witnesses, and advocacy groups often operate under the premise that interrogations are initiated on nothing more than the gut instinct of the detective or the misguided belief that law enforcement officers, through their Reid training, can accurately identify deception.

Still, it cannot be overlooked that an interrogation is rarely the first step in an investigation. Instead, the evidence collected during the course of the investigation may ultimately determine whether a person is selected for interrogation (Newring & O'Donohue, 2008). In the simplest of terms, interviews and interrogations represent a process of inquiry marked by increasingly more persuasive questioning techniques. However, it is the interrogation and the techniques employed during the interrogation portion of the questioning process that have raised concerns by numerous false confession researchers (Guyll et al., 2013; Kassin et al., 2010; Bradford & Goodman-Delahunty, 2008; Klaver et al., 2008; Drizin & Colgan, 2004; Ofshe & Leo, 1997). Some of this concern stems from the historical and unenlightened manner in which criminal subjects were questioned.

In the past, law enforcement officers employed a form of questioning identified as the 'third degree' in which physical and emotional pain was inflicted upon a criminal subject in an attempt to obtain a confession (Kassin & Gudjonsson, 2004). However, U.S. courts have come to reject confessions obtained in such a manner (Kassin, 2005). As a result, law enforcement has since chosen to use more professional and psychologically-based questioning methods (Conti, 1999; Klaver et al., 2008; Narchet et al., 2011). According to Kostelnik and Reppucci (2009), the most commonly cited and most widely disseminated training manual on the interviewing and interrogation of criminal subjects is the Reid Technique. In this technique, law enforcement officers are instructed through a nine-step interrogative process how to socially influence subjects by confronting them with their guilt, refusing to accept denials, offering them sympathy and face-saving explanations for their criminal acts, and then having them document their confession in a written statement (Inbau et al., 2001). While this technique was instrumental in the collective jettisoning of physical and emotional pain in exchange for more psychological approaches (Schatz, 2018), Ofshe and Leo (1997) assert that the Reid Technique is merely a means of injuring the subject without actually leaving a mark. Similarly, Trocino (2016) noted that the new techniques used by law enforcement are "psychologically aggressive" and added that, "The techniques of coercion have evolved from the rack and the thumbscrew to psychological manipulation and coercion that leaves no visible scars" (p.89). In short, it is posited by many in the current academic literature that the law enforcement interrogators of today continue to abuse the subject, but they have gotten much better at hiding evidence of the abuse. While it is difficult to overlook the underlying bias inherent in these positions, these beliefs begin to set the stage for the academic war against law enforcement interrogation.

False Confessions

Throughout the academic literature, readers are constantly reminded that while criminal confessions are powerful, they are also fallible. Simply put, criminal subjects sometimes confess to crimes they did not actually commit (Chapman, 2013). As those who interrogate criminal subjects may know, there are four possible outcomes to a criminal interrogation. Kassin and Gudjonsson (2004) categorized these outcomes as true confessions, false confession, true denials, and false denials. True confessions occur when a truly guilty subject admits to their criminal wrongdoing. False confessions occur when a truly innocent subject falsely accepts responsibility for a crime they did not actually commit. True denials occur when an innocent subject honestly denies their involvement in a criminal act. Lastly, false denials occur when a truly guilty subject falsely claims that they were not involved in the criminal activity under investigation.

According to some false confession experts, it is inherently difficult to identify which type of statement has been provided by a subject. This uncertainty poses a problem for the criminal justice system (Kassin & Gudjonsson, 2004). It has been posited that both true and false denials are not overly critical, as they do not necessarily lead to criminal repercussions for the subject. In other words, a criminal subject is not likely to face punishment for denying their involvement, regardless of whether they are lying or telling the truth. To the contrary, some have suggested that both true and false confessions increase the likelihood that judges and juries will arrive at a guilty verdict (Kassin et al., 2010). Put another way, truthfully or falsely confessing increases the likelihood of successful prosecution. A guilty verdict, in the case of a true confession, demonstrates that the criminal justice system has worked appropriately. Conversely, a guilty verdict, in light of a false confession, can only be considered a travesty of justice.

Case Law Relating to the Admissibility of Confession Evidence

Because confession evidence is so powerful, judicial concern has arisen over the fact that there appears to be an overreliance on confession evidence by juries. As a result, a series of judicial decisions and safeguards have been reached in an attempt to exclude unreliable confessions from being brought before the court as evidence, thereby minimizing the possibility of a wrongful conviction (Kassin et al., 2010). A key safeguard within the U.S. criminal justice system relates to the legal question of whether confession evidence can be presented at trial (Kassin & Gudjonsson, 2004). A great number of legal opinions have helped to shape this question throughout American history. For example, in *Bram v. United States* (1897), the U.S. Supreme Court ruled that for a confession to be admitted as evidence before the Court, the confession must not have been elicited by threat, violence, or any direct or implied promises. The Supreme Court later applied these same conditions to state courts in the case of *Brady v. United States* (1970).

The Supreme Court further addressed the issue of confessions in the case of *Brown v. Mississippi* (1936). In this case, three Black male subjects were taken into custody by police at which time they were denied counsel and then threatened, beaten, and tortured until they each signed a written confession. In *Brown*, the Supreme Court reversed the convictions and ruled that any confession evidence that is obtained through torture and brutality must not be entered as evidence before the court. Four years later, the Supreme Court similarly addressed the role of mental abuse in obtaining confessions in the case of *Chambers v. Florida* (1940). In this case, Robert Darsey, an elderly white man, was robbed and murdered in Pompano Beach, Florida. During a roundup of between 25 and 40 black men, Chambers and his three co-defendants were transported to the Dade County Jail in Miami, Florida, where they were subjected to prolonged interrogation and circumstances designed to inspire terror and encourage confessions. The Supreme Court eventually overturned the convictions of Chambers and his co-defendants and ruled that the prolonged interrogation of these men not only violated their 14th Amendment right to due process, but also raised concerns that their admissions of guilt were compelled and possibly false. In another landmark decision, the Supreme Court ruled in the case of *Culombe v. Connecticut* (1961), that while no clear-cut litmus test exists for the admission of a confession into evidence, such evidence should be excluded if it is obtained by physical violence, a threat of harm or punishment, promises of leniency or prosecutorial immunity, and when the subject is not notified that they have the constitutional right to counsel and to remain silent.

In *Haynes v. Washington* (1963), Haynes was arrested and questioned by police for approximately 16 hours about his involvement in a robbery. Despite his repeated requests, Haynes was denied an opportunity to call an attorney or his wife until he cooperated with law enforcement by providing a written confession. While Haynes was convicted based on his subsequent confession, the Supreme Court overturned his conviction and ruled that his will was overborne and his confession was compelled by a coercive environment and inducements created by law enforcement officers. *Haynes* represented another example of the Supreme Court evaluating the voluntariness of a confession based on a due process standard, this time based on the fact that Haynes was held incommunicado and continuously interrogated in a coercive environment. A year later, in *Escobedo v. Illinois* (1964), the Supreme Court ruled that criminal subjects have the right to counsel during law enforcement interrogations according to the Sixth Amendment.

The rulings in *Culombe* and *Escobedo* served as a precursor to the ruling put forth by the Supreme Court in the landmark decision of *Miranda v. Arizona* (1966). In this case, the Court determined that when a criminal subject is taken into custody, they must be informed of their constitutional rights to silence and to counsel. Now known as the "*Miranda* Warnings," law enforcement officers are required to advise subjects of the previously noted constitutional rights through statements such as: a) you have the right to remain silent; b) anything you say can be used against you in court; c) you have the right to an attorney; and d) if you cannot afford an attorney, one will be appointed for you if you wish (*Miranda v. Arizona,* 1966). While the exact wording of these warnings may vary between law enforcement jurisdictions (Kassin & Gudjonsson, 2004), they are all designed to ensure that the criminal subject has voluntarily and willingly, and with the full knowledge of the meaning of each of these warnings, agreed to speak with a law enforcement officer—thereby permitting any subsequent statements they make to be admitted as evidence before the court. At present, the currently recognized constitutional protections preventing the admission of an involuntary confession as evidence before the court are based upon the Fifth Amendment's privilege against compelled self-incrimination and the Due Process Clause of the Fourteenth Amendment (Joselow, 2019).

Types of False Confessions

Throughout the course of this text, I will outline a number of false assumptions regarding the phenomenon of false confessions. Still, it must be made abundantly clear that innocent subjects *do* sometimes confess to crimes they did not commit. However, not all false confessions are the same and not all can be attributed to the actions of law enforcement interrogators. Three types of false confessions are commonly discussed in the existing academic literature.

Taxonomy of False Confessions

Based on their review of false confession cases and social-psychological theory, Kassin and Wrightsman (1985) created a taxonomy of false confessions in which they identified three specific types of false confessions: a) voluntary false confessions; b) coerced-compliant false confessions, and c) coerced-internalized false confessions.

Voluntary False Confessions

A voluntary false confession is a self-incriminating statement that is given with little to no interrogative pressure from law enforcement (Kassin & Wrightsman, 1985). As noted by Gaines (2018), these types of confessions "are offered freely rather than needing to be extracted by the investigator," and "no deceptive or manipulative tactics are required to convince him of the value of confessing" (p. 177). Kassin and Gudjonsson (2004) suggested that voluntary false confessions may occur for a variety of reasons—such as the subject's pathological need for notoriety; a conscious or unconscious desire to be punished in response to the guilt they harbor for previous transgressions; an inability to differentiate reality from fantasy because of mental illness; and/or a desire to protect the truly guilty party. An example of a voluntary false confession can be observed in the case of Josue Ortiz. According to the National Registry of Exonerations (2020), Miguel and Nelson Camacho were gunned down on the streets of Buffalo, New York on November 11, 2004. A few days later, Ortiz, a 22-year-old who was later diagnosed with schizophrenia and bipolar disorder flagged down a police car and confessed to the shooting. As this confession occurred in the absence of any interrogation, it is impossible to blame interrogation techniques for its elicitation.

The American Psychiatric Association (APA) defines schizophrenia as a chronic brain disorder that may include such symptoms as delusions, hallucinations, disorganized speech, and impaired thought processes (APA, 2021). Similarly, the APA defines bipolar disorder as a brain disorder that causes individuals to experience intense emotional fluctuations, marked changes in energy level, and an overall difficulty in functioning (APA, 2021). In light of such diagnoses, Ortiz's mental health condition undoubtedly had a profound influence on his decision to voluntarily confess to police. Still, not everyone who falsely confesses voluntarily is mentally ill. For example, on September 29, 2013, Juan Silva, Sr. voluntarily traveled to the Milwaukee Police Department and confessed to driving the van that had struck and killed a pedestrian the previous day and injured a second pedestrian before driving off. Silva maintained that the rainy weather, his broken windshield wiper, and his decision to look down at his ringing cell phone contributed to the fatal accident. In June 2015, sixteen months after Silva was sentenced to a five-year prison term, a friend of Silva's wife informed police that Silva had falsely confessed to protect his 20-year-old son who had been driving the van at the time of the accident (NRE, 2020). In this instance, it was Silva's desire to protect his son that led to his decision to falsely confess as opposed to any particular interrogative technique.

In my own experience, I can recall an instance in which I was called upon by a local law enforcement agency to conduct a polygraph examination in regard to an individual who had confessed to killing his neighbor. During his confession to local law enforcement officers, he also admitted to stalking and killing many other young women over several years. The local authorities were uncertain as to the veracity of the subject's claims and before dedicating scarce resources to investigating these other unidentified murders, they requested that I conduct a polygraph examination of the subject to determine whether he was being honest about these homicides. After a failed polygraph examination, I interrogated the subject who then admitted that he had made up the stories about the other murders. When asked why he would do this, the subject advised that he had been a loser for his entire life. As such, he thought that if he admitted to killing numerous other women, at least he could claim that he was a successful serial killer. In this particular example, the subject was motivated to confess by a desire to receive notoriety for his prowess in killing multiple women.

As these cases illustrate, some people falsely confess of their own accord. These types of confessions are not caused by law enforcement, nor are they a result of the interrogative techniques that were employed. Therefore, the interrogative practices employed by investigators in these types of voluntary false confession cases, if any, cannot be blamed for causing the false confessions. This raises a very important question in regard to the claims of false confession researchers. More specifically, if the number of known false confessions purportedly represent the tip of a much larger iceberg of unknown false confessions, how many of these unknown false confessions were made voluntarily and therefore are unattributable to police interrogative practices?

Coerced-Compliant False Confessions

It is important to note that not all false confessions are coerced by the interrogative efforts of law enforcement officers (Chapman, 2013). Some confessions occur as a direct result of the interrogative pressure and techniques employed by law enforcement interrogators. For example, coerced-compliant false confessions occur as a direct result of the interrogative inducements of law enforcement officers (Kassin & Wrightsman, 1985). Kassin and Gudjonsson (2004) suggest that these types of false confessions occur for a variety of reasons. They suggest that these types of false confessors are so anxious to escape the horrible environment of the interrogation room that they will say anything just to be let out of the room. This can be observed in the case of Alonzo Smith. Smith was interrogated by detectives of the Chicago Police Department regarding the murder of James Fullilove, a drug dealer who was found in his apartment with his head submerged in a bathtub full of water in January, 1983. During the course of the interrogation, Smith was seated in a metal chair with his hands cuffed behind his back. Two detectives then struck him repeatedly with a nightstick, including multiple strikes between his legs. Smith was also kicked in the abdomen and had a plastic bag, secured with a thick rubber band, placed over his head as the beatings continued (NRE, 2020). Not surprisingly, Smith falsely confessed in response to the horrendously aversive environment created in the interrogation room.

The second motivation for a Coerced-Compliant False Confession, as noted by Kassin and Gudjonsson (2004), is the subject's desire to avoid the specific or implied threats that the interrogator made during the course of the interrogation. An example of such threats can be observed in the case of Daniel Villegas. According to the National Registry of Exonerations (2020), four men were fired upon in El Paso, Texas on April 10, 1993, as part of a drive-by shooting. Villegas was later brought in for questioning. During the interrogation, the detective threatened to take Villegas into the desert and "beat his ass" if he did not admit to his role in the shooting. He also threatened Villegas with the electric chair if he refused to confess. Villegas later reported that he was "terrified out of his mind," and presumably confessed to avoid the very specific threats put forth by the interrogator (NRE, 2020).

According to Kassin and Gudjonsson (2004), the third motivation behind a Coerced-Compliant False Confession relates to the subject's desire to obtain a specific or implied reward offered by the interrogator during the course of the interrogation. This desire to obtain a specific reward can be observed in the wrongful conviction case of Bobby Johnson. On August 1, 2006, Herbert Fields was shot and killed while sitting in his car in New Haven, Connecticut. Investigators assumed that the killing occurred during a robbery attempt. The detective in the ensuing investigation interrogated Johnson. During the inter-rogation, the detective explained to Johnson that he could possibly receive the death penalty for killing Fields, but the detective promised Johnson he would receive probation if he confessed to the shooting. Johnson then confessed to participating in the shooting death of Fields (NRE, 2020). In essence, Johnson confessed in anticipation that he would receive the specified reward of being sentenced to probation in exchange for his confession.

As the aforementioned cases illustrate, subjects who render a Coerced-Compliant False Confession do so as an act of public compliance, believing that the short-term benefits of confession outweigh the long-term costs associ-ated with continued denial (Kassin & Gudjonsson, 2004). Put another way, these types of confessions occur when a subject knows that they are falsely confessing, but they believe that it is in their best interest to do so (Ofshe & Leo, 1997). In the cases highlighted above, the short-term benefit was to escape additional torture, to avoid being beaten by police and subsequent execution via the electric chair, and to receive a sentence of probation. While Perillo and Kassin (2011) suggest that criminal subjects generally confess as an act of social compliance resulting from the perception that there is no other means to escape their current situation but through confession, I would argue that all three of these subjects falsely confessed to avoid physical pain and/or an ultimate death sentence. I would also posit that the overwhelming majority of modern law enforcement professionals would frown upon treating an interrogation subject in such a manner. Lastly, I challenge false confession researchers, expert witnesses, or advocacy group members to identify an interview/interrogation manual in which beating a subject, threatening them with physical violence, or promising them a lesser sentence in exchange for their confession is taught to law enforcement officers. This begs the question: Do interrogations like those outlined above represent acceptable and commonly-applied interrogative techniques, or are they indicative of police malpractice? This is a question that will be discussed in greater detail later in the book.

Coerced-Internalized False Confessions

Unlike coerced-compliant false confessions in which an innocent subject consciously and deliberately arrives at the decision to falsely confess, Coerced-Internalized False Confessions involve a more serious concern. In these types of confessions, vulnerable individuals respond to highly suggestive and pressure-filled interrogative techniques by not only confessing to a crime they did not commit, but actually coming to believe that they are truly responsible for the criminal act, at times creating false memories in the process (Kassin & Wrightsman, 1985). In other words, the use of highly coercive interrogation techniques on criminal subjects who are considered vulnerable due to their low intelligence, mental health issues, high levels of suggestibility, etc. may cause these vulnerable subjects to become convinced that they actually committed the crime for which they are being interrogated. Ofshe (as cited by Gudjonsson et al., 2014) noted that these particular subjects are not only persuaded by police and come to believe that they actually committed the criminal offense, but they are told by interrogators that there are good reasons for why they cannot recall committing the crime. For example, police may offer to the subject that they simply cannot recall committing the crime because of their history of substance abuse, their deficits in memory, or because the event is too traumatic to recall. Still, the extent to which the subject may internalize the confession may ultimately depend on the duration

17

and intensity of the interrogation (Gudjonsson et al., 2014).

In a 2017 article in the *New Yorker*, Rachel Aviv recounts the story of Ada Joann Taylor who falsely confessed to participating with five other innocent subjects in the 1985 rape and murder of Helen Wilson in Beatrice, Nebraska. Taylor was treated by psychologist Wayne Price, per the recommendation of child protective services, so that she could learn to be a better parent. In treating Taylor, Price diagnosed her with borderline personality disorder and recommended that she surrender her parental rights to her daughter. Because of her trust in Price, she followed his recommendation. After Wilson's death, Burdette Searcey, a former Beatrice Police Department officer and hog farmer, was hired as a Gage County Sheriff's Deputy. Searcey took such an interest in solving Wilson's murder that the Sheriff finally assigned him to the investigation. Searcey's fascination with Wilson's death led him to occasionally pull Price over while he was driving so that Searcey could bounce ideas off of Price who not only provided psychological consulting to area law enforcement agencies, but was also considered the resident behavioral expert in the area. Searcey's investigative focus turned to Taylor after some of her friends reported that she seemed nervous after Wilson's death. Eventually, Searcey obtained a warrant for Taylor's arrest.

During a subsequent interrogation, Taylor, who had experienced a great deal of sexual trauma as a child, repeatedly stated that she could not remember what happened that evening and that she had a history of blocking things out, especially things in her childhood. Searcey suggested that Taylor simply did not want to remember what happened. Taylor then requested a counseling session with Price, at which time Price met with Taylor at the jail. Price often informed inmates at the jail that if they relax, their memories will come back in bits and pieces or even in dreams. During multiple interviews, Taylor advised that she could put herself in Wilson's place because of the repeated sexual abuse she experienced as a child. Additional statements seemed to conflate Taylor's own sexual trauma with Wilson's rape. Searcey then showed her crime scene photographs and fed her facts of the case as Taylor slowly 'remembered' what had taken place. Over multiple interrogations, Taylor described in detail her role in Wilson's death as well as the identities of five others involved in the crime. Taylor became one of the group referred to as the 'Beatrice Six,' all of whom were wrongfully convicted for Wilson's death and were exonerated 19 years later. As of 2017, and despite her exoneration, Taylor still thinks that she can feel the fabric of the throw pillow that she falsely claimed to have held over Wilson's face in 1985 (Aviv, 2017).

The aforementioned vignette not only introduces the interaction between mental illness, suggestibility, and inappropriate questioning techniques by law enforcement and a mental health professional, but it also helps to demonstrate a Coerced-Internalized False Confession. Like Taylor, some subjects become so overwhelmed with the interrogative process that they come to believe that they actually committed a crime in which they had no involvement. While the premise that some people can falsely internalize their guilt may be difficult to believe, false confession researchers suggest that this phenomenon is not necessarily uncommon. Researchers have pointed to laboratory studies in which university students came to internalize their confessions through the interrogation techniques employed against them (Forrest, Wadkins, & Larson, 2006; Klaver et al., 2008; Nash & Wade, 2009; Perillo & Kassin, 2011). Leding (2012) also concluded that the interrogative methods employed by law enforcement officers, while effective in obtaining a truthful confession from a criminal subject, can also cause innocent subjects to confabulate details and go along with the false confession. The likelihood of this occurring is then heightened by such factors as anxiety, fatigue, pressure, confusion, and increased suggestibility (Conti, 1999).

Similar to the other two types of false confessions identified by Kassin and Wrightsman (1985), certain questions arise when considering Coerced-Internalized False Confessions. For example, how frequently do these types of false confessions actually occur? Should it be assumed that because these types of confessions occur within the artificial environment of the university laboratory that they happen with any degree of regularity in the real world? Or, as in the case of Ada JoAnn Taylor, do these types of confession represent a perfect, albeit rare, storm in which highly vulnerable subjects are subjected to police interrogative malpractice? Again, these issues will be discussed in greater depth in future chapters.

Theoretical Explanations of Confession

Although false confessions do occur, the frequency in which they happen is worthy of debate. Many people find it hard to believe that anyone would confess to a crime they did not actually commit. For example, Leo and Liu (2009) conducted a survey with potential jurors regarding their perceptions of false confessions. Participants reported that the possibility that a person would falsely confess to a crime that they did not commit was both unlikely and counterintuitive. These same participants went on to state that they personally would never falsely confess to a criminal act for which they were not involved. In short, despite the efforts of false confession researchers, expert witnesses, and wrongful conviction advocates, it is likely that most jurors may be sitting in the jury box in complete disbelief that anyone would falsely confess outside of being tortured into doing so. As such, researchers and expert witnesses have greatly increased their efforts in trying to educate judges and juries about the false confession phenomenon. Again, in order for the defense to have even a fighting chance against confession evidence, these advocates must convince judges, juries, and the criminal justice system as a whole that false confessions not only occur routinely, but also occurred in the current case before the court. This is their goal and, for many, their livelihood.

Still, the questions relating to motivation are not reserved solely for false confessions. Many people also question why a guilty person would ever truthfully confess, as their confession may guarantee their ultimate prosecution and conviction. Yet, as countless law enforcement officers would likely attest, guilty people confess their criminal actions all the time. The question is why. The following are a few potential explanations for why people may come to truthfully confess their criminal wrongdoing.

Evolutionary Theory

According to Bering and Shackleford (2005), confessions are

20

understandable from an evolutionary psychology perspective. Gold and Weiner, (as cited by Bering & Shackleford, 2005), explained that when a person shows remorse at the time of their confession, others are more likely to believe that the confessor's shame and embarrassment suggests that they have suffered enough and that they are unlikely to recidivate. As a result, the confessor is likely to benefit from a reduction of punishment and feelings of forgiveness from those who receive the confession. From an evolutionary standpoint, these benefits may ultimately save the confessor's life. Similarly, Bering and Shackleford suggested that evolutionary benefits are equally understandable when one considers a confession made to any ally. When a person confesses to an ally, the ally provides them with social aid in the form of: a) physical protection from hostile members of the group who may seek retribution; b) the ally's willingness to speak on behalf of the confessor; and c) the ally's recommendations of alternative and lesser forms of retribution.

From a more practical standpoint, an evolutionary explanation of confessions suggests that a truly guilty subject may confess because they believe that their remorse will cause society to conclude that they are unlikely to commit other crimes. From an evolutionary perspective, the subject equates remorse with a lesser sentence. For those who have ever interrogated a hardcore criminal and received a heavy dosage of 'crocodile tears' at the time of their confession, this concept may be what the subject is trying to tap into.

Without realizing it, interrogators may also be acting in accordance with evolutionary theory when they interact with a subject who is considering confession. For example, it is not uncommon for criminal interrogators to inform a subject that if they confess, the interrogator will be happy to inform the prosecutor that the subject was cooperative and feels remorseful for what they have done. Similarly, interrogators sometimes claim that they will help to tell the subject's story so that all involved understand what happened and why. Lastly, interrogators sometimes intimate that the subject may receive a reduction in their sentence by accepting responsibility for their actions. Still, ethical law enforcement professionals know that they can never promise a criminal subject any specific sentence or legal outcome as they are not in the position, and do not have the authority, to do so. However, these types of statements reflect an interrogator's efforts to present themselves to the subject as an ally who can work and speak on behalf of the subject.

Psychoanalytic Theory

From a psychoanalytic perspective, Reik (as cited by Conti, 1999), suggested that human beings have an unconscious and compulsive need to confess. Reik goes on to suggest that while human beings have instinctual impulses that strive to be expressed, society may come to condemn these expressions. For this reason, the ego can only come to express certain instinctual impulses through the act of confession (Conti, 1999). As a result, confession allows the individual to overcome their own guilt and remorse as the ego attempts to negotiate between the id and the superego (Kassin & Gudjonsson, 2004). Reik believed that the unconscious motivation to confess helps to satisfy the individual's underlying desire for punishment which can only be satisfied through an admission of guilt (Conti, 1999). Berggren (as cited by Kassin & Gudjonsson, 2004), further elaborated that in order to obtain a desired degree of catharsis, the individual must confess to a person in a position of authority such as a member of the clergy or a representative of law enforcement.

Law enforcement officers who routinely conduct interrogations may come to the realization that, deep down, people want to tell the truth. They want to unburden themselves of the guilt they feel over their criminal wrongdoings. Contrary to the anti-law enforcement narrative about how criminal interrogations are conducted, most people do not need to be pushed or coerced into a false confession. From a psychoanalytic perspective, the successful interrogator creates an environment in which the subject feels comfortable submitting to the underlying desire to truthfully confess to what is likely the worst thing they have ever done. Based on the use of psychoanalytic theory to explain the motivation for confession, it is not what is done to the subject that causes them to confess, but their own internal struggle to admit their wrongdoing.

Confession As a Conscious Decision

Whereas psychoanalytic theory looks to the internal processes of a subject, some have suggested that confession is more of a conscious decision-making process. According to Hilgendorf and Irving (as cited by Walsh and Bull, 2012), most criminal subjects make conscious decisions during law enforcement interviews based on their individual perceptions of anticipated outcomes. In putting forth their decision-making model, Hilgendorf and Irving sought to explain an interrogation subject's decision to confess as a series of choices they must make (Bradford & Goodman-Delahunty, 2008). According to this model, the interrogation subject is presented with a series of individual decision-making steps throughout their interaction with law enforcement. For example, should they agree to speak with police? Should they be honest in responding to the questions officers pose to them? And, should they confess to their criminal misdeeds? Each decision is therefore based on the subject's personal perceptions as to the available actions they can take, the anticipated outcomes of their actions, and the values of the anticipated consequences of their behavior (Bradford & Goodman-Delahunty, 2008).

For those who routinely interrogate criminal subjects, this may be the cause for the subject's silence. If an interrogator has ever seen the subject staring at his feet in silence for what seems like an eternity, what they may be witnessing is the outward manifestation of the subject's decision-making process. According to this theoretical explanation, the subject may be engaged in an internal dialogue in which they are weighing the pros and cons of confessing. This is not unlike the cliched Hollywood depictions of an angel on one shoulder and the devil on the other engaging in an open debate of what the person's next steps should be. A successful interrogator may then choose to help the subject in their decision-making by pointing out the benefits of confessing now. Again, contrary to the perceptions of many academics, expert witnesses, and advocates, this assistance does not come in the form of yelling, threatening, or abusive behavior. Rather, this may be the point where an interrogator notes that admitting the truth about what happened allows the subject to control the story, to relieve themselves of the guilt they have been harboring, to potentially negotiate a better deal before their co-defendants confess, to finally bring closure to the matter, et cetera. When presented with a major and difficult decision, whether we realize it or not, we all conduct a cost-benefit analysis. Interrogators must remember that for the subject, this may be the biggest decision they ever make. This theoretical approach to confession helps to highlight the importance of an interrogator being able to thoughtfully weigh in on the subject's internal creation of a pro-con list.

Confession As a Social Interaction

Some researchers have attempted to explain the concept of confession as an intense social interaction between the interrogator and the interrogation subject (Kassin, 2005). Of particular relevance is Latane's (1981) Social Impact Theory. This theory suggests that the actions of other people can influence an individual. Latane proposed that when an individual is the target of the influence of others, the impact will ultimately be determined by the strength, immediacy, and the number of people providing the influence. As these factors increase, so too will the social impact on the individual. Problems arise, however, if these factors increase to a dangerous level. Kassin (2005) suggested that Social Impact Theory can explain the social pressure leading to a false confession based on the strength of the influence employed by police interrogators through their authority, their interrogative methods, and the number of officers that interact with the subject. In essence, it is posited that if the officer is overly authoritative, if they employ overly coercive interrogative techniques, and/or if too many officers are engaged in the interrogation, an innocent person may feel socially pressured to falsely confess.

This approach to explaining the decision to confess may help law enforcement officers decrease the likelihood of obtaining a false confession. By keeping Kassin's (2005) explanation in mind, law enforcement officers should limit their overt displays of authority so as to minimize the likelihood of a false confession. By not displaying their weapon or badge, by dropping their authoritarian tone, and by limiting authoritative symbols in the room like department seals and American flags, law enforcement interrogators may also decrease the pressure on the subject and thereby decrease the likelihood of a false confession. For law enforcement officers who may be called upon to testify to the confession that they have elicited, it is important to be aware that the defense attorney is likely going to question whether the interrogator's gun or badge were showing during the course of the interrogation. This is done in an attempt to make the interrogation room look like a 'pressure cooker' that the defendant was only able to escape by falsely confessing to a crime they didn't actually commit. By dropping the overt signs of authority, the interrogator cannot only counteract this line of attack, but they can also feel more confident that the confession they received was a conscious decision of the subject and not a fearful reaction to overpowering coercion. For these same reasons, law enforcement officers should limit the number of interrogators in the room and avoid badgering the subject into a confession. Essentially, by viewing an interrogation as nothing more than a social interaction, officers can feel more confident in the confessions they elicit.

Cognitive-Behavioral Model

Gudjonsson (1989) proposed a cognitive-behavioral model in attempting to explain the factors that ultimately influence a person's decision to confess during an interrogation. Gudjonsson proposed that when attempting to assess why people confess, the following five factors should be considered: a) the social factors relating to the subject's feelings of isolation, need for approval, and need for affiliation; b) the emotional factors relating to the subject's feelings of distress and anxiety; c) the cognitive factors relating to the subject's thoughts and interpretations of the interrogation situation, to include such considerations as the strength of the evidence against them; d) the situational factors relating to pre-existing circumstances associated with the subject, such as their previous exposure to the legal system; and e) the physiological arousal of the subject to include their heart rate, blood pressure, and perspiration. Each of these considerations is believed to interact in such a way as to cause the interrogation subject to confess. In other words, a law enforcement interrogator should be mindful of the social factors impacting the subject. Does the subject feel isolated from his friends, family, or society? If so, this person may choose to confess to receive acceptance from the officer, the department, and the prosecutor. They may feel that their confession is a sure-fire way to feel like part of the team. While this can be a motivation for the subject to truthfully confess, officers must also be mindful that an excessive need for approval could also lead to a false confession.

From an emotional standpoint, a confession may result when the subject is feeling distressed or anxious. While there may be times during the course of an interrogation in which the officer may seek to increase or decrease the subject's stress based on the subject's behavior, the officer must also be mindful that too much of a good thing can ultimately prove detrimental. For example, if the subject is placed under profound stress, as can be seen in cases of police misconduct or abuse in the interrogation room, the subject may falsely confess as a means of escaping the interrogation. In addition to stress, the subject will also be influenced by cognitive factors during the interrogation. For example, if the evidence against the subject is profoundly overwhelming, they may come to confess because they have no other option but to minimize their future punishment. This is a very important factor for interrogators to keep in mind as the odds of obtaining a truthful confession rise with the amount of evidence. Conversely, some researchers believe that lying about, or exaggerating the amount of evidence against an innocent subject may cause them to falsely confess. This is an argument that will be discussed in greater detail later in the book.

As noted in Gudjonsson's (1989) Cognitive-Behavioral Model, pre-existing factors that are unique to the subject's situation may influence the likelihood of obtaining a confession. One such factor may be the subject's criminal record. As likely experienced by some interrogators, the length of the subject's rap sheet may ultimately influence their decision to confess or deny any criminal involvement. This can go one of two ways. If the subject is a 'frequent flier' in the criminal justice system (i.e., they have been arrested, charged, and prosecuted on multiple occasions previously), they may be unwilling to admit to any wrongdoing because they have come to believe that keeping their mouth shut is their best option. Personally, I have experienced numerous situations with hardcore criminals in which they have told me, "Get the paper and I'll talk." This can be translated to mean that once you can prove that you have enough evidence to convict me by obtaining an indictment, I will tell you what I did so that I can get the best deal possible from the prosecutor. However, it is also possible to be placed in an interrogation room with a 'frequent flier' who, through their previous experiences with the criminal justice system, has come to realize that if they accept responsibility for their actions, they are more likely to obtain more lenient treatment. Either way, it is important for law enforcement officers to be aware that these types of pre-existing situational factors may impact their interrogative success with the subject.

Similar to Gudjonsson's (1989) position that confessions occur as a result of various personal and situational factors, Moston, Stephenson, and Williamson (1992) offered that confessions occur as a result of the interaction of various personal and situational factor like: a) the interrogation subject's background characteristics such as age, sex, and personality; b) the characteristics of the criminal offense such as the nature of the crime and its severity; c) the strength of the evidence against the subject based on their personal perceptions; and d) the questioning styles used by the law enforcement interrogators. While this explanation mirrors Gudjonsson's, in many respects it adds the additional factor of helping determine which interrogative techniques the law enforcement officer ultimately employs.

While the theories and conceptual frameworks outlined above address the issue of both true and false confessions through a variety of perspectives, Kassin and Gudjonsson (2004) noted that these various explanations share certain similarities. More specifically, they note that criminal interrogation subjects make the conscious decision to confess when:

- They are motivated to do so
- When the evidence of their guilt appears significant

- When they have a strong desire to alleviate their shame or guilt
- When they have reached a point where they can no longer handle the stress associated with their isolation and interrogation
- When they are subjected to a myriad of social-psychological interrogative methods
- When the subject comes to believe the benefits of confession outweigh the consequences of continued denial (Kassin and Gudjonsson, 2004)

While these theories and conceptual frameworks attempt to explain why confessions occur, it is important to note that all people are unique. Therefore, different subjects may not arrive at the decision to confess in the same manner and for the same reasons. For that matter, the same subject may not be willing to confess to all interrogators. Since all people are different, their individual characteristics may make them more or less likely to confess, especially in light of the interrogative techniques that are being employed. As nice and convenient as it would be, the simple truth is that not all techniques or methods work on every subject. Law enforcement interrogators must therefore learn to be flexible and be willing to tailor their interrogative strategies to the subject's unique traits, factors, and background.

CHAPTER 2

False Confession Risk Factors: Understanding the Unique Traits of the Subject

As noted from the outset of this text, false confession researchers, expert witnesses, and wrongful conviction advocates frequently blame the actions of law enforcement officers and their interrogative 'tactics' for the elicitation of false confessions. However, it must be noted that the interrogative methods utilized by law enforcement officers are only half of the equation. According to the existing academic literature, two main categories exist for why innocent subjects falsely confess to crimes they didn't commit. The first, and arguably the more important of the two, relates to the personal risk factors of the criminal subject.

Personal Risk Factors for False Confessions

As noted by Kassin (2008), some people are dispositionally more likely to render a false confession due to their inherent malleability arising from various personal characteristics. Simply put, some people have unique factors which cause them to be at greater risk for falsely confessing. The following is a discussion of those factors.

Youth

The existing literature suggests that a subject's status of being a juvenile is one of the key dispositional risk factors for rendering a false confession (Gudjonsson et al., 2016; Lackey, 2020; Schatz, 2018). In concurrence with this position, Drizin and Leo (2004) analyzed 125 false confessions brought about by law enforcement interrogations and reported that a disproportionate number of false confessors (approximately 35%) were juveniles under the age of 17. Similarly, Gross and Shaffer (as cited by Pimentel et al., 2015) concluded after analyzing the National Registry of Exonerations that adolescents are three times more likely than adults to render a false confession. Malloy et al. (2014) presented similar findings after interviewing 193 young men ranging in age from 14 to 17 who had been incarcerated for serious criminal activity. In their study, 17.1% of the participants reported that they had made false confessions to law enforcement officers in the past. It is therefore hard to deny the fact that young people are more likely to falsely confess than their adult counterparts.

The disproportionate number of young people rendering false confessions may begin with arrest frequency. More specifically, Gudjonsson (2010) suggested that young people may be more likely than adults to falsely confess because they are the age group that is more likely to be arrested and therefore at greater risk of being interrogated. This increased likelihood of being interrogated may then interact with the inherent weaknesses associated with human development to produce an increased rate of false confessions. For example, Waxman (2020) reported that young people simply think differently than adults because their prefrontal cortex, which governs critical cognitive functions like foresight, cost-benefit analysis, etc., does not develop sufficiently until late adolescence. This results in the inability of some young people to sufficiently grasp the complexities of the legal system and/or to adequately comprehend the long-term consequences of their actions. As such, juveniles may be more likely than adults to confess to crimes they did not commit in exchange for immediate benefits like ending the interrogation, going home, and so on. Waxman goes on to note that the lack of a fully-developed prefrontal cortex can also cause young people to perceive time differently than adults, thereby making an interrogation lasting only a few hours feel like an unending process. To bring an end to what they perceive to be an interminable ordeal, some juvenile subjects may provide a false confession. It is also suggested that juveniles are more vulnerable to being influenced by others, especially by authority figures. As such, they may be at an increased risk of being influenced by leading questions and then absorbing the information they are being fed by law enforcement officers before regurgitating it back to their interrogators (Waxman, 2020).

The tendency of juveniles to render false confessions may also stem from developmental characteristics associated with adolescence such as impulsivity, a strong susceptibility to social influence, a decreased level of status, and immature judgment (Malloy, Shulman, & Cauffman, 2014). We only need to look back at how we dressed, drove our cars, or acted in public as teenagers to realize that we have all done things as young people that we would never dream of doing in adulthood. It is therefore not surprising that youth also impacts interactions with law enforcement. In fact, it has been concluded that adolescents tend to exhibit poor legal decision-making based on an age-related lack of understanding of the legal system, an inability to fully understand or discern the strength of the evidence against them, and developmental immaturity (Malloy et al., 2014). It has also been suggested that young people may be at an increased risk to falsely confess not only because of their inherent deference to adult authority, but also a misguided loyalty to their friends. In light of the significant amount of time that young people spend with their peers, it is posited that some juveniles falsely confess as a means of protecting a friend who is truly guilty of the crime under investigation. (Pimentel, Arndorfer, & Malloy, 2015).

A real-world example of youth as a risk factor can be observed in the wrongful conviction of 14-year-old Harleme Larry. In Dade City, Florida on July 10, 2010, a young man approached four men drinking beer and then demanded money before shooting and killing one of the men. Two days later, Larry surrendered to police and admitted that he was responsible for the shooting, though he claimed it was in self-defense. Despite giving a recorded confession to police, Larry later testified that his confession was false and that his friend, Derrick Wright, had asked him to take the rap. Larry went on to explain that he and Wright were as close as brothers and Wright had asked Larry to accept responsibility because his young age would result in him having to spend only two years in prison (NRE, 2020).

Theorizing that juveniles may be at an increased risk of falsely confessing due to a strong desire to take the blame for an acquaintance, Pimentel et al. (2015) addressed this issue experimentally with 99 adult college students and 74 adolescent high school students. Each participant was randomly assigned to either receive or not receive a favor from a confederate. Each participant was then put in a position to observe the confederate cheating on a task. The participants were then observed to determine whether they were willing to accept responsibility for the confederate's cheating. Results indicated that 59% of the adolescents took the blame for the confederate's cheating as compared to 39% of adults. Pimentel et al. (2015) therefore concluded that youth is a predisposing characteristic for false confessions based upon the nature of adolescents' peer relationships and their willingness to protect a friend through a false acceptance of responsibility.

While not all adolescents falsely confess to protect a friend, Larry's case clearly illustrates how the poor and immature decision-making of a young person can combine with their desire for acceptance and need for belonging to result in a false confession. As all of the aforementioned information suggests, it is hard to deny that youth is a risk factor for false confessions. However, it is inappropriate and illogical to suggest that the interrogative methodologies employed against the juvenile subject are automatically responsible for the false confession. Like any profession, criminal interrogators tend to stick with what works. In other words, they tend to use the same techniques over and over again. If these techniques have not previously resulted in a false confession from adults, this would suggest that it is the inherent emotional and intellectual shortcomings of juveniles that are at play, not necessarily the interrogative techniques employed. Let's use an analogy to further explain this position.

Consider the interrogative techniques used by law enforcement to be an airplane. The pilot flying this aircraft is the law enforcement interrogator. For the sake of this analogy, let's consider the weather conditions to be the subject. If a subject's status as a juvenile naturally causes the weather to be more severe and dangerous than an adult subject, there are only two possible causes for the ensuing plane crash. We can blame the weather for causing the crash, or we can blame the pilot for making a critical error when flying in such weather conditions. What we cannot blame is the aircraft. Simply put, interrogative methods, like the Reid Technique for example, are simply a means of questioning. If the interrogator is overzealous in using these methods, a false confession may occur. If the subject is highly susceptible to peer influence or suffers from inherent deficiencies in decision-making due to their status as a juvenile, a false confession may also occur. What cannot be blamed is the routine interrogative methods. Put another way, it is fundamentally unsound for academicians, advocates, or expert witnesses to use the false confessions elicited by juveniles to suggest that the routine interrogative techniques used by law enforcement lead to false confessions from adults. It is okay to blame the errors of the pilot or the weather conditions, but don't blame the aircraft. The plane routinely lands safely when flown in normal weather or by an experienced pilot.

Mental Illness

In addition to youth, mental illness has also been identified as a personal characteristic that is likely to increase the probability that a person will render a false confession upon being interrogated by law enforcement (Lackey, 2020). Similar to young people, mentally ill subjects may be at an increased risk of falsely confessing because of their increased arrest rates. Teplin, as cited by Redlich (2004), conducted a study in which it was concluded that persons with mental illness were 67 times more likely to be arrested than individuals without mental health symptoms. In light of this statistic, it is not surprising that mentally ill subjects are disproportionately represented in the ranks of those subjects who have been wrongfully convicted (Redlich, 2004). As previously noted, for a confession to be admitted as evidence within a court of law, admissions must be voluntary and uncoerced (*Bram v. United States*, 1897; *Brady v. United States*, 1970). Although an argument could be made that a mentally ill subject is not competent, and therefore not capable of rendering a voluntary confession, the United States courts have not necessarily agreed with this assumption. For example, in the case of *Colorado v. Connelly* (1986), the defendant, Francis Connelly, raised the argument that the murder confession that he made to police during a schizophrenic episode rendered him incompetent, and his confession should therefore be considered inadmissible. However, the Supreme Court ruled that it cannot automatically be assumed that a subject's confession was a direct result of their mental illness. Instead, it must be demonstrated that the interrogating officers acted inappropriately and employed techniques which coerced the subject to confess (*Colorado v. Connelly*, 1986).

While the ruling in *Connelly* concludes that the interrogative techniques utilized during a law enforcement interrogation are more at issue than a subject's mental health symptoms, it has nevertheless been suggested that the subject's mental illness may make them more susceptible to the interrogative methods used by law enforcement. This begs the question: What is it about the condition of being mentally ill that predisposes a person to falsely confess? Redlich (2004) identified that criminal subjects presenting with mental illness exhibit disorganized thought, poor executive functioning, attention deficits, and impaired decision making that predisposes them to render incriminating statements when interrogated. Redlich, Summers, & Hoover (2010) further identified that subjects with mental illness have inherent vulnerabilities such as proneness to confusion and a lack of assertiveness, both of which place the mentally ill subject at risk for being wrongfully convicted. Because of these types of deficiencies, criminal subjects with mental illness are at an increased risk to admit to crimes they didn't actually commit (Kassin, et al., 2010).

The wrongful conviction case of Eddie Lloyd helps to illustrate the role that mental illness may play in the rendering of a false confession. While being treated in a Detroit, Michigan area hospital for paranoid schizophrenia in 1984, Lloyd wrote to the police with suggestions of how they could solve various crimes in the area, including the brutal murder of a 16-year-old girl in Detroit. On multiple occasions, the police visited Lloyd in the hospital and interrogated him. During these interrogations, police led Lloyd to believe that if he confessed and was arrested, he would help officers 'smoke out' the true offender. Officers then fed Lloyd specific information about the crime. Based on this information and his false beliefs about the motivation behind his confession, Lloyd signed a written statement in which he falsely admitted to his involvement in the crime and then provided a recorded confession as well. Lloyd was subsequently convicted and spent 17 years in prison before being exonerated by DNA evidence (NRE, 2020). In this case, not only did Lloyd's mental illness cause him to become a suspect in this case, but his related lack of competency led to his false confession. While it is hard to argue that the officers in this case engaged in some level of inappropriate conduct, it is hard to blame Lloyd's false confession solely on any particular, and officially sanctioned, interrogative method. In short, an argument could be made that Lloyd's mental health condition played just as much of a role, if not more, in his false confession than the interrogative techniques employed against him.

Cognitive Disabilities

In addition to mental health issues, cognitive deficiencies are also a huge contributor to false confessions. In fact, in their analysis of 125 cases of interrogation-induced false confessions, Drizin and Leo (2004) identified 28 "mentally retarded" subjects who had falsely confessed to law enforcement. This demonstrates that intellectual disabilities are also a dispositional vulnerability for rendering a false confession. Waxman (2020) explained that people with intellectual deficits are often unable to understand or communicate quickly enough to counter the interrogative techniques that are used against them. Similarly, these individuals lack the requisite understanding of their legal rights, the greater criminal justice process, or the anticipated consequences of their actions (Waxman, 2020). Shaw and Budd (as cited by Kassin & Gudjonsson, 2004) similarly reported that intellectually disabled individuals tend to be more compliant with a heightened desire for approval, particularly from persons in a position of authority. As such, when a cognitively challenged subject is put in the interrogation room with an authority figure like a police officer, they are likely to be at greater risk of telling the officer what they want to hear as a means of pleasing the officer. These tendencies may help to explain the disproportionately high number of intellectually deficient subjects in Drizin and Leo's analysis.

An example of how such disabilities can play a profound role in false confession can be seen in the wrongful conviction case of Henry McCollum and his half-brother Leon Brown. On September 26, 1983, the body of an 11-year-old girl was found in a soybean field in Red Springs, North Carolina. The victim was later determined to have been raped and suffocated. Believing that the offender must have been from outside of the community, investigators began looking for anyone from out of town. In addition, based on a rumor that he may be involved because he looked somewhat unusual, police located and questioned McCollum, a mentally-challenged, 19-year-old from New Jersey who was in town visiting his mother. After being interrogated for more than four hours, fed information about the crime by investigators, and promised he could go home if he confessed, McCollum admitted to his involvement in the crime and implicated several others including Brown, his 15-year-old half-brother. Immediately after confessing, McCollum asked investigators if he could now go home. As Brown was also mentally challenged, he confessed to being involved in the crime as well. None of the other boys who were implicated were charged as they had sound alibis. Both McCollum and Brown were convicted based largely on their confessions and spent 30 years in prison before being pardoned by the Governor of North Carolina. Based on their wrongful conviction, the State of North Carolina awarded each $750,000 (NRE, 2020; North Carolina Coalition for Alternatives to the Death Penatly, 2020).

It is important to note that while an individual with an IQ score of between 70 and 75 can be considered intellectually disabled (American Psychiatric Association, 2020), McCollum and Brown had IQs of 51 and 49 respectively. In other words, they both had profound cognitive impairments. While each was awarded $750,000, The Marshall Project reported that within months, hundreds of thousands of dollars of this compensation was siphoned off by people that McCollum and Brown believed were trying to protect them including their sister, a lawyer in Florida, as well as a supposed advocate in Georgia and her partner in New York (Neff, 2018). Based on how McCollum and Brown's cognitive deficiencies interfered with their ability to defend themselves in their personal lives, it is no surprise that they could have been easily coaxed into falsely confessing by law enforcement investigators. Still, it has been suggested that unlike juvenile status or mental illness, law enforcement interrogators often fail to recognize intellectual disabilities in the subjects that they interrogate (Schatz, 2018). This may prevent law enforcement officers from taking necessary precautions that could help preclude the elicitation of a false confession from cognitively-impaired subjects.

Personality Factors

In addition to youth, mental illness, and intellectual disabilities, it is possible for some individuals to be predisposed to rendering a false confession due to their unique personality characteristics. Gudjonsson (as cited by Kassin et al., 2010), suggested that pervasive personality traits like suggestibility and compliance, as well as full-blown personality disorders, can put an individual at risk for a false confession. In surveying 1,080 Icelandic students regarding true and false admissions they may have previously made to teachers, parents, and/or law enforcement, Gudjonsson, Sigurdsson, Bragason, Einarsson, and Valdimarsdottir (2004) identified that false confessions and false denials were significantly associated with antisocial personality traits. In a later survey of 10,472 student participants in Iceland regarding their experiences with law enforcement interrogations and their history of confession, Gudjonsson, Sigurdsson, Asgeirsdottir, and Sigfusdottir (2006) identified that 7.3% of students who reported having been interrogated by police in the past also reported that they had falsely confessed to crimes they had not committed. They further concluded that these same individuals reported having poor self-esteem and increased levels of anxiety, depression, and anger (Gudjonsson et al., 2006). This research suggests that certain personality traits may contribute to a subject's decision to falsely confess.

Based on a previous survey of 1,896 Icelandic students who reported having previously been interrogated by law enforcement, Gudjonsson, Sigurdsson, Asgeirsdottir, and Sigfusdottir (2007) also discovered an association between the decision to falsely confess and unpleasant and traumatic life events such as victimization, death of a loved one, and a history of substance abuse. In considering a potential relationship between false confessions rendered during custodial interrogations and group bullying behavior, Gudjonsson, Sigurdsson, and Sigfusdottir (2010) concluded that individuals who reported a history of being bullied and bullying others were also more psychologically vulnerable to, and likely to give, a false confession during law enforcement interrogation. In relation to specific personality disorders, Gudjonsson et al. (2004) identified that antisocial personality disorder and antisocial personality traits were highly predictive of false confessions, at least with college students in Iceland.

While these studies are presented as a means of demonstrating the type of research and thought that has gone into trying to explain why false confessions occur, it cannot be overlooked that the majority of the aforementioned research relates to youths in Iceland. As Iceland is a very small country with an overwhelmingly homogenous racial makeup, we should be careful in taking any such findings and applying them to such a large and racially/ethnically diverse country like the United States. Similarly, there are obvious and profound differences between adult criminal offenders and young students. Lastly, most of the aforementioned research involves self-report surveys. While relying on what others tell you about themselves is inherently risky, this risk is heightened by the fact that for some of these surveys, researchers were relying on the self-report information from individuals with antisocial personality traits. In other words, these particular respondents are innately untrustworthy by the nature of these specific traits, but the researchers operate under the assumption that there is no reason to believe that youths with antisocial traits would lie about their history of falsely confessing. Like much of the research surrounding the false confession phenomenon, what we are told by the 'experts' must be viewed with a healthy and necessary degree of skepticism.

Compliance and Interrogative Suggestibility

Various other psychological factors have been identified as potential contributors to a person's risk of rendering a false confession. Based on anecdotal evidence observed through the analysis of DNA exoneration cases, Kassin (2008) identified the dispositional variables of compliance and interrogative suggestibility as potential risk factors for false confessions. Gudjonsson (as cited by Kassin & Gudjonsson, 2004), identified that the psychological concept of compliance is comprised of two key components: a) an eagerness to please others in social interactions while protecting one's own self-esteem; and b) a desire to avoid confrontation and conflict when interacting with other people, particularly those who are believed to be in a position of authority. Kassin also suggested that when the subject of a criminal interrogation possesses an increased level of compliance, they are at an increased risk of accepting responsibility for a crime they have not committed.

Simply put, some people are inherently more likely to just go along with what they are told. This can be a problem in the interrogation room. In fact, Gudjonsson and Clark (as cited by Nurmoja & Bachmann, 2008), defined "interrogative suggestibility" as the degree to which a person accepts the information that is communicated to them during a period of formal questioning and which can cause that person to be misled and alter their initial answers. Davis and Leo (as cited by Gudjonsson, Sigurdsson, Sigurdardottir, Steinthorsson, & Sigurdardoeitherttir, 2014) offered that when it comes to criminal interrogation, suggestibility can be viewed as an enduring personality trait which can cause a subject to be more vulnerable to leading questions and interrogative pressure, or it can be an acute state that develops as a result of the interrogative circumstances such as emotional distress and sleep deprivation. Simply put, Davis and Leo are explaining that some people may have a personality that makes them more suggestible during interrogation, or they may be exposed to such interrogative pressure that they become suggestible for that particular interrogation. If we read between the lines, what Davis and Leo are actually suggesting is that *every* person is capable of rendering a false confession. It cannot be overlooked that this is a very beneficial position to have if called upon to offer expert witness testimony in a case regarding a disputed confession.

The individual differences in a criminal subject's levels of suggestibility and compliance come into play when the interrogators employed leading questions or strong custodial pressure during the interrogation (Gudjonsson, 2004). The greatest concern for those individuals with a heightened level of interrogative suggestibility is that they can actually come to have their memories altered by the questions posed to them by law enforcement officers (Kassin, 2008). This is what we saw in the previously-discussed case of Ada Joann Taylor in Beatrice, Nebraska. In light of this willingness to readily agree with persons in authority, both compliance and interrogative suggestibility have come to be considered as dispositional vulnerabilities for false confession (Kassin, 2008).

While suggestibility and compliance may play a role in the elicitation of a false confession from an innocent subject, we must avoid jumping to the conclusion that such personality traits actually *cause* false confessions. This realization is particularly important when it is considered that a defense attorney will have very little difficulty finding a forensic psychologist to administer a Personality Inventory Assessment or Gudjonsson Suggestibility Scale assessment and then report that the subject has a high level of compliance or suggestibility. However, it must be remembered that such assessment measures do not actually identify whether a confession is true or false. They only speak to the personality facets of the subject being assessed. So, while some academic researchers and false confession expert witnesses may claim that high levels of compliance and suggestibility may increase the likelihood of a false confession, it can equally be argued that these personality traits may also increase the likelihood of a *true* confession. In fact, these personality characteristics may cause a truly guilty subject to truthfully confess very quickly and with very little effort from the interrogator. Ironically, compliance and suggestibility may ultimately increase the likelihood of both true and false confessions. As such, the presence of these traits should not be mistakenly used to infer the veracity of the confession.

Additional Dispositional Risk Factors

ADHD Other dispositional vulnerabilities relating to false confessions include Attention Deficit Hyperactivity Disorder (ADHD). In studying male prisoners, Gudjonsson, Sigurdsson, Bragason, and Newton (2008) concluded that ADHD symptoms were significantly associated with the psychological risk factor of compliance. The ADHD symptoms of emotional lability and impulsivity have also been reported to prevent subjects from being able to cope with the strain of police interrogation (Gudjonsson, Sigurdsson, Young, Newton, & Peersen, 2009). Lastly, in surveying individuals diagnosed with ADHD, it was learned that these individuals were more likely to report that they had given a false confession to law enforcement in the past (Gudjonsson et al., 2008).

Drug and Alcohol Intoxication Additional personal risk factors that may cause an innocent person to become predisposed to falsely confessing include drug and alcohol use. Evans, Schreiber Compo, and Russano (2009) reported that criminal subjects who are intoxicated or under the influence of drugs at the time of their interrogation are at a greater risk for providing a false confession. This may stem from the fact that intoxication can make them more easily confused and susceptible to police interrogative techniques (Sigurdsson & Gudjonsson, 2001). False confession may also be more likely among this population because of their withdrawal symptoms. More specifically, if the interrogation lasts long enough that the subject begins going through painful withdrawal symptoms, they may be more inclined to falsely confess just to end the interrogation (Redlich, Kulish, & Steadman, 2011). Lastly, it has also been suggested that intoxicated subjects may be at an increased risk of internalizing their confessions because of their willingness to believe the premise put forth by interrogators that they committed the crime and simply don't remember doing so (Evans et al., 2009).

Race Najdowski (2011) identified that upon analyzing samples of criminal subjects who have rendered false confessions to law enforcement, Blacks are more overrepresented than their White counterparts. As such, Najdowski put forth the idea that race may be a potential risk factor for false confessions and theorized that Black subjects may become so concerned about being perceived in light of negative Black stereotypes that they may actually respond to interrogations with more nonverbal behaviors than Whites. It is possible that law enforcement interrogators may then misidentify these nonverbal behaviors as indicators of deception, assume that the innocent Black subject is guilty, and then subject them to more coercive interrogation techniques than would otherwise be employed against innocent White subjects. This process may eventually result in such a strong motivation to escape the high-pressure interrogation that an innocent Black subject will falsely confess to a crime that they did not commit (Najdowski, 2011).

Recommendations

In reviewing the risk factors above, it readily becomes apparent that for some false confession researchers, nearly everyone is at risk for rendering a false confession. Such a premise will obviously benefit the defense as an expert witness can easily be located and brought before the court to testify that the subject, who had previously confessed his wrongdoing to law enforcement, was ripe for a false confession because he is young, mentally ill, cognitively impaired, has a compliant personality, has a history of drug or alcohol abuse, has been bullied or victimized in the past, has experienced trauma as a child, has low self-esteem, has a history of depression, has anger traits, and/or is African American. Simply put, there will be no problem finding a false confession expert witness who can testify to the subject's predispositional risk factors. Despite the length of this list of personal risk factors, law enforcement interrogators should pay particular attention to the subject's age, mental health, and level of intelligence.

I can recall an incident in which a law enforcement colleague obtained a confession from a criminal subject. Upon being congratulated, the interrogator humbly sloughed off the compliment by stating that he could have painted a face on a tennis ball, thrown it into the interrogation room, and the subject would have confessed his crime to the tennis ball. For those who interrogate criminal subjects routinely, it is common knowledge that some subjects are more willing to confess their misdeeds than others. This is particularly true when the subject is an inherently decent person with little to no exposure to the criminal justice system and who may have simply made a stupid mistake that landed them in the crosshairs of law enforcement. Working bank fraud for a number of years, I have found this to be the case with bank tellers who steal money from their till. In my experience, people who come to be employed by a local bank branch are generally not hardcore criminals by nature. However, earning a relatively low salary while being surrounded by cash can sometimes become a problematic combination. To interrogate such a person can be relatively easy as they are not criminals by nature; they have likely not been in trouble with the law previously; and while they know that what they did was wrong, their criminal act does have some degree of logic. In short, "I didn't have any money, so I took some from work." Such a person may quickly confess to that tennis ball tossed into the room.

Unfortunately, adolescent subjects or subjects with mental health issues and/or cognitive impairments can have a similar response, not because they are truly guilty, but because of their inherent deficiencies. As such, law enforcement interrogators are well-advised to be mindful of the natural weaknesses of these types of subjects. If during the course of the interrogation the subject seems to simply be agreeing with the interrogator's assertions or gives the impression that they are merely trying to please the interrogator, the officer should have concerns. If this occurs, the interrogator should back off of their questioning and reassess whether the subject is providing new information or simply agreeing to the information that they have been provided by the interrogator. Still, despite what some in academia may think, not all interrogators are so ignorant or hungry for a confession that they will overlook the fact that the subject is readily agreeing to everything the interrogator says. In short, if the subject is a minor, has a history of, or presents with mental health issues, or appears significantly intellectually impaired, the officer should be mindful of the very real possibility that the subject may ultimately try to please the interrogator by telling them what they want to hear.

An easy way to check for abnormal compliance from the subject is by testing the subject's level of agreement. More specifically, the interrogator can deliberately misquote information that the subject has already provided and look for disagreement. For example, if the subject had previously informed the interrogator that they drove to the scene of the bank robbery in a red Buick, the interrogator can later summarize the subject's points by clarifying that the subject drove to the bank in a blue Mercury. If the subject corrects the color and make of the vehicle, they are demonstrating an ability to disagree with the interrogator and make corrections when necessary. However, if the subject accepts the interrogator's alteration of the color and make of the vehicle, this may indicate a level of compliance that could suggest that a false confession has been elicited. The same testing can be accomplished by providing the subject with case information that is clearly untrue and implausible to see if the subject readily incorporates that information into their confession.

It is important to note that while age, mental health, and intellectual disabilities should be considered as key risk factors for a false confession, these risk factors should not be considered as automatic disqualifiers to interrogation. According to Innocence Project (2020) data as of April 2020, 21% of wrongful conviction subjects had falsely confessed to their crimes. The obverse of this data means that 79% of wrongful conviction subjects did *not* falsely confess to the crime for which they stood accused. In short, not only did the overwhelming majority of subjects *not* falsely confess, but numerous young, mentally ill, and cognitively impaired subjects also failed to confess falsely. In essence, not all adolescent subjects falsely confess and not all false confessors are adolescents. The same holds true for mentally ill subjects and for subjects with intellectual disabilities. So, while criminal interrogators should be mindful of these three risk factors when interrogating, they should avoid jumping to the false conclusion that any subject with one or more of these risk factors *will* falsely confess. Similarly, it would be inappropriate and untrue for a false confession expert witness to testify that a confession obtained from a young, mentally ill, and/or cognitively impaired subject through lawful interrogative means is likely false. Still, while it is beneficial to draw attention to personal risk factors that may cause an innocent subject to falsely confess, there are others within the ranks of academia and expert witnesses who have found it better to attack law enforcement officers and their 'tactics' of interrogation.

CHAPTER 3

Insights from Interrogative Specialists: Bringing Balance to the Research

A s any law enforcement officer in America can likely attest, enforcing the laws of our great nation is an exhausting and unending process. Criminal activity has existed since humankind has walked the earth. Thankfully, a special group of people has long been called upon to protect the innocent from those who take it upon themselves to rape, pillage, and plunder our communities. Due to the inexhaustible supply of criminal actors and their antisocial actions, law enforcement does not often have the time or resources to study criminality and its related facets. Academics are therefore left to fill this research void. Unfortunately, these academic researchers rarely come from the ranks of law enforcement officers. Regardless of the offense that may be taken, an old adage exists which notes that those who *can* do and those who *can't* teach. To no great surprise, this teaching is closely aligned with academic research. Simply put, it is the teachers, not the law enforcement officers, who often conduct the research. This sadly results in research findings and conclusions that are often inconsistent with the realities of real-world law enforcement. At times, it also leads to an academic bias against police officers and the jobs they are called upon to do. Therefore, academia's conclusion that some individuals possess unique personal characteristics that may predispose them to falsely confessing is one thing, but smearing

the reputations and methods of law enforcement officers who question individuals suspected of committing a crime is quite another. This second line of
attack has served as an impetus for this book.

Because the existing false confession dialogue has largely been one-sided,
the resulting conclusions have relied primarily on biased assumptions made by
the academic researchers exploring the false confession phenomenon and the
expert witnesses who utilize these biased conclusions to repeatedly attack law
enforcement interrogators in open court. The simple fact is that while there has
been an ongoing discussion over the false confession problem, law enforcement has not yet been granted a seat at the table. In an attempt to bring much-
needed balance to the debate over false confessions and factors contributing
to their elicitation, I have conducted my own doctoral research with a focus
on the professional insights of federal law enforcement officers who specialize
in the field of criminal interrogation. Subsequent to this research, I engaged
in an identical study of state law enforcement polygraph examiners who also
specialize in criminal interrogation. As much of the remainder of this text will
compare the findings of academic laboratory experiments with the real-world
insights provided to me by federal and state interrogative specialists, I would
like to more fully explain the nature and methodology of my research.

As previously outlined, a considerable portion of false confession research
has involved laboratory experiments with university students (Forrest et al.,
2012; Guyll et al., 2013; Hasel & Kassin, 2009; Kassin & Fong, 1999; Kassin
& Kiechel, 1996; Kassin & McNall, 1991; Kassin et al., 2005; Kassin &
Norwick, 2004; Kebbell et al., 2006; Klaver et al., 2008; Levine et al., 2010;
Mastroberardino & Marucci, 2013; Narchet et al., 2011; Nash & Wade, 2009;
Newring & O'Donohue, 2008; Perillo & Kassin, 2011; Pimentel et al., 2015;
Russano et al., 2005; Swanner & Beike, 2010; Villar et al., 2013; Woody &
Forrest, 2009). While researchers continue to find value in exploring false
confessions through laboratory research studies, they also readily admit that
the results produced during laboratory experimentation may be difficult to
extrapolate to the real world of law enforcement due to the artificiality of the
laboratory setting, the ethical limitations that preclude a direct replication of

the stressors associated with actual criminal interrogation within a laboratory setting, and the inherent differences between the university student and criminal offender populations (Cole, Teboul, Zulawski, Wicklander, & Sturman, 2013; Gudjonsson, 2010; Gudjonsson et al., 2014; Kassin et al., 2010; Narchet et al., 2011; Stewart, Woody, & Pulos, 2016; Wilford & Wells, 2018). Despite the fact that criminal interrogations in the real world are conducted by law enforcement officers, very few researchers have sought input from officers about their approaches to interrogation, their interrogative methods, and their experiences with false confessions (Frantzen & Can, 2012; Kassin et al., 2007). Even fewer researchers have chosen to direct their inquiries at law enforcement officers who specialize in the interrogation of criminal subjects. Lastly, little to no studies have elected to gather information from law enforcement officers through in-depth qualitative interviews.

Research Questions

In my study, I sought to more fully describe and analyze the interrogation process and related methodologies that are associated with true and false confessions as reported by experienced law enforcement interrogators who specialize in conducting real-world interrogations and who employ interrogative techniques that have led to the elicitation of true, and possibly even false, confessions. Because many false confession researchers have suggested that the actions and interrogative methods of law enforcement officers are largely responsible for false confessions, I designed the following research questions to guide my research:

1. How do federal and state law enforcement polygraph examiners approach the interrogation of criminal subjects to maximize the likelihood of a true confession?
2. To what extent have federal and state law enforcement polygraph examiners experienced false confessions?
3. What were the circumstances in which federal and state law enforcement polygraph examiners experienced false confessions?

Research Tradition

To date, a considerable portion of the existing research has been quantitative in nature and conducted frequently in the form of laboratory experiments with university students. Far fewer researchers have sought to more fully understand the phenomenon of false confessions through direct inquiries made of law enforcement officers who specialize in the interrogation of criminal subjects. Given that I was seeking a more thorough and richer understanding of the false confession phenomenon and the practices of interrogative specialists, I decided to employ a case study approach. In case study research, the researcher thoroughly explores a particular issue, problem, or individual through an in-depth analysis of cases that are bound by a specific time, activity, or contextual framework (Creswell, 2013). To accomplish this, the researcher collects rich and detailed information from sources of information such as interviews, documents, reports, and observations for a select number of cases. With this information, a thorough description of the selected case(s) is provided and themes are identified (Creswell, 2013).

For my study, I served as the main instrument for the collection of data. I accomplished this by conducting in-depth qualitative interviews with state and federal polygraph examiners. State and federal law enforcement polygraph examiners were selected for this study as they are highly trained in the field of both deception detection and criminal interrogation, and they are highly skilled at interrogating criminal subjects subsequent to failed polygraph examinations. It should be noted that while state and federal law enforcement polygraph examiners are trained in the operation of the polygraph instrument and the review of psychophysiological data to determine deception among polygraph examinees, the polygraph technique itself had no bearing on my research design. In fact, many people, including some in law enforcement, may not fully comprehend that administering the polygraph examination to a criminal subject is just one half of the polygraph examiner equation. Yes, for an investigation it is helpful to know whether a particular person was involved in the criminal act being investigated. For example, if a child were to go missing from her home, it is extremely beneficial to rule out the child's parents as suspects in her disappearance. As such, when parents who have no direct involvement in causing their daughter's disappearance take and pass a polygraph examination, it helps investigators to effectively and efficiently direct limited investigative resources in the appropriate direction. The same holds true for the jewelry store employee who passes her polygraph as to whether she was part of the robbery of her store or the child pornography subject who passes his polygraph examination as to whether he has ever had sexual contact with a child.

As demonstrated in the aforementioned examples, polygraph examinations can often be used to remove individuals from the existing list of suspects. Conversely, polygraph examinations can also be used to identify truly guilty subjects. While it is obviously beneficial to know that the father was directly involved in his daughter's disappearance, the jewelry store robbery was an inside job, or the child pornography subject has acted on his sexual interests and engaged a child in sexual activity, a failed polygraph examination does not necessarily advance an investigation. This is where the second half of the polygraph examiner equation comes into play. Quite simply, polygraph examiners tend to be excellent interviewers and interrogators. Whether it is this gift that led them to the polygraph specialization, their honing of their interrogative skill through the repeated questioning of individuals who fail their polygraph examinations, or a combination of the two, polygraph examiners are routinely called upon because they are good at getting people to open up. As such, state and federal law enforcement polygraph examiners were selected for study based on their expertise in interrogating subjects after a failed polygraph examination and the frequency in which they are called upon by other law enforcement officers to interrogate criminal subjects.

I will never forget a question that I received when I was asked to discuss the false confession phenomenon with a group of new criminal profilers. In doing so, I also outlined the information that was provided to me by federal law enforcement polygraph examiners. One of the newer profilers then raised his hand and asked what value could be gained by asking experts in interrogation about false confessions. This question helped to exemplify an underlying flaw in the existing efforts to study false confessions, namely the tendency to focus only on the interrogations that have gone drastically wrong. It is hard to argue that there is tremendous value in learning from the mistakes of others. However, it is ridiculous to suggest that nothing can be learned by experts in a particular field. To the contrary, learning how the most successful people in a specific occupation conduct themselves is known as 'best practices.' For this reason I chose to speak to the best criminal interrogators I could find.

In my study, I served as the primary collector of data in administering the qualitative interviews of state and federal law enforcement polygraph examiners. As such, it became necessary for me to address any potential biases that may have hindered the study. As noted by Frankfort-Nachmias and Nachmias (2008), while personal interviews have the distinct advantage of flexibility that is found to be lacking in other research methodologies, personal interviews also suffer from a lack of standardized data collection. This lack of standardization renders the personal interview approach highly vulnerable to interviewer bias. In an attempt to counteract the possible negative effects of any such biases, I chose to identify and address potential sources of bias. They are as follows:

Based on the fact that I am a career law enforcement officer, a polygraph examiner, and I specialize in the interview and interrogation of criminal subjects, I maintain a worldview that may be inherently different from academic false confession researchers who are not employed in the field of law enforcement, who consult with advocacy groups like the Innocence Project, and/or who routinely testify on behalf of the defense. While some may consider this difference in worldview as a source of potential bias, I consider it a balance to the existing research which has largely ignored the insights of law enforcement officers in the study of false confessions. Despite being professionally trained to avoid biased behavior, I am not immune to the potentiality of biased thoughts. However, during the course of my study, I made every effort to ensure that my own thoughts neither influenced the interviewing of research participants nor affected the collection and analysis of data. To assist in the monitoring of any potentially biased thoughts, I provided interview questions to a trained colleague for review to ensure that no bias appeared in the wording of the questions. Having been trained as a polygraph examiner and interrogator in the identification of verbal and nonverbal cues, I remained vigilant about the existence of such cues in the interviewing of the research participants. Based on Creswell's (2013) recommendation that qualitative researchers utilize the process of reflexivity to continuously examine their own biases, I maintained reflective notes of my personal thoughts, feelings, problems, and prejudices as a means of monitoring potential biases that may negatively impact my research.

Glesne and Peshkin (as cited by Creswell, 2013), referenced the use of 'backyard' research in which studies are conducted in the researcher's own organization or work setting. While this type of research offers a more convenient means of collecting data, it also opens the researcher to potential problems associated with the biased reporting of data. Half of my study can be considered backyard research as my initial study involved me interviewing fellow polygraph examiners employed within my own law enforcement agency. In gaining access to this population, I discussed this research study with the head of the polygraph unit and furnished him a copy of my research plan. The supervisor reviewed my prospectus and sanctioned the anticipated qualitative interviews with the polygraph examiners employed within the agency. I further disclosed the purpose and intentions of my study with multiple layers of management within the organization who also provided approval.

The potential problems associated with this backyard study were minimized by the fact that I had no supervisory, instructor, or administrative power over the members of this population. In addition, I also employed multiple reliability procedures to mitigate qualitative validity concerns associated with this backyard research. More specifically, I: a) checked generated reports to ensure that no obvious mistakes were made during the documentation process; b) routinely compared the collected data with the specified codes as a means of preventing a shift in the meaning of the codes during the coding process; and c) enlisted the assistance of a colleague to cross-check codes to verify that agreement existed in the use of similar codes for the same passages of text.

While some may argue that the negatives of a backyard research design outweigh the benefits, it is important to note that an overwhelming benefit of my study is the fact that I was granted access to an otherwise reluctant and suspicious population. As noted by Ainsworth (2002), law enforcement officers tend to be a closed culture that does not often welcome interruptions from outside entities. For this reason, research involving law enforcement is often limited to those organizations that are willing to invite researchers into their agencies (Kassin et al., 2002). In light of this problem of access, Bull and Soukara (2009) identified that a sufficiently good relationship, which may take many years to establish, must be formed between law enforcement agencies and psychological researchers before they are willing to allow for the comprehensive scrutiny of their interviewing processes. Some may argue that in the case of federal law enforcement agencies, such access may be even more difficult, if not impossible, for a researcher to obtain. However, as I am a sworn law enforcement officer and polygraph examiner employed by the agency from which research participants were initially recruited for my study, the concerns associated with backyard research were outweighed by the unique and unbridled access to an otherwise inaccessible population.

For the second group of participants in my study, I contacted a state law enforcement agency in the midwestern United States who employed 10 polygraph examiners and one supervisor throughout the state. In speaking with the polygraph supervisor, I explained the purpose and nature of my study and asked if his group of polygraph examiners would be willing to participate in the study. The supervisor agreed. It is important to note that for this group of participants, I had a pre-existing relationship with only one participant, but the nature of this relationship was neither close nor continuing. While the secondary study with the state polygraph examiners cannot be considered backyard research, it was my professional role as a federal polygraph examiner that granted me unique access to a group that would likely be unavailable to a traditional academic researcher.

In addition to the clarification of the potential biases I brought to this study, I also employed other validity strategies to ensure accuracy in the findings of both groups. For example, I utilized member checking to verify the accuracy of the findings by providing the participants with the final report and asking them to verify that the findings accurately reflected the information the participants provided during the course of the interview process. I also ensured that rich and detailed descriptions of themes developed through the collected data were used to increase the validity of the findings. As various perspectives were collected during this research, I documented negative or discrepant data as a means of enhancing the overall credibility of the information. As recommended by Creswell (2013), I also used a peer debriefer who reviewed the study and made inquiries, thereby ensuring validity through consistency in interpretation.

Methodology
Participant Selection Logic

For this study, I identified a total of 23 polygraph examiners to participate in qualitative interviews regarding their experiences in conducting interrogations of criminal subjects and obtaining truthful and false confessions. Thirteen of the examiners were employed within a federal law enforcement agency and 10 were employed within a state law enforcement agency in the midwestern United States. I questioned the examiners about the manner in which they approach the interrogation of criminal subjects to maximize the likelihood of a true confession, the extent to which they have experienced false confessions, and the circumstances at the time that they experienced a false confession. As the research questions outlined above required specific knowledge and use of interrogative techniques, the sample from which potential participants could be obtained was relatively small. All polygraph examiners had previously obtained training in interviewing, interrogation, and the administration of polygraph examinations through either the federal polygraph school located at Ft. Jackson, South Carolina or through one of several private polygraph schools sanctioned by the state law enforcement agency. Based on the standardized training processes, as well as the similarity in assigned job responsibilities, I considered the state and federal polygraph examiners in these two agencies to be a homogenous group suitable for this research study.

Because the federal law enforcement agency employed roughly 100 polygraph examiners, it was necessary for me to select a sample from what could be considered a very specialized subgroup. To select participants from the federal law enforcement agency, I employed a purposive sampling method which, according to Patton (2002), involved me using my subjective judgment in an attempt to select sampling units that represent the specified population (Patton, 2002). More specifically, I employed a homogenous sampling method. Homogenous sampling is a purposive sampling method in which the final sample is comprised of units that share similar characteristics or traits. This sampling method is often employed when the research questions specifically relate to the characteristics of a particular group that will later be examined in detail (Patton, 2002). As previously noted, my initial study explored the experiences of federal polygraph examiners, a homogenous group that shares similar backgrounds, training, and job responsibilities. As the research questions outlined above specifically related to this group because of their specialization in criminal interrogation, I believed that a homogenous sampling technique was the most suitable means of sampling for this study. Conversely, since the state law enforcement agency employed 10 non-supervisory polygraph examiners, and because all 10 agreed to participate in the study, I selected all of these examiners to participate in the second study.

In addition to identifying a suitable sampling technique for the initial study, it was also necessary for me to identify a suitable sample size for this research project. A key consideration in selecting an appropriate sample size involves the concept of saturation. Glaser and Strauss (as cited by Guest, Bunce, & Johnson, 2006), identified saturation as the point in data collection when the researcher begins experiencing a continuous collection of the same or similar data with no new data being identified. In their empirical study of saturation and sample size, Guest et al. (2006) operationally defined saturation as the point in which continued data collection and analysis fails to produce the need for additional changes in an established codebook. In my study, saturation occurred when no new information was collected during interviews with federal law enforcement polygraph examiners. In addition, Romney, Batchelder, and Weller (as cited by Guest et al., 2006), developed consensus theory in which they posited that experts tend to agree with one another based upon their shared expertise and, for this reason, relatively small samples may be suitable for the collection of highly accurate information. Guest et al. reported reaching a saturation point after only 12 interviews. For these reasons, I found a sample size of 13 federal law enforcement polygraph examiners to be suitable as a saturation point was realized after 13 interviews from such a homogenous group were conducted. For the second study, a sample size was less of a concern as all 10 of the non-supervisory polygraph examiners employed by the state law enforcement agency agreed to participate in the study.

The final sample between the two studies was comprised of 23 law enforcement polygraph examiners (13 federal and 10 state) who are currently assigned to 22 different cities in 10 different states throughout the United States. Fifteen of the participants were white males; four were white females; two were black males; and two were males of Hispanic descent. The participants ranged in age from 35 to 55, with a mean age of 47. The participants' law enforcement experience ranged from 9 to 31 years, with a mean length of 21.2 years. All but seven of the participants noted that the entirety of their law enforcement experience was gained through employment with their current agency. The participants' experience as a federal or state law enforcement polygraph examiner ranged from 1 to 17 years, with a mean polygraph experience level of 6.4 years. To encourage truthful disclosures from the participants, they were advised in the consent form and reminded prior to the interview that I was not acting in a supervisory capacity within their agency;

their participation in the study had no bearing on their employment, and the information they provided would remain confidential.

Instrumentation

In my study, I employed an interview protocol to assist in the collection of data. Based on my years of law enforcement experience with interviewing and comprehensive note-taking, as well as the bureaucratic problems associated with the audio or video-recording of state and federal law enforcement officers, I decided to record the information I obtained during the qualitative interviews through the use of handwritten notes. I then used these notes to generate a report of interviews from which I identified and analyzed themes. A copy of the interview protocol is presented below.

Qualitative Interview Questions

1. Background

    1.1 Participant information:

- Age
- Gender
- Total length of time in law enforcement
- Length of time as a current agent/trooper
- Length of time as a polygraph examiner

    1.2 Extent of interview/interrogation training

2. Approach to criminal interrogation

    2.1 What is your general approach to interrogating criminal subjects?

    2.2 Why do you think guilty people confess to you?

    2.3 What reasons have people given you for truthfully confessing?

3. False confessions

    3.1 To what extent have you experienced false confessions?

3.2 If you experienced a false confession, what were the circumstances?

3.3 How can you tell if a confession is true or false?

3.4 Why do you think a person would falsely confess to a crime they did not commit?

4. Personal procedures

4.1 How do you go about reviewing a subject's Miranda rights?

4.2 How do you go about documenting your confessions?

4.3 When conducting a polygraph examination, what is your typical length of time between the introduction and the start of the post-test/interrogation?

4.4 How long do your interrogations typically last?

4.5 What do you think is an inappropriate or egregious length of time to interrogate someone?

5. Interrogative Methods

5.1 What interrogative techniques do you believe are effective in eliciting a true confession? Why?

5.2 What interrogative techniques do you believe are ineffective in eliciting a true confession? Why?

5.3 Which interrogative techniques do you believe are likely to cause a false confession? Why?

5.4 What are your thoughts about the following interrogative techniques:
   A. Sleep deprivation?
   B. Offering the subject a deal?
   C. Presenting a subject with false evidence?
   D. Using the 'Bluff Technique'?
   E. Preventing them from speaking to an attorney?

5.1 Which interrogation techniques would you never use? Why?

6. Experiences after the interrogation

6.1   Within the state/federal system, do you believe that a confession ultimately benefits the subject or harms the subject? Why?

6.2   In your experience, is there a difference in how criminal subjects are treated by the state/federal system when they confess as compared to when they continue their denials? If so, what is that difference?

6.3   In your experience, are cases automatically closed once a confession is obtained? If not, what else takes place?

6.4   In your experience, do state/federal prosecutors automatically convict a subject based on his/her confession? If not, what else takes place?

Procedures for Data Collection and Analysis

Because of the decentralized nature of both organizations, it was necessary for me to conduct interviews of participants via telephone as many of them are currently assigned to distant areas or states. The duration of my interviews ranged from 52 to 97 minutes. I documented the information provided by the participants through handwritten notes which totaled 165 pages. These notes were then used to create typed interview reports which totaled 224 pages. I then looked for patterns of responses as they related to the manner in which state and federal law enforcement polygraph examiners approach criminal interrogations; the interrogative techniques that they believe contribute to true confessions; the interrogative techniques that they believe contribute to false confessions; the extent to which they have experienced false confessions; and the circumstances at the time that they experienced a false confession. As patterns of responses were found, I developed a coding scheme in which to classify and organize the data. I also utilized the NVivo qualitative software package to consolidate the large amount of information gleaned from the interviews and to code the information into related chunks of data. NVivo allowed me to more thoroughly search for potential patterns of responses and themes as I continuously reevaluated the codes.

While some, especially those without a research background, likely found this particular chapter less than exciting, I believe that it is important to explain the research methodology that I employed in arriving at my own conclusions. For much of the remainder of this book, I will present the various conclusions and assumptions made by academic researchers, expert witnesses, and advocates about the real-world of criminal interrogation. I will then compare this information to the insights offered by the state and federal law enforcement polygraph examiners with whom I spoke. This will help to demonstrate the often vast disconnect between the conclusions of academics in the laboratory and law enforcement practitioners who actually do the job on a daily basis. Although some areas of agreement do exist, the significant differences in conclusions cannot be overlooked. There are undoubtedly some within the hallowed halls of academia who perceive our country's law enforcement personnel as nothing more than uneducated, societal infantry-men who exist only to ruin your day with a speeding ticket or to destroy your life through abusive and unethical behavior. To the contrary, there are likely those within the thin blue line of law enforcement who operate under the oft-repeated maxim of George Bernard Shaw that, "Those who *can* do, those who *can't* teach." In short, these two disparate groups present profoundly different pictures of what constitutes effective police interrogation and the pesky problem of false confessions.

For too long society has heard only the positions of the academic researcher, the false confession expert witness, and the members of advocacy groups fighting for the release of those who have been wrongfully imprisoned. Their positions have been bolstered by questionable media reporting and deleterious Hollywood portrayals of law enforcement interrogations. It is immaterial whether or not any of these groups are willing to admit to their unique world view and the biases that accompany the lens through which they view law enforcement. The simple fact remains that a palpable anti-law enforcement bias exists within the existing false confession literature.

Unfortunately, this bias has caused many who have chosen to explore the false confession phenomenon to rely on certain assumptions. For the remainder of this book, I will individually address these assumptions and the errors in logic that they have created.

CHAPTER 4

Rethinking the Innocence Project Statistics

Coming Together

U ndoubtedly, many have heard of the noble efforts of the advocacy group known as the Innocence Project. The Innocence Project was founded by Peter Neufeld and Barry Scheck in 1992 to utilize modern advancements in DNA technology to exonerate those individuals who have been wrongfully convicted and to bring about reform within the United States criminal justice system so that similar injustices do not occur in the future (Innocence Project, 2020). As of the writing of this text, the Innocence Project has successfully exonerated 377 wrongfully convicted prisoners (Innocence Project, 2020). It is important for all readers to realize that law enforcement is not necessarily at odds with the goals of these wrongful conviction advocates. If a meaningful discussion is to be held regarding the faults of the criminal justice system, both sides must come to realize the worth of their counterparts.

Those in law enforcement must come to understand that the various members working within the Innocence Project have received a calling to right very specific wrongs. They have dedicated their time, talents, and professional careers to free innocent people from unjustifiable prison sentences. In the same vein, those working with groups like the Innocence Project must also realize that the countless number of individuals working within the law enforcement profession have also dedicated their time, talents, and professional careers to ensure that guilty people are punished for their offenses against our fellow citizens. Unfortunately, when a member is called to either group, it can be very easy to get lost in the arrogance of their own calling. For example, law enforcement officers may immediately come to believe that Innocence Project advocates are nothing but "bleeding heart liberals" who seek to free every prisoner that law enforcement has worked so tirelessly to bring to justice. Conversely, Innocence Project advocates may immediately view all law enforcement officers as the American version of the Nazi Gestapo seeking to imprison every person with whom they come into contact. I can say with complete certainty: Both views are not only biased, but profoundly incorrect.

Without law enforcement, society would degenerate to an 'only the strong survive' mentality in which the most violent and aggressive prey on the meek and mild. The obvious problems associated with this approach are not even worthy of discussion. It is equally important to note that without the efforts of groups like the Innocence Project, 377 innocent people would currently be incarcerated for crimes they did not commit. It is a very simple, yet torturous exercise for any of us to imagine what it would feel like to spend decades behind bars for a crime that we did not actually commit. What those in law enforcement must also consider is the fact that for every person that is wrongfully committed, one truly guilty subject is left on the streets to continue their raping and pillaging of society. Law enforcement officers must also realize that with every proven wrongful conviction, society's trust in their local police deteriorates; the reputation of the lead investigator is impugned; and the investigating agency may be opened to costly civil lawsuits. In short, just as wrongful conviction advocates must admit that society cannot exist without the police, law enforcement officers must similarly admit that wrongful conviction advocates are needed to ensure that the innocent are not punished; the guilty do not remain at large; and society does not lose faith in our law enforcers.

As with any profession, zealots can exist in both groups. There certainly exist law enforcement officers who abuse their power to misguidedly arrest and investigate subjects that *they* believe are guilty, regardless of the existing case facts and evidence. However, there also exist wrongful conviction advocates who see the police as the true offenders and believe that no one should ever be arrested, questioned by police, or incarcerated. Both extremists are wrong, and thankfully, uncommon. So, the discussion about wrongful convictions must begin with both parties stipulating to the fact that not only should the truly innocent *not* be convicted, but the truly guilty *must* be convicted. I contend that any individual who cannot agree to *both* of these assertions regardless of which group they occupy is not suitable to continue their calling. Similarly, any individual who cannot identify the nobility of their counterpart's role within the criminal justice system has become overwhelmed by their own bias.

Despite the importance of both roles, it cannot be forgotten that one of these groups is motivated by advocacy. In essence, an advocate seeks to influence the decision-making of a target institution or system. In the case of the Innocence Project, they readily admit that they seek to bring reform to the criminal justice system, so that innocent people are not wrongly convicted in the future (Innocence Project, 2020). In reading through the 377 cases of wrongfully convicted subjects on their website, the Innocence Project routinely highlights the actions of law enforcement investigators and forensic scientists who overlooked exculpatory evidence, abused their authority, or simply violated the law to ensure the successful arrest and prosecution of an individual they believed to be guilty. Simply put, the Innocence Project website provides countless vignettes in which law enforcement was incorrect in their actions. However, in reading these cases, it also becomes readily apparent that the Innocence Project has also made mistakes, and these mistakes are incessantly repeated throughout the false confession research.

The False Confession Statistic

False confession researchers frequently point to the Innocence Project as their support for claiming that false confessions happen routinely and are a large contributing factor to wrongful convictions. Researchers have repeatedly referenced the claims of the Innocence Project that 25% of wrongful convictions are caused, at least in part, by false confessions (Chapman, 2013; Hasel & Kassin, 2009; Malloy, Shulman, & Cauffman, 2014; Pimentel, Andorfer, & Malloy, 2015; Redlich, 2004; Redlich, Summers, & Hoover, 2010). Over time, this number has been reported as 27% (Trocino, 2016); 28% (Joselow, 2019; Lackey, 2020), and 30% (Bernhard & Miller, 2018; Waxman, 2020; Woody et al., 2018). Despite the frequency with which these numbers are referenced, it is critically important that these concepts not be conflated. For example, this does not mean that between 25% and 30% of all interrogations result in a false confession. It is easy to make this mistake for those who are not familiar with the research. In fact, my wife recently reviewed a doctoral student's dissertation prospectus relating to false confessions in which the student inaccurately reported this statistic in this manner. What the Innocence Project statistic actually means is that between 25% and 30% of individuals *who were proven to be wrongfully convicted* had falsely confessed, at least in part, to the crime. Readers of this text, particularly law enforcement professionals or prosecutors who may not be well-versed in the reading of research, must not mistake this very important difference.

It is also important to be mindful of the caveated verbiage "at least in part", that is routinely provided when reporting the aforementioned statistic. This wording exists to remind consumers of the Innocence Project data that between 25% and 30% of wrongfully convicted subjects were not always successfully prosecuted based on their confessions alone. There are many instances in which the subject not only falsely confessed, but there also existed a false eyewitness identification, flawed testimony about physical evidence from a forensic scientist, etc. Moreover, some of these confessions may not have been a full acceptance of responsibility, but rather admissions to certain aspects of the crime such as being present, overhearing plans of the crime, and so on. Simply put, in those 25% to 30% of wrongful conviction cases, there may have been other contributing factors besides the subject's false confession that led to their wrongful conviction. The following will be an exercise in identifying and deducting these contributing factors from the overall number of false confessions leading to a wrongful conviction.

False Testimony vs. False Confessions

Other concerns exist with the numbers touted by the Innocence Project, namely the operational definition of their concepts. For example, there appears to exist a problem in how the Innocence Project has defined a false confession. While 107 (28%) of the 377 proven cases of wrongful conviction included a false confession, a relatively large number of these cases are actually mislabeled. Kassin and Gudjonsson (2004) define a confession as, "a detailed written or oral statement in which a person admits to having committed some transgression, often acknowledging guilt for a crime" (p. 35). In other words, a criminal confession involves the subject's acceptance of responsibility for a criminal act.

In their featured cases of wrongful conviction, the Innocence Project mislabeled 25 cases as a false confession when in fact they were false confessions rendered by another person. An example of such mislabeling can be observed in the 1976 case of Lewis Fogle who was wrongfully imprisoned for 33 years for the rape and death of 15-year-old Deann Long in Indiana County, Pennsylvania. In this case, an amateur hypnotist and college professor hypnotized and questioned a person of interest who had offered five different statements about Long's murder. In a fifth hypnotized statement years after the murder, the individual identified that brothers Lewis and Dennis Fogle drove the girl to the woods and raped her. Lewis Fogle then reportedly shot Long in the back of the head with a rifle he retrieved from under the front seat of their vehicle. Dennis Fogle was questioned five years after the murder at which time he confessed and gave a statement that was nearly identical to the hypnotized statement. Lewis Fogle was then arrested and charged with murder and rape. While awaiting trial in jail, three men came forward and claimed that Lewis Fogle had confessed to them about killing Long (Innocence Project, 2020).

It is uncertain what the Innocence Project personnel tasked with coding this case may have been thinking. Whether they were referring to the false confession of Dennis Fogle (whose charges were later dismissed for insufficient evidence) or the claims made by the three jailhouse snitches that Lewis Fogle had confessed to the murder while awaiting trial. Innocence Project employees considered this a wrongful conviction based on a false confession. It is important to note that at no time during his own questioning, or during the ensuing legal process, did Lewis Fogle ever confess and accept responsibility for killing Deann Long. To consider his wrongful conviction to be caused in part by a false confession is inaccurate and untrue. If a co-conspirator were to falsely confess and testify that they committed a crime with another subject, this would be a case of 'false testimony,' not 'false confession.' Similarly, if a jailhouse snitch were to falsely claim and testify that a subject confessed to him while incarcerated, this too would be a case of false testimony. The National Registry of Exonerations (NRE), founded in 2012 to provide detailed information about all known exonerations in the U.S. since 1989, agrees with this assertion and identifies Lewis Fogle's wrongful conviction to be a result of, "Perjury or False Accusation," not false confession. Quite simply, the Innocence Project not only mislabeled Fogle's wrongful conviction as being precipitated by a false confession, but they similarly mislabeled 24 other cases in the same manner.

The incorrect counting of some of these cases by the Innocence Project and/or the National Registry of Exonerations can also be caused by an overly inclusive approach to identifying false confessions. Leo (2007) highlights this point by explaining:

> I think they over-count because they count each defendant in
> cases in which there's a false confession about the same crime,
> even if not every defendant made a false confession. So if there
> are four defendants and two falsely confessed and they were
> all exonerated, exculpated, by DNA, the National Registry of
> Exonerations counts all four as false confessions. I would just
> count the two (p. 699).

In the simplest terms possible, if one of the co-defendants falsely confesses, then all of the co-defendants may sometimes be included as false confessors. This approach obviously skews the numbers and is partly responsible for inflating the frequently repeated statistic that 25% to 30% of wrongful convictions are caused by false confessions. I am not suggesting that this inflation was a purposeful undertaking. In social science research, the degree to which different people can arrive at a consensus in rating a particular piece of data is known as interrater reliability. As noted by Lewis-Beck, Bryman, and Liao (2004), "Behavioral scientists often need to evaluate the consistency of raters' judgments pertaining to characteristics of interest" (p. 513). In the case of the Innocence Project, it is highly likely that many different people were responsible for inputting the data from these various wrongful conviction vignettes. In all likelihood, the mislabeling that occurred in identifying cases of false testimony as cases of false confession may simply be a result of poor interrater reliability. Still, regardless of the cause, these 25 cases should be deducted from the overall number of wrongful convictions caused by false confessions.

Updating the Math *While the Innocence Project (2020) claims that 107 of their 377 wrongful conviction cases (28%) involve a false confession, deducting the 25 mislabeled false testimony cases drops the running total of false confessions to 82 out of 377 wrongful convictions, or 21.7%.*

Dream Statements, Equivocal Confessions, and Non-Interrogation Related Confessions

In addition to the mislabeling of false testimony as false confessions, the Innocence Project has also included statements that fall far short of an actual confession. In several additional cases, the wrongfully convicted subject did not actually accept responsibility for the crime, but instead referenced dreams that they had regarding the crime. An example of such a 'dream statement' case can be observed in the wrongful conviction of Steven Linscott who served 10 years in prison for the 1980 rape and murder of Karen Phillips in Oak Park,

Illinois. Linscott was a neighbor of Phillips' and a Bible Study student. He approached police and informed them that he had a dream on the night of Phillips' death (National Registry of Exonerations, 2020). More specifically, Linscott explained that in his dream, a woman had been beaten to death with a long, thin weapon and died in a passive position. Because the murder weapon was identified as a tire iron, and because Phillips' body was found in what was perceived to be a Hindu pose suggestive of the passive acceptance of death, Linscott's dream statement was considered to be a confession. This purported confession was supported by flawed forensic testimony that hair found at the crime scene was similar to Linscott's (Innocence Project, 2020).

If we are to identify a confession as an acceptance of responsibility for a criminal act, it is hard to consider 'dream statements' to be an acceptance of criminal wrongdoing. This is particularly true when various aspects of the dream statement do not match existing case facts. In other words, how can a person say, "I did it" without actually saying, "I did it"? Would the law enforcement officers reading this book feel that they had obtained a confession if their subject stated, "I dreamt of the victim being killed"? Would a prosecutor feel confident walking into court and claiming that the subject's reported dream is synonymous with a confession? The same question arises with equivocal statements like, "I probably did it" or "I guess I did it." Still, the Innocence Project inaccurately labels these statements as false confessions in compiling their wrongful conviction data.

There also exist multiple instances in the Innocence Project cases in which the subject falsely confessed, but the confession did not actually occur in conjunction with an interrogation. For example, Frederic Saecker, while being held in the county jail prior to his trial for an alleged kidnapping and sexual assault of a woman in Wisconsin in 1989, reportedly told a deputy, "I figured it out; I raped the girl, but she liked it." A second deputy reported that Saecker stated shortly before his trial, "That's why I raped her." Despite being diagnosed with organic delusional syndrome and schizophrenia (NRE, 2020), these statements were used against him at trial. A second example involves Cathy Woods who was wrongfully incarcerated for 35 years for the 1976 murder of Michelle Mitchell in Reno, Nevada. Three years after Mitchell's murder, law enforcement officers in Louisiana informed the Reno Police Department that Woods, while being treated as an in-patient in a Louisiana mental hospital, told a hospital employee that she had previously killed a woman in Reno named Michelle. Despite being diagnosed with schizophrenia, falsely claiming that she worked for the FBI, and being unable to provide the location of any evidence (NRE, 2020), the Innocence Project considered this a confession.

It cannot be overlooked that much of the false confession research seeks to blame the interrogative techniques of law enforcement officers for the elicitation of false confessions. However, in the wrongful conviction cases of Saecker and Woods, both subjects voluntarily confessed at a time when they were not actually being interrogated. Even if we ignore the fact that both Saecker and Woods were mentally ill, it is impossible to hold police interrogative practices responsible for these false confessions as neither individual was being interrogated when they confessed. The simple fact is that dream statements and equivocal comments like, "I guess I did it" are not actually confessions. They are not clearly articulated statements provided as an acceptance of responsibility for a criminal transgression.

Let's think of this another way. Assume that you were supposed to meet a friend for lunch at noon. They never showed, they never called, and they did not answer their cell phone when you attempted to call them to determine their whereabouts. You spend an hour waiting for them and then decide to dine by yourself. That evening you finally hear from this person and learn that they simply forgot about your lunch date. We can all assume that an apology would be in order. It is likely that most of us would say something similar to, "Oh my gosh. I am so sorry. I completely forgot. Let me make it up to you." However, instead of hearing this type of statement you heard, "Ya know, I had a dream last night about not showing up for an important business meeting." Or they stated, "I guess I'm sorry." In either instance, do you feel that you received an apology? With either statement, do you feel that this person accepted responsibility for missing your scheduled lunch? In all likelihood, the answer to both of these questions is, "No." Yet the Innocence Project considers these same types of statements in a criminal case to be a confession. An argument could be made in some of these situations that they are only counted as confessions because the police considered it a confession and/ or because the prosecution used these statements at trial. Either way, these statements are simply not confessions and should not be counted as such for the purposes of identifying the frequency of false confessions.

As I will continue to remind readers, it has routinely been suggested in the academic research that the actions of law enforcement officers and the interrogative practices they employ are largely responsible for the elicitation of false confessions (Frantzen & Can, 2012; Hasel & Kassin, 2009; Henkel, Coffman, and Dailey, 2008; Johnson and Drucker, 2009; Kassin, 2012; Kassin, Meissner, & Norwick, 2005; Levine, Kim, & Blair, 2010; Meissner & Kassin, 2002; Narchet et al., 2011; Nash & Wade, 2009; Newring & O'Donohue, 2008; Perillo & Kassin, 2011; Swanner & Beike, 2010). The falsity of this argument will be discussed in greater detail later. However, if this premise is to be believed, we must also deduct from the running total those cases in which a false confession was elicited outside of an interrogation setting. Simply put, if the subject was not being interrogated when they falsely confessed, how can the interrogator or their interrogative 'tactics' be held responsible for the false confession? For this reason, another 8 cases can be deducted from the overall Innocence Project statistics.

Updating the Math *By deducting dream statements, statements that fall short of a confession, and confessions provided outside of the interrogation setting, the running total of false confessions caused by law enforcement interrogative techniques and subsequently leading to a wrongful conviction drops to 74 out of 377 wrongful convictions, or 19.6%.*

Mental Illness and Intellectual Disabilities

As previously discussed, mental illness and intellectual disabilities play a key role in wrongful convictions, especially as they relate to false confessions.

This fact is reinforced by the cases highlighted on the Innocence Project (2020) website. While the concept of mental illness may be a little easier for many in law enforcement to grasp, intellectual disability (previously referred to as "mental retardation") may be more difficult. As outlined earlier, the American Psychiatric Association (2020) reports that an individual with an IQ score of between 70 and 75 can be considered intellectually disabled. It is interesting to note that the Innocence Project identified mental illness and/or intellectual disabilities in 28 of their false confession cases. In other words, per the Innocence Project's own statistics, 26% of the individuals who falsely confessed and were subsequently wrongfully convicted were identified as mentally ill and/or intellectually disabled.

It is not surprising that mental illness and/or intellectual disabilities are present in more than a quarter of false confession cases that have led to wrongful conviction. This is completely consistent with the existing academic research which has noted that the two key personal risk factors for false confession are mental illness (Kassin et al., 2010; Redlich, 2004; Redlich et al., 2010; Redlich et al., 2011) and "mental retardation" (Drizin & Leo, 2004; Redlich et al., 2011). I propose that these conditions have a far greater impact on the rendering of a false confession than the particular interrogative methods employed by the interrogator. This is particularly true based on the fact that the mental health issues presented in many of the Innocence Project false confession cases involve significant diagnoses like bipolar disorder, organic delusional syndrome, and schizophrenia, with many subjects experiencing repeated admissions to psychiatric hospitals. Similarly, while a person with an IQ score of between 70 and 75 can be considered intellectually disabled, nearly 78% of the Innocence Project cases in which an actual IQ score was provided involved IQ scores lower than 70. In fact, the average IQ score of these subjects was less than 65, which can be classified as "mentally deficient." In short, 26% of the false confession subjects presented by the Innocence Project can be considered to have significant mental health issues and cognitive impairments. Again, is the interrogative method the true problem, or is it the subject's decreased level of functioning that is primarily responsible for the false confession? While I will make a more thorough argument later about why mental illness and cognitive impairments are more responsible for false confessions than interrogative methods, for this exercise I believe that it is important to deduct cases with these types of impaired subjects from the overall total in order to obtain a more accurate accounting of false confessions caused primarily by the interrogative practices of law enforcement. To avoid double counting, only 26 of these cases will be deducted from the running total as two of the cases were already counted in previous categories.

Updating the Math *After deducting the 26 cases of false confession rendered by mentally ill and intellectually disabled subjects and not otherwise included in other contributing factor categories, the running total drops to 48 out of 377 cases of wrongful conviction, or 12.7%.*

Youth

Throughout the academic false confession literature, the youth of some criminal subjects has repeatedly been identified as a significant contributing factor for false confessions (Drizin & Leo, 2004; Malloy et al., 2014; Owen-Kostelnik et al., 2006; Pimentel et al., 2015). Not unlike the issues relating to mental illness and intellectual disabilities, this stems from the inherent differences in how juveniles process and respond to the world around them as compared with adults. While I more thoroughly addressed the susceptibility of young people to falsely confess in a previous chapter, the number of Innocence Project false confession cases involving children helps to support this underlying propensity. More specifically, of the 107 cases of false confession provided by the innocence project, 28 (26%) of them were children 17 years of age or younger. In fact, the average age of these false confessors was 15.6.

Similar to the reasoning offered for deducting mentally ill and intellectually deficient subjects, an argument can be made that the subject's status as a juvenile has more of an influence on the decision to falsely confess than

74

the interrogative practices employed against them. For the purposes of this exercise, I will make this exact argument. Since academic researchers, expert witnesses, and advocacy group members often highlight the interrogative practices of law enforcement officers as the primary cause of false confessions, I decided to remove any potentially confounding variables to obtain a better assessment of how frequently law enforcement's interrogative techniques cause false confessions. Although 28 of the Innocence Project's cases of false confession involved subjects 17 years of age or younger, not all of these cases will be deducted from the running total. Because some of these juvenile subjects were also mentally ill, cognitively impaired, did not actually confess, or are otherwise covered in other categories, only 12 juveniles will be deducted from the running total.

Updating the Math *By removing 12 children 17 years of age or younger who are not identified in other contributing factor categories, the running total of false confession cases caused by interrogative methods and leading to a wrongful conviction drops to 36 out of 377 cases, or 9.5%.*

Egregious Police Misconduct

Although many in academia hold the actions and interrogative techniques of law enforcement officers largely responsible for the elicitation of false confessions from innocent subjects (Frantzen & Can, 2012; Hasel & Kassin, 2009; Henkel, Coffman, and Dailey, 2008; Johnson and Drucker, 2009; Kassin, 2012; Kassin, Meissner, & Norwick, 2005; Levine, Kim, & Blair, 2010; Meissner & Kassin, 2002; Narchet et al., 2011; Nash & Wade, 2009; Newring & O'Donohue, 2008; Perillo & Kassin, 2011; Swanner & Beike, 2010), it is important to note that there is a monumental difference between interrogative strategies and police misconduct. This is a point that many false confession researchers, expert witnesses, and advocates either fail to realize or deliberately attempt to conflate. Various interrogative methods such as rationalizing criminal behavior, projecting blame for the crime onto another person, minimizing the seriousness of the offense, etc. have been utilized by successful and ethical law enforcement interrogators with a great deal of success in obtaining truthful confessions. However, it cannot be ignored that law enforcement officers have also engaged in inappropriate behaviors that have clearly resulted in false confessions. A distinction must be made between these two approaches before we can more thoroughly consider the Innocence Project's false confession numbers.

A perfect example of inappropriate interrogative techniques can be observed in the case of Ronald Jones who spent 10 years in prison for the 1985 rape and murder of Debra Smith in Chicago, Illinois. Approximately two weeks after Smith's death, a woman contacted police to report that she had also been raped. This victim went on to identify Jones as her assailant. After being interrogated for 18 hours, during which he was punched in the stomach by police and beaten with a 6-inch long, black object, Jones signed a confession (NRE, 2020). In a similar case in Chicago in 1994, Antwinica Bridgeman's lifeless body was found in the basement of an apartment building by Nevest Coleman. Coleman was subsequently interrogated by police. After sitting in an interrogation room for approximately 30 minutes, a detective entered the room, called him a "lying assed nigger," and then punched him two times in the side of the head with a closed fist. Coleman reported that he was then informed by detectives that if he just went along with their version of events, he would be permitted to go home. Detectives then instructed Coleman on what he was to say; they rehearsed this information with him, and then he provided a court-reported statement in which he implicated Darryl Fulton and another man. Fulton advised that during his own interrogation, after denying involvement in Bridgeman's death, a detective entered the room, hit him in the face, and then threatened to remove Fulton from the station and "put a bullet in his brain" (NRE, 2020).

In light of these accounts, some in law enforcement, particularly those with sterling reputations and a strong adherence to ethical behavior, may immediately discount this information as implausible. Simply put, professional law enforcers may find it hard to believe that one of their own would engage in such outrageous interrogative behavior. Still, there are a few things to keep in mind: 1) As with any profession, unethical law enforcement officers *do* exist and they *have* engaged in this type of behavior; 2) all three of these men were exonerated through DNA evidence, thereby lending credence to their claims that they were abused into rendering a false confession; and 3) these are statements that the Innocence Project are assuming to be true. We can therefore assume that all three of these men, and many others like them, have been physically abused by law enforcement officers in the past.

While it is hard to argue that some unethical and overzealous police officers have historically overstepped their bounds in attempting to obtain the truth, several questions arise from their behavior. First, would any current law enforcement agency find it acceptable to beat and/or threaten to kill a subject in order to obtain a confession? Second, what interview and interrogation regimen or instructors actually teach such an approach? It is impossible to fathom that any law enforcement interrogation course or instructor would actually instruct officers to obtain truthful information through torture or threats. It is equally ludicrous to believe that an ethical law enforcement agency would condone the elicitation of confessions in such a manner. As such, there should be a grand consensus from all of the individuals examining the false confession phenomenon that the interrogative actions taken against Jones, Coleman, and Fulton are not commonly accepted practices, but rather horrendous examples of police malpractice.

As the devil typically resides within the details, we cannot confuse ethical police interrogative techniques with abhorrent misconduct. If false confession researchers and expert witnesses are going to suggest that law enforcement officers' interrogative practices are largely responsible for the elicitation of false confessions, we must first differentiate between appropriate and inappropriate interrogation techniques if we are going to accurately assess the effect of interrogative methods. While academia has largely attacked the nature of commonly accepted interrogative practices like minimization, the Bluff Technique, and the False Evidence Ploy, we must make it a point to separate those practices from torture and abuse. Failing to differentiate between acceptable and unethical methods of interrogation would be akin to suggesting that current teaching techniques can harm children because some teachers engage in sexual activity with their students. When teachers, politicians, medical professionals, media personnel, entertainers, and athletes engage in poor or illegal behavior, the point is quickly made that these reprobates do not reflect the values of the larger group. The same consideration must also be given to law enforcement interrogators. Just because one doctor mistakenly leaves a sponge inside of a patient during surgery does not mean that all doctors are bad. Similarly, just because one interrogator beats a subject into rendering a false confession does not mean that all interrogators are unethical in their practice.

It must also be recognized that the examples of Jones, Coleman, and Fulton outlined above are the exception, not the rule. Because they reflect obvious cases of police interrogative misconduct, they should be deducted from the running total of false confessions before any conclusions are reached about the effects of legitimate police interrogation methods on the decision of innocent people to falsely confess. In reviewing the Innocence Project vignettes, 28 cases involving clear misconduct that were not otherwise captured in another category, were identified. Examples of the misconduct exhibited in these 28 cases include the following behaviors:

- Interrogations lasting between 12 and 40 hours
- Threatening the subject at knifepoint to confess
- Physically striking the subject
- Grabbing the subject by the neck
- Slapping the subject in the face and kicking him in the ribs
- Threatening to kill the subject and make it look like a suicide
- Subjecting the subject to 8 interrogations and 3 polygraph sessions
- Subjecting the subject to 5 polygraph sessions
- Denying the subject food, water, and legal counsel
- Hypnotizing the subject and feeding him case facts to support the confession

The actions outlined above reflect clear police malpractice. Furthermore, it is hard to conceive of a modern law enforcement organization and/or interview training protocol teaching and condoning such behavior by officers. Because such egregious interrogative actions (as opposed to legitimate interrogation techniques) caused the false confession, I decided to remove these cases from the Innocence Project data analysis.

Updating the Math *By removing 28 cases of egregious and physically abusive police misconduct that are not otherwise identified in other contributing factor categories, the running total drops to 8 out of 377 cases of wrongful conviction, or 2.1%.*

Re-Examining the Innocence Project Data

The Innocence Project's statistics are frequently used to support the premise that false confessions are widespread and frequently occurring. In fact, a cursory look at the data could lead to just such a conclusion as 28% of wrongful convictions were reported by the Innocence Project in April 2020 to be caused, at least in part, by false confessions. However, once we remove cases that: a) are mislabeled; b) involve statements that fall short of being an actual confession; c) involve confessions that occurred outside of the interrogative environment; d) were rendered by mentally ill subjects; e) were rendered by intellectually disabled subjects; f) involved juveniles 17 years of age or younger; g) involved egregious examples of police misconduct; or h) involved any combination of these factors, we obtain a far different picture. In essence, when we account for personal risk factors of the subject and/or subjects who were greatly abused or mistreated in the interrogation room, we are left with only 8 subjects who falsely confessed. In other words, if false confession researchers and expert witnesses are looking to blame routine, legitimate, and officially-sanctioned interrogative techniques for causing the elicitation of false confessions from adult subjects who are not mentally ill or intellectually disabled, only 8 such cases have been identified by the Innocence Project to have occurred in the last 47 years.

It is also important to note that of these 8 remaining cases, nearly all of them still involved questionable behavior at the hands of law enforcement. For example, some of these individuals confessed because they were threatened with the death penalty; some of their confessions were inconsistent with the confessions rendered by their co-conspirators; some of their confessions did not match existing case facts, and some of them provided statements that constantly changed. One subject with a fourth grade reading level was interrogated three times before falsely confessing. Another subject was interrogated for nine hours before falsely confessing, though his confession did not completely match existing case facts. Prior to trial, the prosecutor in this case concluded that the statement was actually coerced due to the subject's exhaustion, his high level of susceptibility, and his fear of the death penalty. However, the prosecutor failed to pass this information onto the defense. In other words, the remaining 8 cases are *still* not pure examples of a false confession caused by legitimate police interrogation methods. Still, they were not excluded from the aforementioned exercise because the subject was not reported to have clearly identifiable risk factors, and the law enforcement actions could not readily be identified as egregious.

It is highly coincidental and worthy of consideration that 6 of the 8 remaining false confession subjects were interrogated in one of two different investigations. A criminal investigation in Fairview, North Carolina produced three of these remaining false confessors while a criminal investigation in Forrest County, Mississippi produced three additional false confessors. Although not specified in sufficient detail by the Innocence Project vignettes, it would be a safe assumption that if each of these cases were able to produce three additional false confessions, some sort of police misconduct must have taken place during the course of each investigation, especially since these subjects were not reported to have any of the aforementioned personal risk factors. If we remove these two highly suspicious investigations, we are left with 2 false confession subjects that cannot immediately be placed in any of the risk categories outlined above. This means that only .5% of the wrongful conviction cases reported by the Innocence Project involved false confessions from adults who were not mentally ill, intellectually disabled, and/or were not abused by investigators.

In the simplest of terms, the 25%-30% Innocence Project statistic that is frequently cited by academic researchers is extremely misleading. This is particularly true if this statistic is being used to suggest that there is a link between legitimate interrogative practices and false confessions. Based on the same case information reported by the Innocence Project, it appears that routine and commonly accepted interrogative practices rarely lead to false confessions among adult subjects who are free of profound mental illness and intellectual deficiencies. Put another way, of the 107 wrongfully-convicted false confession subjects identified by the Innocence Project as of April 2020, 99.5% of them were children, mentally ill, intellectually disabled, and/or abused by police prior to rendering a false confession. This is not only a far cry from the 25%-30% statistic that is frequently reported in the existing literature, but it also helps to deduce that police misconduct and the personal risk factors of the subject may have more to do with false confessions than routine police interrogative practices.

Those Who Did Not Confess

While the reevaluation of the statistics outlined above helps to give more insight into the false confession phenomenon when appropriate interrogative techniques are employed, it is also important to highlight a critical, yet inherently overlooked, figure within the Innocence Project data. More specifically, we must consider the subjects who refuse to confess in the first place. When looking at the 377 wrongful conviction cases and 107 false confession cases provided by the Innocence Project, it can immediately be concluded that 270 wrongfully convicted subjects were able to avoid confessing during the course of their investigations/interrogations. This number rises to 295 subjects when we include the 25 mislabeled cases of subjects who did not actually confess. We can also add back in the 8 additional cases of subjects who, instead of providing an outright false confession, merely offered dream statements, unequivocal admissions, or confessed outside of the interrogation setting. That would bring the total number of wrongfully convicted subjects who did not outright confess to 303.

Those law enforcement professionals who have ever been tasked with investigating a violent crime would likely concede that most primary subjects were interviewed and interrogated during the course of the ensuing investigation. If this is true, it means that 80% of the wrongfully convicted subjects identified by the Innocence Project were strong enough to withstand the questioning of law enforcement officers in their case. This includes juvenile subjects, mentally ill subjects, mentally deficient subjects, and subjects who were outright physically or psychologically abused by their interrogators. In other words, even the subjects who were subjected to egregious police malpractice and/or had one or more risk factors, were capable of *not* confessing.

It is possible that some of these subjects may not have confessed because they invoked their Miranda Rights and refused to be questioned by authorities. If so, this is also of great importance as it demonstrates that such individuals were able to withstand law enforcement's purported pressure to interview them. As will be discussed in future chapters, false confession researchers and expert witnesses frequently portray law enforcement interrogators as vicious, unrelenting, and willing to employ whatever means necessary to obtain a confession (Brandl, 2014; Chapman, 2013; Conti, 1999; Kassin, 2012; Lassiter, 2010; Leding, 2012; Leo, 1996; Leo & Davis, 2010; Leo & Drizin, 2010; Narchet et al., 2011; Woody & Forrest, 2009). Similarly, Leo (1996) has compared law enforcement officers to con artists who use trickery and manipulation to get criminal subjects to waive their rights, thereby putting them one step closer to an interrogation. Still, these assumptions do not appear to be supported by the data. The Innocence Project's own data identifies that 80% of wrongfully convicted subjects, despite the highly coercive and manipulative tactics reportedly employed by law enforcement, were able to hold out against the purported arm-twisting of their interrogators. This also demonstrates that when it comes to wrongful convictions, approximately 80% of subjects were convicted for reasons other than a false confession. For the remaining 20%, all but 2 were either juveniles, mentally ill, intellectually deficient, and/or subjected to egregious acts of police misconduct. Based on these numbers, it would be illogical and misleading to conclude that the routine interrogative practices of police overbear the will of ordinary adult subjects or that ordinary adult subjects are likely to render a false confession during a routine interrogation.

Artificial Inflation of the Numbers

Whether a result of the advocacy underlying their efforts, poor inter-rater reliability, minimal practical law enforcement experience, or an outright attempt to mislead the public, the false confession statistics put forth by the Innocence Project continue to remain artificially inflated. In addition to including mislabeled false testimony, statements that fall short of being an actual confession, subject's suffering from profound mental health issues and intellectual deficiencies, juvenile subjects, and clear examples of police misconduct, these numbers are artificially inflated for several other reasons.

The Time Frame Imbalance

While the Innocence Project was founded in 1992, it cannot be overlooked that the cases they helped to resolve date back to as early as January 1973. This is important. If false confession researchers and expert witnesses are seeking to blame the interrogative techniques of law enforcement officers for causing false confessions, we must be aware that some of the cases date back to nearly 50 years ago. In fact, 86 (80%) of the Innocence Project's false confession cases occurred prior to 1995. This begs the question: Is it acceptable to judge the current practices of a profession based on practices that are between 25 and 47 years old? Would we do this with the medical profession? If doctors treated patients with leeches to cure an imbalance of bodily humors generations ago, is it fair or accurate to assume that they continue to engage in these same treatment protocols? For those who do not work in the field of academic research, it may be interesting to know that academia strives to avoid using research that is more than 5-7 years old in their writings. The reason for this is that it would not be academically sound to utilize dated research findings to gauge or support your current research endeavors. Yet, this is exactly what they are doing when they rely on the statistics of the Innocence Project's false confession cases.

The most recent wrongful conviction case involving a false confession cited by the Innocence Project occurred in 2003. Moreover, only 9 of the Innocence Project's false confession cases occurred between 2000 and 2020. In other words, only 8% of the false confessions cited by the Innocence Project have been elicited in the last 20 years. Based on this astronomical statistical imbalance of false confessions occurring over the last 47 years, one can only assume that law enforcement interrogators, like most subject matter experts, have continued to evolve and professionalize their craft over time. It can therefore be deduced that the large volume of earlier false confessions is artificially inflating the overall statistic to make it appear as if false confessions are a frequently occurring problem today. Sadly, many false confession researchers and expert witnesses are more than happy to use such misleading statistics to advance this illusion for their own personal and professional benefit.

The Multi-Subject Case Imbalance

In addition to the problems associated with the dated nature of the Innocence Project's false confession cases, there also exists a problem with the number of cases that have multiple subjects. An example of this problem can be observed in the previously discussed case of the "Beatrice Six" who had falsely confessed to the February 5, 1985 rape and murder of Helen Wilson in Beatrice, Nebraska. This single case led to the wrongful conviction of James Dean, Joseph White, Thomas Winslow, Ada Joann Taylor, Kathy Gonzalez, and Debra Shelden (Innocence Project, 2020). Similarly, Antron McCray, Kevin Richardson, Yusef Salaam, Raymond Santana, and Korey Wise were wrongfully convicted of raping and beating a female jogger in New York City's Central Park on April 19, 1989 after they were coerced into falsely confessing. This group of teenagers became known as the "Central Park Five" (Innocence Project, 2020). Yet another example involves the 1991 rape and murder of Cateresa Matthews in Dixmoor, Illinois. The ensuing investigation led to a series of false confessions and the eventual wrongful conviction of teenagers Jonathan Barr, Robert Taylor, Robert Veal, Shainne Sharp, and James Harden (Innocence Project, 2020). These cases involving multiple subjects serve to skew the Innocence Project data, thereby making it appear as if false confessions are much more common than they actually are. For example, these three separate investigations alone account for 16 false confessions according to the Innocence Project. It is not difficult to see how such multiple-subject cases can artificially inflate the overall false confession statistics. In fact, upon learning that there are 107 cases of wrongful conviction caused by false confessions, readers of the Innocence Project data may jump to the conclusion that this number reflects the work of 107 different investigations. This would be an incorrect assumption. What is particularly interesting is that 9 different investigations put forth by the Innocence Project are responsible for the elicitation of false confessions from 40 different subjects. Put another way, 37% of the total number of false confession cases touted by the Innocence Project are the result of 9 poorly-run investigations. This is significant as it cuts deep into the belief that false confessions are a frequently occurring phenomenon. Let's take a closer look as to why.

In total, the Innocence Project identifies 107 false confession subjects as of April 2020. However, these 107 false confession subjects resulted from only 67 different investigations. More specifically, 9 of these investigations involved 3 or more subjects and accounted for 40 false confession subjects overall. Another 9 of these investigations involved two subjects and accounted for 18 false confession subjects overall. Lastly, 49 of these investigations involved only one subject and accounted for an additional 49 false confessions. When these numbers are combined, we learn that 18 poorly-run investigations led to the elicitation of false confessions from 58 different subjects. In short, 18 investigations caused over half (54%) of the total number of Innocence Project false confession cases. This is noteworthy because it suggests that an unethical interrogator investigating multiple subjects will, not surprisingly, act unethically in multiple interrogations.

Let's consider the following analogy: A professional baseball team has a starting pitcher who tends to be unusually wild with his pitches and hits 4 batters every game. None of the other 4 starting pitchers has a similar problem. Over the course of a month, each of the 5 starting pitchers plays 3 games. That means that the 'wild' pitcher went on to hit 12 players over the last month while his teammates hit 0 batters. If we simply looked at the league statistics, we would observe that while the majority of the teams had only a few hit batters, the team with the wild pitcher has hit 12 batters during the last month. It would be inaccurate to suggest that this team has an overall accuracy problem with its pitching staff or that the team encourages its pitchers to hit batters and then condones such behavior. The simple fact is that *one* pitcher is responsible for *all* of the hit batters. Unfortunately, his 'wildness' is inflating the team's overall accuracy rating.

The same logic holds true for the large number of multi-offender cases in which multiple false confessions were elicited. Simply put, the Innocence Project's false confession statistics demonstrate that we do not have problematic interrogations in 107 cases. Instead, we have problematic interrogations in 67 cases. In essence, these multi-offender cases skew the data to make it appear as if a significantly larger number of interrogators (or departments) are eliciting false confessions than truly are. Again, when we account for the fact that 80% of the Innocence Project's false confession cases occurred more than 25 years ago and 18 cases account for 54% of the total number of false confessions, we being to see that the Innocence Project's statistics may be fostering an inaccurate picture of how widespread the false confession phenomenon is. It is important to note that this inaccurate picture may be further blurred by analyzing the jurisdiction in which these false confessions are occurring.

The Regional Imbalance

Because the Innocence Project's statistics are constantly utilized to assert that false confessions are a frequently occurring phenomenon, it is also important to take a closer look at where these cases have occurred within the

United States. When initially analyzing the total number of false confession cases occurring per state, the Innocence Project reported 67 different false confession cases. As previously highlighted, some of these cases involve one subject falsely confessing and some may involve as many as 6 subjects falsely confessing. However, upon closer analysis, 6 single-subject cases can be deducted as they were mislabeled as a false confession when the subject did not actually render a confession. This brings the total number of different false confession cases occurring throughout the United States between 1973 and 2020 to 61.

It can easily be argued that 61 different cases in which false confessions were rendered over a 47-year period is not an overpowering statistic and certainly is not indicative of a pervasive pattern across the United States. Still, the power of this statistic drops dramatically when we consider that over this 47-year period, the Innocence Project had not identified a single false confession case in 28 states. In other words, 56% of the states have not experienced a wrongful conviction caused by a false confession in the last 47 years according to Innocence Project data. An additional 9 states were identified to have only one false confession during this time period. If we were to operate under the premise that "once is a mistake and twice is a pattern of behavior," 74% of the states do not have a pattern of eliciting false confessions. Again, this hardly speaks to a false confession pandemic.

According to the Innocence Project data, of those states that have had more than one false confession leading to a wrongful conviction in the last 47 years, five states (California, Florida, New Jersey, Oklahoma, and Washington) have experienced two false confession cases; four states (Louisiana, Michigan, Virginia, and Wisconsin) have experienced three false confessions cases, and two states (North Carolina, and Pennsylvania) have experienced four false confession cases. In other words, 11 (22%) of the states are responsible for 30 (49%) of the false confession cases that have been proven by the Innocence Project to have resulted in a wrongful conviction in the last 47 years. What is particularly interesting is the fact that the states of Illinois and New York account for 22 (36%) of the false confession cases during this time period.

In other words, just two states are responsible for more than one-third of the Innocence Project's reported false confession cases.

It cannot go unnoticed that the State of Illinois, in particular the greater Chicago area (to include the cities of Dixmoor, Naperville, Oak Park, Park Forest, and Waukegan) are responsible for 15 (25%) of the false confession cases in the last 47 years as reported by the Innocence Project. While it is astonishing that such a small region is responsible for a quarter of the nation's proven false confession cases, it is not necessarily surprising, in light of the notorious career of former Chicago Police Commander Jon Burge. Burge joined the Chicago Police Department in 1970 and through the 1970s and 1980s, he and the detectives under his command were accused of coercing confessions from more than 100 subjects through physical torture. The torture included the use of cattle prods, smothering subjects with plastic typewriter covers, and placing guns in the mouths of subjects while pretending to play Russian roulette. He was fired from the department in 1993 and was convicted in 2010 of federal obstruction of justice and perjury charges stemming from a civil suit in which he was accused of inflicting cruel and unusual punishment on prisoners (Roberts, 2018). An argument could easily be made that Burge's time as a Commander may have helped to create a culture of abuse that spread throughout the Chicago Police Department and possibly to surrounding jurisdictions. If so, this may account for the disproportionate number of false confession cases occurring in the greater Chicago area between 1978 and 1994.

The potential misdeeds of a particular officer may also help to explain the disproportionate number of false confession cases occurring in and around New York City as reported by the Innocence Project. More specifically, in a 2019 New York Times article, Piccoli wrote about retired New York homicide detective Louis Scarcella. In the article, Piccoli reported that Scarcella was being accused of framing eight people for murder, and that he has had the convictions of multiple subjects in his former cases overturned. In the article, Scarcella denies ever acting unethically in order to obtain a conviction. In addition, Piccoli notes that Scarcella has never been charged with breaking the law or official misconduct. Still, it is important to draw attention to the fact that Scarcella is specifically named in multiple cases highlighted by both the Innocence Project and the National Registry of Exonerations.

The documented misdeeds leading to Burge's conviction and the allegations levied against Scarcella are entirely consistent with the claims of the Innocence Project's cofounder Peter Neufeld. In the 2020 Netflix series *The Innocence Files* (Garbus, Gibney, & Williams, 2020), Neufeld stated, "One of the things that we find at the Innocence Project is that there are certain prosecutors or detectives who engage in serial misconduct." Whether or not it was his intention, Neufeld's statement helps to demonstrate that the collective group of U.S. law enforcement officers and the routine interrogative practices they employ are not necessarily the problem. Instead, it may simply be that a handful of specific investigators and/or departments are disproportionately causing the problem. The regional imbalance of the Innocence Project's data certainly appears to support this premise. When looking at the regional data more closely, it becomes readily apparent that the false confession phenomenon is not as far-reaching and pervasive as academic researchers and expert witnesses would have us believe, and it certainly does not appear to be a national problem.

National Registry of Exonerations

In addition to the Innocence Project, another tremendous source of information on wrongful convictions and their related causes is the National Registry of Exonerations (NRE). The NRE was founded in 2012 and designed to provide detailed information about all exonerations of wrongfully convicted subjects in the United States since 1989. The project is a joint effort of the Newkirk Center for Science & Society at the University of California Irvine, the University of Michigan Law School, and the Michigan State University College of Law (NRE, 2020). To further identify the extent to which false confessions occur, it is helpful to similarly review the data provided by the NRE. As of April 2020, the NRE reported that 2,604 wrongfully convicted subjects within the United States have been exonerated since 1989.

Of these exonerations, 318 subjects were wrongfully convicted, based in part, on their false confessions. From the very outset, this number is interesting. Whereas the Innocence Project reports that 28% of their wrongful conviction cases were caused by false confessions, the NRE's numbers suggest that only 12% of their wrongful conviction cases involved a false confession. The NRE was designed to look at all exonerations in the United States since 1989 which is why their total number of exonerations is seven times higher than the Innocence Project's total number of exonerations. However, we find by multiplying the number of wrongful convictions in such a manner, the overall percentage of false confession cases drops by more than half. While some of this may be explained by the fact that the Innocence Project has a tendency to mislabel their false confession cases, a conclusion that is supported by the NRE data, it also demonstrates that the Innocence Project's reported false confession statistic is grossly exaggerated.

As previously done with the Innocence Project numbers, it is important to further analyze the NRE data to get a better understanding of the false confession phenomenon. While the NRE identifies that 318 of their 2,604 wrongful conviction cases involved false confessions, I found 11 cases to be mislabeled (i.e. they did not actually involve a confession from the subject). Similarly, an additional 9 cases were removed from consideration as they did not necessarily provide conclusive proof that the subject falsely confessed. For example, in one of the NRE cases, a 17-year-old boy confessed to having consensual sex with an underage girl who had gotten pregnant. The girl claimed that she had never had sex with any other person. However, when the baby was born, DNA testing identified that the subject was not the father, and he was released. This does not mean that his confession was false; it just means that he was not the father of the child. In total, there were 9 cases in which conclusive proof of a false confession was not available and these cases were removed from consideration. That brings the overall number of false confessions to 298.

Like the aforementioned review of the Innocence Project data, the NRE cases also included a great number of contributing factors that should be deducted. While some cases involved multiple contributing factors, the following number of cases were deducted from the overall total as they had more to do with the subject's personal risk factors or the use of egregious and unethical interrogative methods by law enforcement officers:

- 115 cases of abuse and egregious police misconduct
- 59 cases involving mentally ill or intellectually deficient subjects
- 45 cases involving children 17 years of age or younger
- 25 cases fell far short of being an actual acceptance of responsibility.
- 10 cases where subjects confessed prior to or outside of an interrogation

In addition to these problematic cases, 7 additional cases were removed because the subject said they never confessed, and while the police claim that they did confess, there was no audio recording, video recording, or written statement to prove that a confession was actually rendered. In some instances, there were no notes or written reports that a confession had ever occurred. In essence, 7 cases were deducted because the subject claimed that they never confessed, and there is no conclusive proof that they did. Lastly, 5 additional cases were removed because the subject reported falsely confessing to protect the truly guilty party. These cases were deducted because the confession was a conscious decision by the subject to take the rap for someone else rather than being a response to any type of interrogation technique.

When the aforementioned categories are removed from the NRE's total number of false confession cases, we are left with 32 subjects. While an argument could be made that this number is still high, it should be highlighted that this number still includes a number of questionable cases. For example, one case involved a subject who was drunk and high at the time of his interrogation. Multiple subjects in other cases were threatened with the electric chair or the death penalty. Another subject had a fourth grade reading level, and there were multiple instances in which the confessions from multiple subjects did not match the case facts and/or the statements of their co-defendants. Finally, in several instances multiple subjects falsely confessed in the same case. This would suggest that unethical interrogative methods must have been employed to get multiple criminal subjects in the same case to falsely confess to an offense that they did not commit. Still, even without deducting any of the remaining 32 false confession cases, this means that over the last 65 years, only 1.2% of the 2,604 exonerations identified by the NRE were elicited from adult subjects who were not mentally ill, did not suffer from serious cognitive deficiencies, and were not physically abused by police. This is relatively consistent with the .5% statistic I identified after analyzing the Innocence Project data.

Not unlike the Innocence Project information, the NRE data is greatly skewed by the time frame in which these confessions were elicited. More specifically, 69% of the NRE false confession cases occurred over 25 years ago and 81% occurred more than 20 years ago. As previously stated, this may suggest that law enforcement officers have continued to professionalize their questioning methods over recent decades. Similar to the data provided by the Innocence Project, the NRE false confession cases also seem to be more of a regional phenomenon with more than 43% of the cases occurring in the states of Illinois and New York. In short, after a more thorough analysis of the NRE data, it again appears that false confessions may not be as frequently occurring as some in academia would have us believe. Furthermore, both data sets may suggest that false confessions ultimately have more to do with abusive police misconduct and high-risk subjects than they have to do with commonly accepted interrogative techniques. Unfortunately, this is not what many academics and expert witnesses want judges and juries to believe.

The Non-False Confession Cases

While false confession cases receive a great deal of attention in the academic literature, the media, and in popular culture, it must be emphasized that they are not the primary reason that wrongful convictions occur. In fact, false confessions are one of the lesser factors contributing to wrongful conviction. To further clarify this point, let's examine the other contributing factors that garner far less attention.

Forensic Science

Faigman, Kaye, Saks, and Sanders (as cited by Kassin & Gudjonsson, 2004), noted that flawed forensic examinations of case evidence can also contribute to the wrongful prosecution and conviction of an innocent person. A review of the Innocence Project cases revealed 171 wrongful convictions that were caused, at least in part, by "Unvalidated or Improper Forensic Science." This means that poor forensic science protocols were used in analyzing evidence, and/or misleading forensic testimony was provided at trial regarding DNA, blood, semen, saliva, hair, fiber, or bite mark evidence. In other words, in 45% of the wrongful conviction cases reported by the Innocence Project, so-called scientific analysis has proven instrumental in wrongfully convicting an innocent person. This is particularly problematic for some in academia as 'science' is supposed to be conclusive and irrefutable. In fact, so unimpeachable is science that Schmid & Betsch (2019) wrote an entire academic article on how to effectively rebut those 'science deniers' who question scientific milestones, spread misinformation, and contradict decades of scientific endeavors. Yet, while DNA science has helped to exonerate scores of wrongfully convicted subjects, 45% of those same subjects were wrongfully convicted, at least in part, because of science.

While this book has not been written to either support or refute the value and legitimacy of forensic scientific analysis, the number of wrongful convictions brought about by such analysis helps to demonstrate that 'science' is far from irrefutable. Still, academics, expert witnesses, and advocates attempt to have their cake and eat it too by disparaging science when it leads to the wrongful conviction of an innocent person and then cheering science when it brings about their exoneration. Either way, the fact remains that the Innocence Project's data identifies that flawed scientific analysis and misleading testimony from forensic scientists are responsible for far more wrongful convictions than false confessions. Therefore, from a strictly statistical perspective, wrongful conviction advocates could better serve the innocent by directing their efforts against those in lab coats rather than those in interrogation rooms.

Still, even in popular culture, shows like *CSI* and *Forensic Files* continue to herald the value of science in bringing justice to the guilty while shows like *The Confession Tapes* and *When They See Us* incessantly remind viewers that law enforcement interrogations cause the innocent to falsely confess. What is the reason for this partiality? Does it reflect society's inherent tendency to hold scientists in higher esteem than police officers? Is it an unhealthy belief in the merits of science? Does it reflect a greater interest or curiosity in forensic science vs. law enforcement? Or, is it a manifestation of an underlying bias against law enforcement? One thing is for certain, when it comes to the problem of wrongful convictions and the data put forth by the Innocence Project, art is definitely not imitating the statistical realities of the criminal justice system.

Eyewitness Misidentification

By far, the largest factor contributing to wrongful convictions is eyewitness misidentification. Eyewitness misidentifications occur when purported eyewitnesses to a criminal event offer inaccurate testimony before the court that the person on trial was responsible for the crime at hand (Kassin, 2005). As of April 2020, the Innocence Project identified that 69% of wrongful convictions are caused by eyewitnesses who inaccurately identify the subject. According to Kassin (2005), eyewitness misidentifications existed in nearly 75% of wrongful conviction cases. With this staggering statistic, it is difficult to believe that so much attention is paid to false confessions and police interrogative techniques. It is also interesting to note the hidden statistic within this statistic.

The Innocence Project data identifies that 259 of their 377 wrongful conviction cases involved eyewitness misidentification. For this discussion, I will break the concept of the eyewitness into two main categories. The first category is the 'observational' eyewitness. These are people who are not involved in the criminal act, but simply observe the preceding behavior, the criminal act itself, or the aftermath. For example, an 'observational' eyewitness may be walking home one evening, hears a woman scream, and then observes a man running with a knife from the alley where the woman's scream emanated. The 'observational' eyewitness then provides a description of the subject to the police and may go on to pick the subject out of a lineup or photo array. During trial, the 'observational' eyewitness may be called upon in court to identify the defendant as the subject they saw running from the scene of the crime on the night in question. Although such testimony is profoundly powerful for a prosecutor, it is also credited with the wrongful conviction of countless innocent people.

The second type of eyewitness is the actual victim. This is the person who is raped, robbed, or assaulted, and then provides an identification of their assailant to the police. Like the 'observational' eyewitness, the 'victim' eyewitness may also pick their attacker out of a lineup or photo array and then identify their attacker in court as the criminal trial progresses. What is not clearly articulated in the Innocence Project data is which type of eyewitness testimony is more likely to contribute to a wrongful conviction. Instead, the Innocence Project and similar advocacy groups tend to combine these individuals into one main group known as 'eyewitnesses.' However, by delving deeper into the available information, we can again identify a noticeable skewing of the data.

While the Innocence Project reports a total of 259 eyewitness identification cases out of their 377 wrongful convictions, breaking these cases down leads to a startling statistic. 'Observational' eyewitness cases account for approximately 17% of these wrongful convictions. Astonishingly, approximately 83% of these types of wrongful convictions are caused by identifications made by 'victim' eyewitnesses. Moreover, nearly all of these types of eyewitnesses are victims of sexual assault. It is unclear why these two distinct types of eyewitnesses are grouped together. However, the profound imbalance of their impact on wrongful convictions cannot go unaddressed. Of even greater concern is the large number of innocent subjects who have spent decades of their lives behind bars because of little more than the victim pointing their finger at the defendant and saying, "You are the one who did this to me."

If academics and advocate groups are truly dedicated to minimizing the wrongful incarceration of innocent subjects, it would make more sense statistically to forgo examining how subjects were questioned by police and instead focus on the people whose inaccurate identifications put the subject in the interrogation room in the first place. Understandably, blaming victims for wrongly identifying their assailants is likely to be met with great resistance. However, the time may come for academics, expert witnesses, wrongful conviction advocates, media outlets, and documentarians to stop largely ignoring the greatest cause of wrongful conviction in favor of focusing on a far lesser contributor. Put another way, if the true motivation is to minimize the number of innocent people who are wrongfully convicted, then advocates should be placing greater doubt in the eyewitness identifications made by sexual assault victims and lesser doubt in the routine interrogative practices of law enforcement officers.

The Iceberg Analogy

As discussed, the inherent inability to identify the extent of the false confession problem has forced many researchers and expert witnesses to rely on the misleading statistics of the Innocence Project to suggest that false confessions occur with great frequency. The fact remains that false confession 'experts' simply don't know. Yet, this does not stop some from suggesting that the numbers reported by groups like the Innocence Project represent only the tip of a vastly larger iceberg of false confessions (Bradford & Goodman-Delahunty, 2008; Drizin & Leo; 2004; Gudjonsson, 2010; Leo, 2007; Leo & Ofshe, 1997; Redlich, et al., 2011; Schatz, 2018; Trocino, 2016). As the previous citations clearly indicate, this 'tip of the iceberg' metaphor is constantly utilized throughout academic research. In reality, what these false confession experts are actually saying is, "We don't know how often false confessions occur, but we know it's a lot." While this claim is designed to be incendiary and to instill doubt in the law enforcement interrogative process, it is also largely inaccurate.

Realizing that I have already engaged in a great deal of math throughout this chapter, I believe that it is also important to give the false confession 'tip of the iceberg' analogy some practical context. Between 1960 and 2018, there have been 70,421,236 violent crimes committed in the United States (Disastercenter.com, 2020). I have already presented a clear argument for why the majority of false confession cases reported by the Innocence Project and the NRE should be deducted from consideration when calculating the effect of routine interrogation techniques on the elicitation of false confessions. However, for the sake of ease, let's simply combine the raw numbers from these groups. If taken together, the Innocence Project and the NRE identified 341 false confession cases occurring from interrogations as far back as 1955. As crime data was only available dating back to 1960, this means that in the last 60 years, only .00048% of violent crimes have resulted in a proven false confession. Let's put this another way. According to what can be proven, less than five-hundredths of one percent of criminal subjects have been proven to have falsely confessed since 1960. Now it must be conceded that there have obviously been false confessions during this same time period which were not proven to be false. As such, that may increase the overall percentage of false confessions. However, it is also important to note that some of the false confessions documented in the NRE data were not related to violent crimes. For example, multiple subjects were found to have falsely confessed in drug possession cases. It is mind boggling to think how much smaller this percentage would actually be if nonviolent offenses were also included in these calculations.

Let's put this statistic into some real-world context. Since 1960, roughly 1,140 Americans have been attacked by sharks (National Geographic, 2020). Similarly, during this same time period, roughly 2,820 Americans have been struck and killed by lightning (National Weather Service, 2020). Even if we fail to deduct from the Innocence Project and NRE data those subjects who were juveniles, mentally ill, cognitively impaired, and those who were beaten by police into falsely confessing, we can conclude that more than 3 times as many Americans have been attacked by sharks and more than 8 times as many Americans have been struck and killed by lightning than have been proven to have falsely confessed during this same time period. If we remove instances of police abuse and subjects with profound risk factors from the analysis and focus only on the false confessions purportedly caused by routine interrogative practices, these comparisons would be even more striking. I do not put forth these statistics to minimize the suffering of those who have been wrongfully convicted. Again, for even a single person to be wrongfully convicted for a crime they did not commit is a tragedy for that person, their family, and the criminal justice system as a whole. Still, we must fight the tendency to extrapolate unique and infrequent events into a persistent nation-wide phenomenon.

It must be recognized that the 'tip of the iceberg' metaphor used in discussing the false confession phenomenon is designed to induce fear within the criminal justice system. It is also not a coincidence that so many false confession researchers and expert witnesses have selected this particular imagery to make their point. The true danger of an iceberg is not the portion visible above the waves, but rather the unknowable and treacherous girth waiting below the surface. This inability to calculate what lurks beneath the waterline is what makes an iceberg truly scary. Those who advocate against the process of criminal interrogation bask in the murkiness of this indeterminable, yet presumptive, collection of false confessions to foster a societal distrust of routine interrogative methods. Again, they create this fear through the questionable argument that while we can't possibly know how many false confessions there are, we are confident that it must be significant. As the analysis in this chapter helps to demonstrate, the number and frequency of false confessions are exaggerated by the very same people who readily admit that they have no idea how frequently they occur. This is the very definition of an irrational fear designed to not only promote panic within the criminal justice system, but to cultivate doubt in the minds of every future juror about the reliability of confession evidence. In reality, this may be the very goal they are seeking to accomplish. Still, unless more substantive proof can be provided, we must all resist the efforts to manipulate and panic our system of justice into making hasty changes to the invaluable investigative technique of criminal interrogation.

CHAPTER 5

Examining the Perspectives of Academia, Expert Witnesses, and Advocates

D espite presenting a vastly different interpretation of the Innocence Project data, it must be remembered that the points made in the previous chapter were not designed to dispute the critically important role played by those working with the Innocence Project and other advocacy groups. Our legal system is designed to have checks and balances to ensure that the truly innocent are not subjected to unwarranted punishment. From time to time, groups like the Innocence Project have helped to right the missteps of the criminal justice system. Still, the nobility of their efforts to free the wrongfully convicted does not make their positions sacrosanct. In order to have a meaningful discussion about the strengths and weaknesses of the American criminal justice system, it is necessary to hear input from all of those who participate in the process. This includes not only law enforcement in general, but criminal interrogators specifically. As will be discussed in this chapter, a war is being waged against those who have been tasked with questioning individuals suspected of engaging in unlawful activity. A key front of this war involves the manner in which law enforcement interrogates criminal subjects. To date, this battle has been waged in only one direction, academia against law enforcement. It therefore becomes critical to identify and draw attention to the fact that a large portion of those working in academia or on behalf of wrongful conviction advocacy groups maintain a distinct and articulable bias against the field of law enforcement. This chapter will highlight that bias.

My Own Worldview

As mentioned in the introduction, I am a career law enforcement officer and have spent more than half of my life in service of the United States. As a military veteran, a sworn law enforcement officer, a polygraph examiner, a crisis negotiator, and a routine interrogator of criminal subjects, I maintain a worldview that is inherently different from that of the academic researchers and expert witnesses who have chosen to research and testify about the false confession phenomenon. While some may consider my unique worldview as a source of bias, I consider it as a balance to the existing conversation about false confessions which has largely ignored the insights of law enforcement officers. Having worked so many years in the criminal justice system, I know firsthand that the overwhelming majority of law enforcement officers with whom I have come into contact are dedicated professionals who strive, often at great sacrifice to themselves and their families, to protect those in their communities. Still, it would be ridiculous to suggest that every law enforcement officer in the United States falls into this category. Not every officer is good at their job or does their job correctly, but this is not unique to the law enforcement profession. There are good doctors and bad doctors. There are good politicians and bad politicians. There are good mechanics and there are bad mechanics. And for anyone who has ever attended college, you are well aware of the fact that there are good professors and bad professors. In fact, a quick perusal of Ratemyprofessors.com will prove this point beyond a shadow of a doubt. Simply put, every type of employment has those who excel in their field and those who should never have been hired in the first place. As such, we should not judge the entire law enforcement field in general, or the interrogation field specifically, based on the actions and missteps of a few bad apples. As outlined in my analysis in the previous chapter, the data suggests that bad officers are the exception, not the rule. Because there are many academics and expert witnesses who would have you believe otherwise, it is of critical importance that we look more deeply into the worldview held by many in academia who are leading the charge against law enforcement interrogators.

In Their Own Words

To identify the bias that exists in the ranks of the false confession researchers and expert witnesses, we need only look to the words they use in examining the criminal justice field and those who have sworn to uphold the laws of our society.

"Tactics"

The first word that immediately rose to my attention in reviewing the false confession literature is 'tactics.' Throughout the existing false confession literature, and almost without exception, the word that is continually used to describe the techniques that law enforcement officers use to interrogate criminal subjects is 'tactics.' An argument can easily be made that the term 'tactic' tends to have an overly aggressive and negative connotation. As one who has served in both the military and law enforcement, this term tends to be utilized for those organizations that are engaged in direct and personal contact with an enemy. As a former member of the United States Army Infantry, we learned countless 'tactics' to dispose of enemy personnel. In law enforcement, the word 'tactics' seems to be reserved for S.W.A.T. teams or those units training to enter buildings, clear rooms, and subdue subjects. In both situations, the term 'tactics' seems appropriate to describe the goals that these types of units are attempting to achieve.

To see the inherent bias in this term, we can try applying it to other professions. For example, would we find it appropriate to suggest that mental health professionals, during the course of their psychological training, learned various 'tactics' to encourage patients to open up about their problems? Can anyone identify a medical school that teaches their students various 'tactics' to remove a cancerous cyst? Is it possible to pinpoint which university professors have learned teaching 'tactics' to more thoroughly explain the intricacies of Aristotle's natural philosophy to students? In reality, countless other professions would likely use terms such as 'techniques', 'strategies', 'tools', or 'methods' to explain what they do. However, when it comes to interrogating a criminal subject, it has been nearly universally agreed upon by academic researchers that law enforcement officers engage only in 'tactics.'

The wide use of this term in the academic literature is not accidental. Instead, it offers a glimpse of just how academics view the art of interviewing and interrogation. To them, questioning a criminal subject is not an effort at establishing the truth, but rather an act of head-to-head combat between a potentially innocent person suspected of engaging in criminal behavior and a law enforcement officer who will stop at nothing in order to obtain a confession. So pervasive is the use of the word 'tactics' to describe law enforcement interrogative methods that I was actually shocked and pleased to observe Leo (2007) use the term "psychological techniques" to describe such methods. Unfortunately, my pleasure was short lived when I read his full observation that "detectives draw on *an arsenal* of psychological techniques to overcome suspect's denials" (p. 703). Whereas other professions may gather various tools for their occupational 'toolboxes,' law enforcement interrogators maintain an 'arsenal,' It seems that despite their best efforts, it is profoundly difficult for many academics to think of criminal interrogation as anything other than direct personal warfare. The constant use of such military-like descriptors helps to demonstrate the underlying bias held by many in academia against law enforcement.

Con Artists

Another key indication of the inherent bias of academic false confession researchers and expert witnesses is the suggestion that law enforcement interrogators are nothing more than con artists. For example, after observing 122 criminal interrogations conducted by 45 police detectives and reviewing 60 hours of videotaped interrogations, Leo (1996) concluded that law enforcement interrogations are, in essence, confidence games in which interrogation subjects are manipulated and their trust is betrayed. Leo identified that the confidence game begins with the recitation of the Miranda warnings where law enforcement officers initiate their cultivation of their unwitting subject. Upon reading the warnings, law enforcement interrogators were reported to subtly employ psychological strategies against the interview subject to convince them to willingly waive their rights and continue speaking with the investigator. In essence, if interrogations are a 'confidence game,' then law enforcement interrogators are 'con artists.' It is hard to ignore the underlying bias in this belief system.

It must be noted that Leo is not alone in his assertion. In fact, his belief that law enforcement interrogators are con artists is doubled down upon by Simon. After shadowing Baltimore Police Department homicide investigators for a year, Simon (as cited by Brandl, 2014) came to a particularly biased and sarcastic conclusion. More specifically, he stated that once law enforcement officers engage in interrogation, they become:

> a salesman, a huckster as thieving and silver-tongued as any man
> who ever moved used cars or aluminum siding, more so, in fact,
> when you consider that he's selling long prison terms to custom-
> ers who have no genuine need for the product (p. 195).

Not only is this statement biased against law enforcement interrogators, it can also be argued that it identifies an inherent unwillingness to accept the fact that some people should be punished for their criminal actions. More specifically, the portion about "selling long prison terms to customers who have no genuine need for the product" suggests that even if you have committed a heinous criminal act, the subject does not need a long prison term. As identified by the adage, "If you can't do the time, don't do the crime," the majority of people, even those engaged in criminality, are well aware of the repercussions of committing a criminal act. Yet, Simon's conclusion can be interpreted to mean that he does not believe in the concept of punishment for criminal wrongdoing. Many would argue that a person who rapes a woman, sexually abuses a child, or murders a fellow citizen is in definite need of a long prison term. If there are those working in the realm of academia or related advocacy groups who honestly believe that no one should be subjected to governmental punishment for their criminal actions, this may help to explain why law enforcement is viewed as an enemy engaging in highly manipulative interrogative 'tactics.' Again, these words reflect an underlying bias in the efforts of many academics and advocates.

Interrogations

Believing that the interrogation 'tactics' employed by police are often responsible for the rendering of false confessions, Kassin (2005) defined the concept of interrogation as:

> a guilt-presumptive process, a theory-driven social interaction
> led by an authority figure who holds a strong a priori belief about
> the target and who measures success by his or her ability to
> extract a confession. It is possible that police who commit them-
> selves to this course of action are, at times, not merely blinded
> by their initial beliefs but motivated to reinforce them (e.g., by a
> desire for closure, to help secure a conviction) (p. 219).

The bias inherent in this definition is also not difficult to see. Kassin is correct in the initial portion of his definition. Interrogations are based on the law enforcement officer's belief that a subject is guilty. This should not come as a shock to anyone as there is no reason to interrogate a subject that you believe is innocent. As many departments and agencies are forced to work with an insufficient amount of personnel and resources, investigators are frequently put in the position of having to carry large caseloads. As such, the thought of wasting time interrogating a person that you believe is innocent is nonsensical and fails to advance any of the investigator's cases. To believe that an interrogation is *not* based on a strong suspicion of guilt would be to suggest that a law enforcement officer would deliberately interrogate a subject that they believe to be innocent just so they can close a case. Such a proposition, by its very nature, is ludicrous. In short, Kassin is absolutely correct in defining an interrogation as a 'guilt-presumptive' process. However, it is the underlying negativity associated with the term 'guilt-presumptive' that makes the definition biased.

Kassin's (2005) definition also begins to evidence some potential bias when he suggests that law enforcement officers gauge their own success by their ability to elicit a confession from a subject. While there is a certain amount of pride associated with convincing a guilty subject to admit to their criminal transgressions, there is no pride in obtaining the same outcome from an innocent subject. It would be safe to assume that most law enforcement investigators have been put in a position where their initial beliefs about a person's guilt changed once they had an opportunity to interview them. In my career, I have certainly entered an interview room with the suspicion that the person sitting inside was involved in the crime at hand, only to have that suspicion flipped on its head after speaking with the subject. Like me, I am sure that countless investigators have had the experience of walking out of an interrogation room and proclaiming, "It's not him." Again, it is a biased assumption to believe that law enforcement officers maintain a belief system of a freight train that can be neither stopped nor turned around. It is also ridiculous to hold law enforcement officers to a higher standard than the rest of the world. To believe that a doctor, psychologist, university professor, or even a cashier does not approach their customer base without any precon- ceived notions about a particular patient, student, or customer is laughable. However, it is profoundly biased to assume that a law enforcement officer, unlike these other professions, can never admit the inaccuracies of their initial assessment and then change their opinion. Simply put, while a strong suspi- cion of guilt is a necessary precondition for an interrogation, it is highly inac- curate and potentially biased to assume that law enforcement's overwhelming desire to be considered successful will trump their ability to admit that they were wrong, even if it means the wrongful conviction of an innocent person.

Interrogative Terminators

Many in academia hold a belief that, like the Terminator character portrayed by Arnold Schwarzenegger, law enforcement interrogators are unrelenting and will stop at nothing until they reach their goal, in this case a confession. To support such a conclusion, they point to clear cases of police malpractice. For example, Kassin (1997) noted that innocent subject Paul Ingram was interrogated on 23 occasions over the course of five months, was subjected to hypnotism, and furnished graphic details of the crime before confessing to raping his daughters as part of a Satanic ritual. Kassin (2007) also wrote about the case of Billy Wayne Cope who confessed to strangling and molesting his daughter after 17 hours of questioning over the course of four days, being held in jail overnight without food or water, being physically isolated from his friends and family, being denied legal counsel, and being falsely advised that he had failed the polygraph examination he had just been administered regarding this issue. Conti (1999) similarly referred to law enforcement's use of the 'wear down' technique in which officers deliberately detain subjects for lengthy periods of time until they confess, adding that an innocent person could be made to confess to almost anything under the stress of constant questioning and suggestion. Lastly, Ofshe and Leo (1997) presented the case of Tom Sawyer who falsely confessed to sexual assault and murder after 16 hours of being interrogated and threatened by law enforcement officers.

An argument could be made that by focusing on proven cases of false confession like those outlined above, false confession researchers have developed a negative view of law enforcement officers and their interrogative methods. This reminds me of when I used to work National Security investigations in Washington, DC. During this phase in my professional career, I was tasked with monitoring the activities of foreign intelligence officers working against our government. I had only worked criminal investigations up to that point, and a co-worker informed me of the inherent difference between criminal cases and National Security cases. This co-worker pointed out that while criminal investigations can be summarized as 'sex, drugs, and rock & roll,' National Security investigations can be summarized as 'ferns, white wine, and quiche.' In other words, this co-worker was suggesting that while criminal investigations focus on a more straightforward game of checkers in trying to determine 'whodunnit,' National Security investigations are much more nuanced and strategic, like a game of chess. In retrospect, he was not wrong in this description.

After working these types of cases for a number of years, I remember coming home and observing that the cord to a floor lamp in my den was out of place. Being that I was in the midst of working against foreign intelligence officers, the first thought that crossed my mind was that someone had 'bugged' the lamp in the study and had failed to appropriately return the cord to the original position. As ridiculous as I knew this idea was, I nonetheless felt compelled to ask my wife about it. In doing so, I received a far more rational explanation . . . she must have knocked the cord out of place while vacuuming earlier in the day. I reference this story only as a means of demonstrating that when you focus on one particular type of work, it can impact how you view the world around you. For example, in attending a party at your home, a mason may walk up to your house and quickly notice that your front steps are beginning to separate from the porch. Conversely, the optometrist who enters your home may immediately recognize that you are wearing the newest eyeglass frames offered by Bausch + Lomb. What is interesting about the two party goers is that they likely won't notice what the other one immediately picked up on. Quite simply, we see what we are most familiar with. This same idea holds true with false confession researchers, expert witnesses, and wrongful conviction advocates. If all they see are false confessions caused by the worst examples of interrogation, they may be conditioned into seeing nothing but false confessions in every interrogation. In other words, they start 'seeing ghosts.' However, it is also possible that there is a more insidious alternative. Maybe they haven't actually become conditioned to see false confessions everywhere. Instead, perhaps they want *everyone else* to see false confessions everywhere. By convincing defense attorneys, judges, potential jurors, the media, and the general public of the omnipresence of false confessions, these academics-turned-expert witnesses can surely stay gainfully, and lucratively, employed. Put another way, if they can successfully convince society that false confessions are a routine occurrence, then their services will be routinely called upon to fight the voluntariness of every law enforcement interrogation.

General Bias Against the Criminal Justice System

If your job causes you to repeatedly focus on those legal cases that have gone horribly wrong, it is not surprising that you may come to develop a negative perception of the criminal justice system. This point is driven home by the words of Innocence Project co-founder Peter Neufeld in the Netflix series *The Innocence Files* (Garbus, Gibney, & Williams, 2020). Upon discussing the constant influx of letters from inmates claiming to be innocent, Neufeld stated:

> As you read any of these letters, you have no idea about the
> duration and density of the journey before us, and you become
> frankly more angry with how foul the criminal justice system
> is. People in the crime lab saying the tire prints match, the shoe
> prints match, the hair matches, the bite marks match. Because of
> these unreliable methods, innocent people are going to prison.
> It's the whole profession. It's the whole system. It's the whole
> methodology. It's all junk.

Do these sound like the words of a man who has maintained his objectivity about either the criminal justice system or those who work on behalf of the prosecution? As mentioned above, the goals of his organization are noble, but statements such as these not only exhibit an undeniable bias, but likely reflect the natural side effects of viewing only the worst cases of police and prosecutorial malpractice. A similar example of the bias that runs through such advocacy groups can be observed in the words of an Innocence Project Volunteer/ Case Expert who was also featured in *The Innocence Files* (Garbus, Gibney, & Williams, 2020). She stated:

> I personally think the justice system just is not fair on so many
> different levels, and so I'm an advocate for reform on pretty
> much every possible thing with the justice system.

Again, these are the words of a person who has chosen to work with the Innocence Project, but appears to be operating under the assumption that the entire criminal justice system is unfair and everything about it must be reformed. Still, these sentiments are not unique to advocates. They can also be observed in academia. For example, Leo (2007) commented at a symposium at the University of Michigan that:

> . . . it's possible in theory that we have the best legal system in
> the world, but I'd want to see some evidence supporting that
> statement, and looking at the wrongful conviction problem in
> America—which has been so well documented by the National
> Registry of Exonerations housed here at the University of
> Michigan—I don't think such a statement is true (p. 694).

Obviously, we live in a country that thankfully affords all citizens the freedom of speech. As such, I have no concerns with what these individuals have to say. However, it is important that law enforcement officers and others working within the criminal justice system be aware of the mindset of the people who are assessing issues, like false confessions, which impact upon the legal system. Being that advocates exist who believe that the entire criminal justice system is wrong, we need to be mindful that such a worldview will naturally impact their approach to, and conclusions about, all criminal justice matters. Quite frankly, a show like *The Innocence Files* is an invaluable resource as it provides an unfettered look into the beliefs and opinions of advocates. Unlike a peer-reviewed journal article in which every word is carefully crafted and reviewed, the more extemporaneous comments of advocates captured on film are more likely to represent their true feelings. However, it is difficult to hear these comments and maintain the belief that they are approaching the false confession problem in an unbiased manner.

It is interesting to note in *The Innocence Files* series that for nearly every wrongfully convicted subject who was profiled, their innocence was proven through the very same processes that caused them to be wrongfully convicted in the first place. To attack these types of methods for their role in the wrongful conviction and then herald them for the exoneration smacks of hypocrisy. Simply put, it is hypocritical on its face to suggest that all forensic science is junk and then use forensic science to exonerate a wrongfully convicted subject. It is hypocritical to suggest that the polygraph technique is junk science and then use the polygraph to help exonerate a wrongfully convicted subject. It is hypocritical to suggest that police interrogative practices are inherently coercive and routinely lead to false confessions and then accept a confession that helps to exonerate a wrongfully convicted subject. In other words, you cannot accept the outcome only when your side wins. Forensic scientific techniques, DNA analysis, polygraph examinations, and criminal confessions cannot be considered valid and reliable only when they serve your particular cause.

In addition to the aforementioned hypocrisy, there are others who conduct research into the phenomenon of false confessions and then routinely testify on behalf of the defense that appear to have little to no confidence in the workings of the American criminal justice system as a whole. More specifically, the language used by some academics seems to underlie a belief that not only are false confessions problematic, but all confessions are problematic. They therefore intimate that no American should ever confess. For example, Davis and Leo (2012) stated:

> To avoid confessing against self-interest, the suspect would be
> best served by avoiding interrogation . . . Suspects can exert their
> *Miranda* rights and refuse questioning without legal counsel.
> But to do so, they must remember everything they know about
> their rights, and understand what those rights are, why they are
> important, and the damaging things that can happen if question-
> ing continues without an attorney present. They must resist inter-
> rogators' efforts to imply that their rights aren't real, and under-

stand that detectives' insinuation of their guilt if they refuse to talk are less important than the long-term damage that can occur if they do. If they do agree to the interrogation, they must control powerful emotions deriving from the events in question and the interrogation itself, control distress, and suppress impulses to do anything to get away. They must control attention and focus on the goal of exoneration, despite powerful forces pulling attention toward the lesser goal of minimizing consequences. They must be able to remember relevant knowledge and use it to critically evaluate the information and arguments presented by interrogators, and recognize when they are being deceived. Moreover, suspects must resist intense pressures to confess from one or more authorities, who presumably have much greater relevant knowledge of evidence against suspects, and other issues, and significant apparent control over their fates (p. 680-681).

It is difficult to interpret such language as anything other than a tutorial for how all criminal subjects, not just those who are innocent, should resist law enforcement's efforts to elicit a confession from them. What is concerning is that these same authors concede that most confessions received by law enforcement officers are likely true. As such, their language could easily be construed as a conscious effort to obstruct justice by interfering with law enforcement's legal efforts to obtain a confession from a criminal subject. This goes far beyond efforts to protect the innocent and speaks to an inherent bias against law enforcement investigators and their sworn duty to protect and serve their neighborhoods, their state, or their country by investigating violations of criminal law and interrogating those who may have done so. In a similar vein, Haney-Caron, Goldstein, and Mesiarik (2018) state:

Talking to police represents a risk because people are more likely to confess, either truly or falsely, if subject to police interrogation (p. 1969).

This particular statement is amazing as it not only highlights that interrogations can lead to false confessions, but it also warns truly guilty subjects that they run the risk of *truthfully* confessing if they agree to speak with police. One would think that obtaining a truthful confession from a truly guilty subject is a good thing. Some may suggest that this is an important first step in ensuring justice for the victim and bringing warranted punishment to the offender. As will be discussed later, some may even argue that a guilty subject's truthful confession helps to ensure that they receive a deal from the prosecutor in exchange for their guilty plea, thereby helping the truly guilty subject to receive less punishment. However, the authors of these types of statements obviously do not share these same feelings. In the simplest terms possible, many academics and wrongful conviction advocates maintain a strong bias against law enforcement. They maintain a fundamental belief that no person, to include the guilty, should ever be questioned by police, let alone confess to their misdeeds. This belief system may explain why so many of them go on to serve as expert witnesses and testify on behalf of the defense. Those employed on behalf of the government must be made aware of this anti-prosecution mindset and the manner in which it fuels the research seeking to explore the false confession phenomenon. Similarly, those working in academia and on behalf of these advocacy groups must also identify their own biases so that they do not come to assume that every interrogation is problematic and every confession is false. Unfortunately, this self-awareness does not yet seem to have occurred as the anti-law enforcement bias appears to have clearly leaked into the research. The next chapters will highlight this point.

CHAPTER 6

Reexamining the Frequency of False Confessions

As previously discussed, a great deal of the false confession academic literature references the statistics of the Innocence Project as a means of suggesting that false confessions not only occur routinely, but that they occur with alarming frequency (Klaver et al., 2008; Narchet et al., 2011). In their study of police interviewing and interrogation, Kassin et al. (2007) embarked upon previously unexplored territory relating to the false confession phenomenon. More specifically, the authors chose to direct their attention to the actual practitioners who conduct interviews and interrogations as opposed to focusing on cases of police malpractice resulting in false confessions or relying on experimentation with university students. Believe it or not, the decision by Kassin et al. to finally seek input from actual police practitioners was the first such study of its kind. In essence, the authors received completed questionnaires from 631 police investigators in the United States and Canada who provided personal information regarding their beliefs about interrogation and the interrogative practices they employ during the course of their investigative duties. Kassin et al. noted that when asked to estimate the frequency with which false confessions occur, their law enforcement survey respondents estimated that 4.78% of subjects who provided self-incriminating statements were innocent of the crime for which they were being interrogated.

The aforementioned number is important to highlight as it gives greater context to the false confession numbers relayed by the Innocence Project. As outlined in a prior chapter, the Innocence Project reported that as of April 2020, 28% of their wrongful conviction cases were caused, at least in part, by false confessions. Again, this number should not be misinterpreted to mean that 28% of all confessions are false. In fact, at least according to the data of Kassin et al. (2007), the law enforcement officers they surveyed estimated that only 4.78% of confessions are false. While some leading the war against law enforcement interrogators may suggest that 4.78% is an astronomically large number, it is equally important to realize that the flip side of this statistic suggests that 95.22% of confessions are true. Before we focus only on the negative aspect of this statistic, we must first ask ourselves how many professions would love to have a 95% success rate? For example, in our nation's history, Lyndon Johnson received the greatest percentage of the popular vote for president with only 61.1% (Statista, 2020). According to the National Center for Education Statistics (2020), only 61% of college students in the United States were able to graduate within a six-year period as of 2017. Lastly, according to Baseball Reference (2020), Ty Cobb had the highest career batting average in Major League Baseball history, and yet he only hit safely 36% of the time. The simple fact is that 95.22% is an astounding success record. However, if we look deeper into the data, this number is still underreported.

While the law enforcement officer respondents in the Kassin et al. (2007) study estimated that false confessions happen approximately 4.78% of the time, a further analysis of the data identifies that 3.80% were estimated to involve a partial admission while only 0.97% gave a full confession. Although the authors did not specifically define what is meant by a 'partial admission,' those who interrogate criminal subjects on a routine basis may conclude that this means an admission that, while helpful, falls far short of a full acceptance of responsibility. For example, perhaps the subject falsely admitted to being at the crime scene, knowing who committed the crime, knowing how the weapon was obtained, et cetera. This is very similar to the earlier analysis of the Innocence Project data in which a considerable percentage of false confessors provided statements that were not actually full admissions of guilt.

What is more interesting about these statistics is the fact that respondents estimated that only .97% of interview subjects gave a full false confession. Looking at the positive side of this statistic allows for the conclusion that, based on the estimations of law enforcement officers surveyed by Kassin et al. (2007), 99.03% of criminal subjects *do not* provide a full false confession upon being interrogated by police. While many people may be comforted by the fact that greater than 99% of criminal subjects don't falsely confess to crimes they didn't commit, academic researchers still manage to snatch only negativity from the jaws of success. More specifically, Kassin et al. looked at the .97% statistic and noted that this number is "significantly greater than 0" (p. 396). Does this represent an inherent bias in the academic study of false confessions, or is law enforcement being set up with an illogical and philosophically unattainable goal that only a 0% rate of false confessions is acceptable? Or, is it possible that what is really at play is an underlying desire that we throw the baby out with the bathwater and get rid of all interrogations so that no person will ever have to fight in court against their own acceptance of responsibility?

As stated earlier, an overwhelming problem for academic researchers, expert witnesses, and advocates is that they simply don't know how often false confessions happen (Conti, 1999; Kassin, 2005; Kassin et al., 2010a; Kassin & Fong, 1999; Malloy et al., 2014). While they would like to believe, or more importantly have *us* believe, that the problem is enormous, the fact is they simply don't know. Like my analysis of the Innocence Project and National Registry of Exonerations data, the law enforcement professionals surveyed by Kassin et al. (2007) identify that false confessions rarely happen. Still, at the conclusion of their study, Kassin et al. recommended that future researchers continue to consult with law enforcement to obtain their perceptions and insights as they relate to criminal interrogations and false confessions. My decision to do exactly that led to conclusions that may continue to hamper the existing 'tip of the iceberg' narrative.

Interrogative Specialists' Experiences with False Confessions

In an attempt to obtain a better picture about the frequency in which false confessions occur, I decided to ask state and federal law enforcement polygraph examiners about their experiences with false confessions. More specifically, I inquired as to the number of times they have experienced false confessions and the circumstances at the time that the false confessions were elicited. The following is a discussion of their responses.

Federal Law Enforcement Polygraph Examiners

Experiences with False Confessions. Upon being questioned about whether they have ever experienced a false confession, all 13 federal law enforcement polygraph examiners reported that, to their knowledge, they have never elicited a false confession, or later learned that a confession that they had elicited was false.

Circumstances at the Time a False Confession was Elicited. Although none of the participants reported experiencing a false confession, four of the participants that I interviewed advised that they had experienced confessions that had bothered them over the course of their careers.

Participant #1:

One participant noted that he had administered a polygraph examination to a 19-year-old male subject who was suspected of having been involved in criminal sexual conduct with a minor. After a failed polygraph examination and subsequent interrogation, the subject gave a simple signed statement which documented that he had engaged in the specified criminal act and had simply forgotten having done so due to his heavy marijuana usage. The participant advised that he had used the theme that the subject had engaged in the criminal act and had forgotten about it due to his heavy marijuana use, but the subject seemed too agreeable to this particular theme. In fact, after the participant introduced this theme to the subject, the subject stated simply, "I guess that is how it happened."

116

The investigators watched the interrogation on camera, and afterwards the participant provided them with the subject's written statement. While the participant did not mistreat the subject in any way, the interrogation felt like the participant was 'intellectually browbeating' the subject with the theme outlined above. The participant noted however, that his 'gut' still said that the subject actually committed the act, and the available evidence supported this conclusion. The participant also noted that the entire polygraph examination, including the interrogation, lasted less than four hours which the participant noted is not an exorbitant length of time. Still, while no exculpatory information has been received to date to suggest that the subject's statement was anything but truthful, the participant offered that this particular confession did not have the same feeling as others he has received, mostly because of how quickly the subject accepted the theme that his marijuana usage had clouded his memory.

Participant #2:

Another participant described a single instance prior to becoming a polygraph examiner in which he wondered about a false confession. The matter involved a female subject who was suspected of mailing a threatening letter. Although there was no direct evidence that the subject had committed the act, the subject's behavior suggested that she was responsible for the crime. The subject later claimed that the confession she had given was false and that she had confessed to the crime out of duress. The participant stated that there was nothing unusual about his interrogation, and his interrogative approach with the woman was consistent with the interrogative approach he used with all subjects. The participant learned from subsequent investigation that the subject likely suffered from mental health issues. In fact, the subject actually served all of her sentence in a psychiatric hospital. The participant also noted that while the subject claimed to have been coerced into a false confession, on the day that the trial was due to begin, the subject pled guilty. The participant added that the only reason he had concerns about this particular situation is because the woman raised the claim that she had falsely confessed and because she had mental health issues that could have potentially caused her to confess for the purpose of gaining notoriety. Despite these concerns, the participant was confident in the subject's guilt and he had no concrete reason to doubt her confession. Moreover, no information had ever been received that would suggest that someone else was responsible for this crime.

Participant #3:

Another participant identified two instances in which he felt he was close to experiencing a false confession. In the first instance, while interrogating a young man about a reported sexual assault of a minor, the subject appeared to become 'really stressed out' after a couple of hours of interrogation. The subject then said to the participant, "Just tell me what you want me to say and I'll say it." Hearing this statement and suspecting that the subject was simply trying to escape the situation and stop the pressure of the interrogation, the participant 'backed off' and re-directed his line of questioning. The participant then informed the subject that he was not going to put words in the subject's mouth. The participant then decreased the pressure in his questioning of the subject at which time the subject confessed to sexually assaulting the minor.

This same participant advised that the second example of a near false confession he had experienced occurred in a manner that was nearly identical to the first. As with the first example, the subject ultimately confessed in the second example as well. While the participant was confident in the confession and guilt of both subjects, these situations came to the participant's mind because both subjects asked the participant to tell them what to say, and in both situations a decrease in the pressure led to their confession. In neither situation did the participant receive any information or evidence that the subjects' confessions were anything but truthful.

Participant #4:

The final participant's experience with a false confession related to an interrogation that he had witnessed. The participant advised that prior to becoming a polygraph examiner, he transported a subject who reported having information about criminal activity to the local State Police office. After being interrogated by a State Police detective, the subject admitted to various criminal acts that he had not committed. While watching the interview/interrogation on camera, the participant observed that the detective clearly intimidated the subject, 'lambasted' him, yelled at him, and fed the subject the information that the detective wanted to hear. Upon driving the subject home, the subject advised the participant that the detective was incessant in his questioning, so the subject decided to tell the detective what he wanted to hear as a means of making the questioning and intimidation stop.

State Law Enforcement Polygraph Examiners

Upon being questioned about whether they had ever experienced a false confession, eight of the participants (80%) advised that while employed as a polygraph examiner with the State Police, they had never knowingly elicited a confession that they later learned was false. The two remaining participants advised that they had elicited a false confession during the course of their careers as a polygraph examiner. The following is the circumstances of those confessions:

Participant #1:

In or about 2007, this participant elicited a false confession from a criminal subject. The case involved the theft of approximately $200 in loose change from a residence. The main suspect in the case was a young male between the ages of 18 and 20 who presented with average intelligence, reported being well-rested, and claimed not to be suffering from any mental health issues. The subject had a history of theft and admitted to being in the house during the time frame in which the money was stolen. Although the evidence against the subject was relatively weak, he admitted to taking the money. A subsequent investigation cleared the subject of any wrongdoing.

Based on the subject's history of theft and his presence in the house, the participant was 'going at him' during the interrogation, and he eventually stated, "Okay, I did it" without any further discussion or additional details.

119

The participant was unable to recall whether the subject provided a written statement, but the participant was suspicious of the subject's confession based on its simplicity. Looking back on this particular interrogation, the participant does not believe that they had done anything out of the ordinary. Moreover, the participant advised that the interrogation lasted approximately 30 minutes. Lastly, the crime was a 90-day misdemeanor that had the subject been convicted of the crime would have likely resulted in probation. The participant theorized that the primary motivation of the subject was that he simply wanted to go home.

Participant #2:

This participant advised that during the course of his career, he has experienced a few instances in which a subject had falsely confessed. In these instances, the subjects defiantly stated something similar to, "Okay . . . I did it" after being interrogated subsequent to a failed polygraph examination. Upon hearing this type of response, the participant informed the subjects that such a confession is 'not going to fly.' In other words, the participant did not accept these confessions.

In one particular instance in or about 2007, this participant also conducted a polygraph examination in regard to the theft of money from the back room of a bar. The subject in the case had failed the polygraph examination and was subsequently interrogated by the participant. The subject then stated something similar to, "Fine, I did it. I just want to leave. Can I go now?" Like the two aforementioned cases, the participant did not accept this confession as truthful. In reflecting upon the aforementioned interrogations, the participant suggested that he was likely using different themes with the subjects at the times that they had given a false confession. Because there was no evidence to corroborate these confessions and because of the participant's doubts about their veracity, all three subjects were permitted to leave.

The participant also recounted a situation in which a woman had entered the State Police post where the participant was assigned and began confessing to participating as an accessory in the killing of babies. It was suspected at the time that the woman was suffering from mental health issues. This suspicion was later confirmed. The woman was neither arrested nor charged for her confession and was instead transported to a mental health facility.

False Confessions Elicited Outside of the Polygraph Context

While only two state law enforcement polygraph examiner participants advised that they had experienced a false confession while employed as a polygraph examiner, two other participants reported experiencing false confessions prior to becoming a polygraph examiner. The following is a discussion of those confessions.

Participant #3:

This participant reported that while investigating narcotics violations as a State Police trooper, they frequently received false confessions. These false confessions always involved the subject's desire to protect another person by 'taking the rap' for them. The participant estimated that this occurred approximately 40% of the time and involved dynamics such as: a) a mother claiming that the seized drugs belonged to her instead of her son; b) a girl-friend claiming drugs belonged to her to protect her boyfriend, or c) a young offender accepting responsibility for the drugs to protect a more senior gang member (or 'OG').

Participant #4:

This participant reported that they received multiple false confessions while working narcotics with the State Police. On each of these occasions, one individual would falsely confess that the drugs discovered by officers belonged to them so as not to get the other person in trouble. Then, while they would initially 'take the hit' for the other person, they would later come off of this story and admit that the drugs did not really belong to them.

Close Calls

While two state law enforcement polygraph examiner participants reported that they had experienced a false confession as a polygraph examiner, and two additional participants reported that they had experienced false confessions while working narcotics with the State Police, two additional participants recounted a situation in which they came close to eliciting a false confession. The following is a discussion of these participants' experiences

Participant #5:

This participant explained that on one occasion, they were in a position where they felt that if they pushed the subject too hard, he could potentially render a false confession. The participant explained that in this particular case, the subject was a juvenile who appeared to just want to be finished with the interrogation. The participant also noted that the interrogation 'didn't feel right.' As a result, the participant backed off of their questioning, and the subject left without confessing. The participant later learned that the case against the subject had been initiated on a false complaint.

Participant #6:

This participant advised that they had also come close to experiencing a false confession. The subject was an Hispanic male whom the participant described as being immature for his age and not overly intelligent. The results of the subject's polygraph test were inconclusive, but the participant decided to interrogate the subject because of the participant's doubts about the truthfulness of the subject's story. Because of the subject's level of intelligence, the participant soon arrived at the conclusion that he could manipulate the subject into saying whatever the participant wanted him to say. As a result of this feeling, the participant contacted their supervisor, and they decided to back off on questioning the subject.

The participant explained that as they were interrogating the subject, it "didn't seem right," and the participant felt that continued interrogation "would not be fair" to the subject. The participant arrived at similar conclusions when previously interrogating two juvenile subjects and an adult female who was 'learning disabled.' With these three subjects, the participant concluded that they were very malleable, and the participant could easily manipulate them as they were simply agreeing with whatever the participant said. Moreover, all three of these individuals gave a confession that sounded similar to "Fine, I did it" or "I'll just say I did it." In these three situations, the participant again backed off for fear of obtaining a false confession. The participant then added, "I'd rather have nothing than a bad confession."

The participant noted that in all of these situations, the participant was using the same interrogative methods as they would use on any criminal subject. For this reason, the participant theorized that these subjects could have falsely confessed not because of what the participant was doing, but because of the type of people the subjects were. Lastly, the participant offered that on approximately five or more previous occasions, they had conducted interrogations in which the person stated something similar to, "You say I did it, fine . . . I did it." The participant did not consider these to be truthful confessions, nor did the participant accept these 'confessions.' The participant concluded by stating that they had never accepted a confession that was later determined to be found false.

Analysis of the Findings

When the information provided by both state and federal law enforcement polygraph examiners is combined, only 4 (17%) of the 23 subjects reported experiencing a known false confession. For some it may seem unbelievable that so few false confessions had been experienced by these participants, especially in light of the constant drumbeat by some academic researchers, expert witnesses, and advocates that false confessions happen on a routine basis. However, when we consider the risk factors associated with false confessions, this number is a little more understandable. As previously noted, youth (Drizin & Leo, 2014; Malloy et al., 2014; Owen-Kostelnik et al., 2006; Pimentel et al., 2015); mental illness (Kassin et al., 2010; Redlich, 2004; Redlich et al., 2010; Redlich et al., 2011); intellectual deficits (Drizin & Leo, 2004; Redlich et al., 2011); and drug or alcohol intoxication at the time of the interrogation (Evans et al., 2009) are four key risk factors that cause a criminal subject to be more inclined to accept responsibility for a crime they did not actually commit. In the field of polygraph, examiners are taught that the subject must not only voluntarily agree to be tested by means of the polygraph, but they must also be suitable for testing. As such, polygraph examiners ask questions during the pre-test phase of the examination regarding the subject's age, education level, mental health history, and substance use. Not only does this line of questioning help to gather critical background information about the subject, but it also allows the examiner to identify whether the subject is suitable for testing. In short, the polygraph examiners interviewed for my study may not experience many false confessions because the same risk factors that predispose a subject to falsely confess are the same risk factors that could render the subject unsuitable for testing.

The information provided by the participants in my study also clearly demonstrates that law enforcement officers who specialize in interrogation have an awareness of when a confession does not 'feel right.' Simply put, they reported that they can identify when a subject is malleable and can be pushed into simply agreeing with the interrogator. Overall, the information provided by all of these participants can be summarized in the following four key points:

1. Participants expressed an ability to sense when something was wrong with the interrogation.

2. Participants' natural response to a malleable subject was to back off of their interrogative pressure.

3. Participants refused to accept confessions that they believed were suspicious.

4. When additional investigation was conducted and ultimately cleared the subject, suspicious confessions were not used to prosecute these innocent subjects.

This information is completely inconsistent with the belief system held by many in academia that law enforcement officers care only about the confession; they will say and do anything to obtain it; they will close their case once it is obtained; and the confession will automatically be used to convict the innocent.

The information provided by the subjects in my study also further supports the premise that the false confessions that were elicited by participants had more to do with the subject than the interrogative methods. For some, this involved immaturity, mental illness, low intelligence, a desire to please the interrogator, or a desire to protect the truly guilty person. Also interesting is the fact that the participants who had elicited a false confession did not report using any new or unusual interrogative technique. This too, may suggest that the key risk factor for false confessions is the subject's unique traits, not the method of interrogation. In other words, whether a polygraph examiner or an investigator routinely questions criminal subjects, interrogators tend to use the same general questioning techniques and approaches over and over again. Through the mere process of repetition, they each develop their own unique spiel and means of doing things . . . and they tend to stick with what works. Like a baseball pitcher, they may have a variety of pitches that they can call upon, but they still continue to throw in a generally consistent manner. In light of this reality, it becomes curious how they can obtain a confession from a criminal subject on Monday and have Tuesday's subject walk out of the room without confessing. In other words, why does one person confess to an interrogator and another person doesn't? Clearly the difference must be the subject.

Even the most arrogant of interrogators cannot realistically claim that they have a 100% confession rate. Some truly guilty subjects truthfully confess and others 'lawyer up' or walk out of the room without confessing. If an officer uses the same general interrogative techniques on each subject he questions, there must be a unique personal difference between the confessors and the non-confessors that would help to explain their ultimate decision to confess or resist. Perhaps it is an underlying weakness in personality or character that causes the truly guilty subject to confess to the examiner. Perhaps it is an underlying strength and firm resolve that allows the truly guilty subject to resist interrogative efforts and maintain their innocence. Or, maybe it is the true confessor who is strong and the false denier who is weak. Regardless of the explanation, if the interrogative techniques used by an interrogator are relatively consistent, then it is the uniqueness of the subject that must ultimately play a role in deciding whether or not to confess. This same rationale can be used for the innocent individuals who may be mistakenly interrogated by law enforcement. Again, if not all innocent people falsely confess, and if the interrogator's questioning techniques are held generally consistent, then there must be inherent differences between the innocent who truthfully maintain their innocence and the innocent who falsely confess. More precisely, there must be a profound difference in those who choose to falsely confess as even the Innocence Project data identifies that most innocent people are able to avoid such false admissions.

Another issue to consider may be the seriousness of the crime for which the subject is being interrogated. For example, one of the participants highlighted above noted that their subject may have falsely confessed after only 30 minutes of interrogation not only because he wanted to go home, but because he was being questioned about the minor infraction of stealing $200 in loose change from a residence (a 90-day misdemeanor). It is hard to believe that a significant number of interrogative 'tactics' were employed in such a brief period of time. As such, this false confession may have had more to do with the inconsequential nature of being accused of stealing loose change than it did with trying to escape the aversive nature of the interrogation room. As I will discuss in a future chapter, the decision to falsely confess in light of a minor confession may help to explain why so many false confessions are obtained from college students within the laboratory setting.

The information provided in the aforementioned interviews of federal and state law enforcement polygraph examiners appears to lend credence to the position that false confessions occur infrequently. It should be noted that these law enforcement officers specialize in criminal interrogation and engage in this activity on a routine basis. As such, they have participated in far more interrogations than the average law enforcement officer. In fact, some have conducted hundreds of interrogations each year. By sheer volume alone, these individuals have a greater opportunity to experience false confessions than their non-polygraph examiner counterparts. Yet a review of the research demonstrates a very low level of false confessions reported by this population. As I have previously outlined, the Innocence Project data reflects a low level of false confessions; the National Registry of Exonerations identifies a low level of false confessions; the study conducted by Kassin et al. (2007) reports a low level of false confessions, and now the interrogative specialists interviewed for my study identify a low level of false confessions. This consensus suggests that the claims that innocent subjects routinely confess to crimes they did not commit is yet another false assumption.

CHAPTER 7

Does Law Enforcement Actually Trick Subjects Into Waiving Their Rights?

An important consideration that may ultimately influence a false confession is the subject's decision to waive their *Miranda* rights. As previously noted, the Supreme Court's ruling in the landmark case of *Miranda v. Arizona* (1966) has helped to establish very specific warnings that must be provided to an interview subject once they are taken into custody to ensure that any statements that the interview subject may give are voluntary. A subject's decision to waive their rights has come to be viewed as a critical juncture in the interrogation process and one that Kassin and Norwick (2004) refer to as a 'risky choice.' Historically, gaining access to the interrogation room for the purpose of conducting social science research has been extremely difficult (Kassin & Norwick, 2004). In his seminal work, Leo (1996) was given the opportunity to personally observe 122 criminal interrogations conducted by 45 police detectives. He also reviewed 60 hours of videotaped interrogations provided by two additional police departments. This study marked the first time that such research had been conducted since the 1960s. Upon completing his observations, Leo concluded that law enforcement interrogations are, in essence, confidence games in which interrogation subjects are manipulated and their trust is betrayed. Leo also identified that the confidence game begins with the recitation of the *Miranda* warnings whereupon law enforcement officers start their cultivation of the unwitting subject. Upon reading the warnings, law enforcement interrogators were reported to subtly employ psychological strategies against the interview subject to convince them to willingly waive their rights and continue speaking with the investigator. Leo also noted that the psychological techniques used by law enforcement to this end included strategically building rapport, offering sympathy, pretending to be an ally, minimizing the importance of the *Miranda* warnings, subtly nodding as they read the warnings to the subject, and/or referring to the process of reading the *Miranda* warnings as a mere formality.

To more fully understand how law enforcement polygraph examiners review the rights of a criminal subject prior to a polygraph examination, I asked state and federal law enforcement polygraph examiners to outline their personal procedures for reviewing subjects' Miranda rights. Many of the participants reported that they immediately present the Miranda rights review to the polygraph subjects as an administrative duty that the participant must first complete before a polygraph examination can be administered. The participants reported a variety of explanations that they provide to polygraph subjects for why the Miranda rights must be reviewed at the outset of the polygraph process. These explanations include: a) the subject maintains certain rights as a United States citizen; b) the polygraph is a voluntary process and their consent is needed prior to testing; and c) the subject is presently being questioned in a federal law enforcement office which necessitates a review of the subject's rights prior to questioning. The majority of the participants advised that they also inform the subject that they are not under arrest and are free to leave at any time. Some participants reported that they go so far as to show the subject where the exit is located, even demonstrating that the door is unlocked.

All of the participants reported that in reviewing the subject's Miranda rights, they utilize their agency's standard advice of rights form which they either provide to the subject as a hard copy or that they display on the screen of their laptop computers where the subject can see. Nearly all of the participants advised that they read the rights aloud to the subject as the subject follows along, with most participants explaining each right individually. Only one participant offered that he typically allows his subjects to read the Miranda warnings to themselves after first confirming that they can read and write English. Many of the participants advised that they ask questions to verify the subject's intelligence and English proficiency as a means of ensuring that they understand the rights that are about to be reviewed. Some participants clarified that they verify the subject's intelligence to combat any potential defense challenges claiming that the subject did not actually understand their Miranda rights at the time that they were reviewed. Nearly all of the participants reported that they then verify that the subject understood their rights and ask if additional clarification about the meaning of any particular right is needed.

In obtaining the subject's waiver of their rights, most participants reported that they have the subject read the waiver portion of the form aloud so that the participant can verify the subject's English proficiency; their ability to comprehend the material; and to confirm that the subject was paying attention. All of the participants reported that once the rights are reviewed, the subject's questions have been answered, and the subject has expressed their willingness to waive their rights, the participant will have the subject sign the form. Several of the participants stated that they often have the lead investigator witness the review of the Miranda rights in anticipation that the subject's future defense attorney will try and claim that the rights were not reviewed with their client, or that their client did not understand the rights. The participants will then have the lead investigator sign the form as a witness. While being questioned about their personal procedures for reviewing Miranda rights, many of the participants noted that they take the Miranda review process very seriously because it is necessary to both ensure that the subject's waiver of their rights is voluntary and to prevent any future legal challenges from defense attorneys.

Leo (1996) asserts that the interrogation con game begins when law enforcement interrogators manipulate unsuspecting subjects into naively waiving their Miranda rights. It does not appear that this presumption accurately reflects the methods of the interrogative specialists whom I interviewed. The fact that state and federal law enforcement polygraph examiners find great value in being straightforward in their review of a subject's Miranda rights directly contradicts Leo's (1996) portrayal of law enforcement interrogators as con artists who slyly manipulate criminal subjects into waiving these constitutional rights. The insights offered by the participants in my study also contradict Leo's claims that interrogators employ psychological strategies to convince an unwitting subject to waive their rights. The interrogative specialists in my study reported that they frankly, and in a straightforward manner, inform subjects that they must be advised of their rights prior to questioning because they are entitled to these rights as an American citizen; because they must voluntarily agree to participate in the polygraph process; and/or because they are being questioned within the confines of a law enforcement office. Participants also reported that they inform the subject that they are free to leave at any time, with some actually pointing out the location of the exit and highlighting the fact that the doors are unlocked. These explanations, when combined with the participants' efforts to verify the subjects' understanding of their rights after they have been reviewed, also appear to run contrary to Leo's belief that law enforcement officers con unwitting subjects into waiving their rights by minimizing the importance of these rights.

Leo (1996) claimed that the confidence game run by law enforcement interrogators also involves their minimization of the Miranda process by referring to it as a mere legal formality. In my study, many of the participants reported that they do, in fact, present the Miranda rights review process as an administrative duty that must be completed prior to the polygraph. While some may readily jump to their feet and claim victory in light of this revelation, I contend that identifying the Miranda process as an administrative duty is actually a factual statement. Based on countless legal rulings, as well as many departmental policies, the Miranda review *is*, in fact, a mandatory administrative process. This is particularly true for the agencies from which the participants in my study were recruited. In fact, the Miranda review process is so administratively ingrained in both organizations that pre-printed standardized forms are used by the participants to unequivocally explain Miranda rights to criminal subjects. Therefore, presenting the Miranda review as a formal process does not appear to be an act of manipulation as much as it appears to be an honest explanation of what is required by both law and departmental policy prior to the administration of a polygraph examination or interrogation. The formality of these rights is not unique to the two organizations from which I recruited interview subjects. Anyone who has worked in and around law enforcement has undoubtedly seen some type of Miranda rights form available to nearly every law enforcement agency. In fact, some law enforcement officers carry a laminated card in their wallet or credentials so that they can read a subject their rights verbatim and without error. In my own experience, I have even observed officers who have the Miranda warnings printed on the back of their business cards. The fact that these rights are formally written down in so many places helps to clearly demonstrate that yes, reading a suspect their rights is a formality that must take place prior to questioning.

Going beyond how the Miranda rights are actually reviewed, Davis and Leo (2012) also suggested that law enforcement interrogators employ strategies to give subjects the illusion that questioning is inevitable; questioning cannot be refused; and subjects do not actually have the right to invoke their Miranda rights and terminate the interview. Similarly, Leo (2001) presumed that law enforcement officers may elicit an 'implicit waiver' in which they read the subject their rights and proceed with questioning as if the subject did not have a choice to refuse. Contrary to these presumptions, the participants in my study reported that their Miranda review process involves a word-for-word and unequivocal recitation of a subject's constitutional rights followed by an equally unequivocal, voluntary, and informed waiver from the subject. As noted by many of the participants, they are keenly aware that their actions in the interrogation room will eventually be scrutinized by defense attorneys. For this reason, they seek a waiver of rights that is informed, voluntary, and able to withstand any future legal challenges. The participants' process of reading the subject their rights verbatim from a standardized form, further clarifying their rights, asking if the subject understands their rights, and answering any questions the subject may have about their rights, does not appear to reflect either the confidence game suggested by Leo (1996), the illusion of inevitable questioning put forth by Davis and Leo (2012), or the 'implicit waiver' reported by Leo (2001). In short, some false confession researchers may actually be exhibiting their own anti-law enforcement bias by seeing manipulation and 'Jedi mind tricks' in something as simple and straightforward as the review of an advice of rights form.

Frequency in Which Rights Are Waived

While false confession researchers like to suggest that law enforcement officers engage in trickery as a means of getting criminal subjects to waive their rights, the simple fact is that the majority of interview subjects choose to waive their rights and continue speaking with law enforcement. In surveying 631 law enforcement officers about their interviewing and interrogation practices, law enforcement respondents reported that approximately 81% of the subjects they interview elect to waive their rights prior to being interviewed (Kassin et al., 2007). Some researchers have suggested that this willingness to waive one's Miranda rights puts the interview subject at risk of truthfully or falsely confessing (Kassin, 2005; Kassin & Norwick, 2004). This fact is particularly troubling based on Leo's (1996) conclusion that innocent subjects are even more likely to waive their rights than their guilty counterparts. It is therefore argued that this increased likelihood that innocent subjects will waive their Miranda rights and continue speaking with police places innocent subjects at an increased danger of rendering a false confession (Kassin, 2005; Kassin & Norwick, 2004; Leo, 1996). Again, this conclusion seems to be built upon a belief system that no citizen, regardless of their guilt or innocence, should ever agree to speak with a police officer. It also reeks of an assumption that police will aggressively interrogate every citizen who agrees to speak with them regardless of their guilt. Lastly, this conclusion assumes that the interrogative methods employed by law enforcement and the related pressure to confess cannot be resisted by any citizen, irrespective of their guilt or innocence

In essence, academic researchers and expert witnesses are arguing that if a citizen waives their rights, they get one step closer to speaking with police. If they speak to police, they are one step closer to being interrogated. If they are interrogated, they are one step closer to being subjected to problematic interrogative methods and overpowering interrogative pressure. If they are subjected to interrogative techniques and pressure to confess, they are one step closer to either a true or false confession. Ultimately, this is what they are striving for—no confessions ever. As such, some have chosen to start from the very beginning and recommend that citizens never waive their rights to prevent the start of the process. How far back will they focus their efforts? The simple fact is that some academic researchers, expert witnesses, and advocates have decided to combat the false confession issue through a scorched-earth approach in which all interrogations should be prevented to preclude the outside possibility that even a single innocent person may falsely confess. The Miranda review process therefore became an excellent starting point for this undertaking.

Based on the frequency with which interview subjects waive their rights and Leo's (1996) conclusion that law enforcement officers employ psychological strategies to coax interview subjects to waive their rights, Kassin and Norwick (2004) conducted a study with 144 college students who were randomly assigned to enter a room and either steal a $100 bill from a drawer (the guilty group) or to simply open and shut a drawer without taking anything (the innocent group). Upon being interviewed about the mock theft, the participants were read one of three Miranda warnings. The 'Neutral' Miranda warning involved simply reading the Miranda rights to the subject. The 'Sympathy-Minimization' Miranda warning involved the Miranda rights being described to the subject as a mere formality, after which subjects were offered a drink of water, encouraged to relax, and informed that the subsequent questioning session was an opportunity for them to tell their side of the story. The 'Hostile-Closed Minded' Miranda warning involved the interviewer first stating that the subject was guilty, and the interviewer was not interested in hearing any lies from the participant; then the interviewer actually reviewed the Miranda rights. At the conclusion of each of the Miranda warning conditions, the participants were provided a form and asked to indicate their willingness to waive their rights in light of the type of Miranda warning they were given and the reasons that contributed to their decision.

In this study, Kassin and Norwick (2004) identified that 58% of all suspects chose to waive their rights. However, there was no support for Kassin and Norwick's hypothesis that sympathy and a minimization of the importance of the *Miranda* warnings would increase the likelihood that participants would waive their rights. In other words, college students participating in the study were not any more likely to waive their rights when they were treated with sympathy or when the Miranda rights were described as a mere formality. This contradicts Leo's (1996) belief that it is the manipulation employed by law enforcement that induces people to waive their rights and continue speaking with police.

While the majority of all participants in Kassin and Norwick's (2004) study waived their rights, it is important to note that only 36% of the participants in the guilty group chose to waive their rights. These individuals suggested that they chose to waive their rights because they believed that the interviewer would infer that they were guilty if they did not do so. Conversely, 64% of the guilty participants elected not to waive their rights believing that remaining silent was in their best interest. These last two statistics are important as they identify that none of the guilty subjects were impacted by how the Miranda rights were reviewed with them. It did not matter if they were read the Miranda rights in a neutral manner, a hostile manner, or in a sympathetic manner. Nearly two thirds of the guilty subjects thought it was in their best interest to avoid speaking with interrogators and approximately one third only decided to talk with interrogators for fear of being perceived as guilty. This helps to demonstrate that the guilty subject's decision to speak with, or not speak with, law enforcement has more to do with the conscious and deliberate decision-making of the subject, not the reported trickery employed by law enforcement.

Kassin and Norwick (2004) also noted that it was of particular concern that 81% of the innocent participants chose to waive their rights, with 72% reporting that they waived their rights because they had nothing to hide. Kassin (2005) refers to this as the 'phenomenology of innocence.' Through this conceptual framework, Kassin explained that innocent subjects operate under the misperception that their innocence will protect them from negative outcomes. Believing in the protective nature of their own innocence can then cause these subjects to make decisions that ultimately increase the possibility that they may incriminate themselves during an unwarranted interrogation. Moreover, it has been suggested that if an innocent subject agrees to be interviewed by law enforcement officers, the subject's behavior will constantly be assessed for signs of deception that will then trigger the use of more and stronger interrogative methods (Meissner & Kassin, 2002; Narchet et al., 2011).

Kassin and Norwick's (2004) findings also indicate that the innocent subjects, like the guilty subjects, were not tricked or manipulated by police into waiving their rights. Instead, they appear to have made a conscious decision to speak with law enforcement because they are confident in their innocence regarding the crime for which they will be questioned. It is therefore a tremendous leap to assume that the confidence they hold in their own innocence places them at an increased risk for a false confession. This presupposition relies on the false assumption that law enforcement officers armed with case facts, evidence, experience, and possibly even results from a polygraph examination, cannot accurately identify deception when they see it. In other words, it assumes that if you agree to speak with police, you will automatically be judged as guilty and subjected to an interrogation. Similarly, it relies on the false assumption that law enforcement interrogation techniques are so overwhelmingly powerful that innocent subjects are unable to resist the urge to falsely confess. Lastly, it falsely assumes that the law enforcement officer will never stop interrogating, and the innocent subject will never stop answering questions, until a confession, albeit a false confession, is finally rendered.

Kassin's (2005) concept of the 'phenomenology of innocence' actually sets up a fallacy of causation by suggesting that since innocent people some-times falsely confess to crimes they did not commit, an innocent person is more likely to falsely confess by waiving their rights to not be interrogated. Couldn't we also create the concept of 'phenomenology of technology dis-interest' to help explain why false confessions occur? Under this concept we could argue that an innocent subject's disinterest in technology also places them at risk for a false confession? For example, if an innocent subject embraced modern technology like Caller ID or the Ring Video Doorbell, they would be aware that the police were looking for them and they could easily avoid answering their phone or opening their front door so as not to speak with police in the first place. Again, how far back are we going to trace the false confession causes? The simple fact remains: there is a long series of events between agreeing to talk with police and the rendering of a false confession.

It is also important to note that in the real world of criminal interroga-tion, both innocent and guilty subjects routinely ask for an attorney, ask to leave the room, indicate that they no longer wish to speak with officers, or in some way bring an end to the interrogation without actually confessing. Similarly, law enforcement interrogators also frequently end the interrogation without obtaining a confession because they come to the realization that the subject before them is innocent; they are unable to make any headway with the subject; or they simply run out of energy. Not every interrogation leads to a confession. Therefore, the belief that an innocent person's decision to waive their rights places them one step closer to falsely confessing is both weak and misleading. Instead, what may actually be desired by some academics, expert witnesses, and advocates is that *no* person, regardless of their innocence or guilt, should *ever* speak to police outside of the presence of an attorney. This concept is not only illogical, but it is incompatible with the concept of justice. Unfortunately for these individuals, it appears that the decision to waive one's Miranda rights remains a personal decision of the subject. Moreover, based on Kassin and Norwick's (2004) findings, it is a decision that does not read-ily appear to be influenced by the trickery and psychological manipulation of law enforcement officers as posited by Leo (1996). It is therefore a false assumption that law enforcement officers routinely trick people into waiving their rights.

CHAPTER 8

Reconsidering Law Enforcement's Ability to Identify Deception

When a false confession expert witness employed by the defense approaches a case, they have two options available in order to conclude that the subject's confession may be false. As previously discussed, the first option relates to the risk factors of the subject. In short, the defense's expert witness can take the stand and make claims that the subject in this case, due to his unique combination of risk factors, was ripe for a false confession. The second approach they can take is to directly attack the actions and interrogative techniques utilized by the law enforcement interrogator. As noted by Kassin et al. (2010), a criminal interrogation is a process designed to overcome the denials of subjects who are believed to be guilty so that a legally admissible admission of wrongdoing can be used as evidence against them at trial. For some researchers, the subject's wrongful conviction in light of their false confession marks the end of a series of poor decision-making by various entities within the criminal justice system. Understanding the points in the process in which poor decisions are made will help to give context to academia's overall perception of the problem.

False Confessions as a Breakdown in Legal Decision-Making

Kassin (2005) proposed a conceptual framework in which he identified false confessions as a breakdown at various decision-making points through-out the American legal process. He identified these points as follows:

1. Law enforcement interviewers target innocent people for interroga-tions because innocent people are incapable of accurately assessing deception.

2. Innocent people subject themselves to criminal interrogation by naively waving their constitutional rights to remain silent and to seek legal counsel.

3. Once in the interrogation room, innocent people unwittingly appear anxious and defensive which makes them appear guilty.

4. Innocent people can then be induced into falsely confessing by law enforcement's use of deceptive and psychologically oriented inter-rogation methods.

5. Law enforcement officers, attorneys, and triers of fact are incapable of accurately identifying false confessions when they see them.

Following this sequential process of decision-making errors allows read-ers to understand how an innocent subject winds up falsely confessing to a crime they did not commit. Exploring these decision-making points will help to explain the concepts put forth by some false confession researchers and later testified to by expert witnesses. In addition, it will help to demonstrate some of the flawed experimental designs that academic researchers have created to study the false confession phenomenon and the false assumptions they have formed regarding law enforcement officers and how they question criminal subjects.

Police Cannot Accurately Identify Deception

Prior to the onset of an interrogation, a pre-interrogation interview is typically conducted with the subject. During the interview phase, the ques-tioning is predominantly neutral and geared toward gathering information from the subject (Inbau et al., 2001). This is a critical point in the questioning process because this interview ultimately determines whether the individual will be subjected to an interrogation (Inbau et al., 2001). The key factor in determining whether an interrogation is warranted stems from indications that the interview subject is being deceptive in their responses (Inbau et al., 2001). Essentially, the reason law enforcement officers begin an interrogation is because they surmise through verbal and/or nonverbal clues that the subject is lying. I contend that available physical evidence, witness statements, co-conspirator admissions, and case facts also contribute to an officer's determination of a subject's truthfulness. However, false confession researchers, expert witnesses, and advocates like to ignore the case information available to the interrogator and instead highlight how poor law enforcement is at identifying deception. It has been suggested that while law enforcement officers are inherently unskilled at identifying deception, they claim to have a great deal of confidence in their ability to identify when a subject is lying to them (Kassin, 2005). Because the ability to identify deception is such a critical juncture in the interrogation process (Willen & Stromwall, 2012), a sizeable amount of false confession research has been directed at law enforcement's accuracy in identifying deception in interview subjects.

Human Accuracy in Detecting Deception

While law enforcement officers have historically reported a keen ability to detect deception in the subjects they interview (Frantzen & Can, 2012; Hill & Moston, 2011; Kassin et al., 2007); Kassin and Fong (1999) suggested that this confidence may be misplaced. This is particularly concerning as the judgment of law enforcement officers is the key determining factor as to whether a criminal subject should ultimately be interrogated (Meissner & Kassin, 2002). In an early review of accuracy in deception detection, Zuckerman, DePaulo, and Rosenthal (1981) focused on three specific issues: a) strategies people employ to deceive and the behaviors associated with their efforts at deceiving; b) behaviors associated with the judging of deception; and c) accuracy associated with detecting lies. Through their review, Zuckerman et al. (1981) concluded that human beings' ability to accurately identify deception is only slightly better than chance. Put another way, human beings might as well flip a coin when it comes to identifying whether the person they are talking to is lying.

Zuckerman et al. (1981) also concluded that the ability to accurately identify deception is determined by the channels available to the individual assessing the subject's honesty. Two particularly telling channels include body cues and speech cues, both of which increase the assessor's likelihood of accurately identifying deception when available. Within the field of law enforcement, these are frequently referred to as verbal and nonverbal cues. The adeptness in which an individual can construe and interpret the verbal nuances of a subject's speech ultimately determines their success in identifying deception (Zuckerman et al., 1981). It is not uncommon to hear our friends and loved ones express a keen ability to identify when their children are lying to them or when a politician or spouse of a murder victim is being dishonest when interviewed on television news magazines. As someone who has spent a career in law enforcement, I can attest to the fact that law enforcement officers, based on their training and/or investigative experiences, can be even more brazen in expressing their deception detection abilities.

Through a meta-analysis of research relating to accurately identifying deception, Bond and DePaulo (2006) concluded that when people are not given special training to detect deception, they can distinguish between truth and deception with an accuracy rate of approximately 54%. More specifically, they found that human beings can correctly identify truthful information with an accuracy rate of approximately 61% and lies with an accuracy rate of approximately 47%. In short, untrained laypeople are better at identifying when someone is being truthful than when they are lying. Bond and DePaulo also concluded that when an individual is motivated by a strong need to be believed, they tend to appear more deceptive. This is particularly problematic within the criminal justice context as innocent subjects obviously have a strong desire for the law enforcement officer to believe that they are innocent. As opposed to accepting the strength of their denials as proof of their innocence, human beings tend to take on the Shakespearean "the lady

144

doth protest too much" approach by assuming that their overacting is actually a sign of deception. This may explain why some people may be less inclined to believe a person who makes comments like, "I swear on the lives of my children that I didn't do it" or "I swear on a stack of Bibles that I am innocent." Although Bond and DePaulo's findings are not specifically directed toward law enforcement officers, they are concerning as they identify human weaknesses that may inherently influence law enforcement officers tasked with identifying and interpreting verbal and non-verbal cues in deciding whether a criminal subject should be interrogated. It is therefore important to identify the effect that training, experience, and specialization may have on a law enforcement officer's ability to accurately identify deception.

The Ability of Law Enforcement to Identify Deception

As earlier research efforts noted the weakness of human beings in assessing deception, later efforts focused on the same ability in law enforcement, especially as it relates to their training. First on the chopping block was the Reid interrogation technique. Trocino (2016) identified the basic tenant of the Reid Technique as the ability of officers to identify deception among criminal subjects. He then suggests that if students of the Reid Technique believe that they can accurately identify deception, they may come to falsely believe that anything that does not fit the narrative that an interrogation subject is guilty must be a lie. In Trocino's words, "This pathology proves the old adage that if one is a hammer, the entire world looks like a nail" (p. 95). This type of anti-Reid sentiment led researchers to test just how good law enforcement officers, especially those who have been trained in such techniques, truly are at identifying deception. For example, Kassin and Fong (1999) examined through laboratory experimentation the abilities of people to distinguish true and false denials rendered during the course of a criminal interrogation. In this experiment, 16 male college student participants engaged in various mock crimes such as vandalism, shoplifting, breaking & entering, and computer break-in, and were subsequently subjected to a mock arrest and questioning session. Innocent participants were instructed to be honest while guilty participants were instructed to lie to the interrogator by denying their involvement. To increase the consequences associated with honest and deceptive responses, those participants who were ultimately judged as guilty were to be detained at the campus security office for five minutes while those who were ultimately judged as innocent would receive $5. Forty additional college student participants were randomly assigned to receive 30 minutes of Reid interrogation training or to receive no training at all. These 40 participants were then shown videos of the interrogations of each of the 16 participants who participated in the mock criminal activity. After reviewing each interrogation, which ranged from 3.5 to 6 minutes, the 40 observing participants were asked to identify which denials were true and which were false.

Kassin and Fong identified that the observers were unable to distinguish between truthful and deceptive subjects, and that the Reid-trained participants were not only less accurate than those in the naïve control group at distinguishing between true and false denials, but they were more confident in their judgments. Based on these findings, Kassin and Fong concluded that the Reid Technique may not be effective and may actually prove to be counterproductive as a method for accurately identifying truthful and deceptive responses from an interview subject. The importance of this conclusion bears repeating. Through this laboratory experimentation, these two academic researchers concluded that the Reid Technique may actually make law enforcement officers worse at identifying deception. It is ludicrous laboratory experiments like this one that have helped to cast such a negative shadow upon the wildly successful Reid Technique and the ability of law enforcement officers to identify deception.

As law enforcement officers, prosecutors, and others within the criminal justice system tend not to be huge consumers of academic research, let's take a closer look at what actually took place in this particular experiment. Kassin and Fong (1999) took 16 college students and had them engage in mock crimes. In other words, they took 16 noncriminals and had them engage in pretend crimes. So, from the outset, this was a group of people who did not, in any way, represent real-world criminal subjects, and they pretended to engage in criminal activity. The participants who were pre-selected to pose as guilty subjects were then informed that if during the course of their ensuing interrogation they were correctly identified as being guilty by the interrogator, they would spend 5 minutes in the campus security office. Now, it is important for those not familiar with the ethical constraints of laboratory experimentation to know that it is not ethically permissible to cause physical, emotional, or psychological harm to a test subject. As such, it is logical and appropriate that this is the extent of the punishment that could be handed out to a participant who was accurately identified as being guilty. What is not logical is the premise that spending 5 minutes in the campus security office is either a threatening punishment or even remotely reflects the threat of a lengthy prison term faced by a real-world criminal subject.

The absurdity of this experiment continues with the application of the Reid Technique. As mentioned, 40 additional college students were randomly assigned to receive or not receive training in the Reid Technique. To replicate the training and experience of law enforcement officers, those students receiving training were given 30 minutes in the Reid Technique. Any law enforcement officer who has ever received Reid training or some other type of interview and interrogation training can readily attest to the fact that it takes at least 30 minutes to get through the lecturer's introduction on the first day of the training course. Yet, it was posited that 30 minutes of Reid training in this particular experiment sufficiently reflected the realities of a 40-hour course in criminal interviewing and interrogation and a career of perfecting the skills learned in such a course.

The ridiculous nature of the experiment continues when each of the assessors are directed to watch a video ranging from 3.5 to 6 minutes of a non-law enforcement officer interrogating a non-criminal about a pretend crime. Again, those who have ever interviewed or interrogated a criminal subject in the real world would likely agree that it takes between 3 and 6 minutes just to complete the Miranda review process. Yet for this experiment, this is the total duration of the actual interrogation video that they are asked to review before making a ruling as to the fake criminal's level of honesty regarding their involvement, or lack of involvement, in the pretend crime. I posit that it is completely inappropriate, and borderline unethical, to draw any conclusions about the deception detection abilities of actual law enforcement officers and/or the effects of the Reid Technique on these abilities, based on such an unrealistic and non-representative laboratory experiment. However, academia, expert witnesses, and advocates exhibit no outward concern about doing just that. What will become increasingly clear throughout this text is the fact that enormous leaps are being made between academic laboratory research and the real-world interrogation of criminal subjects by law enforcement professionals. Nevertheless, it is this type of fraudulent research that is being used to fuel the legal attacks against American law enforcement officers and the interrogative techniques they employ.

Building on research like that of Kassin and Fong (1999), Meissner and Kassin (2002) addressed the ability of law enforcement officers to accurately identify deception by comparing the judgments of actual police investigators to trained and naïve college students while simultaneously examining the impact that experience and training may have on judgment accuracy. Their sample was comprised of 44 law enforcement investigators (25 local officers from Florida and 19 local officers from Ontario) who were then shown the 3.5 to 6.0-minute interrogation videos from the Kassin and Fong experiment. Participants were then asked to judge whether the subjects were truthful or deceptive in their denials. When compared to the responses of the college student participants in Kassin and Fong's earlier experiment, results indicated that neither training nor prior experience as a law enforcement officer appeared to increase accuracy in identifying deception. Meissner and Kassin also concluded that experience and training appeared to increase the likelihood that a law enforcement officer would view an interrogation subject as deceitful. Meissner and Kassin's findings therefore seemed to support previous research that suggested that law enforcement officers maintain an investigator bias that causes them to see deception in others.

If Meissner and Kassin's findings are to be believed, law enforcement officers' increased tendency to see deception in others may translate into an increase in subjecting innocent people to unwarranted interrogations. The logic of such research works as follows: a) we can conclude that law enforcement officers are bad at detecting deception; b) their training and experiences make them more prone to distrust the subject they are interviewing; c) because they misperceive an innocent person to be lying, they initiate an unwarranted interrogation of an innocent subject; and d) the innocent subject is placed that much closer to a false confession. However, we have to return to the problematic nature of the experiment. First, these researchers asked law enforcement officers to watch a video of an interrogation that lasted for less than 6 minutes. In this situation, the officer has no actual contact with the subject and has no control over the interview. By the very nature of this design, the officer does not have access to all nonverbal behavior. Does the interrogation subject engage in toe tapping, scratching, preening, covering his mouth, start touching his face, or otherwise exhibit a change in demeanor, behavior, or emotion at certain questions? Subtle nonverbal clues like this can be missed when you are not in the actual presence of another person. Similarly, the officer does not have any control over the questions that are being asked. As such, they cannot ask known truth questions to compare those responses to the answers on suspected lie questions. Lastly, how much data can be collected from a subject in as little as 3.5 minutes? Would it be fair to test the diagnostic abilities of a medical doctor or psychologist by having them watch a 3.5 minute video of a pretend patient? How good would these professionals be in the same situation?

The very nature of this research design is also profoundly problematic. As previously mentioned, the videos involve the interrogation of a college student pretending to be a criminal and pretending to have engaged in a criminal act. They are then subjected to a pretend interrogation by a pretend law enforcement interrogator. By its very nature, every aspect of this study is fake. The researchers then task a law enforcement professional who is trained and experienced at detecting deception to identify whether the fake criminal who is being interrogated by a fake law enforcement officer about a fake crime is being truthful. While the researchers feel quite comfortable in assuming that law enforcement officers maintain a bias that causes them to see deception in others, perhaps what is actually taking place is the officer's correct assessment that the entire video recording is based on a lie. In reality, it may be that the true bias in this study is the anti-law enforcement bias maintained by the academic researchers and false confession experts designing these experiments and testifying about their flawed conclusions in open court.

The Problem with Testing Detection Deception in the Laboratory

As noted by Bradford and Goodman-Delahunty (2008), if the ability to correctly identify deception within an everyday social context is important, this same ability is of critical importance when the initiation of a criminal interrogation rests on the accuracy of this final assessment. In reviewing 39 studies relating to the abilities of laypeople to identify deception, Vrij (as cited by Bradford & Goodman-Delahunty, 2008), noted that a considerable portion of the empirical research involved research participants being shown videotapes of interviews with innocent and guilty subjects and then asking them to identify both the accuracy of the statements and the cues that contributed to their assessment. Vrij identified a mean accuracy rate in these studies which hovered only slightly above chance. The inherent unfairness in testing the deception detection abilities of a law enforcement officer under such limiting and contrived conditions is akin to showing a baseball commentator one recorded inning of a baseball game and then asking them to conclusively identify which team won the game. To use a more academic example, it would be like providing a university professor with a single homework assignment for a student and then asking them to identify whether the student passed the course. In both of these analogies, the baseball commentator and the university professor would require vastly greater amounts of information before arriving at a well-informed conclusion. However, greater and more varied information is exactly what is withheld from the law enforcement officers in the types of deception detection studies outlined above. Without additional information, what researchers are actually testing is how well a person can guess. Even more interestingly, they then seem shocked that, like calling a coin toss in the air, the accuracy rates hover around 50%. Based on this overreliance on artificial and illogical laboratory experiments, we should all question the frequent academic conclusion that law enforcement officers are inherently unreliable, and at times, actually worse than untrained college students in their ability to accurately identify deception.

As stated above, an argument could be easily made that the deception assessments made by university research participants who received 30 minutes of interview training, or the responses of university research participants who participated in mock crimes of no real consequence, may not be suitable for drawing conclusions about the deception detection accuracy of law enforcement officers. In fact, this very argument was made by O'Sullivan, Frank, Hurley, and Tiwana (2009) who suggested that the tendency of most lie detection researchers to rely on university student participants may have contributed to the false conclusion that human beings, to include law enforcement professionals, are only slightly better than chance at identifying deception. O'Sullivan et al. noted that the experimental studies specifically designed to test law enforcement's ability to accurately identify deception and the lies on which officers are asked to render judgements do not actually reflect the lies they observe within their profession. In a meta-analysis of deception detection research, O'Sullivan et al. concluded that when law enforcement officers are tasked with identifying deception in high stakes lies like those involving serious rewards or punishments for the interrogation subject, they are significantly more accurate than those officers who are tested in low stakes situations. In other words, law enforcement officers are better at identifying lies when the outcome is arrest, prosecution, a lengthy prison term, embarrassment in the community, loss of employment, and possibly the loss of friends and family as opposed to sitting in the campus security office for five minutes.

Based on the position that the significance of the lie matters when assessing law enforcement's ability to accurately identify deception, Frantzen and Can (2012) sought to compare lie detection confidence levels between violent crime and property crime detectives while similarly comparing lie detection confidence levels for law enforcement officers engaged in custodial and non-custodial interviews. Frantzen and Can also sought to analyze the relationship between officers' lie detection confidence levels based on the interrogative technique that was employed. While many of the previous researchers had focused upon experimental research with university students in controlled settings, Frantzen and Can chose to seek the insights of law enforcement officers by collecting self-report surveys from 135 detectives in local (i.e. municipal and county) law enforcement agencies in Texas. In analyzing this data, they determined that respondents had a mean lie detection confidence level of 75% which is significantly higher than chance and notably higher than the lie detection abilities reported in experimental research studies. Simply put, law enforcement officers reported a much higher level of deception detection ability than what was found in the artificial environment of the laboratory.

Frantzen and Can (2012) concluded that this high degree of confidence was due in part to the fact that law enforcement officers, by the very nature of their profession, have access to corroborating evidence like witness statements and physical evidence that is likely to support their lie detection judgments. While false confession researchers like to suggest that innocent people may be unnecessarily subjected to criminal interrogations due to the inability of law enforcement to accurately identify deception, they fail to take into account the fact that lies are not always simply identified by the interrogator's hunch or gut instinct. It is also important to note that interrogation is rarely the first step in an investigation (Newring & O'Donohue, 2008). Because interrogations often tend to occur toward the end of an investigation, officers are able to enter the interrogation room with a great deal of evidence and information that may help to disprove false statements made by the subject. In simplest terms, while the laboratory seeks to identify how well a law enforcement officer can guess whether a person is lying based on viewing a 5-minute video, the real world permits an officer to access additional case facts and evidence, control the line of questioning, and view all verbal and nonverbal behavior before determining whether an interrogation is necessary. Again, this questionable laboratory research has caused many academics, expert witnesses, and advocates to falsely conclude that law enforcement officers make the decision to interrogate on nothing more than a feeling that the subject is lying.

The assertion that law enforcement officers cannot accurately identify deception is deserving of debate and must not be accepted at face value. This assertion is a convenient proposition as it supports the overarching argument against criminal interrogation. After all, who would support the interrogation of criminal subjects when the basis for the interrogation is inherently flawed? It is therefore of great benefit to expert witnesses to be able to take the stand and reference research which concludes that law enforcement officers are not only incapable of identifying deception, but their training and experience may actually make them worse at doing so. However, law enforcement officers and prosecutors must be made aware that the detection deception research on which these conclusions are based is highly dubious. As such, it is demeaning, insulting, illogical, and self-serving for academics, expert witnesses, and advocates to continue to foster the flawed premise that law enforcement officers are incapable of accurately identifying deception and may actually be worse than college students in these efforts.

CHAPTER 9

How Long Are Subjects Kept in the Interrogation Room?

A conceptual framework exists in the study of false confessions in which researchers suggest that the actions of law enforcement interrogators, as well as the interrogative tactics they employ, are predominantly responsible for false confessions, and potentially wrongful convictions within the United States criminal justice system (Gudjonsson, 2010; Joselow, 2019; Leo, 2007). The tendency to blame law enforcement interrogative methods for false confessions exists despite the fact that these same interrogative techniques have also proved successful in the elicitation of confessions from truly guilty parties (Conti, 1999; Russano et al., 2005). The following is a discussion of the law enforcement actions and methods that false confession researchers find particularly problematic.

"Isolation"

As previously discussed, Inbau et al. (2001) created an effective interrogative process known as the Reid Technique that has been taught to countless law enforcement officers for decades. Kassin and Gudjonsson (2004) suggested that the 9-step process comprising the Reid Technique can be broken down into three primary processes: isolation, confrontation, and minimization. As recommended by Inbau et al., when criminal subjects are taken in for questioning, they are generally separated from friends, family, and social support networks so that they can be questioned privately. This separation is designed to ensure privacy and to permit the law enforcement officer to maintain control over the interview and interrogation process. However, false confession researchers like to refer to this aspect of the Reid Technique as 'isolation.' For example, Kassin et al. (2010) suggested that rather than talking to a subject in privacy, what law enforcement is actually attempting to accomplish is a steady increase of the stress associated with the subject's continued denials by holding them incommunicado in an unfamiliar environment. Kassin (2008) also suggested that isolation increases both the subject's anxiety level and their desire to escape the interrogation process. In light of the stress associated with isolation, Kassin and Gudjonsson (2004) concluded that the likelihood of a false confession increases as the duration of the interrogation increases.

Again, the manner in which some false confession researchers, expert witnesses, and advocates choose to reframe the routine aspects of law enforcement is somewhat biased. If you can think back to the last time that you accompanied a loved one to a doctor's appointment and watched as they were called back into the office, did you interpret this innocuous act as the 'isolation' of your loved one? How about when a university professor recommends to a student that they discuss disputed exam questions during the professor's office hours? Is the professor trying to 'isolate' the student from the rest of the class? When you were taken to the back office at the dealership to discuss whether you wanted the extended warranty and undercoating on your new vehicle, were they 'isolating' you from the rest of the customers? Quite simply, in life we do many things in private, and we would not consider them an act of isolation. Yet this is the picture that some false confession researchers like to paint of the interrogation process. Like the word 'tactics,' describing the interview process as an act of 'isolation' also welcomes an inherently negative connotation. But is this really what is taking place? In reality, there are times when interviews are conducted within a person's home, their place of business, or even on a public sidewalk. In these instances, general information may be collected. However, there also comes a time when more in-depth discussions need to be had. This is why the car salesman does not discuss a final price and sales agreement with you while standing in the middle of the parking lot. The same holds true in the field of law enforcement. There comes a time when it is necessary to actually sit down and have more detailed private discussions.

What some academics, expert witnesses, and advocates often overlook is the very nature of law enforcement discussions. Suppose for instance that the current investigation relates to the suspicion that the husband/father of the house is believed to have been downloading child pornography. Three considerations arise in such a case. First, the revelation that this activity has been taking place will likely not be well received by the rest of the family and may serve to bring a great deal of shame upon the subject. As such, this is a matter that the subject may wish to discuss privately and away from his wife and children. Secondly, with his wife and children looking on, the subject is unlikely to admit to his wrongdoing based on the shame that such an acknowledgment is likely to bring. Lastly, broaching this issue in the presence of the subject's family is likely to elicit an emotional response from family members which could, in turn, result in a potentially violent confrontation between family members and the subject, family members and the police, or even suicidal attempts from the subject. In essence, while some researchers and expert witnesses may like to portray a private interview as an act of 'isolation,' in reality a private interview room protects the privacy of the subject, increases the likelihood of candid responses from the subject, and helps to ensure the safety of the subject, the subject's family, and investigators.

Duration

In addition to being 'isolated' in the interrogation room, some academics, expert witnesses, and advocates also like to point to the amount of time that a subject spends in the interrogation room as a potential cause for false confession. For example, after reviewing 600 audio- and video-recorded police interviews in England between 1989 and 1990, Baldwin (1993) concluded that nearly 75% of the interviews lasted less than 30 minutes. In a similar study in which 50 audiotaped police interviews in England relating to a variety of criminal offenses were reviewed, Bull and Soukara (2009) determined that the interviews ranged from 5 minutes to 3 hours. Citing various observational studies, Kassin et al. (2007) noted that routine law enforcement interrogations in the United States range between 20 minutes and one hour. What these studies suggest is that law enforcement interviews and interrogations, even across countries, are generally not lengthy affairs. Still, it has been posited that the likelihood of a false confession increases with the length of the interrogation.

In their analysis of 125 confirmed cases of false confessions caused by law enforcement interrogation techniques, Drizin and Leo (2004) identified that the mean duration of these interrogations was 16.3 hours with 34% lasting between 6 and 12 hours and 39% lasting between 12 and 24 hours. Although not clearly specified, this means that 27% of these false confession cases involved interrogations that lasted for more than 24 hours. It has been theorized that as an interrogation drags on, the subject becomes increasingly more uncomfortable, fatigued, and anxious (Davis & Leo, 2012). For these reasons, it is not surprising that false confessions tend to occur during interrogations that last for prolonged periods of time (Kassin et al., 2010). During extremely long periods of interrogation, sleep deprivation may also further compromise a subject's ability to resist falsely confessing (Kassin et al., 2010). Based on the profound differences in the length of routine police interrogations and those interrogations resulting in a false confession, it appears that law enforcement officers should avoid keeping criminal subjects in the interrogation room for egregious lengths of time so as to minimize the likelihood of eliciting a false confession. The question becomes: Are 16-hour interrogations typical for law enforcement officers, or do they represent police misconduct?

Duration of Polygraph Pre-Test Interviews

In an attempt to answer the question posed above, I first queried state and federal law enforcement polygraph examiners about the average length of time between the polygraph examiner and the subject being introduced and the start of the post-test interrogation. For the purpose of this study, this period of time was referred to as the polygraph 'pre-test.' This is the portion of the polygraph examination in which the examiner: a) collects basic background information from the subject; b) provides an explanation of the polygraph instrumentation and process; c) obtains the subject's version of events; and d) reviews test questions with the subject. Several of the participants reported that it is difficult to confidently identify the average length of their pre-test interviews because various factors can influence how long this period of time may last. For example, participants suggested that this period of time may last longer if: a) the case is particularly complex; b) the subject is talkative; c) the subject is providing a significant amount of previously undisclosed information; and/or d) the interrogator senses that he or she may be able to convince the subject to confess their crimes prior to the actual administration of the polygraph examination.

According to federal law enforcement polygraph examiners, the shortest average pre-test interview was reported to be approximately 45 minutes while the longest average pre-test interview was reported to be between 2.5 and 3 hours. The majority of federal examiners estimated their pre-tests to last between 1 hour and 2 hours in length. State law enforcement polygraph examiners generally reported a longer pre-test interview process with an average of between 1¾ hours and 3 hours. However, the majority of state examiners estimated their pre-test to last between 2 and 2.5 hours. Polygraph pre-test interviews cannot be considered 'routine' as the examiner engages in tasks like explaining the polygraph components and reviewing test questions. These things do not occur in a typical law enforcement interview. Even so, it is important to note that the lengths of state and federal law enforcement polygraph examiner's pre-test interviews are not inconsistent with the duration of routine law enforcement interviews identified by both Kassin et al. (2007) and Bull and Soukara (2009).

Duration of Polygraph Post-Test Interviews

I also asked state and federal law enforcement polygraph examiners to estimate the average duration of their post-test interrogations. Many of the participants reported that it is difficult to give an exact average of how long their interrogations last as there is a great deal of variance. Some of the federal examiners noted that they have interrogated subjects for as little as a couple of minutes to as long as 18 hours, with most estimating that their interrogations rarely go beyond 4 or 5 hours. The majority of the federal examiners suggested that their average interrogations last between 2 and 3 hours. The average length of post-test interrogations for state law enforcement polygraph examinations were reported to be between 30 minutes and 2 hours. In essence, while their lengths of pre-test interviews and post-test interrogations differ, federal examiners identified that their total polygraph examinations generally last between 3 and 5 hours while state examiners' total polygraph examinations generally last between 2½ and 4½ hours. These nearly identical numbers offer excellent insight into the duration of typical criminal polygraph examinations.

The aforementioned information is important as it demonstrates a great deal of overall consistency between state polygraph examinations and federal polygraph examinations. It also identifies that law enforcement professionals who specialize in criminal interrogation typically interrogate for no longer than 3 hours and rarely longer than 5 hours. This would suggest that Drizin and Leo's (2004) observation that interrogations in false confession cases averaging 16.3 hours clearly reflects police misconduct as opposed to normal interrogation procedures. To further support this conclusion, both state and federal examiners frequently expressed an awareness that overly lengthy interrogations tend to: a) result in an incessant rehashing of ideas; b) prove unproductive in developing additional information; and c) provide support to anticipated defense claims that the subject was coerced into confessing. While some participants expressed a willingness to talk with a criminal subject for as long as they are willing to keep talking, many of those who specialize in criminal interrogation reported that extremely long interrogations may ultimately prove counterproductive. In short, it appears that interrogative specialists express a ready awareness of how long they are interrogating a criminal subject, and they strive to avoid such lengthy periods of inquiry to:

a) prevent unproductive questioning; and b) to preclude future legal attacks from defense attorneys who will likely allege that their client was harangued for an egregious length of time.

It is hard not to be astounded by the fact that false confession interrogations averaged 16.3 hours. When I have given presentations on false confessions to law enforcement officers, this statistic consistently results in a similar expression of incredulity. To obtain greater insight about the perception of this statistic among interrogative specialists, I decided to ask state and federal law enforcement polygraph examiners what they thought constitutes an excessive or egregious amount of time to interrogate a criminal subject. Similar to other questions, many of the participants noted that this is a difficult question to answer as various factors may influence what is considered egregious. Such factors may include the nature of the case, the extent to which the subject was interviewed by investigators prior to the polygraph, and the characteristics of the subject. For example, one participant noted that if the case involves allegations of child pornography, this may require a longer interrogation as these types of criminal subjects are much more reluctant to admit their embarrassing and taboo sexual attraction to children. Conversely, many participants suggested that if the subject suffers from mental health issues, if the subject has a poor ability to deal with stress, if the subject is being yelled at by the interrogator, and/or if there is a high degree of coercion, then it will be necessary to terminate the interrogation much sooner.

The majority of the participants offered that the ultimate determinants of how long an interrogation should last also depends upon the following key factors:

1. Does the subject continue to remain in the interrogation room voluntarily?
2. Does the subject express a willingness to continue speaking with the interrogator voluntarily?
3. Is the subject regularly receiving food, water, cigarette, and bathroom breaks?

4. Is the subject continuing to provide useful information?

5. Is the case critically important and time sensitive like a kidnapping or missing child?

Some federal examiners reported that if these conditions are met, interrogations lasting as long as 6 to 8 hours, or even longer, are acceptable. However, if these conditions were not met, some participants reported that interrogations lasting between 5 and 8 hours may be considered egregious. The largest number of participants suggested that interrogations in which the aforementioned conditions are not met become egregious when they last longer than 8 hours. For state examiners, 63% reported that even if these conditions were met, they would consider interrogations lasting longer than 6 hours to be egregious. Another 37% considered anything longer than 6 to 8 hours would be considered egregious.

What is interesting about these findings is the fact that the 16.3-hour false confession interrogations noted by Drizin and Leo (2004) are between 5 and 8 times longer than the average interrogation reported by federal law enforcement polygraph examiners. Similarly, these 16.3-hour interrogations are between 8 and 32 times longer than the average interrogation reported by state law enforcement polygraph examiners. Lastly, for both state and federal law enforcement polygraph examiners, the 16.3-hour false confession interrogations reported by Drizin and Leo are more than double the length of what these interrogative specialists already consider egregious. In short, if those who specialize in criminal interrogation believe that interrogations lasting more than 8 hours are excessive, 16.3 hours can be considered nothing less than an abysmal abuse of power. One thing was made abundantly clear while interviewing these participants: They are aware of the duration of their interrogations and they are well-acquainted with the fact that they could face criticism while on the witness stand for keeping a subject in the interrogation room for too long.

While polygraph examiners who specialize in interrogating criminal subjects appear to be keenly aware of the negatives associated with overly lengthy interrogations, it is unknown whether other law enforcement officers share that same insight. It is therefore critically important that all law enforcement officers tasked with interrogating a criminal subject be mindful of how long they interrogate; the problems and lack of productivity associated with excessively long interrogations; and the likely legal challenges and criticisms they may face if they allow their questioning to go on for too long. It can be expected, whether a subject is interrogated for 10 minutes or 10 hours, that the defense will have no other option available to them but to claim that their client was interrogated far longer than they should have been. As such, the defense attorney will engage in this routine and foreseeable avenue of attack. I personally experienced such a ridiculous argument when being cross examined by the defense attorney for a subject who confessed to me *in 10 minutes* that he had sexually abused his stepson years earlier. If a defense attorney can attack a 10-minute interrogation, think of what they will do with an interrogation lasting for several hours.

Defense Games

Although the results of a polygraph examination are not generally presented in court, the statements made by the subject during the course of the examination *can* be admitted. In the defense attorney's attempts to suppress their client's incriminating statements, it has been my experience that defense attorneys like to question polygraph examiners on the stand about the total length of their 'interview' with a subject. They do so knowing full well that a polygraph examiner cannot identify the full nature of their profession or disclose the fact that a polygraph examination was administered to their client as this revelation can cause a mistrial. In light of these circumstances, polygraph examiners are placed in the difficult position of explaining to the jury that they were called upon by investigators to interview the subject because of their interrogative prowess while strategically concealing the fact of being a polygraph examiner. Being aware of the legal minefield in which the examiner finds himself, it is not uncommon for the defense attorney to try and goad the examiner into revealing their true specialization. They will do this by asking the polygraph examiner on the stand such questions as, "Why is it that they wanted *you* to interrogate the subject?" and "What specific skills do *you* have that the investigators needed *you* to question my client?" These questions are designed to either make the examiner slip up and utter the forbidden P word (polygraph) or to give the jury the impression that the examiner is the 'go-to water boarder' who is brought in to torture confessions from criminal subjects when traditional interviewing techniques have failed. In essence, this becomes a legal game reminiscent of tickling your sibling in church knowing that they are forbidden from laughing out loud.

The games played by the defense then continue with a direct attack on the length of the 'interview.' Although the defense attorney is aware of the fact that a sizeable portion of the examiner's 'interview' of their client involved a polygraph pre-test and the administration of a polygraph examination, they will feign shock when the examiner reports that the 'interview' of their client lasted for more than a few hours. The games will continue as the defense attorney inquires as to what possibly could have taken place in that 4-hour time period, knowing that the polygraph itself took up a significant period of time but cannot be referenced. While in reality the actual interrogation may have only lasted for 45 minutes, the defense will make a big show for the jury that their client was 'isolated' in the interrogation room for hour after hour. It is important to remember that this entire charade is designed to accomplish one goal: to create the impression for the jury that the subject's confession was false and coerced during a never-ending interrogation. And, if the defense is lucky enough and/or their client's finances permit, the defense will retain the services of an academic researcher or false confession expert who can use the inherently flawed academic research to support this illusion.

For those law enforcement officers who are not specialized in the field of polygraph, it should be expected that the defense will engage in the same types of attacks against their non-polygraph interrogations. As such, all law enforcement officers would be well-advised to avoid lengthy interrogations not only to minimize the likelihood of eliciting a false confession, but also to help insulate officers from the anticipated insinuations that will surely be mounted by the defense. Similarly, while it is important as a human being to ensure that a criminal subject is given adequate water, food, bathroom breaks, and opportunities to smoke a cigarette, these actions also help to counteract the abusive picture the defense attorney will try and paint about the interrogative setting. Still, it should not be forgotten that the average length of interrogations leading to a false confession is 16.3 hours (Drizin & Leo, 2004). This is not only an outrageous length of time to interrogate a subject, but it also directly contradicts the defense's anticipated argument that a routine 5-hour interrogation may have caused their client to falsely confess to a crime they did not commit. This statistic should be remembered by law enforcement officers and routinely cited by prosecutors at trial. Quite simply, it is a false assumption to believe that law enforcement officers 'isolate' subjects in the interrogation room for egregious periods of time in order to elicit a confession. This incessant narrative may, in reality, reflect an inherent bias held by many academic researchers studying the false confession phenomenon and eagerly repeated by defense attorneys and expert witnesses in their attacks on law enforcement interrogations. For certain, outrageously lengthy interrogations have been conducted by law enforcement officers. However, these egregiously long interrogations are rare; they represent clear examples of police malpractice; and they do not automatically lead to false confessions. As noted by Kassin et al. (2007), "Proven false confession stories represent an inherently biased sample of cases" (p. 384). It would therefore be false to assume that this biased sample reflects the routine interrogative practices of American law enforcement officers.

CHAPTER 10

How Far Will Law Enforcement Officers Really Go to Get a Confession?

It is reported throughout the academic literature that law enforcement officers engage in a wide array of problematic and overly coercive interrogative methods. Some of these problematic interrogative techniques are identified as 'good cop/bad cop' (Newring & O'Donohue, 2008); sleep deprivation (Davis & O'Donohue, 2004); subjecting subjects to extremely lengthy interrogations (Chapman, 2013); manipulating the subject through psychological coercion (Leo & Drizin, 2010); increasing pressure on the subject (Najdowski, 2011); offering the subject a deal in exchange for their confession (Russano et al., 2005); employing deception and deceit (Conti, 1999); using trickery (Kassin et al., 2007); lying to the subject's loved ones about the subject's guilt (Chapman, 2013); minimizing a subject's sensory stimulation through physical isolation (Conti, 1999); and subjecting subjects to numerous interrogation sessions (Chapman, 2013). These researchers present a picture of law enforcement interrogators as single-minded individuals who will say and do anything, without stopping, until a confession is obtained. Trocino (2016) referred to this as a "win at all costs mind set" (p. 99). Similarly, Leding (2012) stated that because the law enforcement officer has already determined the subject to be guilty and will not accept the subject's denials, the interrogator "will use whatever means necessary to elicit a confession" (p. 265). Bull and Milne (as cited by Lassiter, 2010), suggested that law enforcement in the United States has developed an ethos of interviewing in which a confession is the primary goal and a close-minded, oppressive, and suggestive interviewing style is then employed to obtain the highly desired confession. The problem then becomes that this overwhelming desire to elicit the confession leads to an increase in coercive interrogation techniques which, in turn, can cause an innocent subject to falsely confess. The following is a discussion of some of the problematic techniques that officers are reported to utilize in order to force a confession out of a criminal subject.

Sleep Deprivation

The academic research has identified a handful of particularly problematic interrogative practices that are reportedly engaged in by law enforcement interrogators. One particularly troublesome approach is that of sleep deprivation. As previously discussed, Drizin and Leo (2004) identified that the average length of a criminal interrogation resulting in a false confession was 16.3 hours. Over such a long interrogative period, it is not illogical to assume that the subject of the interrogation will become increasingly more fatigued as the questioning process drags on. Conti (1999) has referred to the deliberate detention of criminal subjects for lengthy periods of time until they confess to a specified transgression as the 'wear down' technique. As noted by Kassin and Gudjonsson (2004), the longer a criminal subject is isolated in the interrogation room, the more desperate they become to escape. Moreover, this type of 'wear down' or sleep deprivation may further compromise a subject's ability to resist falsely confessing (Kassin et al., 2010). Kassin, Appleby, and Perillo (2010) also referenced various studies which indicated that depriving a person of sleep can impair their decision-making, make them more susceptible to influence, and impact their ability to sustain attention. Frenda et al. (2016) offered that "sleep deprivation sets the stage for a false confession by impairing complex decision making abilities—specifically, the ability to anticipate risks and consequences, inhibit behavioral impulses, and resist suggestive influences" (p. 2048). In light of these claims, it is not surprising that the Innocence Project and the National Registry of Exonerations offer numerous case vignettes of false confessors who were held in interrogation rooms for inordinate lengths of time.

In an attempt to better understand whether interrogative specialists consider this an effective or suitable interrogative technique, I asked state and federal law enforcement polygraph examiners about whether they found sleep deprivation to be an appropriate interrogative method for questioning criminal subjects. For the purpose of this question, 'sleep deprivation' was defined for the participants as deliberately keeping a subject awake to weaken their mental state and increase the likelihood of a confession. Nearly all of the participants identified this technique as unacceptable. While a variety of reasons were offered for this conclusion, they generally fell into the following categories: a) ethical concerns; b) effects on the subject; and c) anticipated repercussions.

Ethical Concerns. In explaining why they find sleep deprivation to be unacceptable, state and federal participants repeatedly referenced the ethical concerns that come along with such a practice. In general, some of the participants explained that to deliberately deprive an interrogation subject of sleep is simply "unethical" and "morally wrong." Multiple participants based their position on the fact that this technique essentially deprives a subject of a "necessity" and a "biological need." Other participants described sleep deprivation as "unfair," "Gestapo-type tactics," and "against my moral compass." One participant even joked that she personally has no interest in staying up all night waiting for a criminal subject's mental state to weaken, noting that she would rather go home and get some sleep herself.

Effects on the Subject. The federal and state law enforcement polygraph examiners I interviewed also expressed concerns about the effects that sleep deprivation may have on the subject. For example, one participant noted that people need to sleep, and a person's brain does irrational things when it is sleep-deprived. For this reason, many of the participants noted that when a subject is in such a weakened state, the veracity of their information cannot be trusted. Participants also suggested that because human beings need to sleep, they may ultimately choose to confess simply to escape the interrogation and give themselves an opportunity to rest. Many of the participants explained that depriving a subject of sleep negatively impacts the subject by severely weakening their mental and psychological state. It was further suggested that sleep deprivation is akin to being intoxicated and not having the ability to make good decisions. In fact, one participant explained that when a person is sleep deprived, their "brain isn't working at the level it should be." Others offered that in this condition, the subject is not in their right mind, not thinking clearly, and not lucid enough to make an informed decision. One participant actually referred to such a technique as "almost a form of torture." Similarly, another participant admitted that even he personally would say anything just to get some sleep. As such, depriving a subject of sleep would put the subject at a disadvantage and render them "incoherent."

Anticipated Repercussions. Participants also reported that sleep deprivation is likely to have various negative repercussions for not only the subject, but also for the interrogator. For example, some participants identified that if a subject were to render a confession after being deprived of sleep, the information provided would no longer be useful because the subject would not have made the admissions of his/her own free will. In other words, the subject would simply be telling the interrogator what they want to hear so that he/she can get some rest. As a result, multiple participants expressed their concern with the sleep deprivation technique because of the likelihood that it could lead to a false confession. In fact, one participant suggested that if a subject was sleep deprived, the interrogator may be likely to elicit a confession that sounds something like, "Yep, I did it" with very little supporting details. In addition to the effects that the sleep deprivation technique has on criminal subjects, some participants noted that it can also have negative repercussions for the interrogator. More specifically, some participants explained that an interrogation obtained through sleep deprivation will undoubtedly be challenged in court, and the defense attorney will likely introduce doubt as to why the subject confessed. As cautioned by one particular participant, using sleep deprivation will cause the defense attorney to "tear you up on the stand."

Notably, several participants offered that they viewed sleep deprivation to be an acceptable practice as it is not illegal to keep a person awake to answer questions. However, one of these participants also advised that depriving a person of sleep is not necessary to obtain a truthful confession, so he tends to avoid using this approach. Multiple participants also advised that as long as the subject remains in the interrogation room voluntarily, they would be willing to continue the interrogation even if it was late at night and both the interrogator and the subject were tired. Some participants also reported that interrogating a tired subject is even less of a concern when the criminal case is important, and exigent circumstances exist such as in a case of kidnapping where time is of the essence. Still, the overwhelming majority of participants stated that they find this practice unacceptable and they would never use it. In fact, one of the participants stated, "We are in the truth-seeking business, not the confession-seeking business." Under this premise, he suggested that doing things correctly and legally to get to the truth is more important than obtaining a confession of questionable veracity via unacceptable practices. So, while Frenda et al. (2016) claim that "the interrogation of unrested, possibly sleep-deprived, suspects is not out of the ordinary and may even be commonplace" (p. 2047), the interrogative specialists I interviewed reported that they are overwhelmingly opposed to the practice because it is unethical; it leads to the collection of questionable information; it can encourage a false confession; and it can lead to future legal issues for the interrogator. In short, those who specialize in interrogation do not appear to rely on wearing a subject down in order to obtain a truthful confession.

Offering the Subject a Deal

Another technique that some false confession researchers believe to be routinely used by law enforcement interrogators is the offering of a deal to the subject in exchange for their confession (Russano et al., 2005; Swanner & Beike, 2010). Such a deal may involve the offering of incentives of decreased punishment in exchange for a confession (Swanner & Beike, 2010) or outright suggesting that the subject can go home once they confess their crimes (Drizin & Colgan, 2004). In a novel experimental paradigm used with 330 undergraduate students, Russano et al. studied the influence of psychologically based interrogation techniques on the likelihood of true and false confessions. The participants were paired with a confederate, and both were instructed to solve various logic problems, some of which were to be solved individually and some of which were to be solved jointly. In the 'guilty' condition, the confederate violated experimental rules by asking the unwitting participant for help on an individual problem. The participants who provided the answer were considered 'guilty.' In the 'innocent' condition, the confederate did not ask the participant for help. All of the participants were then interrogated. Unlike Kassin and Kiechel's (1996) often-cited ALT key experiment in which university participants were interrogated about pressing a forbidden computer key and crashing the computer system, Russano et al. considered their experimental paradigm to be more realistic as the crime of cheating was more serious in nature and required an intentional act. At the conclusion of their experiment, Russano et al. identified that when participants were offered a specific deal of leniency, they were 1.43 times more likely to confess (54.1% vs. 37.8%).

While experiments like these have caused some in the academic literature to have concerns over the interrogative technique of offering subjects a deal in exchange for their confession, proven cases of false confession have also demonstrated that law enforcement does employ this technique from time to time. For example, on August 1, 2006, 70-year-old Hebert Fields was shot and killed in New Haven, Connecticut while sitting in his car. The ensuing investigation eventually focused on 16-year-old Bobby Johnson who was advised during his second interrogation that he faced the death penalty for his supposed involvement in the crime. The detective in the case (who was later fired for stealing from the department), then promised Johnson he would get probation if he just confessed. Not surprisingly, Johnson, who was reported to have an IQ of 69, confessed to the murder. His confession was instrumental in his wrongful conviction and he spent 8 years in prison before having his conviction vacated (National Registry of Exonerations, 2020).

Although these types of worst case examples of criminal interrogation suggest that police may sometimes offer subjects a deal in exchange for their confession, I sought to more thoroughly understand how interrogative specialists view such a practice. As such, I asked the state and federal law enforcement polygraph examiners in my study whether they found the technique of offering the subject a deal in exchange for their confession to be an acceptable practice. Every participant questioned about this technique identified it as *unacceptable*. All of the participants suggested that they are not in a position to offer the subject a deal, nor do they have the authority to do so. As plainly stated by one participant, "We can't do that." Instead, participants repeatedly explained that the ability to offer the subject a deal is "up to the powers that be" such as the prosecutor or the judge. In fact, multiple participants advised that they make it a point to specifically inform the subject that they cannot offer the subject a deal or promise them anything. As noted by one participant, since they do not have the authority to speak on behalf of the court or the prosecutor, any deal that he would offer would constitute a "blatant lie." Multiple participants also advised that offering the subject a deal without the authorization or concurrence of a prosecutor could be considered "unconstitutional", "illegal", and "unethical." Over the years, I have had the joy of working cases with a partner and close friend who made it a point of informing interrogations subjects, "I cannot make you any promises. In fact, if anybody in law enforcement ever told you they could promise you something, they are lying."

Multiple state and federal participants in my study also suggested that offering the subject a deal without prior authorization from a prosecutor may potentially lead to a false confession if the subject is falsely led to believe that they can avoid punishment by simply confessing. Lastly, one participant stated that offering the subject a deal without prosecutorial concurrence and authorization was not only illegal, but it gives a 'black eye' to the interrogator, his agency, and law enforcement as a whole. Despite the vehemence with which state and federal participants reported that they are not authorized to offer criminal subjects a deal in exchange for their confession, multiple participants advised that they do say things to the subject to encourage their confession, but still fall far short of a promise or a deal. For example, one federal participant advised that he truthfully informs subjects that the court is set up to give the subject a certain degree of credit through the Federal Sentencing Guidelines for confessing and accepting responsibility for their criminal actions. In short, within the federal criminal justice system, criminal subjects who truthfully accept responsibility for their actions can receive a significant reduction in their sentence. As such, many federal investigators use this reality in their interrogative discussions. Other participants advised that the only thing they promise the subject is that the participant will act as the subject's spokesperson and present the subject's information to the prosecutor in a positive light. Another participant reported that while she never promises a subject anything, the best thing she can tell a subject is that they will ultimately be better off if they choose to confess. The support for this type of approach will be further explored in the chapter relating to how true confessors are treated within the criminal justice system.

While discussing the concept of offering the subject a deal, one state law enforcement polygraph examiner in my study identified that he clearly explains to criminal subjects that he does not make deals and then adds, "I'm not telling you that I can sprinkle fairy dust on this and make it go away." This participant then offers to the subject that if they accept responsibility for their criminal actions, he would be willing to tell those who make the deals (the prosecutors) that the subject was honest and regrets his actions. This same participant offered that while he cannot specifically offer the subject a deal, he finds it acceptable to tell a subject that if they are honest about what happened, "maybe we can work a deal for you." Another participant explained that while he would never offer the subject a deal, he would tell the subject that there are other people who have the authority to make deals and they may consider the subject's willingness to cooperate. Overall, the participants in my study unanimously advised that offering a subject a deal in exchange

174

for their confession is "unacceptable," but several explained that they would be willing to pass the subject's acceptance of responsibility on to those who can make such deals.

There are some within academia who would claim that the underlying problem with these promises to tell judges and prosecutors of a subject's cooperation is that it implies that the subject will ultimately be treated in a more lenient manner. Redlich et al. (2011) referred to this as "pragmatically implied leniency" and noted that it is a highly prevalent interrogative technique. While various researchers have suggested that promises of leniency are particularly coercive, especially those in which the officer assures the subject that a lighter sentence will be recommended (Joselow, 2019), it is important to note that the interrogative specialists whom I interviewed reported that they deliberately avoid making such promises for the various reasons outlined above. In essence, what some academic researchers are suggesting is that, not only can explicit promises of leniency cause an innocent person to falsely confess to a crime, but the same result can occur if the subject merely interprets the interrogator's words to mean that they may be treated more leniently. The question therefore becomes: Is it problematic to *infer* that the subject's cooperation may help them in the long run? Joselow (2019) cited *State v. Jackson* in which the Supreme Court in North Carolina ruled that the subject's confession was not coerced despite the fact that while the subject was assured that the court would view him as cooperative if he were to confess his criminal wrongdoing, the subject was not outright promised a lighter sentence in exchange for his confession. In short, it appears that courts *do* differentiate between explicit and inferred promises of leniency. In addition, interrogative specialists may feel comfortable inferring that the subject's cooperation may ultimately benefit them based on their real-world experiences of criminal confessors receiving better treatment and lighter sentences as a result of their confessions. This issue will be discussed in greater detail later.

Denying a Subject the Right to Speak with an Attorney

My review of the false confession research identified that law enforcement officers are believed to engage in the practice of preventing criminal subjects from speaking to their attorney during the course of an interrogation. For example, Kassin (2007) wrote on the case of Billy Wayne Cope who was interrogated for numerous hours, held overnight in jail without food or water, and prevented from speaking with an attorney before falsely confessing to causing the death of his 12-year-old daughter. The National Registry of Exonerations also provides case vignettes of innocent people who go on to falsely confess after being denied an opportunity to consult with legal counsel. For example, Eddie Lowery, a soldier at Fort Riley, Kansas, was interrogated all day without food and when he asked to speak with an attorney, was told that he did not need one. Lowery eventually falsely confessed and spent nine years in prison for the July 1981 murder of a 74-year-old woman in Ogden, Kansas (NRE, 2020). Similarly, Anthony Moore was interrogated by police in regard to the November 1992 murder of a retired police officer during the armed robbery of a Radio Shack in Manhattan, New York. Moore eventually went on to confess falsely despite repeatedly asking to speak with an attorney and being denied. Moore eventually spent three years in prison before being exonerated (NRE, 2020).

What these case vignettes illustrate is how police officers have denied criminal subjects an opportunity to speak with an attorney when they specifically requested to do so. It is unclear whether these denials occur as a strategy to give subjects the impression that they do not actually have the right to invoke their right to an attorney as suggested by Davis and Leo (2012), or whether they occur as an outright refusal as observed in the cases of Cope, Lowery, and Moore. In either event, some academic researchers, expert witnesses, and advocates believe that denying a subject the right to speak with an attorney is a routine law enforcement practice. To more thoroughly explore this premise, I decided to ask state and federal law enforcement polygraph examiners about their impressions regarding this presumed practice. Upon being questioned about this approach, every participant immediately advised that denying a criminal subject an opportunity to consult with their attorney is an unacceptable practice. The following is a discussion of the reasons participants offered for why they would never engage in such a practice.

Illegality. All 23 of the participants immediately reported that denying a subject access to an attorney was an unacceptable practice as it violates the subject's constitutional rights. Some participants further reported that this practice is 'unethical,' and it violates the rights specifically explained to the subject during the *Miranda* review process. It also stands in stark contrast to the participants' profession as a law enforcement officer in which they swore to uphold the Constitution. As noted by one participant, not allowing the subject to confer with his attorney is "against everything we stand for." Another participant identified that the ability of a criminal subject to speak to an attorney is their "number one right." Yet another participant noted that this right is "a line that's drawn deep in the sand." Still other participants stated that if a law enforcement officer violates this right, they are "making bad case law" and they "don't want to be that person" because they would be committing a "color of law violation" and essentially, "Your name is done in law enforcement."

Immediate Termination of the Interrogation. In being queried about this supposed interrogative approach, the majority of the participants readily expressed that once a subject requests to speak with their attorney, the interrogation process must be terminated. Such an invocation of a subject's right to counsel was described by participants as "a bright line in the sand," which clearly indicates that as an interrogator, "I'm finished talking to him," or more specifically, "game over."

Future Legal Challenges. Participants reported that engaging in such a practice will undoubtedly lead to legal challenges from the defense which could foreseeably lead to the suppression of the confession, thereby rendering this important piece of evidence unusable. One particular participant highlighted the point that the confessional end does not justify the interrogative means by stating, "It is our job to get information that can be used. If it can't be used, what good is it?" Other participants explained that they want to do their job in the right way, maintain their integrity, and avoid giving ammunition to defense attorneys to question them on the stand. As summarized by one participant, "It's not worth (losing) my job or my way of making a living".

The Invocation Must Be Unequivocal. Despite the unanimity in expressing how and why denying the subject an opportunity to speak with their attorney is unacceptable, several participants noted that it is important that such an invocation of one's rights be clearly articulated. In other words, some participants suggested that a subject's request to speak with an attorney must be unequivocal. They noted that a question like, "Do you think I need an attorney?" does not rise to the level of an unequivocal invocation of one's right to counsel. In light of such ambiguity, the majority of the participants advised that they would continue the interrogation until an unambiguous request to speak with counsel is made. However, the participants frequently noted that their actions in light of a subject's request to speak with an attorney will have future legal ramifications. In demonstrating this awareness, one participant stated, "I will be on the stand one day and I don't want to give the appearance that I acted unethically or crossed the line."

Based on the responses of the interrogative specialists I interviewed, as well as my personal experiences working in law enforcement, a subject's unequivocal request to speak with an attorney is not taken lightly. Ignoring such a request not only violates the subject's constitutional rights, but it can lead to a host of problems for the interrogator including being grilled on the stand by the defense attorney, being named in a civil suit, and being punished by one's department, among other possibilities. Just as importantly, it can lead to a confession being suppressed by the court, thereby rendering a valuable piece of evidence unusable. While casting aside a subject's request for an attorney may make for good television, many in law enforcement take such an invocation seriously. Still, it is not coincidental that many of the false confession cases outlined in both the Innocence Project and the National Registry of Exonerations data involve officers denying subjects an opportunity to speak with an attorney. After all, many of these same cases involve other problematic behaviors such as physically assaulting the subject, making false promises, threatening the subject, engaging in egregiously long periods of questioning, et cetera. In light of my own experiences with law enforcement officers and the responses provided to me by those skilled in the art of criminal interrogation, denying the subject an opportunity to speak with their attorney, like other problematic interrogative behaviors, represents a clear act of police malpractice rather than an officially sanctioned interrogative protocol.

Is There Anything You Wouldn't Do?

The information outlined above clearly indicates that those who specialize in the interrogation of criminal subjects find sleep deprivation, offering the subject a deal in exchange for their confession, or denying a subject an opportunity to speak with an attorney to be profoundly unacceptable practices. This runs counter to many academic researchers, expert witnesses, and advocates who presume that law enforcement will do anything in order to obtain a confession. However, I decided to gain a deeper insight into this premise by asking state and federal law enforcement polygraph examiners if there is anything they would intentionally avoid doing while in an interrogation room. The following is a discussion of their responses.

Torture. Nearly every participant readily identified that they would never torture a subject. The participants identified that this includes any activity that would cause the subject physical or psychological harm.

Deprivation. The majority of the participants also identified that they would never deprive the subject of such basic necessities as sleep, water, food, or bathroom breaks. Similarly, many of the participants reported that they would never deny the subject of such constitutional rights as their right to speak with an attorney or their right to end the interrogation.

False Evidence. Most, but not all, of the participants advised that they would never deliberately provide false evidence to a criminal subject in light of the risks associated with this technique. For example, participants noted that if they get caught lying about evidence by the subject, they could lose credibility with the subject, destroy rapport with the subject, cause the subject to become more resolute in their denials, or cause the subject to end the interrogation prematurely. Some participants also noted that this technique is unethical and may cause the subject to falsely confess. While some of the interrogative specialists that I interviewed seem to be in agreement that presenting a subject with false evidence of their guilt could possibly lead to a false confession, many others reported that they would avoid using this technique because of the ramifications associated with getting caught in a lie by the interrogation subject.

Displays of Aggression and Coercion. Many participants stated that they would never act toward the subject in an aggressive manner. This includes such behaviors as yelling or screaming at the subject, pounding on the table, exhibiting hostility or anger toward the subject, belittling the subject, physically or psychologically coercing the subject, and/or attempting to wear the subject down in order to obtain a confession. Participants also reported that they would never threaten a subject or their family, make false or unauthorized promises to the subject, or engage in any activity that could be considered coercive and possibly overcome the subject's free will. Participants further clarified that they would not do anything in the interrogation room that would preclude a subject's confession from being anything but truthful and voluntary.

Unethical and Illegal Behavior. Participants frequently reported that they would never engage in any behavior in the interrogation room that could be considered unethical or illegal such as misrepresenting what the subject said in the interrogation room, feeding them information about the case to bolster the subject's confession, or pushing the subject to simply agree with what the participant wants them to say. As one participant stated, "I'm really guarded in what I do because it can affect that person's life." Another participant noted that the type of behaviors outlined above can "jeopardize my job." As such, he advised that he would never engage in such behavior.

Summary

My review of the false confession research identified various questionable interrogative tactics that law enforcement officers reportedly employ during the course of a criminal interrogation, many of which were identified during a review of known cases of false confession. These questionable tactics include sleep deprivation (Guyll et al., 2013; Kassin et al., 2010a; Newring & O'Donohue, 2008); offering the subject a deal in exchange for their confession (Drizin & Colgan, 2004; Russano et al., 2005; Swanner & Beike, 2010); and denying the subject an opportunity to speak with their attorney (Kassin, 2007). However, when law enforcement officers who specialize in criminal interrogation were consulted on these specific techniques, these questionable techniques were quickly repudiated. Depriving a subject of sleep to wear them down was found to be unethical because it deprives the subject of a basic necessity and renders the information they provide questionable and likely involuntary. Similarly, offering the subject a deal in exchange for their confession was roundly considered unacceptable as law enforcement officers do not have the authority to make such deals, thereby making this practice unethical and illegal. Lastly, denying the subject an opportunity to consult with an attorney was unanimously considered unacceptable as it violates the subject's constitutional rights and destroys the reputation of the officer and their department.

It is equally important to note that the participants in my study identified numerous behaviors and techniques that they would never employ inside of the interrogation room. While Kassin et al. (2010) identified law enforcement's history of using physically coercive acts such as beating subjects, simulating drowning, putting cigarettes out on their bare skin, and withholding basic necessities like food, water, and sleep, nearly every participant in my study readily advised that they would never engage in torture or engage in any activity that could cause the subject physical or psychological pain. The majority of the participants also advised that they would never deprive the subject of either basic needs like sleep, water, food, or bathroom breaks; nor would they ever deprive someone of their constitutional rights like the right to speak with counsel and/or terminate the interview. These findings are consistent with the claims made by various researchers that abusive tactics have since been replaced with more psychologically-based techniques in light of various legal rulings (Conti, 1999; Kassin et al., 2010a; Klaver et al., 2008; Narchet et al., 2011).

The participants identified various other techniques they would never use during the course of the interrogation. For example, participants frequently reported that they would never conduct themselves in a manner that could be considered unethical, illegal, or for which they will have to answer during cross examination. Such behaviors included yelling, screaming, pounding on the table, exhibiting hostility or anger, threatening the subject or their family, making false or unauthorized promises to the subject, presenting subjects with false evidence, or engaging in any activity that could possibly overcome the subject's free will. Many participants clarified that engaging in this type of behavior during an interrogation could make the subject's subsequent confession untruthful and involuntary which would render the statement useless. The ready ability of participants to identify so many interrogative actions in which they would never engage strongly contradicts Leding's (2012) position that law enforcement interrogators "will use whatever means necessary to elicit a confession" (p. 265).

The information provided by the state and federal interrogative specialists that I interviewed help to demonstrate that some academic researchers, expert witnesses, and advocates may be operating under an inaccurate and biased perception of how law enforcement officers interrogate as a result of their tendency to focus on those interrogations that have gone drastically wrong. While the positions put forth by these interrogative specialists are not meant to reflect how every law enforcement officer in the United States questions criminal subjects, they do offer some real-world insight as to how responsible interrogators operate. What does become increasingly clearer is that it is erroneous to conclude that law enforcement officers are so hell-bent on obtaining a confession that they will risk the well-being of the criminal subject, the admissibility of the confession, the reputation of their agency, or their personal careers by engaging in questionable activity to achieve this goal. As the cases found in the Innocence Project and National Registry of Exonerations databases clearly indicate, some law enforcement officers have made mistakes or engaged in unethical behavior during the course of their jobs. However, inappropriate behavior in pursuit of a desired goal is not unique to the law enforcement profession. Even the Houston Astros were found to have engaged in stealing signs in order to win baseball games. This does not mean that all Major League Baseball players cheat. In fact, this doesn't even mean that all of the players on the Houston Astros cheat. It is also important to remember that these unethical and disturbing interrogative practices, many of which are presented in the Innocence Project and NRE vignettes, date back to the 1970s and 1980s. Simply put, some academic researchers, expert witnesses, and advocates are routinely operating under the false assumption that present day law enforcement, as a monolithic profession, will say and do anything to elicit a criminal confession.

CHAPTER 11

Why Do Criminal Subjects Truthfully Confess?

B ased on anecdotal evidence from cases of wrongful conviction proven through DNA evidence, some interrogative techniques employed by law enforcement officers are believed to be overly coercive (Kassin, 2008; Kassin et al., 2010). In the academic literature, it has also been suggested that because of the pressure that is placed upon law enforcement officers to get subjects to confess, officers are often led to engage in coercive interrogative tactics that can cause an innocent person to falsely confess (Russano et al., 2005). When suspects are determined to be deceptive during a pre-interrogation interview, law enforcement officers reportedly begin questioning subjects in a much more confrontational manner while employing a variety of techniques designed to exert social influence upon the subject. Kassin, Appleby, and Perillo (2010) note that this transition from interview to interrogation is not a subtle one. Instead, the officer moves drastically from assessing the subject during the interview process to single-mindedly pursuing a confession during the interrogation phase (Kassin et al., 2010). As the pressure of the interrogation is ratcheted up, so too is the pressure experienced by the subject (Najdowski, 2011).

After studying interrogation manuals, Ofshe (as cited by Chapman, 2013), concluded that many interrogative methods require a subject to be "persuaded" to confess by convincing them that their situation is hopeless. This can be accomplished by either inventing evidence of their guilt or by distorting key case facts. Subjects can also be persuaded to confess by manipulating their feelings of guilt and distress. Lastly, interrogative persuasion can be accomplished by pressuring the subject to consider the benefits of confessing, most notably the potential for less severe punishment (Chapman, 2013). In essence, it is a common perception in the academic literature that law enforcement interrogators employ intense psychological pressure which, at times, causes some people to falsely confess (Kassin & Gudjonsson, 2004). According to Davis and Leo (2012), interrogation is designed to increase anxiety, guilt, and other negative emotions while increasing the subject's impulse to escape. Moreover, the interrogator employs interrogation tactics to convince the subject that a confession will benefit the subject in the long run (Davis & Leo, 2012).

As noted by Narchet et al. (2011), once an investigator determines that a subject is being deceptive, a more aggressive interrogation process is initiated in which increased social pressure and manipulative interrogative methods are employed. The law enforcement officer then chooses one or more interrogative techniques that they believe will yield an incriminating response from the subject (Frantzen, 2010). As recently as the 1930s, these techniques involved such physically and psychologically coercive acts as beating a subject, simulated drowning, putting lighted cigarettes out on their body, whipping them with a rubber hose, explicitly threatening them with harm, shining a blinding light in their eyes, and withholding sleep, food, and water (Kassin et al., 2010). Because of various legal rulings and court cases, these abusive techniques have been replaced by more psychologically-oriented methods (Conti, 1999; Kassin et al., 2010; Klaver et al., 2008; Narchet et al., 2011) that are believed to convince the subject that the benefits of confession outweigh any perceived disadvantages (Moston & Stephenson, 1992) and that confession is ultimately in the subject's best interest (Kassin et al., 2010). Kassin et al. therefore suggested that law enforcement officers approach confessions with the sole focus of raising the anxiety and despair associated with the subject's continued denials.

One interrogative means of increasing anxiety and despair among criminal subjects is maximization (Kassin & McNall, 1991). Maximization techniques involve questioning methods designed to scare and intimidate the subject by directly confronting them with accusations of guilt, exaggerating the seriousness of their purported criminal actions, and refusing to accept their denials (Russano et al., 2005). Leo (2007) described these as techniques designed to "suggest that the suspect will face a bad or perhaps the worst possible outcome if he or she does not make or agree to an incriminating statement" and that these strategies "can imply harsher treatment, confinement, punishment, sentencing and/or other negative outcomes if the suspect fails to comply and confess" (p. 713). Leo (as cited by Woody and Forrest, 2009) went on to suggest that few people fully understand the coercive nature of police interrogation methods and the degree of manipulation and deception that is employed during the interrogative process. Similarly, Bull and Milne (as cited by Lassiter, 2010) suggested that law enforcement in the United States has developed an ethos of interviewing in which a confession is the primary goal and a close-minded, oppressive, and suggestive interviewing style is then employed to obtain the highly sought-after confession. It is possible that American law enforcement officers are perceived in such a manner because of the nature of their interrogation training. As noted by Kassin et al. (2010), police officers in the U.S. only receive brief interrogation training while at the academy, and perhaps some specialized training when they are promoted to their detective bureaus. As a result, it has been suggested that police may resort to overbearing and threatening interrogation techniques because they don't know any better.

Kassin and Gudjonsson (2004) have also suggested that people confess either truthfully or falsely because the interrogation room becomes so aversive that they will say anything just to escape or because they are simply trying to avoid a punishment that the interrogator has either hinted at or outright threatened to inflict if the subject continues their denials. When combined with the constant portrayal of law enforcement interrogators as vicious and unrelenting in their pursuit of a confession (Brandl, 2014; Chapman, 2013;

Conti, 1999; Kassin, 2012; Lassiter, 2010; Leding, 2012; Leo, 1996; Leo & Davis, 2010; Leo & Drizin, 2010; Narchet et al., 2011; Woody & Forrest, 2009), we are left with the Hollywood portrayal of an intimidating cop, slamming the table with his fist under the blinding glare of a bare, swinging lightbulb. Unfortunately, many of the Innocence Project and National Registry of Exonerations false confession cases involved this type of police brutality. While law enforcement is not permitted to use physical violence or explicit threats or promises in exchange for a confession, police are generally free to interrogate subjects through deceptive, exhausting, and aversive tactics for as long as the suspect does not invoke his rights or demand that the interrogation be ended (Davis & Leo, 2012). Moreover, it has been suggested that this interrogative behavior can be engaged in with virtually no risk that the elicited confession will be ruled involuntary and excluded from trial (Davis & Leo, 2012).

In essence, there exists within the academic literature a belief that law enforcement interrogators think it best to lie to subjects, wear them down through long sessions of questioning, and/or engage in techniques that cause the interrogation room to become profoundly unpleasant, all in an attempt to force a criminal subject to confess. As with other stereotypes, we have to question whether this reflects the reality of criminal interrogation or whether researchers have developed a biased and negative view of American law enforcement by focusing almost exclusively on unethical criminal interrogations using unsanctioned practices and techniques. This may explain why Frantzen (2010) recommended that researchers pay more attention to the interrogative methods that law enforcement officers find effective and ineffective. Still, it should be noted that relatively little information has been collected from law enforcement officers regarding how they perceive the factors that impact the criminal interrogation of a subject (Kassin et al., 2007). When cops are consulted, a different picture begins to develop as to how criminal subjects are questioned.

Asking the Cops

In the first study of its kind in the United States, Kassin et al. (2007) conducted a self-report survey of police practices and beliefs by obtaining and analyzing 631 surveys from law enforcement officers within the United States and Canada. Kassin et al. asked respondents about a variety of issues relating to criminal interrogation to include the interrogative methods that officers use to obtain truthful confessions. It is interesting to note that 73% of law enforcement respondents reported that they have "never" intimidated a criminal subject during an interrogation. This suggests that law enforcement officers approach interrogations differently and employ less coercive interrogative methods than what some false confession researchers claim. Building on the research of Kassin et al. (2007), Frantzen (2010), collected self-report data from 43 police investigators in Texas and followed up by personally interviewing 18 of the respondents. Their line of questioning was designed to help identify law enforcements' perceptions of strategies that influence criminal interrogations. The participating officers were specifically questioned about the following interrogative methods and their opinions on the effectiveness of each:

- Appealing to the subject's conscience
- Appealing to the subject's guilt
- Explaining to the subject the importance of their cooperation
- Identifying contradictions in the subject's account of events
- Highlighting the interrogator's expertise or authority
- Confronting the subject with actual evidence of their guilt
- Praising or flattering the subject
- Offering moral justifications and/or psychological rationalizations for the crime
- Minimizing the moral seriousness of the criminal act
- Undermining the subject's confidence in his denials
- Invoking metaphors of guilt
- Employing the Reid Technique of interrogation

Results indicated that offering moral justifications and/or psychological rationalizations for the subject's criminal act, as well as confronting the subject with existing evidence of his guilt, were perceived by participating law enforcement officers to be the most effective interrogative strategies. In addition, the participants found it beneficial to appeal to the subject's conscience and to build rapport with the subject. Appealing to the importance of cooperation and minimizing the moral seriousness of the offense were also reported to be effective by law enforcement participants. Conversely, Frantzen (2010) reported that participants identified that appealing to the detective's expertise or authority and using praise or flattery on the subject were not overly effective approaches to an interrogation. In other words, the participants in Frantzen's (2010) study reported that, rather than trying to intimidate, threaten, or strike the subject, they rely on presenting the subject with evidence of their guilt and rationalizing why they committed the crime. These findings are noteworthy in that, despite the horror stories of police interrogation atrocities as outlined by advocacy groups and some false confession researchers, law enforcement officers did not report relying on coercion to obtain confessions.

In light of these studies, it appears that researchers consulting with law enforcement officers receive a different picture of how law enforcement officers approach interrogations and question criminal subjects. Contrary to many academic perceptions, law enforcement officers report that they choose positive interactions with criminal subjects over combative approaches. Upon hearing this, it is highly likely that many academic researchers, expert witnesses, and advocates will reflexively argue that law enforcement officers are never going to tell the truth about what they do in the interrogation room and are likely engaging in impression management. Still, the information reported by law enforcement officers as to how they interrogate has received support and corroboration from an interesting and counterintuitive source, namely those who have found themselves on the other side of the interrogation room table.

Dominance vs. Humanity

In an attempt to identify their perceptions of interrogation techniques, Holmberg and Christianson (2002) surveyed 83 men who had been convicted of murder or sexual offenses. Upon analyzing the surveys, Holmberg and Christianson identified two primary interviewing approaches used by law enforcement officers as reported by these convicted individuals. The first approach was marked by the concept of 'dominance.' In this type of approach, the interrogator was emotional, impatient, and aggressive in condemning the subject for his criminal wrongdoing and offered the subject little time to reflect or make comments. The second approach was marked by the concept of 'humanity' in which the interrogator exhibited an interest in the subject as a human being and showed concern about the subject's needs. Results indicated that when the interrogator acted in a dominant manner, the murderer and sexual offender respondents reported feeling greater fear, stress, and paralysis that precluded them from confessing. In other words, when an interrogator exhibited aggressiveness, impatience, or emotionalism toward the subject at the time that they were interrogated, these subjects were less likely to confess. Conversely, when the interrogator treated the subject with humanity and respect, participants reported that they were more likely to confess to their criminal offenses (Holmberg and Christianson, 2002).

Kebbell, Hurren, and Mazerolle (as cited by Walsh & Bull, 2012) similarly reported that inmates were more likely to be compliant with interviewers when the interviewer exhibited compassion, understanding, and honesty toward them. Conversely, inmates reported that they became more resistant toward the interviewer when the interviewer was aggressive, dishonest, judgmental, and/or appeared to be biased toward the inmate's guilt. Findings like these indicate that both interrogators and subjects realize that it is humane treatment and respect, not coercion and trickery, that lead criminal subjects to truthfully admit their misdeeds. While this is completely inconsistent with the portrayal of the interrogations conducted by American law enforcement officers put forth by many academics and expert witnesses, it should really not come as a big surprise. As children, most of us learned the Golden Rule and the importance of treating others like you would like to be treated. As demonstrated in movies like *The Devil Wears Prada, Horrible Bosses,* and *Office Space,* Hollywood seems hellbent in fostering the idea that power is consistent with mean and abusive behavior. Yet even in these fictional portrayals, the recipients of such behavior respond in quite negative ways. The same holds true in the real world of criminal interrogation. According to not only the police, but also the subjects that they interrogate, mean and abusive behavior results in negative and uncooperative responses. This may explain why law enforcement officers consistently identify the benefit of treating criminal subjects with respect and humanity.

General Approach to the Interrogation

In my study, I sought to more fully understand how experts in the field of criminal interrogation approach their task of questioning criminal subjects. As such, I asked state and federal law enforcement polygraph examiners a variety of questions relating to their theoretical approach toward interrogating criminal subjects. The participants offered a variety of descriptions of how they conduct themselves when performing a criminal interrogation. My review of these descriptions revealed that the interrogative approaches offered by participants appear to center around three general interrogative aspects: 1) the tone of the interrogation; 2) the manner in which the interrogators present themselves; and 3) the way participants treat the subject.

Tone of the Interrogation

In describing the tone of their interrogations, the state and federal law enforcement polygraph examiners I interviewed frequently used terms like "low key," "reserved," "laid back," "conversational," "non-confrontational," "informal," and "soft." Contrary to the assertion that criminal interrogations are aggressive and are hostile interactions between the law enforcement officer and the criminal subject, the participants in my study described their questioning approach far differently. Repeatedly, these interrogative

192

specialists noted the importance of being approachable and non-threatening so as to encourage the criminal subject to open up and discuss their criminal transgressions.

How Participants Present Themselves

Whereas some have suggested that a criminal interrogation is marked by heated confrontation, direct accusations, and a dogged pursuit of the truth by an intimidating law enforcement officer, the interrogative experts interviewed for my study reported a vastly different presentation. In describing the manner in which they present themselves to criminal subjects, the participants used terms like "friendly," "nice," "neutral," "non-confrontational," "calming" and "objective." These descriptions marked the prevailing sentiment that people are unlikely to interact with individuals who are mean to them and/or appear to have a pre-existing bias against them.

How Participants Treat Subjects

The participants in my study used a variety of terms to describe how they treat criminal subjects during an interrogation. The most frequently occurring descriptions identified that the participants treat criminal subjects with "respect" and "dignity" while creating an environment that is "nonjudgmental." Some of the participants further explained that they attempt to present themselves as a "good listener" who desires to hear the subject's side of the story and to more fully understand them. Lastly, participants explained that when interrogating a criminal subject, they present themselves in a manner similar to that of a "father confessor," an "ally," a "therapist," a "priest," "a counselor," a "father figure," and the "guy in the white hat." As one participant explained, taking on these types of roles causes the subject to be more receptive to the interrogator. Another participant explained that instead of going after the subject, the participant likes to "bring them to me." More specifically, this particular participant noted that they try to create an environment of trust in which the subject feels comfortable admitting to their crime.

Regardless of whether they worked for a federal or a state law enforcement agency, the interrogative experts interviewed in my study reported treating criminal subjects in a very similar manner. The similarities in their interrogative approaches can be observed in two nearly identical statements made by both a federal and state examiner more than 18 months apart. One federal examiner described their general approach to criminal interrogation by claiming, "You get a lot farther with sugar than salt." This explanation was entirely consistent with the response of a state examiner who described their interrogative approach by noting, "You get more with honey than vinegar." As these statements suggest, both groups noted the importance of developing a positive relationship with the subject in order to obtain information rather than trying to force or intimidate information from the subject.

Participant Opinions on Why Subjects Confess to Them

In an attempt to more fully understand why criminal subjects truthfully confess, participants in my study were also questioned as to why they believe criminal subjects ultimately decide to confess to them. The following is a list of their responses.

Trust. The most frequently cited answer given by participants for why criminal subjects truthfully confess referenced the concept of trust. Whether this was described as a strong sense of rapport developed between the subject and the participant, or whether it was described as being "straightforward," "up front," "honest," or "credible" with the subject, many of the participants suggested that guilty people confess to them because the subject comes to trust them. Multiple participants noted that criminal subjects can easily detect insincerity among law enforcement officers. For this reason, it was recommended that interrogators be sincere when interacting with the subject.

Kindness. Another frequently cited reason as to why guilty people confess involves the participant simply being "nice" to the subject. Similar descriptions offered by the participants included being "fair," "respectful," and "not a jerk." Regardless of the descriptions used, many of the participants posited that guilty people confess to them because they treat the subject kindly and humanely. Treating subjects nicely and respectfully may be closely associated with why various participants believed that guilty subjects confess to them because they come to "like" the interrogator and because the subject feels "comfortable" talking to them.

Some participants clarified that many subjects have had only negative experiences when dealing with law enforcement. These interactions likely involved a degrading and overbearing style of questioning. For this reason, it is important for the interrogator to differentiate themselves from other law enforcement officers. Treating the subject with empathy, kindness, and humanity increases rapport, allows the subject to feel more positive toward the interrogator, and creates a more comfortable environment. As rapport, positive feelings, and comfort levels increase, the barriers to a truthful confession slowly begin to erode.

An Environment Free of Judgment. Many participants identified the importance of creating an environment in which the subject does not feel judged for their criminal actions. Some participants suggested that they minimize the seriousness of the offense. Others identified that they offer rationalizations for why the subject may have engaged in the criminal actions. As noted by one participant, it is important for the subject to feel as if they have "an out." Similarly, another participant offered that it is helpful to reframe the subject's criminal actions. In other words, when it comes to the criminal offense under investigation, it may be easier for the subject to say that the offense was a result of intoxication as opposed to evil intentions. This approach allows the criminal subject to admit their wrongdoing without feeling like a bad person and/or feeling as if they are being judged by the interrogator.

Desire to Confess. Participants also noted that some subjects confess because they have a strong underlying desire to relieve themselves of the guilt that they are feeling and they are simply looking for a way to do so. One participant offered that people have confessed to him because he has afforded them an opportunity to unburden themselves, and he therefore has "given them the lifeline that they've been waiting for."

Lying Is No Longer an Option. Some participants suggested that subjects choose to confess because they have come to the realization that they cannot lie to the participant any longer, and they therefore have no other choice but to confess. In other words, the subject came to the realization that continued denial is no longer viable, and it is far better to accept responsibility for their actions.

Allowing Them to Explain "Why." Some participants explained that they approach the interrogation process as an opportunity for the criminal subject to explain their side of the story. Up to this point in the investigation, it is likely that the victim's account of the event is the only perspective that investigators have received. As such, some participants noted the value of allowing the subject an opportunity to not only explain what happened, but in the event of a confession, *why* it happened. This ability to give their side of the story and explain the motivation behind their actions was reported by some participants to be an important catalyst in obtaining a truthful confession. Still, despite these explanations for why criminal subjects truthfully confess, one participant reported that some people will naturally confess to anyone who is decent to them while others will never confess to anyone. This participant went on to say that the majority of subjects fall somewhere in between.

Reasons Given by Subjects for Truthfully Confessing

Many participants reported that they make it a point of asking criminal subjects why they chose to confess. Some participants also noted that criminal subjects sometimes offer such explanations without being prompted by the interrogator. My review of these explanations identified four basic categories of why criminal subjects reportedly confessed after being interrogated by the participants: 1) how the subject was treated by the participant; 2) the environment created by the participant; 3) what the participant did that others in law enforcement have not; and 4) the subject's personal motivations.

How the Subject Was Treated by the Participant. Many of the participants reported that when they asked criminal subjects why they decided to confess, subjects often referenced the manner in which they were treated by the interrogator. The type of treatment that led to the subject's decision to confess included the following:

Being Treated Well. A majority of the participants advised that subjects informed them that they confessed because the participant treated them well. Subjects have given various descriptions of what it means to have been treated well by the participant. This includes such explanations as, "You were nice to me;" "You treated me like a person;" "You didn't judge me;" "You treated me fairly;" or "You were professional to me."

Being Nonjudgmental. Multiple participants advised that subjects reported that they had chosen to confess to the participant because the participant did not belittle them or judge them for the criminal actions they committed. In other words, despite the interrogator asking them about their involvement in a criminal act, the subject was never made to feel bad about themselves for what they did.

Respect. Respect also seemed to be a recurring explanation for why criminal subjects chose to confess during the course of an interrogation. For example, one participant noted that criminal subjects reported confessing to the participant because, "You treated me like a man." Other participants identified that subjects have chosen to confess to them "because you bought me lunch," and because the participant "couldn't have treated (the subject) any better."

Professionalism. It was also reported by federal and state polygraph examiners that subjects claimed to have confessed because they were treated professionally and because the participant thoroughly explained to the subject what was going to take place during the course of the polygraph examination.

The Environment Created by the Participant. My review of the participants' responses identified that many subjects reportedly confessed because of the welcoming environment created by the interrogator. For example, participants shared that subjects claimed to have confessed because, "You're like a therapist;" "You seem to understand;" "I feel comfortable talking to you;" and "I've never been able to talk about this with anyone." Several participants noted that subjects reported confessing because the participant made it feel as if the time was right to do so and because the participant actually listened to the subject. This desire to be heard and understood can be observed in such subject statements as, "You're the only person that ever listened to me;" "You asked me and then listened to what I said;" and "You're the first one who has taken the time to talk to me about this." The desire of some criminal subjects to be understood can also be observed in the response of one participant who advised that he often hears from subjects, "I wish I could talk to you more." Similarly, another participant recounted a criminal subject who explained that the participant "understood her plight" and her time spent with the participant "was a road to healing." It was at this point that the criminal subject asked to hug the participant. In fact, multiple subjects reported hugging certain subjects after the interrogation.

What the Participant Did That Others in Law Enforcement Have Not. Many participants reported hearing from subjects that they had chosen to confess because the participant did not behave like other law enforcement officers. For example, some participants reported receiving explanations from subjects for why they had chosen to confess like, "Because you didn't yell at me like the other people did" and "You're the only person in law enforcement that I have trusted." The importance that subjects place on the ability to trust interrogators can also be observed in the words of one participant who noted that subjects have reported confessing to him because "I felt that you weren't bullshitting me." Participants similarly advised that subjects informed them that they confessed to the participants because no other law enforcement officer bothered to ask them what happened and because the subjects were afraid to disclose this information to other law enforcement officers.

The Subject's Personal Motivations. In addition to the various reasons for confessing outlined above, many participants identified that subjects often confess to them because of underlying personal motivations. The following is a list of subjects' motivations as reported by the participants.

Guilt. Sometimes subjects are anxious to relieve themselves of the burden that their criminal actions and their repeated denials place upon them. Because of this internal pressure, some subjects look to the interrogator and the interrogation as a conduit or opportunity to relieve themselves of this strain. This can be observed in subjects' explanations previously provided to participants to include, "I've been wanting to get this off of my chest;" "I've been carrying this around for a long time;" "I've been looking to get it off my chest and this was the first opportunity;" "It felt like a good time to turn over a new leaf;" and it was time to move on with their lives. At times, the subject feels guilty for the crime that they committed, and they desperately want to rid themselves of the burden of their guilt. As a result, participants advised that the interrogation room can serve as the perfect avenue for criminal subjects to unburden themselves of this guilt. In addition to the guilt over their criminal actions, subjects sometimes reported confessing because they felt guilty lying to the participant. This can result in not only a confession, but an apology to the interrogator for lying to them and not admitting their criminal transgressions earlier.

Nobody Ever Asked Me. Participants offered that guilty subjects sometimes choose to confess during the course of an interrogation because, "No one ever asked me about it" prior to the interrogation.

Inevitable Detection. Participants also suggested that subjects sometimes confess because they assumed that they would eventually be caught, so continued denials were useless.

Effective Interrogative Approaches

Based on the aforementioned impressions of why criminal subjects truthfully confess, I also inquired of the interrogative specialists in my study what interrogative approaches they feel are most effective in eliciting a truthful confession. Participants noted a large number of techniques that seemed to fall into two relatively distinct categories. The first category related to how interrogators conduct themselves and how they treat the subject. I identified this category as "interpersonal approaches." The second category involved actual "interrogative strategies" employed by the participants and designed to encourage the subject to admit to their criminal wrongdoing. The following is a discussion of these two categories.

Interpersonal Approaches

The following is a discussion of the interrogative techniques relating to how the participant interacts with the subject to effectively elicit a truthful confession.

Understanding and Empathy. The most frequently reported interpersonal approach employed by the federal law enforcement polygraph examiners I spoke with involved understanding and empathizing with the subject. The majority of the participants identified that when interrogating a criminal subject, they take care to try and understand the subject's point of view, a process that multiple participants referred to as "empathy." This motivation to understand others was described by one participant as her desire to hear the subject's side of the story and to understand why they did what they did. She further noted that in her experience, subjects actually do have reasons for their criminal actions and, as a federal law enforcement polygraph examiner, she strives to understand these reasons. Another participant expressed that his attempts at using empathy with a criminal subject involves asking himself, "What would I want if I was in the (polygraph) chair? How would I want to be treated?" Yet another participant reported that he routinely informs criminal subjects that he is not there to judge them, but to simply try and understand why things happened.

While understanding the subject may ultimately benefit the interrogator by providing valuable insight as to what the subject did and why they did it, participants also noted that this desire to understand may also benefit the subject. One participant suggested that all people desire to be understood and that, "We all need affirmation." He then added that if an interrogator can provide that needed affirmation during the course of the interrogation, then they are much more likely to be successful in having the subject tell their side of the story. Another participant similarly described that his efforts to understand and empathize with subjects during the course of an interrogation resemble "more of a therapist approach as opposed to the traditional law enforcement approach." Despite the importance participants placed on empathy and understanding, they frequently noted that the understanding and empathy must be genuine in order to be successful. As offered by one participant, an interrogator has to be careful not to fake empathy as a criminal subject "can see through it in a heartbeat."

The state law enforcement polygraph examiners I interviewed similarly reported that the most effective interpersonal approach they employ is showing the subject understanding and empathy. The majority of the participants explained that criminal subjects are more likely to truthfully confess if the interrogator expresses "empathy" and "sympathy" toward them. More specifically, the interrogator must strive to give the subject the impression that they understand the subject. Participants further explained that this sense of understanding can be obtained by showing the subject "compassion" and demonstrating a "willingness to listen" to the subject. As noted by several participants, an interrogator is much more likely to obtain a truthful confession from a criminal subject if they do "the opposite of what cops do." In other words, whereas most law enforcement officers may give subjects the impression that all they care about is locking the subject up, an effective interrogator must instead present themselves as being on the side of the subject and "just another guy." In fact, one participant offered that they actually make it a point to differentiate themselves from other officers by informing the subject that as a polygraph examiner, they are not like other officers who drive around in fancy patrol cars arresting people.

Friendliness. For both federal and state participants, the next most frequently cited interpersonal approach involved interacting with the subject in a friendly manner. Many participants advised that to effectively elicit a truthful confession, it is necessary to engage the subject with friendliness. This includes treating the subject with "respect" and treating them as a "human being." Participants reported that being friendly is important because "people confess to people they like." It was similarly offered that, "the nice guy gets the confession," and "people don't talk to people they don't like." In light of such beliefs, many of the participants stated that they strive to be friendly toward the subject because it serves to put the subject at ease; it leads to the subject's development of positive feelings toward the interrogator; and it encourages the subject to speak with the interrogator by making the subject feel more comfortable. One participant similarly noted that she has found it effective to be likable with the subject by being nice, soft-spoken, and approachable. Another participant identified that he tries to be a priest, a counselor, a father, and a friend to the subject as they are more likely to be receptive to, and speak openly with, someone they like and trust. As one particular participant noted, he finds it more effective to talk to the subject "like you're in your living room having a beer with them." It is this type of treatment that encourages a criminal subject to continue talking with the participant and to be more forthcoming about their criminal wrongdoing.

While the merits of acting in a friendly manner toward the subject were repeatedly referenced, it was also noted on multiple occasions that friend-liness must be expressed at the outset of the interrogation and not held in reserve. More specifically, participants noted that while it may be necessary to become confrontational with a criminal subject, especially in light of con-tinued denials and inconsistencies, it is easier to go from friendly to confron-tational than it is to go from confrontational to friendly. Participants also put forth that there must be a balance between being friendly and professional. The dangers of being overly friendly with a subject was described by some participants as being too "buddy-buddy," a mistake that can cause the inter-rogator to lose control of the interrogation.

Rapport Building. Another effective interpersonal approach noted by par-ticipants related to building rapport with the subject. In fact, one participant reported that the most important technique for obtaining a truthful confession may be to build rapport with the subject. This is because people are more likely to open up to a person when they are getting along with them. As one participant clarified, "They will tell their best friend things that they would never tell anyone else." This participant further explained that building rapport allows for the collection of more information about the subject and what is important to them. This information can then be used for the development of theme material that can be used during the course of the interrogation. Other participants similarly expressed the importance of rapport building. For example, one participant suggested that because people tend to be attached to, and talkative with people with whom they share a commonality, the participant has found it beneficial to try and find commonalities with a subject on which they can connect. Another participant similarly offered that when interrogating a criminal subject, the participant looks for commonalities with the subject in an attempt to develop rapport with them. In my own interrogative experiences, I have been able to foster rapport through shared hobbies, interest in the same types of movies, shared experiences as a parent, similar political views, and even a mutual love of the Philadelphia Eagles. Through this search for commonalities and the development of rapport, interrogators can make a connection with the subject and avoid making the subject feel blamed or judged for the criminal acts they have committed. This personal connection makes it easier for a criminal subject to confess their crimes. As a result, the law enforcement interrogators who are better at building rapport with a criminal subject tend to be better at eliciting confessions.

In addition to searching for commonalities between the subject and the interrogator, participants noted that rapport can sometimes be easily established with the simplest of gestures. For example, one participant stated that an easy way to begin establishing rapport with a subject involves shaking the subject's hand when first meeting them. The participant added that this is particularly important with inmates who may not be used to being shown this type of respect. Similarly, I can personally recall interviewing a bank robbery subject who had confessed his involvement in a series of bank robberies. We were looking to try and convince this subject to cooperate further against his co-conspirators, so my partner and I traveled to the county jail a few days later to continue speaking with him. Coincidentally, it happened to be the subject's birthday on the day of the follow-up interview. Immediately outside of the interrogation room was a soda machine, and I decided to buy the subject a can of Coke. As I entered the room, I handed the subject the can and said, "Happy Birthday." I will never forget how this giant man who now stood accused of entering multiple banks with a firearm looked up from where he sat, took the can in his handcuffed hands and said, "Aww man, you nice to me." From that point forward, my partner and I had a tremendous working relationship with this individual and to this day, we both joke that he will probably call us when he is eventually released from federal prison.

Now some cynical academics who have chosen to dedicate their lives to studying law enforcement interrogation generally, and false confessions specifically, may likely jump to the conclusion that my decision to purchase a can of soda was simply a trick designed to encourage a confession. In full disclosure, I made this purchase as a Christian. Like others in law enforcement, I can sympathize with the position that criminal subjects find themselves in. It must be a terrible feeling to be awakened from a sound sleep by pounding on your door followed by the call of, "Police, search warrant." It does not take a bleeding heart to appreciate the flood of emotions that accompany such a startling stimulus. This is why I repeatedly explain to the subjects I test that while it is a pleasure to meet them, I am sorry that it has to be under the circumstances outlined above. This is often followed by an offer of water, food, and/or an opportunity to use the restroom. Not only do these gestures represent a human exchange of kindness, but they mark the onset of rapport building. It should also be highlighted that these gestures are not relegated to law enforcement interviews. As a psychologist, my wife routinely makes these same offers to the patients arriving at her office. In fact, a trip to the car dealership to have your oil changed will likely result in you watching television in a comfortable chair with a cup of coffee and the promise of a pastry as you await the return of your vehicle. Regardless of how rapport is built, many of the state and federal law enforcement examiners in my study identified that building rapport is crucial in decreasing the subject's anxiety level and making the subject feel that they are working with the interrogator rather than against them.

Being Nonjudgmental. The state and federal polygraph examiners I interviewed also identified that the interrogator's ability to remain nonjudgmental of the subject during the course of the interrogation is a key interpersonal approach. Many participants suggested that creating an environment in which the subject can feel comfortable in truthfully disclosing their criminal actions without the fear of being judged by the interrogator is critically important. One participant noted that from the outset of the interrogation, he explains to the subject that he is not there to judge them, but to understand what has taken place. Another participant advised that they try to create a nonjudgmental environment by informing subjects at the beginning of the examination process that there is "nothing you can tell me that I haven't heard before." It was a recurring theme among the participants that if the interrogator is successful at making a connection with the subject while giving the appearance that the interrogator is accepting and nonjudgmental of the information that the subject is providing, then the interrogator is much more likely to have the subject openly disclose their criminal activities.

Trust and Respect. In addition to the interpersonal approaches discussed above, the participants reported that treating a subject with trust and respect is very important if a truthful confession is to be successfully elicited. As noted by one participant, if a subject does not trust the interrogator, they will not feel comfortable telling their story. The importance of trust was expressed by another participant who suggested that if the interrogator is caught in a lie, the subject will no longer trust the interrogator and then "shut down." This participant added that if the subject believes that you are trying to trick them, then you are simply "one more law enforcement officer who is out to get them." It is therefore of the utmost importance that the interrogator be straightforward with the subject. In this participant's experience, criminal subjects appreciate her straightforwardness. She added that people generally want to get the load off of their chest and it feels good to "vent" if you trust the person to whom you are venting. For this reason, this participant advised that she strives to develop a trusting relationship with the subject. Another participant similarly highlighted the importance that trust plays during the course of an interrogation. He suggested that in creating an environment of trust, he immediately explains to the subject that the participant will be honest with them if the subject provides that same honesty in return. This participant further explained that it is necessary for the participant to create an environment where the subject comes to respect and trust him if the interrogation is going to be effective.

As suggested by this last comment, respect is directly associated with trust when it comes to the interrogation of a criminal subject. This may help to explain why many of the participants identified respect as a key interpersonal approach. One participant advised that he makes great effort during the course of a criminal interrogation to create an environment of "mutual respect" between himself and the subject. Another participant offered that by treating a subject respectfully, the subject is not only put at ease, but they feel more comfortable talking to the participant. Yet another participant suggested that the need for respect is nearly universal. This participant reported that if you treat a person with respect and dignity, you will likely receive the same from them in return. In his experience, respect is particularly important with the Hispanic and Native American cultures, as well as those who have already come into contact with the criminal justice system. The need for mutual respect between the subject and the interrogator was succinctly expressed by still another participant who stated, "People confess to people they respect."

Advocates and Allies. Another frequently reported interpersonal approach that effectively leads to the elicitation of truthful confessions includes being an "advocate" or "ally" for the subject. This interpersonal approach involves the creation of an environment of teamwork between the interrogator and the subject. One of the participants explained that he accomplishes this by fully explaining to the subject what the participant will be doing during their time together and that the participant is working on the subject's behalf. Another participant explained that he attempts to create such an environment by utilizing rapport building strategies to allow the subject to feel that they are engaged together in the interrogation process. Participants also noted that it is important for the subject to know that the participant is not there to hurt the subject, but to serve as an ally and to help the subject to the extent that the participant can do so.

In attempting to convince the subject to talk to him, one participant explained that he sets out to prove to the subject that the participant is his "biggest ally." In a similar vein, another participant stated that she presents herself as an "advocate" for the subject in that she is the only person who can get the facts of the subject's situation across to the investigators working the case. She also makes it a point to inform the subject that she does not "get paid any more money" if the subject confesses. Instead, the participant is able to advocate for the subject by helping the subject tell their story. While very few of the participants stated that they ever become confrontational with a subject, one participant noted that even when it is necessary to more directly confront a subject, he does so as an advocate. For example, upon hearing something contradictory in the subject's statement, the participant may say something similar to, "I have to challenge you with what you just said because the prosecutor isn't going to be able to make sense of this." Overall, the participants frequently reported that working as an advocate or ally with the subject is much more effective in eliciting a confession than working against the subject as an adversary.

As with other strategies put forth by the interrogative specialists with whom I spoke, some studying police interrogation and false confessions in academia are likely to point to this approach as simply continued trickery on behalf of the interrogator. More specifically, they are likely to claim that interrogators merely try to dupe the naïve criminal subject into believing that the officer is working on their behalf when, in reality, they are trying to 'snooker' them into confessing. This overly negative view requires that a key assumption be made. It presumes that a truthful confession does nothing but hurt the subject and that admitting to one's criminal transgression is ultimately against the subject's best interest. This assumption is reflective of an underlying disbelief in the premise that there should be repercussions for one's criminal behavior. As will be discussed in an upcoming chapter, the experiences of the state and federal law enforcement polygraph examiners that I interviewed suggest that those who truthfully confess to their criminal wrongdoings experience a far better outcome than those who falsely maintain their innocence. As such, if the subject is truly guilty of committing the crime under investigation, our criminal justice system requires that they receive some sort of punishment. Since the interrogative specialists that I interviewed, and likely countless others in law enforcement, have experiences that suggest true confessors receive lighter sentences, it is not hard to see why law enforcement interrogators can readily and genuinely claim to be acting as an advocate or ally for the subject.

Being Professional. In addition to the interpersonal approaches already discussed, the participants in my study offered various others that can be effective in eliciting a truthful confession from a criminal subject. One such approach relates to the interrogator interacting with the subject in a "professional" manner. While the attributes of being friendly with the subject have already been discussed, one participant suggested that there must be a balance between the interrogator's friendliness and his or her professionalism. The concept of professionalism was described in various ways by the participants. For example, multiple participants suggested that it is more appropriate and effective to address the subject in a "low key" and "conversational" tone as opposed to being confrontational, raising your voice, and being "in your face." Similarly, participants suggested that maintaining "neutrality" with a subject can be effective as it serves to increase the interrogator's credibility with the subject. Simply put, participants noted that the interrogator's level of professionalism when interacting with a criminal subject can ultimately have an impact on the subject's decision to confess.

The need for professionalism among interrogators should not come as a surprise to anyone. Regardless of the profession, we tend to trust those who present themselves in a professional manner. This is why mechanics, landscapers, heating and cooling technicians, and pest control specialists tend to wear uniforms, so that we perceive them to be professionals and come to have more confidence in their abilities. The comedian Jeff Foxworthy makes fun of this point when joking about southern accents and claiming in his deepest southern drawl that no one wants to hear their brain surgeon say, "A'ight, now what we're gonna do is saw the top of your head off, root around there with a stick, and see if we can't find that dag burn clot." Quite simply, professionalism goes a long way. Looking back to the first 2020 Presidential debate between Donald Trump and Joe Biden, onlookers were aghast to see a President who would not stop interrupting and a former Vice President who told the leader of the free world to "shut up man." Post-debate reports found many people questioning the capabilities of both men. Viewers would likely have come away with much more confidence in both candidates if they applied the interrogative recommendations of using a "low key" and "conversational tone" as opposed to being confrontational, raising your voice, and being "in your face."

Being Genuine. While the participants identified a variety of interpersonal approaches that are likely to increase the elicitation of a truthful confession, they also noted that these efforts to engage with the subject on an interpersonal level must be authentic. Being "straightforward", "up front", and "genuine" with the subject, as opposed to the use of manipulation and trickery, were often cited by participants as a necessary component for a successful interrogation. Participants frequently reported that it is important for interrogators to be themselves when engaging a criminal subject in an interrogation. In fact, one participant offered that upon becoming a polygraph examiner, the participant's biggest fear was that he was going to have to be someone that he is not. He further clarified that while he was concerned that he would have to be aggressive or act like a "jerk" in order to obtain confessions, he was pleased to learn that being himself and acting toward the subject with kindness is a more effective approach. The premise of being "straight-forward" and "up front" with a subject was more thoroughly described by one participant as acting in an "honest" and "credible" manner to include explaining to the subject how the federal criminal justice system works, how their cooperation will benefit them as they traverse the system, and how the information provided by the subject will ultimately be furnished to the federal prosecutor by the participant.

Interrogative Strategies

My review of participant responses identified that while interpersonal approaches were more frequently referenced as being effective in eliciting a truthful confession from a criminal subject, there are also interrogative strategies that can equally prove effective. It is important to note that several participants reported that the strategies they choose to employ depend on the subject, their backgrounds, and their education level, among other factors. Some participants actually referred to some of these strategies as aspects of the Reid technique. The following is a discussion of the successful interrogative strategies identified by the participants.

Themes. The most frequently referenced interrogative strategy deemed to be effective in eliciting a truthful confession by participants relates to the use of themes during the interrogative process. The majority of the participants reported using this technique. *Theming* was defined by one participant as offering the subject an "out" or a "face-saving way" of explaining their criminal activity which serves to minimize the seriousness of the subject's criminal acts. Themes were also described by participants as "hooks," "rationalizations," or potential explanations for why the subject may have committed the crime other than the fact that they are simply a bad person. Similarly, themes were described as stories that an interrogator can tell to provide the subject with the "lifeline" they are looking for. For example, one participant explained that if it becomes apparent that the subject's family is important to them, using a theme that involves the subject's family may be effective

210

in convincing them to confess. Another participant identified his particular process of theme development as "cognitive dissonance" in which he seeks to overcome a subject's need for self-preservation by creating a rational explanation for the subject's criminal actions that is less stressful. In essence, this participant redefines *why* the subject engaged in the specified criminal behavior as opposed to focusing on *whether* the subject actually committed the crime. This creates an environment in which the subject can be honest about their criminal actions without feeling judged by the participant.

In developing themes, participants reported that they attempt to identify logical explanations for why the subject may have committed the crime and then present those potential explanations to the subject. However, one participant noted that it is important for the themes to be meaningful to the subject and reflect why the subject may have engaged in the crime based on what the interrogator was able to learn about the subject during interview preparation and during the pre-test interview. Such possible explanations include suggesting to the subject that they committed the crime due to stress, substance abuse, or financial problems. For this reason, this participant noted that it is critically important to try and learn as much information as possible about the subject prior to the polygraph test and to pay attention to what the subject is actually saying during the pre-test interview as this will increase the effectiveness of the eventual themes developed by the interrogator.

Participants also identified themes as being effective because they offer the subject a nicer way to confess to what they did. As opposed to suggesting that the subject is a criminal, themes give the subject an "avenue out" that makes the subject look better in admitting his crimes. Themes can also address how the subject will feel better if they admit to their criminal actions. Lastly, participants reported that themes are effective in eliciting a truthful confession because they serve to rationalize why the subject committed the crime, minimize the seriousness of the offense, and project the blame onto someone or something other than the subject. This process of rationalization, minimization, and projection helps subjects to more easily explain and justify their criminal behavior in a "face-saving way" while still acknowledging that the crimes they have committed are wrong. Participants explained that these types of themes help to make the subject feel that while they may have done something bad, they are not a bad person. As noted by one participant, "Even the biggest creeps don't want to be made to feel like a creep."

- Minimization – Participants described the act of minimization as attempting to decrease the seriousness of a subject's criminal actions. As one participant noted, this can include highlighting that the subject's criminal act "only happened once." In other words, the interrogator may find it beneficial to suggest to the subject that he is not a "thief"; he simply took money from his employer on this one occasion. Simply put, minimization helps the subject to realize that their criminal act could have been much worse (i.e., it could have involved the theft of more money, the harming of more victims, the infliction of greater pain upon a victim, et cetera). Minimization therefore helps to encourage the subject to confess by making the crime seem less serious than the subject may have thought prior to entering the interrogation room.

- Rationalization – This may involve the interrogator suggesting that anyone in the subject's position would have likely acted in the same way as the subject. For example, the interrogator could suggest that anyone suffering from the same level of financial distress as the subject would have taken money from their employer as well. As grotesque as it may seem to some, it can also involve the interrogator suggesting to an individual suspected of shooting a rival gang member that others who have been so disrespected would likely have stood up in the same way to defend their reputations and their community. In essence, rationalization is designed to help encourage the subject to confess by removing the perception that the subject's criminal actions were not monstrous, but rather a rational response to an irrational situation.

- Projection – With this type of theme, the interrogator encourages the subject to truthfully confess to their criminal wrongdoing by suggesting that the subject may have committed the specified criminal act due to outside influences. For example, the interrogator could offer that if the credit card companies did not charge such high interest rates, or if the subject's employer did not pay him such a paltry salary, the subject would not have to resort to stealing from work to pay his bills. Projection can also involve blaming the victim for the role they played in their own victimization. An example of this may include blaming the victim of the assault for instigating the initial confrontation.

While some in academia may foreseeably jump to the conclusion that the themes outlined above are simply manipulations employed by unrelenting law enforcement interrogators to trick an unsuspecting subject into a confession, it is important to note that these concepts are neither new, nor unique to the field of interrogation. In actuality, these themes are completely consistent with the defense mechanisms developed by Sigmund Freud and extrapolated upon by his daughter, Anna Freud, in her work *The Ego and the Mechanisms of Defense*. As noted by Whitbourne (2011), Freudian defense mechanisms are a part of everyday life and are utilized by everyone at some point. Whitbourne goes on to explain that Freud's defense mechanisms are unconscious protective measures employed to prevent individuals from connecting with their "ravenous instinctual desires" while also protecting them from the anxiety associated with confronting one's "weaknesses and foibles" (2011, p. 1). While Freud and his followers suggested that defense mechanisms are used to combat sexual or aggressive feeling, Whitbourne offered that they are a common means of dealing with unpleasant emotions and can be applied to a wide range of reactions brought about by feelings of insecurity and anxiety. As such, the interrogative themes of rationalization, minimization, and projection are essentially the repurposed defense mechanisms of Sigmund and Anna Freud. In short, suggesting that the subject's crimes are not as serious as initially perceived, placing responsibility for the crimes on another person, and/or suggesting that the crimes were rational under the circumstances, are simply attempts to tap into the inherent desire of human beings to avoid the unpleasantness that comes with the realization that they have made a terrible, albeit criminal, error that has drawn the attention of law enforcement.

Allowing the Subject to Speak and Then Highlighting Inconsistencies. Participants also frequently noted the value of allowing the subject to talk during the course of the initial interview and early on in the interrogation as this allows for the collection of important information and the identification of any potential holes in the subject's story. One participant referred to this as a "free narrative" approach and involves the interrogator simply directing the subject to, "Tell me what happened." Another participant advised that they encourage the subject to talk by employing "active listening skills." Still another participant reported that they encourage the subject to talk by strategically using silence so that the subject will feel encouraged to fill the silence with additional discussion. In essence, many participants advised that they prefer to let the subject tell their story while the participant listens care-fully for information that does not seem consistent or logical. One participant described this process as allowing the subject to "roll out his lies."

Upon identifying inconsistencies or misstatements in their stories, the participants then expose and attack these obvious attempts at deception. Participants noted that this strategy of "trapping them in a known lie" is particularly effective when it is combined with the fact that the subject has just failed a polygraph examination. One participant referred to this strategy as a "one-two punch." Highlighting inconsistencies in a subject's statement also convinces the subject that the interrogator is not "buying" their lies and that continued deceit is no longer an option. Another participant stated that consistently identifying a subject's deception and confronting them on this deception can also decrease the subject's motivation to continue lying and encourage them to respond honestly from that point forward.

Presentation of Evidence of Guilt. Some participants suggested that presenting a subject with case facts that indicate their guilt can prove effective in eliciting a truthful confession from a criminal subject. Some participants reported that it is extremely effective to present the subject with case facts that clearly identify the subject's guilt as this can increase the likelihood of obtaining a confession. Presenting such proof of guilt could be especially effective if the subject was not aware that the interrogator was in possession of such information. Participants identified that this type of evidence may include cell phone evidence, photographs, surveillance video, GPS data, or other information that may conclusively identify, or strongly suggest, that the subject is responsible for the criminal act under investigation. Participants suggested that upon being presented with such evidence, the subject knows that "the jig is up" and a truthful confession is more likely to occur. Participants further noted that when the interrogator presents this evidence or case facts to the subject in the form of a surprise revelation, it can be particularly effective in eliciting a truthful confession. In addition, participants offered that because the evidence and case facts indicate that the subject is guilty of the crime, interrogators can then try to convince the subject that it would be of greater benefit for the subject to tell their side of the story as opposed to relying on others, particularly victims and co-conspirators, to do so.

Miscellaneous Interrogative Strategies. The state and federal law enforcement polygraph examiners interviewed in my study also provided the following list of additional techniques that they find effective in eliciting a truthful confession.

Alternative Questions. This technique involves presenting the subject with two opposing options of why they may have engaged in the specified criminal act, with one of the options proving to be more appealing than the other. More specifically, it includes such approaches as asking the subject whether he routinely commits the specified criminal act or whether it only happened on one occasion. For example, "Are you a serial rapist or did you just misinterpret what this particular girl was telling you on your date?" This approach is somewhat of a melding of the themes of minimization and rationalization. More specifically, by offering the subject a horrendous worst-case explanation for his criminal act (i.e., "You are a lifelong child predator") and a more palatable explanation (i.e., "You had a one-time momentary lapse in judgment with one child"), a guilty subject can rationalize his behavior and minimize the overall seriousness of the criminal act by selecting the more palatable option.

"Get out in front." This technique involves explaining to the subject the importance of telling the truth about their criminal act and presenting their side of the story so that others cannot make assumptions about what occurred. In other words, in this approach, the interrogator encourages the subject to be proactive and explain what happened so that others (i.e. the victim, witnesses, the prosecutor, et cetera) do not tell the subject's story for him. This is a variation of the "alternative question" in the fact that the subject can choose between offering his account of the crime or relying on what can only be assumed to be a more damning and damaging telling of the story by those who do not have the subject's best interest at heart.

Explaining Why. This involves the interrogator encouraging the subject to admit to their criminal behavior so that they can explain *why* the crime occurred. This is bolstered by the premise that an explanation helps to give the subject's actions context. This approach is particularly helpful in crimes where motivation is important such as the difference between murder, manslaughter, and criminally negligent homicide.

Emotional Approach. This involves the interrogator asking the subject to consider how society will view them, how their family will view them, or how they will view themselves regarding their criminal actions. This may also involve the interrogator explaining the circumstances of the crime to the subject so that he can see the crime from the victim's perspective.

Possibility of Future Polygraph Testing. This involves the interrogator (especially a polygraph examiner) giving the subject the impression that future polygraph testing will take place. The interrogator then suggests that they want the subject to pass any future polygraph examination and by disclosing additional information, the subject can increase the likelihood of passing any future tests.

Proxemics. This involves the interrogator strategically moving toward or away from a subject during the course of the interrogation or gently touching a male subject's knee when they lose themselves in thought.

Walking the Subject Through Individual Aspects of the Crime. This involves the interrogator gradually moving the subject from "I did nothing" to "This is what I did." This may also be described as "chipping away" at the subject's denials by getting them to admit to individual parts of the crime. For example, if the subject initially states that he has no involvement in the crime, the interrogator may first strive to get the subject to admit to being in the vicinity of the crime when it occurred. After that, the interrogator may then slowly move to getting the subject to admit to having contact with the victim on the night of the offense, and so on.

Shutting Down Denials. This involves the interrogator minimizing the subject's opportunities to deny their criminal actions so as not to strengthen their denials.

The Desire to Confess. Regardless of the interpersonal approach or interrogative strategy employed by the interrogator, the federal and state law enforcement polygraph examiners I interviewed suggested that a truthful confession must ultimately be desired by the subject. In other words, the subject must want to confess and their confession must be voluntary. As such, participants offered that people need a reason to confess. Some participants reported that it is necessary to convince the subject that confessing their criminal actions will ultimately benefit them. Sometimes this benefit may involve the realization that within the state and federal systems, a confession leads to a decrease in their eventual sentence. At other times, the benefit may be the suggestion that the subject will feel better upon admitting and taking responsibility for their criminal wrongdoings. Regardless of how the benefit is presented, one participant reported that he always makes the subject's confession feel like a positive release and a positive endpoint to the interrogation process. This is not an uncommon result of confession. In my personal experience, I have had many criminal subjects hug me, thank me, shake my hand, and explain to me that the questioning session felt like therapy after they gave their confession. In fact, I actually had a criminal subject involved in the threatening of a public official leave me a voicemail message thanking me for talking to him and ultimately changing his life after he confessed his misdeeds to me days earlier. These responses to interrogation should not come as a surprise in light of the benefits associated with religious and psychotherapeutic confessions outlined in an earlier chapter. In short, it is important to recognize that just as a confessor may experience a positive emotional release in church or in their therapist's office, catharsis can also be experienced by those who confess within the interrogation room.

Ineffective Interrogative Approaches

Law enforcement is not unlike other professions. Whether an engineer at Ford Motor Company, a high school football coach, an advertising executive, a professional chef, or a drycleaner, people tend to know what works and what does not work within their respective fields. It is therefore reasonable to suggest that law enforcement officers are inherently capable of differentiating between effective and ineffective interrogative techniques. Like other professions, this knowledge is sometimes handed down from senior employees to newer members of the team, and sometimes it is handed down through official edicts or policies. In an attempt to identify whether the interrogative specialists I interviewed also understood what doesn't work in the interrogation room, I asked them to explain what interrogative strategies are ineffective at eliciting a confession. The following is a discussion of what the participants in my study found to be ineffective when trying to elicit a truthful confession.

Disrespectful Behavior. Upon being questioned about ineffective interrogative methods, the majority of the participants responded by focusing on interrogator behaviors that can be considered disrespectful. Participants offered a variety of names to describe this type of behavior such as being "hardcore," "hard-nosed," "in-your-face," "old school," employing the

"Sipowicz Routine," or playing "Good Cop/Bad Cop." This type of behavior was more thoroughly defined in the following ways:

- Yelling or screaming at the subject
- Threatening the subject
- Being abrasive
- Badgering, bullying, or using a "Did you do it? Did you do it?" approach
- Degrading the subject or calling them names
- Looking down on the subject, judging them, or being condescending
- Acting as an authoritarian

Participants frequently reported that if the subject is being yelled at by the interrogator, there is no incentive for them to talk. As rhetorically asked by one participant, "Why would they talk to you?" in light of such disrespect. Participants also reported that interrogative methods in which the interrogator is "loud," "aggressive," yells at the subject, or calls them a "liar" are ineffective at eliciting a confession because nobody wants to be on the receiving end of this type of behavior. Participants further explained that people have an underlying human desire to be respected. As a result, when people are treated disrespectfully, they "shut down," and they tend to exit the interrogation room. As suggested by one participant, it is very hard for an interrogator to "come back from being an unpleasant person." Similarly, it was succinctly and colorfully reported by one participant that "mean people suck," and "nobody wants to talk to somebody who makes them feel like shit." Another participant stated that "nobody will tell you the worst thing they've done in their life" if they are treated in such a manner. As put by yet another participant, "Nobody wants to tell a drill instructor that they touched a 2-year-old girl."

From an interpersonal perspective, a participant suggested that yelling and screaming at a subject is ineffective because nothing is being communicated between the subject and the interrogator. Moreover, this type of behavior indicates that the interrogator has lost control of what they intended to do, which is to have the subject tell their side of the story. Another participant offered that this type of "TV stuff" indicates that the interrogator is "losing his cool," that he or she is no longer in charge of the interrogation, and the subject "got your goat." It was suggested by many of the participants that these types of behaviors prevent the interrogation room from feeling like a safe place to talk and decrease the likelihood of successfully eliciting a confession. They also noted that being disrespectful to a criminal subject who has had previous experiences with the criminal justice system is particularly ineffective because many criminal subjects already have the perception that law enforcement is bad, and this type of behavior will confirm those biased perceptions. Participants added that yelling at a subject and acting toward them in an aggressive manner will cause the subject to shut the interrogator out, increase their defiance, and strengthen their denials. While this behavior may resemble "all the things you see on TV," participants advised that it does not actually work in convincing a subject to confess to their criminal activity.

It was further noted that disrespectful behavior from the interrogator also demonstrates a lack of respect for the subject which, in turn, can cause the subject to lose respect for the interrogator. This behavior was also reported to give the subject the impression that the interrogator is not actually interested in the truth, but simply wants the subject to tell them what the interrogator wants to hear. It was also suggested that for those who have already been involved in the criminal justice system, such disrespectful behavior will ring hollow as an experienced criminal will be well aware of what the interrogator legally can and cannot do. It was also posited that the use of this type of behavior is exaggerated in the media and within popular culture. Therefore, a subject may perceive the interrogator as being disingenuous if such disrespectful behavior were to be exhibited. Lastly, it was noted that this type of behavior creates a confrontational and volatile environment which could encourage the subject to falsely confess as a means of ending the interrogation. In other words, if we are unlikely to deal with a mechanic, a mortgage broker, a sales associate, or even a spouse who treat us disrespectfully, why should it be assumed that similar treatment at the hands of a law enforcement interrogator would encourage the subject to stay in the room and continue speaking with police.

Anger, Insincerity, and Disinterest. Participants reported that a confession is also unlikely to occur if the interrogator acts in an angry, argumentative, insincere, biased, disinterested, or egotistical manner with the subject. Showing anger toward a subject or becoming argumentative with a subject was reported to cause subjects to become "defensive" and disinclined to talk to the interrogator. Similarly, being insincere, showing a lack of interest in the subject by not listening to them, leaving the room, texting, and giving the subject the appearance that all the interrogator cares about is getting a confession from the subject and then going home, will cause the subject to distrust the interrogator and decrease the likelihood of a confession.

Lying to the Subject. Participants reported that deception at the hands of the interrogator is also an ineffective approach in eliciting a truthful confession. For example, if the interrogator is dishonest with the subject or acts in a disingenuous manner, the subject will come to distrust the interrogator and likely disengage or outright end the questioning. Multiple participants identified the presentation of false evidence to the subject as a particularly problematic form of deception. If caught in this or any other type of lie during the course of the interrogation, the interrogator will destroy all of the trust and rapport that they strove so hard to create during the course of the interrogation. Similarly, presenting false evidence can cause a subject to walk out of the room, or possibly even falsely confess, just to end the interrogation. For these reasons, one participant described lying to a subject during the course of an interrogation as simply "bad practice."

Coercion and Physical Harm. In addition to the aforementioned behavior, participants offered that using overly coercive techniques or even physically harming the subject are ineffective approaches and may cause the subject to stop talking to the interrogator or possibly even render a false confession as a way of ending the interrogation. Rather than coercing a confession, one participant replied, "You have to sell somebody a reason to get over the self-preservation hump" which is always present during a criminal interrogation. Therefore, when it comes to confessing, an effective interrogator will help a subject to see "what's in it for them" rather than trying to force it out of them. In short, trying to force a confession via physical intimidation or heavy coercion is likely to result in an abrupt end to the questioning session. This runs counter to what some in academia frequently claim about false confessions and their causes.

Badgering, Intimidating, and Judging the Subject. In addition to actually physically harming the subject, some participants suggested that it is equally ineffective to badger, intimidate, judge, or threaten the subject. "Badgering" a subject was defined by one participant as "beating them over and over" with the fact that they had failed a polygraph examination. "Intimidation" was clarified by participants to include, verbally abusing a subject, keeping them in the interrogation room for a prolonged period of time without giving them breaks, playing "good cop/bad cop" with the subject, and/or forcing the subject into a corner where they are pressured into making a decision that is not of their own volition. While some in academia operate under the assumption that playing "good cop/bad cop" is a routine interrogative practice, one participant identified this approach as being particularly ineffective because (thanks to movies and television) everyone knows what the interrogator is attempting to do.

Multiple participants also referenced the ineffectiveness of judging the subject. Participants further described this as belittling the subject and making them feel bad about themselves for the criminal act that they committed. It is not difficult to identify the ineffectiveness of such an approach. Imagine a law enforcement officer seeking to obtain a confession from a suspected child molester by commenting, "So you like to touch kids, huh? You're a sick little freak, aren't you?" As highlighted by some of the interrogative specialists I interviewed, no subject is going to admit their wrongdoing after being judged in such a manner. In fact, such a comment may likely result in the subject ending the interrogation.

Participants offered that threatening a subject may involve an interrogator stating, "If I find that you are lying to me, I'm going to make it my personal business to screw you." Some participants also noted that it is possible to threaten the subject through their family. For example, an interrogator may try to force a confession from a criminal subject by threatening to direct the investigation toward the subject's wife, children, friends, or other relatives. An example of this may involve the interrogator stating, "If you don't tell me what I want to hear, I'm going to do everything in my power to make sure that your wife is charged with this as well." Multiple participants reported that threatening a subject or their family has little value as such actions will likely cause the subject to end the interrogation or render a false confession to avoid getting their friends and relatives in trouble.

False Evidence, False Promises, and Feeding Information. In addition to the methods outlined above, participants in my study reported that it is ineffective to present the subject with false evidence, to make false promises to the subject, and/or to feed the subject case facts and information. As previously mentioned, presenting the subject with false evidence of their guilt was found to be ineffective in eliciting a true confession because the interrogator could easily be identified as lying which could cause the subject to distrust the interrogator. Furthermore, the interrogator will lose all credibility with the subject, and rapport will immediately be destroyed. Some participants also noted that making false promises to the subject is an ineffective interrogative strategy. Such promises include statements that if the subject only confesses, he can go home; he can avoid being charged; he will receive a lesser sentence, and so forth. Lastly, participants reported that it is ineffective to "feed" a subject information about the case so that their confession matches existing case facts and available evidence. These approaches were reported to be ineffective because of the likelihood that they could lead to a false confession.

What Works

As discussed earlier, many false confession researchers have suggested that it is the interrogative methods used by law enforcement that are actually responsible for causing false confessions (Frantzen & Can, 2012; Hasel & Kassin, 2009; Kassin, 2012; Kassin et al., 2005; Levine et al., 2010; Meissner & Kassin, 2002; Nash & Wade, 2009; Perillo & Kassin, 2011). Whereas law enforcement previously employed the 'third degree' to coerce criminal subjects into confessing (Kassin et al., 2010), these overtly abusive methods have more recently been replaced with more psychologically-oriented methods (Conti, 1999; Kassin et al., 2010a; Klaver et al., 2008; Narchet et al., 2011). Though beatings and physical intimidation have largely fallen by the wayside, some academic researchers, expert witnesses, and advocates maintain that police interrogators simply found new ways to increase the pressure on a subject until they finally confess, sometimes falsely. Upon interviewing state and federal officers who specialize in the interrogation of criminal subjects, it became clear that these professionals share a common view of what is, and what is not, effective in the interrogation room. Repeatedly, these experts reported that exhibiting understanding and empathy toward the subject is the most effective interpersonal approach to interrogation. By trying to understand the subject's point of view and empathizing with their situation, criminal interrogators stand a far better chance of convincing the subject to openly discuss their criminal transgressions. Acting kindly toward a criminal subject, building rapport, and being nonjudgmental about their misdeeds all help to create an environment of trust and respect between the interrogator and the subject. Still, it is important that law enforcement interrogators remain professional in their interactions with a criminal subject. This includes not only treating the subject respectfully and ethically, but also taking care to avoid becoming inappropriately close or "chummy" with the subject. Lastly, participants noted the importance of being genuine when interacting with the subject. An interrogation is not a play requiring a bold and brilliant acting performance from the officer. Instead, it demands genuine concern from the interrogator. A first-time offender will feel and appreciate an officer's sincere concern while a repeat offender will easily identify when the officer is being disingenuous. It is therefore critical that the officer be themself and be genuine when interacting with a criminal subject. As noted by a close friend and clinical psychologist, this approach of creating an alliance while maintaining appropriate boundaries is completely consistent with the goals of a clinical therapist.

This point hit home for me in the investigation of a cold-case homicide which had gone unsolved for nearly 10 years. In this particular case, a 20-year-old woman had gone missing until her decomposed body was found two weeks later in a field. In being asked to assist local law enforcement with the investigation, my partner and I came to focus on two friends who were potential subjects in the woman's disappearance and murder. Upon finally convincing one of the friends to come into our office for an interview, my partner and I eventually began interrogating this individual about his involvement in the woman's death. After several hours, the subject advised that he would tell us everything that had transpired if he could just go home and tell his wife first. With no other options available to us, we escorted the subject from our office with the agreement that he would come in the next day and provide the details of what had taken place. Before he left, we highlighted to the subject how unusual this arrangement was and the level of trust that we were placing in him. The subject then left our office with the promise that he would return the next day and fully disclose what he knew.

Not surprisingly, this decision to allow a key suspect in a 10-year-old murder investigation to walk out the door led to a great deal of debate between my partner and me on whether he would actually return to our office as agreed upon. To our shock and profound pleasure, the subject showed up at our office the following day as promised. Over the next couple of hours, he somberly recounted how his friend had killed the victim in the subject's house, carried her lifeless body from the residence, placed her body in the trunk of his car, and departed the area. The subject then testified against his friend at trial and was instrumental in his friend's subsequent murder conviction. After the subject provided the details of the victim's death, his knowledge of the crime, and his failure to come forward with the information years earlier, my partner and I asked him why he finally chose to provide this information after hiding it so successfully for 10 years. Looking at us from across the table, the subject said simply, "I just felt like I could trust you guys."

I provide this story to demonstrate the importance of being genuine with an interrogation subject. Not only had this person hidden from law enforcement for over a decade, but he also managed to keep this information to himself during that time. He neither discussed it with the killer, nor did he disclose it to a friend or family member. After speaking with this individual for numerous hours, he likely could be diagnosed with Paranoid Personality Disorder. He was in no way inclined to share the worst day of his life with any other person, let alone two law enforcement officers. However, it was ultimately the genuineness with which we interacted with him and the trust that developed from this honesty that led to the elicitation of this critical information. If not, the crime would likely remain unsolved as only two people in the world knew what had happened that day. Over the years, my partner and I have experienced a great deal of success in convincing criminal subjects to tell us about the mistakes they have made. Moreover, we have come to realize that being genuine is not only important, but it has been readily recognized by those subjects we have questioned. In its purest form, an interrogation is a deep, personal, and positive interaction between individuals. The pathway to such a connection is paved with the genuineness of the interrogator.

Undoubtedly, the aforementioned statement is likely to be met with an eyeroll or 'humph' from those in academia who claim to be experts in criminal interrogation, despite never actually having conducted one. Some academics, expert witnesses, and advocates may also argue that these comments simply exemplify the psychologically-oriented tactics that have replaced the 'third degree.' However, the participants I interviewed repeatedly noted how important it is for their interactions with the subject to be genuine. In reality, these behaviors may not be calculated and psychologically-manipulative interrogative tactics employed during the course of an interrogation, but rather the inherent personality traits of those drawn to the specialty of criminal interrogation. One participant demonstrated this possibility when he reported that he was so concerned that he would have to be mean and aggressive to criminal subjects that he was pleased and relieved to learn that he could simply be himself and act toward subjects with kindness and still elicit confessions. Many other participants echoed this sentiment through the use of such words as being "honest," "credible," and "straightforward." Contrary to the likely biased perceptions of some false confession researchers, experts, and advocates, the insights of the participants in my study suggest that law enforcement interrogative specialists are not attempting to manipulate subjects, but are instead being genuinely kind and respectful when interacting with them.

In addition to how they present themselves and interact with criminal subjects, the participants also identified interrogative strategies that they believe are particularly effective when questioning a criminal subject. Participants most frequently identified the use of themes as an effective interrogative strategy. According to Kassin (2008), this approach is consistent with the minimization portion of the Reid Technique in which law enforcement interrogators attempt to morally justify the subject's criminal actions. Kassin et al. (2010) identified that such minimizations include rationalizing the crime and providing alternative explanations for the criminal act by offering that the crime may have been committed accidentally or out of self-defense. The participants in my study described their use of themes in very much the same way. For example, participants described themes as an "out" or a "face-saving way" for a criminal subject to explain their criminal actions, thereby minimizing the seriousness of the offense.

While some false confession researchers suggest that minimizing the offense is actually designed to infer that the subject will be treated in a lenient fashion if they choose to confess (Kassin, 2008; Kassin et al., 2010a; Kassin & McNall, 1991; Narchet et al., 2011; Newring & O'Donohue, 2008; Russano et al., 2005), the participants in my study frequently reported that their themes are designed to create an environment in which the subject can honestly disclose his criminal actions without the fear of being judged. In addition, as opposed to offering explanations that infer judicial leniency such as 'accidents' or 'self-defense,' participants often reported that they seek to identify logical and meaningful explanations for why the subject may have committed the offense. As noted by one participant, themes are only effective if they are meaningful to the subject. Themes were also identified as being effective because they offer the subject a nicer way to reframe what they have done by rationalizing their motivations for committing the crime, minimizing the seriousness of the offense, and projecting the blame onto someone or something else. As opposed to inferring the promise of leniency, the participants in my study reported that themes encourage honesty from the subject by removing barriers such as condemnation, recrimination, and judgment that may preclude forthrightness. It therefore appears that these efforts to reduce the subject's shame through the use of themes are different from minimization purportedly designed to infer future judicial leniency.

Participants identified additional interrogative strategies that are effective in eliciting a truthful confession including attacking inconsistencies in the subject's statement and presenting them with true and clear evidence of their guilt. Participants noted that these approaches may help convince the subject that lying is no longer an option and that the time has come to be honest about their criminal actions. This is consistent with Perillo and Kassin's (2011) conclusion that criminal subjects generally confess as an act of social compliance brought about by the realization that there is no other means to escape their current situation but through confession. These strategies are also consistent with the conclusion that criminal subjects are more likely to confess when the evidence against them is strong (Baldwin, 1993; Kebbell et al., 2006; Moston & Engelberg, 2011; Moston et al., 1992).

The interpersonal approaches and interrogative strategies identified as effective by participants closely resemble some of the interrogative techniques Kassin et al. (2007) listed in their survey of predominantly local law enforcement officers. Upon querying respondents about a myriad of interrogative techniques, Kassin et al. (2007) presented the following techniques in order of their frequency of usage: a) identifying contradictions in the suspect's story,

b) establishing rapport and gaining the suspect's trust, c) confronting the suspect with evidence of his guilt, d) offering the suspect sympathy, moral justifications and excuses, and e) minimizing the moral seriousness of the offense. These techniques closely reflect some of the interpersonal approaches and interrogative strategies noted by the participants in my study to be effective in eliciting a truthful confession. This suggests that there may be some level of consistency in how local law enforcement officers and federal law enforcement polygraph examiners interrogate.

The effective interpersonal approaches and interrogative strategies reported by the participants in my study also closely resemble the findings of Bull and Soukara (2009) who reviewed interviews by law enforcement officers in England and identified that these officers frequently a) presented the subject with evidence, b) emphasized contradictions in the subject's statement, c) challenged the subject's account of events, d) showed concern for the subject, and e) suggested scenarios of what may have occurred. In reviewing audiotaped interviews of English police officers, Bull and Soukara (2009) also concluded that criminal subjects were more responsive to and cooperative with the interviewer when the interviewer was open-minded, flexible, responsive to the subject, and took time to build rapport. In short, even law enforcement officers in other countries see the benefit of treating criminal subjects with decency and respect. This position is also supported by the insights offered by real-world criminal subjects. For example, Kebbell, Hurren, and Mazerolle (2006) consulted with serious criminal offenders in prison who reported that they tended to be more compliant with particular interviewing styles. More specifically, these offenders explained that they were more cooperative with law enforcement officers who were compassionate, understanding, non-aggressive, honest, non-judgmental, and were clear and straightforward in their explanation of the ensuing process. Quite simply, the information provided by the interrogative specialists interviewed for my study is very similar to not only the experiences of law enforcement interrogators in other countries, but also the experiences of actual criminal subjects questioned by law enforcement. Together, these sources combine to reiterate what most of us already know: Treating someone with kindness and respect encourages a positive connection.

Evidence Strength

In addition to how interrogators treat subjects and the interrogative approaches they employ, it has also been suggested that evidence strength is the ultimate determinant of whether a guilty subject truthfully confesses. For example, in their study involving Australian students engaged in mock criminal activity, Kebbell et al. (2006) reported that the subject's perception of the strength of the evidence against them was the largest determinant of whether a confession was rendered by the subject. In their review of the relevant literature, Moston and Engelberg (2011) also identified that confessions are more likely to occur when the evidence presented to a criminal subject is strong. In my experience, there have been cases in which the evidence against a subject is so strong that the subject's confession is irrelevant. However, I conducted an interrogation in these situations anyway based on the premise that a confession not only saves the government the time and effort associated with taking a matter to trial, but it increases the likelihood that a subject will receive some form of benefit for their truthful admission of wrongdoing. Still, due to the strength of the evidence in these cases, I made it clear to the subject from the outset that the evidence against them was so overwhelming that their confession was not needed to successfully prosecute them. This then leads to systematically presenting the subject with the evidence of their guilt. These are very easy interrogations to conduct as the proof of guilt is in the evidentiary pudding. All that is left is to truthfully identify to the subject that the best option available to them is to confess their criminal actions and start making efforts to work a deal with the prosecutor.

Like many decisions we make in life, some are easier than others, but not necessarily because they are unimportant. Sometimes critical choices like the decision to move, change careers, break up with a significant other, or place a loved one in a nursing home are made that much easier by the circumstances surrounding the issue. When the Pro-Con list is made, the final tally helps to clarify the path that needs to be taken. The available evidence in some cases may ultimately prove to be the North Star for the criminal subject who finds themself contemplating the path of continued denial versus the path of confession. This is why confessions are not always the start of a criminal matter, but rather the culmination of a thorough investigation. Therefore, there may be times in which the interrogative methods employed by a law enforcement officer may be less important than the existing evidence against the subject. Conversely, as the strength of the evidence decreases, the interrogative prowess of the officer must increase if a confession is to be elicited. As outlined above, the state and federal polygraph examiners that I interviewed identified that interpersonal considerations such as understanding, empathy, friendliness, trust, respect, rapport building, professionalism, and being nonjudgmental increase the likelihood of eliciting a confession. While some academic researchers and expert witnesses may sneer at these claims, it is important to note that these interrogative specialists are not alone in their perceptions.

Foreign Law Enforcement's Perceptions of What Works

Bull and Soukara (2009) conducted four interrelated research studies that sought to explore what actually occurs within the interrogation room. In the first study, law enforcement officers from a relatively large police department in England, who routinely interview criminal subjects, were questioned about what they believed were the most necessary skills an interrogator must possess in order to be effective. Participants identified preparation, knowledge of the topic, the ability to build rapport with the subject, listening, questioning, flexibility, open-mindedness, and compassion/empathy as the most critical skills for effective interrogation (Bull & Soukara, 2009). When questioned about the techniques they tended to employ when dealing with an uncooperative subject, most participants reported that presenting evidence of guilt to the subject had the greatest impact. When asked about the importance of obtaining a confession from the subject, almost all of the participants replied that it was, "Not at all important." The participants also noted that it is critical for officers to enter the interview/interrogation room free of bias. Similarly,

Soukara, Bull, and Vrij, (as cited by Bull & Soukara, 2009), noted that law enforcement participants reported that their interrogative actions were not typically influenced by the way the subject looked or behaved. These findings obtained from real-world law enforcement interrogators in the United Kingdom stand in stark contrast to the descriptions of American law enforcement officers and their interrogative methods as presented by many false confession researchers.

In a second study, Bull and Soukara (2009) analyzed 80 of the 200 interviews provided by law enforcement officers relating to a variety of criminal offenses ranging from reckless driving to homicide. The interviews were rated on the prevalence of the 17 most commonly identified interrogative methodologies in the existing research. These techniques, and the percentage of the 80 law enforcement officers who reported using these techniques, are as follows: a) presenting the subject with evidence (79); b) open-ended questions (79); c) leading questions (73); d) repetitive questioning (67); e) emphasizing contradictions in the subject's statement (>50%); f) positively confronting the subject with accusations of their guilt (>50%); g) challenging the subject's account of events; h) gentle prodding (<50%); i) showing concern for the subject (<50%); j) interrupting the subject (<50%); k) suggesting scenarios of what may have occurred (<50%); l) handling the subject's mood (<50%); m) remaining silent (<50%); n) maximizing the offense (1); o) minimizing the offense (Never); p) intimidating the subject (Never); and q) suggesting that the situation is futile (Never). Of the 80 interviews that were examined, 31 people rendered a confession. Bull and Soukara noted that 5 of the confessions happened very early in the interview. In addition, it was reported that many of the techniques outlined above were used during interviews in which no confession was obtained. Lastly, there did not appear to be a positive correlation between the use of the interrogative techniques listed above and the elicitation of confessions (Bull & Soukara, 2009).

Contrary to previous findings, the work of Bull and Soukara (2009) highlights that many interrogative techniques employed in real-world criminal interrogations do not automatically lead to confessions, and some people confess in the absence of these techniques. This point bears repeating. Some of the interrogative methods outlined above did not lead to a confession, and some people chose to confess even when none of these techniques were used. This again suggests that interrogative methods are not always the ultimate determinant of whether a confession is elicited. Logic would therefore suggest that the same holds true for false confessions. No interrogative technique automatically leads to a false confession, and some people falsely confess prior to any specific interrogative techniques being employed. In both instances, this would suggest that it is the subject who ultimately determines whether a confession, true or false, is rendered. In fact, Bull and Soukara (2009) noted that the only statistically significant correlation between interrogative techniques and confession was a negative one relating to challenging the subject's account of events. Bull and Soukara suggested that when interrogators chose to challenge a subject's depiction of events, they were less likely to render a confession. Thus, it appears that in the real world of law enforcement interrogation, confronting a subject more harshly may actually make them less likely to confess.

In a third study, Bull and Soukara (2009) examined 50 additional audio-taped interviews provided by police to identify any potential relationships between the interviewer's behavior and the behavior of the subject. Bull and Soukara focused on the following interview skills: a) rapport building; b) communication; c) open-mindedness; d) presumptiveness (assuming guilt); e) flexibility (the ability to change interview techniques to fit the subject's behavior/attitude); and f) responsiveness to the subject (displaying a positive reaction to the subject's behavior/attitude). Bull and Soukara also evaluated the following behaviors of the interview subject: a) cooperation; b) responsiveness to the interviewer; c) plausibility of the subject's account; and d) resistance (unwillingness to answer questions). Upon examining the relationship between interviewer and subject behaviors, Bull and Soukara concluded that subjects were more responsive to, and cooperative with the interviewer when the interviewer was open-minded, flexible, responsive to the subject, and took time to build rapport. Similar to the findings of the previous study,

Bull and Soukara again presented a different picture of what takes place in a real-world criminal interrogation.

In their final study, Bull and Soukara (2009) selected 40 additional interviews from the 200 provided by police in which a confession occurred toward the middle or end of the interview. These interviews were selected under the premise that interrogative techniques are more likely to have contributed to the confession since the confession occurred later in the interview. The interrogative techniques that were employed and the frequency in which they were noted are as follows: a) disclosure of evidence (100%); b) open-ended questions (100%); c) repetitive questions (93%); d) leading questions (75%); e) handling the subject's mood (73%); f) emphasizing contradictions in the subject's statement (65%); g) positively confronting the subject with accusations of their guilt (60%); h) interrupting the subject (55%); i) remaining silent (35%); j) challenging the subject's account of events (28%); k) suggesting scenarios of what may have occurred (20%); l) gentle prodding (15%); m) showing concern for the subject (10%); and n) suggesting that the situation is futile (3%). Bull and Soukara offered that these findings appear to indicate that a subject's ultimate decision of whether to confess may be at least partially influenced by the strategies of presenting the subject with evidence of their guilt, using open-ended questions, and asking repetitive questions. It was also noted by Bull and Soukara that the interrogative tactics of greatest concern to some false confession researchers such as the Bluff Technique, false evidence ploys, minimization, and so on, were rarely present in actual police interviews in the United Kingdom. In light of these findings, there appears to be a disconnect between the perceptions of criminal interrogation held by some false confession researchers and what actually occurs when criminal offenders are interrogated by law enforcement personnel. Moreover, the interrogative techniques believed by law enforcement officers in the United Kingdom to be effective are quite similar to those reported by the state and federal law enforcement polygraph examiners in my study.

Contrary to the conclusions of many false confession researchers who believe that law enforcement interrogators rely on coercive, deceitful, and manipulative tactics to elicit confessions (Frantzen & Can, 2012; Hasel & Kassin, 2009; Henkel et al., 2008; Johnson & Drucker, 2009; Kassin, 2012; Kassin et al., 2005; Levine et al., 2010; Meissner & Kassin, 2002; Narchet et al., 2011; Nash & Wade, 2009; Newring & O'Donohue, 2008; Perillo & Kassin, 2011; Swanner & Beike, 2010), real-world law enforcement officers offer a marked contrast of what they believe is effective in the interrogation room when academic researchers actually take the time to obtain their insights. It is also important to note that law enforcement officers who routinely interrogate criminal subjects are similarly capable of articulating what doesn't work when questioning criminal subjects (e.g., being disrespectful toward the subject, showing anger, exhibiting disinterest, being dishonest, acting in a judgmental manner, being overly coercive, or physically intimidating the subject). Lastly, multiple participants in my study noted that it is ineffective and unethical to present the subject with false evidence or feed them information about the investigation as these actions can potentially lead to a false confession. In light of the information provided in this chapter, it would be inappropriate and inaccurate to falsely assume that law enforcement officers, particularly those who specialize in criminal interrogation, lack an awareness of what is effective and ineffective when interrogating criminal subjects.

Summary

As previously noted, the law enforcement interrogation process is often portrayed as being so coercive, threatening, and manipulative, that criminal subjects will confess, both truthfully and falsely, solely as a means of escaping the interrogation room. Moreover, American law enforcement officers are often perceived to be guided by the belief that confessions are the primary goal of an interrogation and a close-minded, oppressive, and suggestive interviewing style is employed to obtain that confession. While it has been suggested that the problems associated with criminal interrogation in the United States may stem from the relative lack of interrogation training received by officers, it appears that when law enforcement officers who are highly trained and skilled in criminal interrogation are queried, they are able to outline a very deliberate and well-considered approach to questioning criminal subjects. Furthermore, these methods of interrogation appear more consistent with treating others as you would like to be treated than they do the 'third degree' approach of physically harming or intimidating a helpless subject until a confession is elicited. They also run counter to the positions of academic researchers like Ofshe and Leo (1997) who claim that while police no longer physically abuse subjects, modern interrogation methods still harm the subject without actually leaving a mark on their body.

Whereas many false confession researchers and expert witnesses have posited that coercion, manipulation, threats, and an overall authoritative attitude are the primary weapons of the law enforcement interrogator, the interrogative experts interviewed for my study clearly identify the value of being "laid back," "low key," "non-confrontational," and even "soft" in their questioning of a criminal subject. They report accomplishing this by being "friendly," "nice," and "neutral" and treating the subject with "kindness," "respect," and "dignity." As opposed to acting as an overbearing and authoritative police officer, the interrogative specialists interviewed in my study choose to present themselves as a "father figure," "therapist," or "counselor." These participants constantly repeated the uncomplicated reality that people will not talk to people they do not like or trust. In essence, when it comes to the search for a criminal confession, these interrogative specialists report that it is not the vinegar that brings the flies, but the honey.

It cannot be ignored that these approaches to criminal interrogation are entirely consistent with countless other professions that bring people into direct contact with the public. More specifically, it begs the questions: How many people would seek the services of a doctor, therapist, financial advisor, attorney, or even vacuum cleaner salesperson who treats them in a confrontational, condescending, authoritative, or threatening manner? Similarly, how many professions teach their personnel to yell at, intimidate, or threaten their client base as a means of closing the deal, making the sale, or encouraging compliance? An argument can easily be made that people are unlikely to

236

confide in a friend or family member who judges them for their misdeeds and acts toward them in a hostile and combative way.

When questioned about their beliefs as to why criminal subjects have confessed to them in the past, the interrogative specialists in my study repeatedly pointed to the importance of trust. If a criminal subject is going to confess, the majority of participants reported that the subject must come to trust the interrogator. In addition, treating the subject with kindness was reported to increase rapport between the subject and the interrogator; allowed the subject to develop positive feelings toward the interrogator; and permitted the creation of a comfortable and nonjudgmental environment for subjects to disclose their wrongdoings. As reported by some participants, this type of positive interaction with the subject may allow the interrogator to differentiate themselves from other law enforcement officers who may have mistreated the subject in some way in the past. As explained by one participant, if an interrogator is going to be successful in getting the subject to disclose their criminal activity, "You have to be a person to them and not just another cop."

As identified by multiple interrogative specialists in my study, the environment created by the interrogator is of critical importance. Popular culture is full of innumerable portrayals of the handcuffed subject placed at a spartan table, illuminated by a bare swinging lightbulb, and being barraged with questions from an intimidating detective who slams his fists on the table while looming over the subject. However, those who specialize in criminal interrogation reported creating a vastly different environment. The participants in this study often suggested that confessions come from subjects who do not feel judged for their criminal transgressions. Sometimes this nonjudgmental environment is created by minimizing the seriousness of the offense. Other times it can be accomplished by offering the subject alternative and more palatable explanations for their behavior. For example, interrogators can suggest that the misdeed was a result of the subject's alcohol consumption, their misinterpretation of the victim's behavior, or simply bad luck and poor timing. Multiple participants described this as giving the subject "an out", so that they can accept responsibility without feeling guilty or judged. Lastly, multiple participants pointed to the fact that confessions are more likely to occur when the interrogator is able to create an environment in which the subject feels that they are being afforded an opportunity to tell their side of the story.

Despite the interrogative approaches outlined above, some participants suggested that the internal motivations of the subject may ultimately play a role in their decision to confess. Whether as a result of the interrogator's actions or in response to the subject's personal decision-making process, it was posited that subjects sometimes confess as a means of alleviating themselves of the guilt surrounding their criminal wrongdoing. At times, the interrogation room may represent the first opportunity that the subject has been given to discuss their role in the crime at hand. Similarly, the decision to confess may come from the subject's belief that lying in light of the existing evidence or circumstances is no longer an option. Lastly, the decision to confess may reflect the subject's realization that it is far better to confess than to face the grim realities of the remaining alternatives.

It is important to note that while some assumptions about why criminal subjects ultimately confess may stem from the personal experiences of the interrogative specialists interviewed for my study, many participants also reported that they make it a practice of asking subjects why they decided to confess. Those who engage in this practice reported similar explanations behind the subject's decision to confess. These responses centered around the interrogator's respectful, fair, professional, and non-judgmental treatment of the subject during the interrogation process. Relatedly, this type of treatment was reported by subjects to make them feel comfortable, listened to, and understood. In fact, some subjects advised that they found the interrogation process to be therapeutic and a motivation to change the manner in which they had been living their lives. Other subjects reported to participants that they were ultimately treated far differently by the participant than others in law enforcement with whom they had previously come into contact. Lastly, some subjects explained to participants that they decided to confess because they could no longer hold onto their guilt; they knew that their detection was

inevitable; and/or they were finally afforded an opportunity to explain their actions.

Based on the information provided by the state and federal interrogative specialists interviewed for my study, it becomes clear that a kinder and gentler approach is the preferred manner of interrogating a criminal subject. Subjects are more likely to confess their wrongdoings if they are treated well and provided an environment that is free of judgment. Contrary to the picture presented by many academic researchers, expert witnesses, and advocates, it is not the heavy-handed cop that obtains the truthful confession. Threats and intimidation are not effective techniques in the interrogation room and are unlikely to encourage cooperation and disclosure from a criminal subject. As noted by one participant, "The nice guy gets the confession." In light of these insights, it is a false assumption to conclude that criminal subjects only confess because law enforcement officers intimidate or threaten them into doing so.

CHAPTER 12

Can Any One Particular Interrogative Technique Cause a False Confession?

Throughout the academic literature, and as will be presented throughout this book, researchers have offered countless explanations for what they believe causes an innocent person to falsely confess. For example, it has been suggested that false confessions can occur when various interrogative techniques are employed such as the False Evidence Ploy (Janda, 2015; Kassin, 2008; Kassin & Kiechel, 1996; Woody et al., 2018), the Bluff Technique (Perillo & Kassin, 2011); offering incentives of decreased punishment in exchange for a confession (Swanner & Beike, 2010); and using minimization interrogation techniques (Narchet et al., 2011; Newring & O'Donohue, 2008). Still, as noted by Frantzen and Can (2012), relatively little research has explored law enforcement's perceptions of the interviewing and interrogation of criminal subjects and few studies have actually consulted with law enforcement about what proves productive in the interrogation room (Frantzen, 2010). In fact, it was not until Kassin et al. (2007) conducted a national survey of law enforcement officers regarding their use of specific interrogative techniques that such insight was sought in a meaningful way in the United States. As discussed in the preceding chapter, while law enforcement officers may not generally have the abilities or occupational freedom to conduct their own research, this should not suggest that they are unaware of what causes false confessions. Furthermore, a scientific laboratory study with university students is not always necessary to identify the most effective techniques in any particular profession. In fact, trial and error, personal experience, and the generational transmission of best practices throughout the workforce are likely more important in teaching occupational practitioners what does and does not work in their respective fields. For example, while working with a landscaping crew going through college, I was quickly taught that trimming with the right side of the weed eater head blows grass clippings away from the flower bed while trimming on the opposite side blows grass clippings into the bed. As efficiency matters when cutting a large number of lawns each day, not having to blow grass clippings out of a flower bed at the end of a job proved to save a great deal of time. While this was clearly a 'best practice' that was handed down to me and every new employee that came after me, I am nearly certain that it was not discovered in an academic journal by my landscaper boss as he sipped on a cup of Earl Grey tea. In short, the conclusions of academic researchers are not always needed in order to do one's job effectively.

Since academia has largely been responsible for exploring the potential causes of false confessions, there may be an underlying academic arrogance that law enforcement is clueless about such causes. In an attempt to assess whether law enforcement officers are aware of what may cause an innocent person to falsely confess, I decided to ask the state and federal law enforcement polygraph examiners in my study for their insights. Their responses as to what they believe may cause a false confession generally fell into three categories: a) the techniques that were used; b) the vulnerabilities of the subject; and c) the subject's personal motivations. The following is a more thorough discussion of their responses.

Techniques That Were Used

Participants readily identified that the actions and interrogative methods of the law enforcement officer can influence whether a criminal subject ultimately confesses falsely. The following is a list of the actions and methods that the interrogative specialists I interviewed suggested were most likely to contribute to a false confession.

Stress and Coercion. Most of the participants identified that false confessions can sometimes be caused by the inappropriate, unethical, and possibly illegal behavior of the interrogator. Most frequently, participants reported that if the interrogator employs a great deal of coercion, it is possible that a false confession may be elicited. According to the participants, a stressful or coercive environment may include an interrogator or multiple interrogators using hostile, aggressive, or overbearing interrogative techniques such as being verbally abusive, physically abusive, or intimidating the subject through the use of threats against the subject or their family. Participants referred to this type of an approach as "browbeating" a subject. Other participants noted that this can include such behavior as yelling or screaming at the subject, scaring the subject, badgering the subject, "getting in the face" of a subject, or "pushing too hard." One participant seemed to sum things up by stating that a subject may falsely confess if the interrogator makes them feel "over-pressured." Acting toward the subject in such a manner can create so much stress for the subject and place them under such an inordinate degree of duress that the subject will do and say anything, to include giving a false confession, just to end the interrogation. This type of an environment may also put the subject in a position where they feel that they have no other choice but to confess. Some of the participants described this type of an approach as "unscrupulous" and a clear indicator of the interrogator's "unprofessionalism."

An example of how this approach can lead to a false confession can be observed in the wrongful conviction case of Michael Shelton. On March 21, 1992, the bodies of 17-year-old Leslie Murphy and 14-year-old Stephen Neighbors were found along a gravel road near Moody, Texas. Both victims had been shot in the back. In March 1993, James Pitts Jr., an acquaintance of Neighbors, was reinterviewed after being cleared as a suspect the previous year. Pitts (who was later determined to have an IQ of 68) reportedly "lost it" during the interview and admitted to being with both victims before they

243

were killed. This led to four days of interrogation in which Pitts offered five different versions of events, to include claims that he and three others were involved in the victims' murders. More specifically, Pitts confessed that he, James Long, Michael Shelton, and Richard Kussmaul had raped Murphy and that Kussmaul then shot both victims to death. Although he falsely confessed to being involved in the crime, Shelton testified that he only did so because the lead detective "was cussing at me and told me he knows I did it and he said if I don't come clean, he was going to make sure I got the death penalty . . . I had a two-week-old daughter at the time, and he said he would make sure she would be turned over to (Child Protective Services) and my ex-wife would go to prison because she must have known something about the murders, too." Shelton was later convicted and sentenced to 20 years in prison for his involvement in the murders. He was eventually exonerated in 2019 (National Registry of Exonerations, 2020). It is hard to ignore the role that the profound stress and coercion placed upon Shelton by detectives played in his decision to falsely confess in this case.

False Promises. Participants offered that making false promises to the subject could also potentially contribute to a false confession. Of particular concern are promises in which the subject is led to believe that if they simply confess to the crime at hand, the interrogator will allow them to go home. Participants similarly suggested that false confessions may occur if an interrogator promises the subject that if they confess they will receive a lesser charge or a lesser sentence. It was offered that such promises may sound similar to, "Tell me you did this and I can make it all go away;" "You can go home if you confess;" or "Tell me why you did this and I'll let you go." In light of such promises, an innocent subject may choose to falsely confess not only to end the interrogation, but under the inaccurate belief that their confession will allow them to avoid prosecution. Clearly such a promise is not only false, but egregious.

The impact that false promises can have on a subject's decision to falsely confess is exemplified in James Long's wrongful conviction as a co-defendant in the aforementioned murders of Leslie Murphy and Stephen Neighbors in Moody, Texas in 1992. Like Michael Shelton discussed above, Long also falsely confessed in this case. Long testified that he falsely confessed to being involved in the deaths of Murphy and Neighbors, "because I was scared of going to prison or, worse, getting the death penalty." In fact, Long advised that the lead detective in the case grabbed Long's arm and showed him the vein that would be used to facilitate the lethal injection that he would receive if he did not confess to his role in the crimes. Long also reported that the detective and the prosecutor promised him probation if he were to confess. Long then testified that, "I was willing to say anything they wanted me to say because I thought I was getting probation and no prison time." He added, "I had two small children and I was afraid of going to prison for life or, worse, getting executed." Like Shelton, Long was convicted and sentenced to 20 years in prison for his involvement in the murders, but was later exonerated in 2019 (National Registry of Exonerations, 2020). As can easily be identified, Long's confession was directly influenced by the false promise that if he just confessed, he would be given probation and avoid a prison sentence.

False Evidence. Participants reported that another interrogative approach that may contribute to the elicitation of a false confession included the presentation of false evidence. Regarding the presentation of false evidence, some participants suggested that the use of "crazy lies" like suggesting that DNA analysis conclusively revealed that the subject was at the scene of the crime, could potentially cause an innocent person to falsely confess. Participants stated that such problematic lies about false evidence may sound like, "We have all of this evidence against you, and you will get the death penalty unless you tell me," or "We found your DNA, and the prosecutor is going to charge you right now." Participants stated that the problem with lying to a subject to such an extent is that it causes the subject to feel trapped. However, one participant noted that in her experience as a federal law enforcement polygraph examiner, by the time the subject is brought in for a polygraph examination, the evidence against the subject has generally already been established with them. In other words, the lead investigator has most likely already questioned the subject and presented them with evidence of their guilt, only to have them deny their involvement and yet agree to a polygraph examination as a means of clearing things up. In these types of scenarios, it may be inherently more difficult for a polygraph examiner to lie about the existence of additional evidence.

Pushing for Agreement. Participants also noted that it is problematic and inappropriate for an interrogator to question a criminal subject by pushing them to simply agree with the interrogator's presumptions. For example, participants suggested that if the interrogator attempts to lead or sway the subject into confessing by asking closed-ended questions and feeding them case information, it is possible that a false confession could be elicited. As noted by one particular participant, a false confession may occur if the interrogator feeds case facts to the subject so that the subject can simply "regurgitate" the information back to the interrogator in the form of a confession. Participants similarly identified that it is concerning when an interrogator creates the written confession for the subject and then simply forces them to sign it. Participants described this type of behavior as "clumsy police work" in which the interrogator assumes that the subject is guilty and then believes that it is their responsibility to get the subject to admit to it. In essence, one participant offered that conducting an interrogation in such a manner forces the subject into a corner where they are pushed to make a decision that is not of their own volition and could potentially lead to a false confession.

An example of how a law enforcement interrogator might simply push for agreement from a subject can be observed in the wrongful conviction case of Charles Johnson. On December 4, 1995, two owners of a car dealership in Chicago, Illinois were shot to death by two men who were believed to have visited the dealership shortly before the shooting. On the following day, 17-year-old Troshawn McCoy was arrested based on an anonymous tip. After being interrogated, McCoy falsely confessed to being involved in the murders and implicated several others to include 19-year-old Charles Johnson. Johnson claimed that during his interrogation, he was provided with what he was told were his release papers which he was asked to sign. Johnson signed the paper but then disavowed the document when he discovered that it was a confession written by investigators. Based on his 'confession,' Johnson was convicted and sentenced to life without parole. Johnson was later exonerated in 2017 (National Registry of Exonerations, 2020). While this is a particularly outrageous example of an interrogator trying to trick a subject into confessing, it helps to exemplify inappropriate interrogations in which officers seek not to identify the truth, but rather to push criminal subjects to agree with investigators' assumptions about the crime. Luckily, such unethical interrogative behavior appears to be the exception, not the rule.

Lengthy Periods of Interrogation. Participants identified that lengthy periods of interrogation may also contribute to the elicitation of a false confession. For example, participants suggested that a false confession may possibly occur if the subject is isolated in an interrogation room for an extremely long period of time without sufficient water, bathroom, and meal breaks. Multiple participants offered that if the subject is interrogated for 10 to 12 hours or longer without requisite breaks, it is possible that the subject may simply give up and decide to confess falsely without thinking of potential legal ramifications, all in an effort to end the interrogation. As noted by some participants, lengthy periods of questioning can cause the subject to become fatigued and psychologically "worn down". This is particularly true if the subject's biological needs are not met during the course of the interrogation (e.g. they are deprived of food, sleep, etc.). In light of these problematic techniques, innocent subjects may become motivated to falsely confess just as a means of ending the interrogation so that they can sleep, eat, use the bathroom, and so on. Participants likened this type of an approach to "brow beating" or "torture" in that the subject will simply say anything to end the questioning and attend to their physiological needs. This possible contributor to false confessions is consistent with the observation of Drizin and Leo (2004) who reported that the average length of an interrogation resulting in a false confession is 16.3 hours.

Vulnerabilities of the Subject

Despite the problematic interrogative actions outlined above, many of the participants in my study reported that false confessions are not always influenced by the actions of the interrogator. Instead, they suggested that false confessions can also be caused by the personal characteristics of the subject. The following is a discussion of the subject characteristics believed by participants to contribute to the decision to falsely confess.

Low Intelligence, Mental Illness, and Youth. The majority of the participants reported that a false confession is more likely to occur if the person is uneducated, has a low IQ, or has been diagnosed with learning disabilities. Similarly, the majority of the participants also suggested that if the subject is suffering from a mental health condition or psychosis, it is possible that a false confession could be elicited from the subject. Many of the participants noted that the youth and immaturity of the subject may also be a potential contributor to false confessions. In addition to biological youth, some participants noted that it can be problematic if the subject has "mental immaturity." Participants offered that intelligence, mental illness, youth, and immaturity may be of concern because they can cause the subject to be more easily manipulated by an interrogator who is overly aggressive in their interrogative approach. It is important to note that these observations are entirely consistent with the primary subject risk factors routinely put forth by false confession academic researchers and expert witnesses. Similarly, they reflect the key risk factors apparent in the cases of those who have been wrongfully convicted subsequent to a false confession and highlighted by both the Innocence Project and the National Registry of Exonerations.

Personality and Substance Abuse. Participants reported that the subject's personality may also be a potential cause of false confessions. More specifically, participants suggested that if the subject is a "pleaser" who simply seeks to agree with the interrogator's assertions, a false confession may occur. Similarly, if the subject is the type of person who desires attention and notoriety, they too may be more likely to confess to something they did not do as a means of obtaining recognition. Lastly, multiple participants offered that a subject may potentially give a false confession if they are under the influence of drugs or alcohol at the time of the interrogation, though they would likely not be polygraphed in this condition.

The Subject's Personal Motivations

In addition to problematic interrogative techniques and the personal risk factors of the subject, some of the state and federal law enforcement polygraph examiners I interviewed explained that false confessions can occur as a direct response to the subject's personal motivations. The following is a discussion of some of the motivations they believe can cause an innocent criminal subject to falsely confess.

Protecting the Truly Guilty. The most frequently reported motivation that may cause a criminal subject to falsely confess is the desire to protect the truly guilty party. This may occur when the truly guilty party is a close friend, a family member, a sexual partner, a fellow gang member, et cetera. In fact, some participants offered that taking responsibility for a crime they did not commit may be considered by some subjects to be a "badge of honor," especially if it increases their status within a criminal organization or gang. Another participant also suggested that falsely confessing to a crime may prevent a "beef" between an innocent and guilty subject. In other words, it may sometimes be more advantageous for an innocent person to accept responsibility for a crime they did not commit than to tell the truth and become an enemy of the person or group that actually committed the crime.

Protecting Oneself. Participants also suggested that an innocent subject may rationally decide to falsely confess as a means of guaranteeing a lesser punishment or sentence. In these instances, the subject may think, "Nobody believes me, so I might as well admit to a lesser offense." Similarly, an individual who is more experienced with the criminal justice system may choose to falsely confess to prevent the interrogator from pressing further and obtaining a truthful confession to a more serious crime because they know that the false confession will not hold up under legal scrutiny. Such an individual may give a vague false confession in an attempt to shut the interview down by essentially giving an inexperienced interrogator "something that is nothing." Put another way, knowing that the false confession they give will eventually be suppressed by the court, an experienced criminal subject may throw the interrogator a bone to forego a deeper interrogative dive into other crimes for which they are truly guilty. In these cases, a false confession can be used as a mechanism for the subject to avoid rendering a true confession.

Miscellaneous Personal Motivations. Participants identified other potential motivations for why a subject may consciously decide to confess falsely. For example, one participant advised that an innocent subject may deliberately confess to a crime they did not commit as a way of obtaining attention for themselves. Another participant stated that in rare situations, it is possible that an innocent subject's life may be so bad that they falsely confess to a crime to facilitate their incarceration, thereby obtaining guaranteed shelter and regular meals. It was suggested that this may be particularly true with homeless and/or mentally ill offenders who are simply looking for "three hots and a cot" and thereby conclude that a false confession will lead to immediate food and shelter.

Areas of Agreement

While some academics and expert witnesses may perceive law enforcement officers as unthinking automatons who blindly pursue the coveted confession as a means of quickly closing their cases, those who specialize in criminal interrogation offered clearly articulable explanations for why someone would falsely confess to a crime they did not commit. The responses of the interrogative specialists I interviewed clearly demonstrate that they not only have an awareness that false confessions exist, but they can readily identify the interrogative actions, subject traits, and internal subject motivations that may cause them. What is even more interesting is the fact that these explanations, by and large, match the positions put forth by academic researchers. Not unlike those in academia who study the false confession phenomenon, the participants in my study identified that the actions of the interrogator may have an impact. These actions were identified as: a) stress and coercion brought about by aggression, physical abuse, threats, or generally unscrupulous and unprofessional behavior; b) the presentation of false evidence or otherwise falsely giving the subject the impression that the evidence of their guilt is overwhelming; c) making false promises like the subject can go home, charges will be dropped, or no punishment will be meted out if the subject just confesses; d) simply pushing to have the subject agree with the interrogator's belief as to what had occurred, and e) interrogating the subject for lengthy periods of time. Participants also identified many characteristics or factors specific to the subject that may contribute to the elicitation of a false confession. These characteristics and factors were identified as: a) low intelligence, b) mental illness, c) youth, d) substance abuse, e) a personality in which the subject desires to please the interrogator, f) the desire to protect the truly guilty party, and g) the desire to protect oneself. These responses are consistent with the findings of many false confession researchers. For example, low intelligence/mental retardation (Drizin & Leo, 2004; Kassin & Gudjonsson, 2004; Redlich et al., 2011); mental illness (Redlich, 2004; Redlich et al., 2010); adolescence/youth (Drizin & Leo, 2004; Malloy et al., 2014; Owen-Kostelnik et al., 2006; Pimentel et al., 2015); substance abuse (Evans et al., 2009; Gudjonsson et al., 2007); predisposing personality traits (Gudjonsson et al., 2006; Kassin, 2008; Kassin & Gudjonsson, 2004); and the desire to take the blame for a friend (Pimentel et al., 2015) were all suggested by false confession experts to be potential causes of false confessions.

In the simplest of terms, those law enforcement officers who specialize in criminal interrogation may have a keen awareness of what causes a false confession and therefore actively seek to avoid the pitfalls that contribute to their elicitation. Despite this apparent area of agreement between law enforcement interrogators and academic researchers, it appears that the interrogative methods employed by the officer may actually play less of a role in causing false confessions than what some in academia claim. For example, Leo (2007) stated:

> False confessions and false statements, of course, will occur in response to traditionally-coercive methods of interrogation such as the use of physical violence, threats of immediate physical harm, excessively long or incommunicado interrogation, or deprivation of essential necessities such as food, water, and/or sleep (p.709).

Such "traditionally-coercive methods of interrogation" are completely consistent with many of the problematic interrogative methods likely to cause a false confession outlined by the state and federal law enforcement polygraph examiners I interviewed. Still, Leo (2007) correctly noted that these techniques no longer appear to be commonplace in the United States. Therefore, since false confessions continue to be a problem and "traditionally-coercive" interrogative techniques are rarely used currently, it seems that false confessions may have more to do with the subject than with the interrogative methods used to question them.

Interrogative Techniques May Not Be the Problem

As outlined above, there are a great number of areas on which academia and law enforcement can agree when it comes to identifying what causes an otherwise innocent person to accept responsibility for a criminal act they did not commit. However, within the existing false confession literature, a great deal of attention continues to be directed toward how law enforcement officers interrogate. This research and the questionable conclusions reached have led to widespread legal attacks on the way law enforcement interrogates and the methods they use. The success of these attacks can be readily observed in the March 2017 decision of Wicklander-Zulawski & Associates, one of the largest firms offering interview and interrogation training to law enforcement officers, to stop teaching the Reid Technique to police officers (Schatz, 2018). In my own experience, I have taken the stand to discuss confessions that criminal subjects have provided to me, only to be asked by the defense attorney if I have ever been trained in the Reid Technique. This area of questioning is obviously posed as if to suggest that participating in such training is akin to being a potential spreader of the COVID-19 virus.

It cannot be overlooked that both academic researchers and law enforcement interrogation specialists have posited that there are various reasons beyond the interrogator's actions and techniques that cause false confessions. For example, Pimentel et al. (2015) identified that according to empirical research, "a substantial number of false confessions are given to protect another individual" (p. 226). Similarly, Gudjonsson (2010) reported finding that the desire to protect a peer was present in approximately 60% of instances of false confession reported by Icelandic youth. If a subject consciously decides to confess to protect someone else, it is illogical to blame the interrogative techniques that were employed for causing the false confession. It is also important to remember that some people confess voluntarily. In fact, Redlich et al. (2010) reported that "voluntary false confessions are the most common type of false confession" (p. 80). The frequency with which false confessions occur can even be observed, though conspicuously ignored by some academic researchers, in university laboratory experiments. For example, Wilford and Wells (2018) employed a modified cheating paradigm to investigate the similarities and differences between pleas and confessions. In doing so, they noted that 23.7% of the university students participating in the experiment falsely confessed without even being subjected to the interrogative technique used in the experiment. Walsh and Bull (2010) referenced various other researchers in concluding that "some suspects enter the interview room having decided to confess and will carry out this decision irrespective of the investigator's performance" (p. 319). In a comparable vein, Kassin (2005) stated, "whatever techniques are used in the interrogation room, one could argue that, voluntarily or under pressure, people will still at times confess to crimes they did not commit" (p. 225). Simply put, innocent people often choose to falsely confess voluntarily regardless of what interrogative methods are used against them. In these situations, it is again difficult to hold either the interrogator or their chosen interrogative techniques responsible for the false confession.

Once we exclude false confessions made voluntarily, false confessions made to protect the truly guilty party, and false confessions made to gain notoriety for the subject, only then can we start considering the interrogative techniques employed during the interrogation as a potential contributor to the false confession. However, we must also assess whether it is the interrogative technique that caused the false confession or whether it is the extreme application of these techniques that caused the problem. Consider the following analogy. Absent a profound allergy to chocolate, chocolate cake in and of itself does not kill people. However, if you decide to eat a whole chocolate cake at the end of every meal, you could possibly develop Type II diabetes and/or become morbidly obese and die as a result of either of these conditions. This reflects the old adage that too much of a good thing is anything but. The question therefore becomes: Did chocolate cake kill you or did *too much* chocolate cake kill you?

The same question must be asked in regard to police interrogative techniques and the elicitation of false confessions. Do interrogative techniques cause false confessions, or does the extreme application of interrogative techniques cause false confessions? Kassin et al. (2010) noted that, "when used in the extreme, certain interrogation tactics can cause even ordinary innocent adults to confess" (p. 44). Similarly, Leding (2012) suggested that it is "in extreme cases" that interrogative techniques can cause a false confession (p. 263). Hill and Moston (2011) also noted that "police interviewing malpractice" is actually what's at play when false confessions are elicited (p. 73). Frantzen (2010) also referred to the types of interrogations that cause false confessions as "horror stories" (p. 227). However, perhaps the best explanation of the cause of false confessions can be observed in the words of Johnson and Drucker (2009) regarding the presentation of false evidence to a subject:

> It is not suggested here that this particular interrogation tactic
> alone (or any specific one alone) will coerce or cause a false

confession. Rather, the accumulation of several of these tactics
over the course of a prolonged interrogation can diminish the
suspect's will and resistance, and gain compliance, so that they
begin to entertain hypothetical notions of their guilt which interrogators build upon (p. 57).

Whether they mean to or not, what these researchers correctly identify is
that false confessions are not caused by the simple use of a routine interrogative approach during a typical questioning session. In other words, it would
be inappropriate, misleading, and inaccurate for an expert witness to enter the
courtroom and suggest to the judge or jury that the defendant's confession
may be false because the officer employed the False Evidence Ploy, or the
Bluff Technique, or a minimization strategy. Instead, if the subject: a) did
not falsely confess voluntarily; b) did not falsely confess to gain notoriety;
c) did not falsely confess to protect the truly guilty party; d) was not an adolescent; e) was not mentally ill; f) was not intellectually disabled; or g) did
not have a personality that makes them predisposed to please authority, it
must be assumed that he falsely confessed because the officer went overboard
in his interrogation. Again, it is "extreme" interrogative techniques, "police
interviewing malpractice," and interrogative "horror stories" that are at play.
As agreed upon by both academic researchers and the interrogative specialists in my study, this extreme interrogative behavior may take the form of: a)
threatening the subject; b) yelling at the subject; c) intimidating the subject;
d) creating an overly stressful or coercive environment; e) presenting the subject with "crazy lies" about DNA evidence; f) promising the subject that they
can go home or they will avoid prosecution if they confess; and g) pushing the
subject to simply agree with law enforcement's beliefs about what happened,
all while keeping the subject in the interrogation room for 16.3 hours or more.

This indicates that normal interrogative techniques are not responsible
for false confessions just as a piece of chocolate cake at a friend's birthday
party is not responsible for causing death. It is only when the interrogator
abusively applies these techniques that normally-functioning adults run

the risk of falsely confessing. What is profoundly misleading is to conduct unrealistic laboratory experiments with college students in which a particular interrogative approach is applied and then jump to the conclusion that because some of the student participants falsely confessed to an insignificant mock crime in the lab that a real-world criminal subject being questioned about the murder of a child will also falsely confess when presented with that same interrogative technique. It is equally misleading to look at interrogative 'horror stories,' pick out one technique, and hold it accountable for the resulting false confession. Yet this is exactly what is done when some researchers draw conclusions about the false confession phenomenon after focusing their attention on interrogations that have gone drastically wrong and involved abusive behavior by law enforcement interrogators.

As an example of this latter approach to studying false confessions, Johnson and Drucker (2009) looked at the wrongful conviction cases of Byron Halsey and Jeffrey Deskovic. Halsey was questioned in regard to the 1985 murder of the 7 and 8-year-old children of the woman he lived with in Plainfield, New Jersey. On the first day, Halsey was questioned for 13.5 hours and was found to be unsuitable for polygraph testing because of his fatigue and alcohol consumption. On the following day he was with officers for another 17 hours. During this time, he was administered a polygraph examination. Officers advised that Halsey then went into a "trance," started speaking "gibberish," began crying, and made incriminating statements that did not match case facts. For nearly six hours, two officers sat with Halsey and drafted a five-page confession that matched the existing case facts. It is also important to point out that Halsey had learning disabilities and a sixth grade education. Eventually, Halsey was exonerated, but not before he spent 19 years in prison for the murder of the children (Johnson & Drucker, 2009).

In 1989, 15-year-old Angela Correa was found strangled and beaten to death in the area of Peekskill, New York. Jeffrey Deskovic, a 16-year-old student at Correa's school, soon became a person of interest in her death due to his attendance at three of Correa's wakes and what appeared to investigators to be an unusually high degree of emotion from Deskovic who had no previous relationship with the victim. Over the course of approximately six weeks, Deskovic had numerous contacts with investigators, some of which were initiated by Deskovic. During some of these contacts, officers interviewed Deskovic for numerous hours and, on January 25, 1990, Deskovic agreed to submit to a polygraph examination. After being informed that he had failed the examination, and after being subjected to a lengthy interrogation, Deskovic confessed to raping and killing Correa (Johnson & Drucker, 2009). According to Deskovic, during his interrogation, the interrogator invaded Deskovic's personal space and yelled at him. The interrogator also informed Deskovic that police were going to hurt him if he didn't confess. The interrogator also stated, "What do you mean you didn't do it? You just told me you did it through the polygraph test. We just want you to verbally confirm it." The interrogator then promised Deskovic that he could go home if he just confessed. Upon confessing, officers fed Deskovic case facts to support his confession (Deskovic, 2015). Deskovic was later exonerated after spending 16 years in prison (Johnson & Drucker, 2009).

Both of these cases help to demonstrate that when risky subjects are subjected to police malpractice, false confessions *can* occur. It is hard to look at either of these cases without seeing inappropriate and unethical law enforcement conduct. However, it would be misleading to review these cases, 'cherry pick' one particular and routine interrogative technique that was employed, and claim that the technique contributed in any meaningful way to the false confession. In fact, Halsey was interrogated for 30 hours over a 40-hour period and Deskovic was interrogated for an untold number of hours over repeated questioning sessions. Over the course of such egregiously long interrogations, it is highly likely that officers threw everything but the kitchen sink into their questioning sessions. It would therefore be misleading and inaccurate to say that because officers, at one point, bluffed Halsey or Deskovic, that the Bluff Technique caused their false confession. It would be more accurate to conclude that the false confession occurred as a result of risky individuals being subjected to ridiculously long and repeated periods of questioning in which they were threatened, given false promises, and fed information until a confession that matched case facts was provided.

To blame a single and commonly-accepted interrogative technique for eliciting a false confession would be like blaming the football team's loss on the field goal kicker who missed an extra point on the last play of the game, especially when the quarterback threw four interceptions, and the running back fumbled three times in the previous four quarters. Law enforcement officers, prosecutors, judges, and juries must resist the temptation to accept the suggestion of academic researchers and expert witnesses that because a particular interrogative technique was previously used in a horrendously abusive interrogation fraught with countless examples of police misconduct, that same technique may be responsible for a false confession in the current case before the court. There is a monumental difference between a technique being 'used' during a false confession interrogation and a technique 'causing' the false confession. This is particularly true when such egregious behavior was engaged in by the interrogators. In short, while analyzing proven cases of false confessions can identify *the presence* of a particular interrogative technique, and an artificial experiment can show the effect that the technique may have on *college students in a university laboratory*, neither are sufficient to show that the technique actually *causes* a false confession in the real world of the criminal justice system. It is therefore a false assumption to suggest that a single interrogative technique can cause a false confession.

CHAPTER 13

Reconsidering the Reid Technique's Impact on False Confessions

I t is likely that the overwhelming majority of individuals reading this text, especially those associated with the criminal justice system, have heard of the Reid Technique. This may stem from the fact that within recent years, the Reid Technique has come to be associated with overly coercive interrogative tactics that too frequently cause the elicitation of false confessions. Personally, when I am called upon to testify in court about a confession that I have elicited during the course of a polygraph examination, it is not uncommon for the defense attorney to ask if I have ever been trained in the Reid Technique. The reason for this question is obvious. The defense attorney is trying to suggest that I am well-versed in water boarding, torture, or otherwise forcing a criminal subject to confess against their will. This repeated question from defense attorneys helps to demonstrate just how negative a reputation the Reid Technique has received in recent years and how toxic they believe this method of questioning subjects has become. But what is driving this assumption?

While there are a number of techniques for interviewing a criminal subject, perhaps the most influential process in North America is the Reid Technique (Kassin et al., 2010). In fact, this process has been taught to more than 300,000 interrogators (Schatz, 2018). According to Kostelnik and

Reppucci (2009), the Reid Technique is the most commonly cited and most widely disseminated training manual on the interviewing and interrogation of criminal subjects. In the Reid Technique, law enforcement officers are taught to question subjects in a two-part process that starts with a non-confrontational interview and leads to the interrogation of those determined to be guilty during the interview phase (Kassin et al, 2010). Inbau et al. (2001) describe the Reid Technique as a nine-step process for successfully interrogating a criminal subject. Newring and O'Donohue (2008) provide the following summary of these steps:

1. Direct, positive confrontation
2. Theme development
3. Handling denials
4. Overcoming objections
5. Procurement and retention of a suspect's attention
6. Handling suspect's passive mood
7. Presenting an alternative question
8. Having the suspect orally relate various details of the offense
9. Converting an oral confession into a written confession

Kassin and Fong (1999) summarize these steps even further by explaining that the technique is a process of social influence in which the interrogator directly confronts the subject with their guilt, refuses to accept their denials, offers them face-saving alternative explanations for their criminal actions, and then convinces them to document their criminal misdeeds in a written confession. Leo (as cited by Schatz, 2018) noted that Reid and Inbau, the creators of the Reid Technique, found physical violence and intense psychological duress to be inappropriate and therefore developed an effective alternative for law enforcement officers to elicit confessions. In short, the Reid Technique was instrumental in bringing an end to the 'third degree' approach to questioning criminal subjects. Despite the debt of gratitude owed to Reid and Inbau for this advancement, some in academia continue to criticize this highly successful means of interrogation. For example, Ofshe and Leo (1997) maintain that psychological approaches to interrogation, like those put forth in the Reid Technique, are merely a means of injuring the interrogation subject without leaving a physical mark. They believe that law enforcement has foregone the infliction of physical pain to coerce confessions in exchange for the infliction of psychological suffering, the scars of which are not so easily detected.

Kassin and Gudjonsson (2004) suggested that the Reid Technique can essentially be broken down into three primary processes: isolation, confrontation, and minimization. As recommended by Inbau et al. (2001), when criminal subjects are taken in for questioning, they are generally separated from friends, family, and social support networks, so that they can be questioned privately. This separation is designed to ensure privacy, to permit the law enforcement officer to maintain control over the interview and interrogation process, and to increase the stress associated with the subject's continued denials by holding them incommunicado in an unfamiliar environment (Kassin et al., 2010). As previously discussed, the use of words like 'isolation' and 'incommunicado' to describe the private questioning of a criminal subject are not only designed to be inflammatory, but they serve as a manifestation of what may be an underlying anti-law enforcement bias and belief that no criminal subject should ever be questioned by police as such questioning may lead to the subject confessing against their own self-interest.

Directly confronting a guilty subject with evidence of their guilt is another key component of the Reid Technique of interviewing and interrogation (Inbau et al., 2001). The confrontation process involves the law enforcement interrogator directly accusing the subject of participating in the criminal matter at hand and possibly supporting these assertions with real or fictitious evidence (Kassin, 2008). In the minimization portion of the Reid Technique, the law enforcement interrogator applies various methods in an attempt to morally justify the subject's criminal actions (Kassin, 2008). These methods include offering the subject sympathy; giving the appearance of understanding; rationalizing the crime; and providing alternative explanations for the criminal act by suggesting that the act was committed accidentally or out of self-defense (Kassin et al., 2010). These aspects of the Reid Technique appear quite consistent with the effective interrogative techniques outlined by the federal and state law enforcement polygraph examiners I interviewed in my study. The question becomes, if the Reid Technique was instrumental in ending the physical abuse of criminal subjects, and if it is so successful in eliciting truthful confessions, why do so many academics and expert witnesses seek to discredit this method?

The Reported Problems with the Reid Technique

While the Reid Technique has been taught to countless law enforcement officers across the world, many academic researchers continue to suggest that it is fraught with problems. For example, Kassin (2008) suggested that isolating a person from their friends, family, and support network, especially over prolonged periods of time, serves to increase the subject's anxiety level and their desire to escape the interrogation process. Therefore, it has been suggested that innocent people may falsely confess to a crime they didn't actually commit simply as a means of escaping the horrendous environment caused by such isolation. Similarly, it has been posited that strong assertions of guilt, such as those made when using the Reid Technique to directly confront a criminal subject, can increase the subject's feelings of despair. This can then increase the likelihood of a false confession (Kassin, 2008). Aronson (as cited by Kassin & Gudjonsson, 2004), suggested that when a person considers the anticipated outcome as inevitable, they may come to agree with the anticipated outcome. When applied to criminal interrogation, Aronson's premise maintains that when a criminal subject comes to believe that their admission of guilt is inevitable, they will eventually acquiesce and provide a confession. This may therefore explain why an interrogator's direct confrontation of a criminal subject may increase the likelihood of a false confession. Lastly, it has been suggested that through the minimization strategies taught in the Reid Technique, a subject may come to infer that if they simply confess, they will be treated in a more lenient fashion (Kassin, 2008; Kassin et al., 2010a; Kassin & McNall, 1991; Narchet et al., 2011). This hope of more lenient treatment may help to explain why a person is likely to falsely confess when presented with minimization strategies like those put forth in the Reid Technique.

Academic researchers, through their ready access to university laboratory test subjects, have also sought to explain the inherent problems of the Reid Technique. For example, Kassin and McNall (1991) hypothesized that using minimization strategies like offering the subject sympathy, giving them excuses for their criminal behavior, blaming the crime on someone else, or attempting to morally justify their crime can cause criminal subjects to expect leniency from the criminal justice system once they confess. In their laboratory experiment, 75 college students were randomly assigned to read a transcript of a criminal interrogation in which one of five different interrogative techniques were used. Minimization was one of these techniques. After reading the transcript, each student was directed to complete a questionnaire in which they were asked to rate on a 10-point scale whether they thought the subject in the transcript would receive a harsh or lenient sentence if they confess. Students were also asked to rate the following aspects present in the interrogation transcript:

- The amount of pressure that was placed on the subject to confess through the use of the minimization technique
- How eager the interrogator appeared to be for the subject to confess
- How fair, aggressive, and likable they found the interrogator to be

Lastly, students were asked to estimate how many guilty and innocent subjects would likely confess if they were exposed to the same interrogative technique. Let me rephrase this last set of instructions to clarify the experiment. The researchers asked college students how likely *they* thought 100 truly guilty and truly innocent subjects would be to confess if the interrogator minimized the moral seriousness of the crime.

While some may find it difficult to understand the validity of this research design based on the fact that college students are being asked to guess how real-world criminal subjects may feel, it is interesting to note what the students reported. More specifically, students reported that the interrogator who employed minimization techniques appeared more sympathetic to the subject and less eager for the subject to confess. In addition, they found the use of the minimization technique made the overall interrogation appear less coercive. Finally, students estimated that very few innocent subjects would falsely confess in light of minimization techniques (Kassin & McNall, 1991). One would think that this would be a positive sign for the use of minimization strategies as taught in the Reid Technique. However, in their conclusion, Kassin and McNall stated that minimization techniques can be hazardous as they give criminal subjects the impression that their sentence will be more lenient, and therefore may coax innocent people into falsely confessing. Despite the fact that Kassin and McNall readily admit that this conclusion is 'speculative,' many academic researchers continue to use these questionable types of conclusions to support their attacks on the Reid Technique.

As previously noted, Kassin and Fong (1999) gave college students 30 minutes of Reid Training before watching 3.5 to 6-minute videotaped interrogations conducted by college students of other college students who had been directed to engage in a mock crime. Their conclusion? The Reid Technique is ineffective in helping law enforcement officers to identify deception, and may actually make them worse at doing so. Similarly, Newring and O'Donohue (2008) experimented by having college students interrogated for between 5 and 7 minutes regarding whether they pressed the ALT Key on the computer keyboard before concluding that the Reid Technique may cause both false confessions and the false implication of others. In an attempt to collect real-world insight from law enforcement practitioners, Kostelnik and Reppucci (2009) sought to analyze the difference between officers who have been trained in the Reid Technique and those who have not regarding their sensitivity to the developmental maturity of juvenile interrogation subjects. They surveyed 1,828 police officers (514 of whom had been trained in the Reid Technique) about their perceptions and practices when interrogating children, adolescents, and adults. While this study is noteworthy in the fact that it is one of the few studies that have sought input from actual law enforcement officers regarding interrogation techniques and perceptions, the study focused primarily on juveniles. The sample was also predominantly comprised of patrol officers who are less likely to have received specialized training in interrogation and may therefore be less likely to engage in criminal interrogations than their investigator counterparts. This study is also limited by the fact that it fails to address any specific interrogation techniques. As such, it is difficult to identify exactly what participants may have been considering when questioned about interrogations and interrogative strategies. Still, these weaknesses in the design did not stop Kostelnik and Repucci from concluding that officers trained in the Reid Technique may be less sensitive to the developmental maturity and competencies of young subjects, and may typically not consider these factors when selecting psychologically coercive interrogation strategies.

The academic vehemence against the Reid Technique can also be observed in the words of Trocino (2016) in his primer on false confessions. For example, when discussing the process of moving from an interview to an interrogation based on the interrogator's identification of deception in the subject, Trocino states, "This is the psychological equivalent from moving from browbeating to the rack or thumbscrew" (p. 94). Trocino goes on to claim that not only are the interrogative methods of the Reid Technique profoundly coercive and abusive, but disciples of the Reid Technique are taught to lie in court by claiming that the interrogation was a nonchalant and consensual conversation between the interrogator and the subject. More specifically, Trocino asserts, "The Reid Technique trains its pupils in the art of propaganda to minimize the coercion inherent in the interrogations" (p. 96). It is difficult to overlook the anti-Reid, and perhaps the anti-interrogation bias dripping from this type of verbiage. Still, their point is abundantly clear. Many false confession researchers, expert witnesses, and defense attorneys *hate* the Reid Technique. In fact, this method of interrogation has become so maligned that defense attorneys have come to view it as patient zero in the subsequent line of contact tracing. Not unlike medical professionals during the COVID-19 pandemic who sought to trace the spread of the Coronavirus, defense attorneys and their expert witnesses now suggest that any law enforcement officer who has come into contact with the dreaded Reid Technique are now potential spreaders of the false confession virus. For them, the equation is very simple:

Law Enforcement Officer + Reid Technique + Criminal Subject = False Confession

In addition to the negative views of the Reid Technique put forth within the academic research, the media has also popularized this perspective as well. For example, the *New York Times* reported on a lawsuit filed by John E. Reid and Associates in October 2019 regarding negative comments made about the Reid Technique in the Netflix series *When They See Us*, a dramatization of the Central Park Jogger case in which six teenage boys falsely confessed to raping and killing a jogger in New York City in 1989. In the series, one of the show's characters referred to the harsh questioning methods employed against the teenage subjects as "the Reid Technique." More specifically, in the fourth episode of the series, one of the characters states to another, "You squeezed statements out of them after 42 hours of questioning and coercing, without food, bathroom breaks. Withholding parental supervision. The Reid Technique has been universally rejected. That's truth to you?" Despite this Hollywood characterization, John E. Reid and Associates maintained in the lawsuit that the Reid Technique prohibits "striking or assaulting a subject, making any promises of leniency, denying a subject any rights, conducting excessively long interrogations, or denying a subject any physical needs" as is depicted in the series. For this reason, John E. Reid and Associates maintained that the Netflix series has misrepresented what is taught in the Reid interrogative method (Fortin, 2019). Still, it appears that this line of dialogue in *When They See Us* is popular culture's reflection of the underlying and increasing distrust of the Reid Technique within the criminal justice system. But, is this distrust justified? If this criticism and distrust is being fueled by the flawed research designs and questionable conclusions of some academic researchers, the skewed interpretations of false confession expert witnesses, the desperate 'Hail Mary' legal arguments of defense attorneys, and/or the emotional and biased protestations of advocacy groups, I contend that the answer to this question is a resounding, "No." So, what is the real reason behind the anti-Reid movement?

The Reid Technique Works When Used Correctly

As noted by Johnson and Drucker (2009), "The Inbau-Reid modern psychological interrogation approach can be effective in securing 'confessions' from suspects" (p. 68). In other words, even academia has to admit that the Reid Technique works. Moreover, the creators of this interrogative technique have maintained in their training that nothing should ever be said or done during the interrogative process that would lead an innocent person to confess falsely (Johnson & Drucker, 2009). While the book *Criminal Interrogation and Confessions*, co-written by Inbau and Reid, is now in its fifth edition, the authors have warned since the first edition in 1962 that physical abuse of a subject can lead to false confessions (Fortin, 2019). This demonstrates that from its earliest beginnings, the Reid Technique and those who have taught it to countless law enforcement officers around the world, have acknowledged the existence of false confessions and have actively warned against methods that could cause false confessions to be elicited. In short, the Reid Technique does not actually teach abusive interrogative strategies to law enforcement. In fact, John E. Reid and Associates has argued that false confessions occur not when the Reid Technique is employed, but when the Reid Technique is employed incorrectly, such as when investigators physically abuse a subject or fail to take appropriate precautions when dealing with adolescent subjects (Fortin, 2019).

The Reid Technique boasts a success rate in obtaining confessions from criminal subjects 85-90% of the time when properly employed (Sanow, 2011). More specifically, it is suggested that the Reid Technique should be thought of:

> in the same way as the basic negotiation techniques used by
> crisis negotiators: know when to talk and when to listen; know

what "hooks" to listen for; know what changes to look for, when the changes should occur; know when to be stern, frank, open, honest, insistent, and when to interrupt; know what to ignore and what to cut off; and know when to be caring, empathetic and understanding (Sanow, 2011, p. 1).

As stated above, the methods of the Reid Technique are not unusual or overly coercive. In fact, even those in academia are forced to note the simple fact that the Reid Technique teaches students to interrogate in an ethical manner. For example, Leo (2007) admits that, "The Reid and Associates police interrogation training manual specifically recommends that police interrogate for no longer than four hours absent 'exceptional situations' and that 'most cases require considerably fewer than four hours'" (p. 711). Schatz (2018) highlights that, "The Reid Method handbook considers it 'highly important' to 'let the confessor supply the details of the occurrence'" and "The truthfulness of a confession should be questioned . . . when the suspect is unable to provide any corroboration beyond the statement, 'I did it'" (p. 667). Similarly, Schatz states that, "The Reid handbook itself recognizes that a suspect with a 'mental . . . condition may offer misleading behaviors'" (p. 666). Even when it comes to making sure officers don't deliberately or accidentally feed case facts to criminal subjects to bolster their confessions, Joselow (2019) concedes that, "the Reid Technique and other police training emphasize avoidance of disclosing key facts in order to properly test a suspect's knowledge" (p. 1648). Lastly, in discussing the inappropriateness of threatening subjects or promising them leniency, Redlich et al. (2011) cited the following passage from the Reid manual:

> Psychologically, a promise of leniency has a much lesser persuasive impact on a person's decision to confess than when the promise is coupled with a threat... Because this incentive could cause an innocent person to confess, it is improper (p. 414).

While it is important to note that the creators of the Reid Technique go out of their way to ensure that the end users of their method employ the technique in a proper and ethical manner, it may be even more important to realize that some of the biggest detractors of the Reid Technique (i.e., academics studying the false confession phenomenon) are keenly aware of this fact. In other words, the Reid Technique thoroughly disavows unethical and abusive interrogative behavior and many in academia know it. Yet, this does not stop some academic researchers, expert witnesses, defense attorneys, and even Hollywood production companies from continuing to advance the lie that the Reid Technique is synonymous with the overly abusive and coercive questioning of criminal subjects. The reason for this persistent attack may stem from the very success of the technique itself.

In taking the time to actually consult with law enforcement officers, Frantzen (2010) noted that offering criminal subjects moral justifications and psychological excuses, as is taught in the Reid Technique, are among the most effective interrogative strategies. Goodman (2006) also concluded that the Reid Technique is not an inherently coercive method of interrogation and, when used appropriately, it does not violate a subject's Fifth Amendment right against self-incrimination or their Fourteenth Amendment right to due process. Similarly, Frumkin (2019) stated that, "The Reid interrogation method and its various offshoots are highly effective and serve the purpose of getting truly guilty individuals to confess" (p. 15). Even in my own study, the state and federal law enforcement polygraph examiners I interviewed identified that Reid-like methods are very helpful in encouraging a truly guilty subject to admit to their criminal transgressions.

The reason that the Reid Technique has proven to be so popular is based on the fact that many law enforcement officers, especially those who routinely employ the Reid Technique, find it to be highly effective. In short . . . it works. This may not only explain why it has been taught to innumerable law enforcement officers across the world for the last 70 years, but also why courts refuse to dismiss the technique outright as overly coercive. It may very well be that the U.S. court system's refusal to universally dismiss the Reid Technique as overly coercive may have served to delineate the location of the current battlefield. It appears that some academic researchers, expert witnesses, and defense attorneys have come to realize that if there is any chance of mounting an effective legal defense for those subjects who have chosen to confess their criminal misdeeds to law enforcement, triers of fact must become convinced that the Reid Technique and similar interrogative methods are instruments of abject oppression. Interestingly enough, the success of the Reid Technique may actually be measured by the very fervor with which it is attacked. In light of the obvious bias against not only law enforcement, but quite possibly against the successful prosecution of criminal subjects in general, it is not surprising that some have set their sights on the very interrogative method that has proven to be so successful in eliciting truthful confessions. Moreover, it seems as if the agreed upon means of convincing judges and juries of the evils of the Reid Technique is to use inherently flawed academic research designs and their questionable conclusions as proof that the Reid Technique causes innocent people in the real world to falsely confess.

Despite the attack on the Reid Technique, it should be noted that it is not uncommon for law enforcement interrogators to pick and choose from various interrogative methods in developing their own unique style of questioning. This process is quite similar to how each of us has learned to write. In elementary school, we each learned how to make our letters in the same way. In fact, it is highly probable that your classroom had the capital and lowercase version of each letter hanging as a border over the chalkboard. You may have even been tested on how to correctly write your letters with the teacher paying particular attention to whether you touched the top, bottom, and middle lines in the appropriate places. Notwithstanding these efforts to conform our penmanship, as adults our handwriting is nearly as unique as our own fingerprints. Some people can develop immaculate handwriting worthy of a wedding announcement while others develop a style that falls somewhere between chicken scratch and a doctor's handwritten prescription. The same is true of interrogation. Interrogators may be taught the Reid Technique, but later borrow from other techniques, employ methods recommended by fellow officers, and make modifications based on their own interrogative experiences. What's left is a uniquely personal approach to questioning criminal subjects.

Sometimes this makes them better interrogators; sometimes it makes them less effective interrogators; and unfortunately it sometimes, in extreme situations, makes them abusive interrogators. For those who become unethical and abusive in their questioning methods, we cannot assume that because they were at one time trained in the Reid Technique, that the Reid Technique is responsible for their immoral, unethical, and illegal interrogative methods, just as we cannot blame your first-grade teacher for your atrocious penmanship. In both situations, you were taught how to do it correctly. It is ultimately up to you, as an individual, to decide what you do with the instruction you received. This may be why Goodman (2006) suggested that interrogations should be judged on a case-by-case basis to determine if a particular subject's will was overborne during their interrogation rather than broadly defining all psychological interrogative methods, like those taught in the Reid Technique, as coercive. This may also explain why Schatz (2018) made it a point to highlight these words found in the Reid manual:

> When a false confession occurs, it is not the technique that is the genesis, but rather the introduction of an element, most frequently a threat of harm and/or promise of leniency, that violates the best practices described in this text (p. 665).

The truth of this point can immediately be observed in my earlier analysis of the false confession cases presented by the Innocence Project and the National Registry of Exonerations. As was previously discussed, a significant proportion of these cases involved not the use of the Reid Technique, but rather outrageously barbarous methods of questioning. In fact, Redlich et al. (2011) cite Leo in noting that, "In proven false confession cases, police have exerted tremendous amounts of pressure to induce suspects to confess" (p. 395). Beating subjects with nightsticks, threatening to shoot them in the desert, shoving a gun in their mouth, and attempting to suffocate them with a plastic typewriter cover are clearly not taught or recommended in the Reid Technique. As highlighted above, the Reid Technique helped to bring about an end to such abusive interrogative practices. Being that this abusive behavior has largely dissipated, it is now necessary for some academic researchers and expert witnesses to attack the psychological aspects of interrogation.

It is undeniable that there exist academic researchers, expert witnesses, and advocates who hold an open distaste for law enforcement's efforts to elicit truthful confessions, prosecutor's desires to prosecute guilty subjects, and the criminal justice system's responsibility to punish convicted subjects. In fact, even Kassin (2005) notes that, "a warehouse of psychology research suggests that once people form an impression, they unwittingly seek, interpret, and create behavioral data that verify it" (p. 219). If this is true and a bias against the criminal justice system is held by some, there exists a clear motivation for these researchers, expert witnesses, and advocates to attack the most widely-taught and arguably the most effective interrogative method. Afterall, if doubt in the Reid Technique can be fostered, then doubt can be fostered in the minds of every judge and jury presented with a confession elicited by a law enforcement officer who was once trained in the Reid Technique. If this doubt can be successfully cultivated, it becomes a gift that keeps on giving. Still, this is an intellectually lazy argument as it is far easier to cast blame on an entire interrogative method than it is to prove that one particular interrogation was conducted in an abusive and overly coercive manner. Sadly, too many training organizations, consulting firms, and law enforcement agencies have already sought to distance themselves from the time-tested Reid Technique because of the faulty conclusions of flawed academic laboratory experiments with college students. What these groups fail to realize is that when the attack on the Reid Technique is completed, these same academic researchers, expert witnesses, and advocates will redirect their focus on the next successful inter-rogation method. Winston Churchill once defined an appeaser as "one who feeds a crocodile, hoping it will eat him last." For those who have swallowed hook, line, and sinker the false assumption that the Reid Technique causes false confessions, you may want to listen carefully for the growl and hiss behind you . . . it may just be the academic crocodile.

CHAPTER 14

Re-Evaluating the Effects of False Evidence on False Confessions

hroughout the academic literature, it has been suggested that law enforcement officers routinely employ deception in their questioning of criminal subjects. As noted by Gaines (2018), police interrogators routinely employ deceptive techniques "in order to convince the suspect that confession itself is the only way to escape what would otherwise be a far worse outcome" (p. 176). Leo (2007) adds that "police are allowed to lie about anything in the interrogation room so long as it does not violate the Fourteenth Amendment due process voluntariness standard" (p. 717). In fact, the frequency in which law enforcement officers lie to criminal subjects has been depicted as so common and pervasive that American citizens may have come to expect this type of behavior from police. For example, Henkel, Coffman, and Dailey (2008) surveyed citizens across several states and found that the majority of respondents believed that interrogators routinely lie to criminal subjects, especially in regard to the existence of physical evidence that purportedly proves their guilt. Ridiculous and unrepresentative Hollywood portrayals of criminal interrogations also further promote this belief system. Some false confession researchers have gone on to suggest that the deceptive practices utilized by law enforcement officers are unfortunately responsible for the elicitation of false confessions from innocent subjects (Drizin & Colgan, 2004; Forrest, Woody, Brady, Batterman, Stastny, & Bruns, 2012; Gudjonsson, 2003; Kassin, 2005; Perillo & Kassin, 2011).

Lying about the existence of evidence has been reported by some academics to be particularly problematic. However, this approach has not been expressly repudiated by either law enforcement agencies or by the courts. As noted by Kassin (2008):

> American police are permitted to bolster their accusations by
> telling suspects that there is incontrovertible evidence of their
> guilt (e.g., a hair sample, eyewitness identification, or failed lie-
> detector test) – even if no such evidence exists (p. 250).

Both Lackey (2020) and Janda (2015) point to the case of *Frazier v. Cupp* (1969) in highlighting that the Supreme Court has not only deemed it permissible for American law enforcement officers to lie to criminal subjects, but they also clarified that police deception, on its own, does not render a confession involuntary. Still, when it comes to lying about evidence, some courts have drawn a clear distinction between instances in which law enforcement lies about the existence of evidence and situations in which they actually manufacture fake evidence (Janda, 2015). In other words, while it may be permissible to bluff a subject by stating that DNA evidence was found at the scene of the crime, some courts frown on the creation of tangible documents supporting this bluff, such as the creation of phony laboratory reports to bolster the false evidence claims. Janda also identified that some courts have attempted to establish a clear distinction between 'intrinsic' and 'extrinsic' forms of police deception. For example, intrinsic deception was described as untruthful statements or misrepresentations regarding the existence of incriminating evidence (i.e., "We found your fingerprint at the scene of the crime"). Conversely, extrinsic deception was described as deception unrelated to the offense (i.e., promising the subject that a confession will guarantee them salvation, promising them mental health treatment in exchange for their confession, and lying about legal concepts). Janda goes on to identify that in the case of *State v. Kelekolio* (1993), the court reasoned that extrinsic deception is particularly concerning as it is more likely to lead to the elicitation of a false confession. Still, despite conclusory statements like these, Janda is clear in his exasperation that no state court has successfully laid out a comprehensive method for identifying whether a particular interrogative technique is likely to cause a false confession. Instead, while courts may question whether a confession elicited through a deceptive interrogative technique is reliable, they appear to be hesitant to conclusively state that a specific technique is likely to cause an innocent person to confess falsely.

The reluctance of courts to identify specific interrogative techniques as likely to cause a false confession has led many academics to advocate for such conclusions through their inherently flawed research. This advocacy can be readily observed in the continued academic assertion that presenting false evidence to an innocent criminal subject can cause them to falsely confess. A variety of reasons has been offered to support this claim. For example, it has been suggested that fabricated evidence may cause an innocent subject to feel that his situation is hopeless (Gudjonsson, 2003). It has also been theorized that criminal subjects may falsely confess in light of fabricated evidence because they believe that once the evidence is reviewed, their innocence will be proven (Kassin, 2005). In short, some academic researchers, expert witnesses, and advocates have frequently claimed that this form of deception is particularly dangerous. The following is a discussion of some primary techniques that law enforcement reportedly uses to mislead criminal subjects about the evidence against them.

False Evidence Ploy

Kassin (2008) identified the False Evidence Ploy (FEP) as a particularly concerning interrogative strategy. In fact, there exists a substantial body of academic research that purportedly demonstrates that FEPs increase false confession rates (Nash & Wade, 2009; Woody et al., 2018). In this type of approach, law enforcement interrogators attempt to strengthen their accusations by presenting the subject with purportedly overwhelming evidence of their guilt when such evidence does not actually exist (Perillo & Kassin, 2011).

This technique may involve the interrogator falsely informing the subject that their fingerprints, blood, or hair was found at the scene of the crime; an eye-witness has positively identified the subject as the perpetrator; or the subject has failed a polygraph examination relating to their involvement in the criminal act (Perillo & Kassin, 2011). Proof that FEPs can cause false confessions has often been found in existing cases of wrongful conviction. For example, after reviewing false confession wrongful conviction cases in the U.S., it was identified that the FEP technique was employed in numerous cases (Drizin & Leo, 2004; Leo & Ofshe, 1998). Kassin (2005) went even further by claiming that the FEP technique was implicated in the overwhelming majority of cases of false confessions rendered as a result of police inducement.

In addition to FEPs being present in proven cases of false confession, the ability of this technique to reportedly cause false confessions has also been studied by academic researchers within university laboratories. To investigate the relationship between FEPs and false confessions, Kassin and Kiechel (1996) created a seminal research study in which university students were told that they were participating in a computer-based study of reaction times. At the outset of the experiment, students were warned not to press the ALT key on the computer's keyboard as a glitch in the software would cause the computer to crash. Experimenters then deliberately crashed the computer and interrogated the innocent participants about pressing the forbidden ALT key. Half of the participants were presented with false eyewitness testimony that they had been observed pressing the ALT key. Based on the results, Kassin and Kiechel concluded that the presentation of false evidence, particularly false eyewitness testimony, increased the likelihood of a false confession. The ALT key paradigm led to multiple other studies in which the same research design or a similar derivative was used to investigate other factors that may potentially contribute to the rendering of a false confession (Forrest et al., 2006; Forrest, Wadkins, & Miller, 2002; Horselenberg, Merckelbach, & Josephs, 2003; Redlich & Goodman, 2003). In using variations of the ALT key paradigm, researchers have purportedly replicated the effects of FEPs on the elicitation of false confessions (Kassin, 2008). Simply put, many academic researchers, expert witnesses, and advocates appear to operate in near unanimity that presenting subjects with false evidence routinely leads to false confessions.

According to academic researchers studying the false confession phenomenon, the ability of FEPs to increase false confession rates is only half of the problematic equation. The other concern relates to the frequency with which this interrogative technique is employed. Henkel et al. (2008) suggested that the use of the FEP in law enforcement interrogations is commonplace. Similarly, Kassin et al. (2007) documented the fact that nearly all of the law enforcement officers they surveyed (92%) reported using this technique at least some of the time. In essence, the underlying logic goes something like this . . . If cops routinely use FEPs and FEPs cause false confessions, then it can be assumed that false confessions happen routinely. However, while there may be more than one way to skin the idiomatic cat, it should be noted that there is also more than one way to present false evidence to an interrogation subject.

Types of False Evidence Ploys

When FEPs are discussed, it is not uncommon for minds to immediately gravitate to false law enforcement claims that a fingerprint was located at the scene or DNA evidence was retrieved from the victim. Still, it must be highlighted that evidence comes in many forms. So too does the presentation of false evidence. In recognizing this fact, Leo (as cited by Forrest et al., 2012), categorized FEPs into three individual categories:

- Demeanor FEPs. Leo (as cited by Forrest et al., 2012), described Demeanor FEPs as false claims made by interrogators that the subject's appearance or behavior are indicative of the subject's guilt. An example of this type of FEP might sound like this: "It is obvious that you are lying, it's written on your face." (Moston & Stephenson, 1993, p. 107). These types of deceptions give subjects the impression that they are subconsciously leaking out some physical or behavioral clues that the interrogator is able to pick up on. In my experience, I have referenced the look in a person's eyes, the supposed weight on their shoulders, the 'obvious' cathartic release when they have offered an admission, and so on. This type of FEP can be particularly effective in encouraging a subject to provide further information about their wrongdoing by convincing them that their own body and mannerisms are betraying them.

- Testimonial FEPs. According to Leo (as cited by Forrest et al., 2012), Testimonial FEPs involve the interrogator falsely claiming that an eyewitness, co-conspirator, or surveillance video has placed the subject at the scene of the criminal offense. This type of FEP may sound like this: "I know that you committed this crime because two people have already told us that they saw you do it." These types of deceptions suggest that someone or something has identified the subject's involvement. These can be particularly effective as they tap into the subject's inherent and unrelenting fear that maybe someone saw them. This is an even greater worry in light of the modern omnipresence of surveillance cameras, monitors, and cell phone videos. For those who may have engaged in a criminal act with others, Testimonial FEPs also capitalize on a subject's underlying misgivings of whether their co-conspirators can be trusted to keep their mouths shut. Simply put, the strength of these FEPs resides in their very plausibility.

- Scientific FEPs. Leo (as cited by Forrest et al., 2012) described Scientific FEPs as false claims made by the interrogator that the subject has left unequivocal physical evidence like blood or a fingerprint at the crime scene. This type of FEP may sound like this: "We know that you committed this crime because we found your fingerprint on the handle of the knife." Nash and Wade (2009) suggest that the presentation of this type of supposed evidence is designed to elicit a confession by convincing the subject that the evidence against them is overwhelming and conclusive. When FEPs are discussed in the academic literature, it is this type of scientific evidence that is being referenced and it is this type of deception that is most highly protested.

Doctored Video Evidence

While FEPs have been shown to encourage false confessions, Nash and Wade (2009) expanded this concept by investigating whether being presented doctored video evidence, or being informed that video evidence exists, would cause subjects to believe that they are guilty of the specified transgression. In their experimental design, Nash and Wade filmed university students as they participated in a computerized gambling task in which they were instructed to take fake money from a specified stack of cash (identified as the "bank") when correctly answering a question. This was signified by a green check mark appearing on the monitor. Participants were further instructed that when a question was answered incorrectly, they were to return money to the bank. This was signified by a red X appearing on the monitor. The participants were later accused of taking money from the bank even though they had incorrectly answered a question. All of the participants were then told that a video exists in which they are seen taking the money after an incorrectly answered question. Half of the participants were shown a doctored video of them taking money after an incorrectly answered question (i.e., the video was doctored by replacing the green check mark with a red X on the monitor, thereby making it appear as if the participant was taking money from the bank when the question was answered incorrectly). The results indicated that 100% of the participants in each group signed a written confession that they had incorrectly taken the money. Of even greater concern is the fact that the majority of each group (60% and 67%) internalized the confession by coming to believe in their own guilt. It was therefore concluded that the existence of doctored-video evidence can elicit false confessions (Nash & Wade, 2009).

To overcome the potential argument that taking money from the bank on one occasion may have merely been an accidental transgression, Nash and Wade (2009) conducted a second experiment in which participants were accused of incorrectly taking money from the bank on three separate occasions, a reportedly less plausible transgression. In the group that viewed doctored video evidence depicting them incorrectly taking money on three occasions, as well as the group that was simply informed that such evidence exists, 93% signed a written confession that they had incorrectly taken money on all three occasions. For the group that was merely told that this evidence exists, 60% internalized their confession while 87% of those who observed the video internalized their confession. Nash and Wade therefore concluded that even in the event of a less plausible transgression, doctored video evidence can elicit false confessions.

Bluff Technique

The ALT key paradigm put forth by Kassin and Kiechel (1996) was also employed in the study of a lesser form of the FEP identified as the Bluff Technique. According to Perillo and Kassin (2011), the Bluff Technique is a less deceptive version of the FEP in which interrogators pretend to have evidence without specifically stating that this evidence necessarily incriminates the subject. An example may sound something like this: "We have discovered several fingerprints at the crime scene, and they have been sent to the laboratory for analysis." Unlike an FEP in which false evidence is provided that conclusively links the subject to the crime, the Bluff Technique merely gives the subject the impression that future discovery of their guilt is imminent. Perillo and Kassin then conducted a series of three experiments to explore the effects of the Bluff Technique with university students. Two of the experiments involved the ALT key paradigm, and the third involved a version of the cheating paradigm put forth by Russano et al. (2005). In the first two studies, the participants were instructed that they would be participating in a reaction time study and were warned not to press the ALT key because it would cause the computer to crash and research data would be lost. As in previous studies, the computer was deliberately crashed by researchers at which time the participants were questioned about pressing the ALT key. During the course of the ensuing interrogation, some of the participants were 'bluffed.' More specifically, they were falsely informed that their keystrokes had been recorded on a server that could only be accessed once the professor arrived on scene and entered a password. Once the server was accessed, there would be conclusive proof of whether the student did, in fact, press the ALT key. The results of these two studies indicated that participants were more likely to confess when told that their keystrokes had been recorded on a server. Of those who received the Bluff Technique, 75% cited the bluff as the reason they falsely confessed. Interestingly, the false confessors added that they believed that once the actual evidence was analyzed, their innocence would be proven and they would be exonerated.

In the third study, participants who were purportedly recruited to study individual and joint problem-solving tasks, were randomly assigned to either a control group or to a group in which they would be asked by a confederate to help them cheat during the study. In half of the interrogations, the Bluff Technique was employed by informing participants that a hidden camera had been running and was downloaded directly to a hard drive that would soon be accessed. Results indicated that the Bluff Technique caused 50% of the innocents to falsely confess to cheating with 88% citing the Bluff Technique as a reason for their false confession. These findings supported the hypothesis that the Bluff Technique harms the innocent by falsely giving them the impression that an analysis of the bluffed evidence will serve to exonerate them.

The Problem with the Laboratory

A major problem for not only law enforcement officers, but also prosecutors, is their lack of familiarity with research. They hear that an expert witness will be testifying on behalf of the defense, and they become stymied by the expert's reference to the research that supports their conclusions. Sadly, too much deference is given to academic researchers who take the stand and suggest that the confession that was rendered in a particular case may likely have been false. In short, the word 'research' scares both investigators and prosecutors. However, it should never be forgotten that research is not sacrosanct and it is more than deserving of criticism and questioning. The aforementioned studies are a perfect example of this.

Despite the unbridled acclaim heaped upon Kassin and Kiechel (1996) after their creation of the ALT key experiment and the countless other research experiments that followed suit, there are significant problems with this experiment. For example, the participants in this experiment were, as always, college students. It is impossible to avoid seeing the inherent differences between real-world criminal subjects and those individuals who graduated high school, applied to and were accepted at a university, and then volunteered to assist academic researchers in a laboratory study. From the very outset, it is inappropriate to suggest that the decisions and actions of university students in any way reflect the decisions and actions of their criminal counterparts. Similarly, it is important to note that the students in the ALT Key experiment were not accused of engaging in a criminal act. Remember, pressing a forbidden computer key is not criminal in nature. As such, it would also be inappropriate to suggest that what college students do in regard to a non-criminal act has any correlation to what criminal subjects may do when confronted with allegations that they have violated criminal law.

It should also be considered that pressing a computer key, even one that you were instructed not to touch, is not inherently associated with any significant repercussions. Therefore, it would be inappropriate to equate a college student accused of engaging in a non-criminal act that is devoid of any significant repercussions with a criminal subject who stands accused of committing an actual crime that, if found guilty, can be expected to lead to a lengthy prison sentence. In addition, as anyone who has ever typed on a computer has realized, it is sometimes possible to accidentally press the wrong key. These accidents are called 'typos.' In Kassin and Kiechel's (1996) experiment, students were asked to press particular keys while engaged in a reaction time study. As a result, it is not out of the question that a student may think that it is possible that they accidentally pressed the ALT key as they rushed to complete their task. To the contrary, it is improbable for a criminal subject accused of engaging in a bank robbery to similarly conclude that they may have accidentally robbed the bank. In short, it becomes a question of volition. It would therefore be inappropriate to associate an interrogation for a non-criminal act that may have happened accidentally with a criminal act that would have been committed intentionally. Finally, the interrogations conducted in the Kassin and Kiechel experiment were not only conducted by non-law enforcement officers, but they occurred over the course of just a few minutes. This is intrinsically different from a law enforcement interrogation that may have lasted over the course of several hours.

On its face, the renowned ALT Key experiment has absolutely nothing to do with the real world of criminal behavior, criminal investigation, or criminal interrogation. Yet, researchers have no problem pointing to such an unrealistic laboratory experiment to conclude that the use of the FEP can cause a criminal subject to falsely confess to a crime they did not commit. In reality, all that can reliably be concluded from this study is that when college students were falsely informed that they were observed pressing a forbidden computer key (possibly by accident), college students were more likely to falsely confess to doing so. As such, law enforcement officers, prosecutors, judges, and juries should be cautioned about automatically accepting the premise from academic researchers or expert witnesses that the same outcome can be anticipated when applied to a genuine interrogation of an actual criminal subject accused of committing a real-world felony.

The same holds true for the doctored video evidence experiment conducted by Nash and Wade (2009). Again, we are presented with college students engaged in a non-criminal act, although this time it involved taking fake money from different piles. As before, the college students are not criminals; their actions are not criminal; and the repercussions for their 'theft' are non-existent. Like the ALT key experiment, the participants are put in a position where their 'theft' very easily could have occurred accidentally, which may explain why they chose to falsely confess rather than question the doctored video. It is also possible that because there was no anticipated punishment for their 'theft,' participants simply did not care enough about falsely confessing to question the doctored video. I wonder if they would have falsely confessed so readily if they thought that their 'theft' could lead to a failing semester grade or expulsion from the university? Regardless, it is equally inappropriate to apply these findings to the real world of law enforcement. To do so would presuppose that an innocent person would falsely confess to robbing a bank because the police showed him a doctored surveillance video of him conducting the robbery. Again, while this may work with an unimportant and plausible accident, is it likely to work with a premeditated and volitional act of criminality?

As noted above, Perillo and Kassin (2011) reapplied the ALT Key experiment and then added a cheating experiment in an attempt to study the impact of the Bluff Technique. The same problems associated with the artificial laboratory environment continue to exist within this study. However, in this experiment, participants were bluffed into believing that their keystrokes had been recorded on a server which would be analyzed once the professor arrived and entered a required password. Researchers concluded that bluffing a student into believing that such evidence exists increased the likelihood of false confessions. Furthermore, it was highlighted that some students actually confessed falsely because they knew that they would be proven innocent once the keystroke data was reviewed. This led to the outrageous conclusion that some innocent criminal subjects may falsely confess *now* because they know that the evidence will exonerate them *later*. This may be the case for a disinterested university student who may have accidentally hit a computer key but is not expected to face any punishment, and simply does not feel like waiting around until the professor arrives on scene. However, it is hard to accept that an innocent criminal subject would confess to stabbing his wife to death, be handcuffed and arrested, be subjected to pre-trial detention, risk losing his job, face the scorn of his friends, family, and community, and then undergo a thorough lambasting by the media, all under the hope and belief that a future investigation will exonerate him. At best, such a ridiculous interpretation of human behavior is an understandable result of studying such a complex phenomenon in the artificial setting of a university laboratory. At worst, it is a concerted effort by some in academia to defraud judges and juries about the true meaning of their research.

It is also interesting to note that in the study by Perillo and Kassin (2011), 75% of the innocent students who refused to confess falsely also cited the Bluff Technique as their reason *not* to confess. In other words, three quarters of the innocent participants who did not falsely confess likely concluded that there was no reason to falsely confess as they would soon be proven innocent when the professor arrived and accessed the keystroke data on the server. This may be a more pragmatic view of how real-world criminal subjects react to the Bluff Technique. More specifically, their denials may be strengthened in the realization that no incriminating evidence will be uncovered. Although not stressed by the researchers, it cannot be overlooked that the overwhelming majority of innocent students who maintained their innocence did so because they knew that their innocence would be proven. In addition, almost as an afterthought, the authors noted that some participants explained that they deliberately chose to falsely confess because there were low stakes associated with their confession. In other words, these students thought, "What the hell? It's not like I'm going to get into any trouble over this." Buried in a very brief sentence at the tail end of their article, Perillo and Kassin offer a stark yet inconvenient fact; it's very easy to admit to an act that carries no meaningful repercussions.

It is also important to note that at least one attempt to replicate Perillo and Kassin's (2011) study has fallen short. For example, Wilford and Wells (2018) sought to distinguish between false confessions and false guilty pleas in light of the Bluff Technique. In doing so, they employed a cheating paradigm similar to that used by Perillo and Kassin. More specifically, Wilford and Wells recruited 422 undergraduate students to participate in a study regarding how different personality types solve problems individually and in pairs. Each student was introduced to a confederate who was secretly working with the researchers. This confederate encouraged participants to cheat by providing an answer to a problem that was supposed to be solved individually. Those students who helped the confederate cheat were considered guilty. During the subsequent 'interrogation,' some of the students were bluffed into believing that the session was automatically recorded by a pre-existing security camera and that the camera fed directly into a locked server that recorded the video and could only be accessed by an off-campus security firm. In the bluff group, students were told that the professor was already in the process of contacting the security firm to obtain the video that will ultimately determine whether or not the student cheated. Students in the 'No Bluff' category were not presented with this deception.

While similar to the research of Perillo and Kassin (2011), the study by Wilford and Wells (2018) led to two important outcomes. First, Wilford and Wells hypothesized that the bluff outlined above would increase the rate of false confessions from students who did not actually cheat. In discussing their results, they noted that "the false confession rate rose when participants were in the bluff versus the no-bluff condition" (p. 163). Although this may seem like a success to those who propose that the Bluff Technique causes innocent subjects to falsely confess, it is critically important to highlight the end of the aforementioned sentence. While Wilford and Wells *did* observe that bluffed students confessed more than those who were not bluffed, they went on to clarify that "this increase was not statistically significant" (p, 163). In other words, they were "unable to replicate the results of Perillo and Kassin" (p. 166) as the impact of the Bluff Technique on their innocent participants was not as overwhelming as the impact on Perillo and Kassin's participants. Even more interesting is the fact that while Kassin and Perillo reported that not a single 'No Bluff' participant in their study confessed falsely, Wilford and Wells had 23.7% of their 'No Bluff' students falsely confess. Think of that: Wilford and Wells had nearly 24% of their participants falsely confess even though they were never bluffed.

The study by Wilford and Wells (2018) helps to demonstrate that not only may the Bluff Technique *not* be as impactful as originally reported, but some college students were likely to falsely confess for no real reason at all. When this last point is combined with the inherently unrealistic and unimportant nature of academic research designs, it becomes clearer why false confessions may be so easy to elicit in the confines of the university laboratory. As previously discussed, the ethical constraints of human subject research preclude the application of punishment that even remotely begins to approximate the punishments handed down by the criminal justice system. Still, one particular experiment sought to address such issues and, upon bringing even the slightest dose of realism to the laboratory, students began acting in a more realistic and understandable manner.

"I Didn't Break That Lamp!"

In 2013, Cole et al. correctly noted that if empirical research into criminal interrogation is to yield meaningful results, subjects must be placed in various situations in which both innocent and guilty subjects are interrogated. Unfortunately, the ability to do so is greatly hindered by ethical constraints which can render research designs unrealistic and unrepresentative. In light of this reality, Cole et al. turned their attention to the seminal ALT key design conducted by Kassin and Kiechel (1996) which not only served as the impetus for so many other research studies, but also became the basis for the overarching assertion that false confessions are easy to obtain. Cole et al. highlighted that because of the high plausibility that a person may have *accidentally* pressed the wrong key during the typing test portion of the ALT key study, the participants in the study were experiencing a high degree of *uncertainty* about their guilt or innocence. In other words, they suggested that the reason that so many students confessed falsely in the ALT key experiment is because students could not be certain as to whether or not they actually pressed the forbidden ALT key. Still, many researchers largely ignore this sense of uncertainty and instead blame the FEP technique for eliciting false confessions. Sadly, this potentially deliberate oversight has not stopped some academic researchers and expert witnesses from trumpeting the incessant assertion that presenting false evidence during the course of an interrogation can lead to a false confession.

To combat these extraordinary protestations against the interrogative technique of presenting a subject with false evidence of their guilt, Cole et al. (2013) replicated Kassin and Kiechel's (1996) experiment. However, in doing so they made a monumental change to the paradigm. Unlike so many subsequent studies that continued to use the transgression of pressing a forbidden computer key, Cole et al. decided to wrongly accuse students of breaking a lamp. Why is this important? While it is distinctly possible that students in Kassin and Kiechel's study may have accidentally pressed the ALT key without even knowing that they had done so, the students in the Cole et al. study would know conclusively that they had *not* broken the lamp. In their study, 55 college students were recruited through flyers posted around campus. In the flyers, participants were directed to contact the lead researcher to set up an individual appointment in which they would be asked to complete a survey and discuss some of their answers with researchers. Upon arriving for their appointment, participants were escorted to a room down the hall where they could complete their survey in private. The participants entered the room by themselves with instructions to report back to the researcher when they finished the survey. Within the room was a table, chairs, and a broken green banker's desk lamp lying on its side amid broken pieces of glass.

As participants completed their surveys and exited the room to find the researcher, the researcher met them at the door and led the participants back into the room to discuss their survey responses. Upon entering the room, the researcher feigned surprise over the broken lamp and asked each participant, "Did you knock over the lamp?" After receiving the initial denial, the researcher then asked each participant, "Are you sure?" At this point, half of the participants were presented with incriminating false evidence. More specifically, an administrative assistant seated down the hall falsely claimed, "I heard the lamp break while you were in there." The other half of the participants were not presented with this false evidence. Both groups were then asked again, "Are you sure you didn't break the lamp?" After this last accusatory question, the researcher ended the experiment, informed the participants of the nature of the study, and asked them about their perceptions. All of the participants advised that they were aware of the broken lamp and all were certain that they were not responsible for breaking it. Most of the participants explained that while they felt some degree of stress over being falsely accused of breaking the lamp, the majority of the participants did not believe that they would experience any repercussions or punishment.

According to a subsequent analysis of the data by Cole et al. (2013), not a single participant confessed to breaking the lamp or provided any indication that they were somehow responsible. Instead, only strong claims of innocence were received, even when the administrative assistant falsely claimed to have heard the lamp break while the participant was in the room. Cole et al. posited that no false confessions were elicited from these participants because they were absolutely certain that they were not responsible for breaking the lamp. Conversely, they offered that the reason Kassin and Kiechel, as well as the multitude of other researchers that employed a similar typing test, so readily received false confessions was because participants were uncertain of their actual guilt or innocence. In essence, this study suggests that when people are certain of their innocence, they are less likely to confess, even when presented with false evidence. As such, the questionable nature of the ALT key research design has led to an invalid and oft-repeated assertion within the existing literature that false confessions can easily and routinely be elicited when subjects are presented with false evidence.

The work of Cole et al. (2013) helps to demonstrate that when laboratory research even slightly begins to approach the realities of criminal behavior and the criminal justice system, college students act in profoundly different ways. Of course, it is easy to elicit a false confession from a college student who is questioned about pressing a forbidden computer key during a typing test. They simply don't know whether or not they pressed it. Even more importantly, it is highly probable that they did press the ALT key without knowing it. We can expect that false confessions would be even more likely to occur if students knew that they would not be punished for their admissions. Alas, neither of these conditions exist in the real world of criminal investigation. Absent profound mental illness, most subjects know whether or not they committed the crime for which they are now being interrogated. Similarly, unless they are falsely promised immunity from prosecution, most know that their admission of wrongdoing will lead to some form of punishment. This is why laboratory studies designed to examine criminal interrogation and false confessions are so fatally flawed and why their conclusions must be met with a great deal of skepticism. Adding even a minor dose of reality to these designs changes these conclusions in undeniable, though perhaps inconvenient, ways for many academic researchers and expert witnesses. The same holds true when actual interrogative practitioners are questioned about false evidence techniques.

Asking the Experts

In light of the academic concerns over presenting subjects with false evidence of their guilt, however misguided they may be, I decided to ask state and federal law enforcement polygraph examiners in my study for their insights regarding these techniques. The following is a discussion of their responses.

False Evidence Ploy

In inquiring about their thoughts on the FEP technique, I offered participants in my study an example. The example was similar to, "I know that you are responsible for this crime because we found DNA on the victim's body, sent it to the laboratory, and it was conclusively determined that the DNA belongs to you." Upon being questioned about their opinions on this technique, the number of participants who found the FEP technique acceptable was nearly equally split with the number of participants who found it unacceptable. Multiple participants similarly reported that they found the technique both acceptable and unacceptable depending on the circumstances.

The FEP Technique Is Acceptable

Participants offered various reasons for why they found the FEP technique to be an acceptable and justifiable interrogative strategy. The following is a discussion of those reasons:

- <u>It is acceptable to lie in an interrogation</u>. Some participants noted that the FEP technique is acceptable as it is legally permissible for an interrogator to lie to a subject during an interrogation. This point is not unique to the interrogative specialists whom I interviewed. In fact, it is often repeated within the academic literature that lying to a criminal subject has largely been found to be legally permissible by U.S. courts (Janda, 2015; Lackey, 2020; Leo, 2007). For this reason, a number of the state and federal law enforcement polygraph examiners in my study did not have a problem with this type of lie. This is also consistent with an analysis of unpublished research by Stewart et al. (2016) who found that while judges do recognize the deception inherent in the FEP technique, they do not perceive such lies as coercive. In short, it appears that both interrogative specialists and judges do not immediately balk at the idea of presenting subjects with false evidence of their guilt.

- <u>The subject still has options</u>. One participant identified that the FEP technique is acceptable because the lie does not necessarily trap the subject in a box. To the contrary, the subject still has the following options available to them: a) they can admit their crimes; b) they can offer an excuse or possible explanation as to why the evidence against them exists; or c) they can continue to completely deny their involvement in the criminal act. These available options may help to explain why FEPs have not been automatically and unanimously identified as overly coercive by the legal system.

- <u>It only works on the guilty</u>. The FEP technique was found to be acceptable by one participant because of the nature of the technique itself. This participant suggested that if the subject did not commit the crime, then the presentation of false evidence will not cause them concern since they would be certain that they are not responsible for the criminal act. Moreover, it was suggested that an innocent subject will remain confident of their innocence in light of the false evidence because they will know that they were not there and they will conclude that the interrogator is "full of crap." As such, innocent subjects presented with false evidence are unlikely to render a false confession. Conversely, the truly guilty subject would have a great deal of concern in the presence of the false evidence that was presented because they would know that they had, in fact, committed the crime under investigation. This is consistent with the findings of Redlich et al. (2011) who, after comparing true and false confessions among individuals with serious mental illness, concluded that subjects who truly confessed perceived the proof against them to be significantly greater than those who confessed falsely. Redlich et al. added that this was not surprising "given that in false confessions cases, there should be no "real" evidence" (p. 414). We can therefore extrapolate this point to mean that false evidence (which may in fact be true evidence) holds greater sway over a guilty subject than false evidence (which cannot possibly be true) holds over an innocent subject. Simply put, the FEP technique is likely to only work on the guilty.

To illustrate this point, the aforementioned participant in my study noted a situation in which he used the FEP technique with a subject who ultimately proved to be innocent. Upon hearing the false evidence that the participant provided, the subject responded to him by stating simply, "Good luck with that" and then ended the interrogation. For this particular participant, this situation served as an example of how an innocent person will not be swayed by false evidence of their purported guilt. Another participant reported that he employed the FEP technique during an interrogation he conducted prior to becoming a polygraph examiner. This participant explained that he had created a false laboratory report that indicated that the suspected bank robber's fingerprints were located on a bank robbery demand note. Although the participant never showed the subject the lab report, he informed the subject that he had the report in his possession at which time the subject subsequently confessed. This participant offered this situation as an example of how the FEP technique can work on a truly guilty party. In this particular case, the subject did not even need to review the fabricated laboratory report before confessing because he was certain of his guilt and the faked evidence he was presented was distinctly plausible.

The FEP Technique Is Unacceptable

While many of the participants identified the FEP technique as acceptable, a nearly equal number of participants identified it as an unacceptable interrogative method. Participants offered various reasons for this conclusion.

- Catching you in a lie. Despite the fact that some participants have used the FEP technique in the past, many of the participants offered that it is a technique that can easily backfire. For example, some participants suggested that anyone with some level of intelligence who identified the presentation of false evidence as a lie would likely be strengthened in their denials because they would know that the interrogator was lying to them. Participants offered examples of how this could occur by suggesting that the subject may never have touched the victim's body, or they may have worn gloves or a condom during the commission of the crime. If the interrogator then falsely claimed that the subject's fingerprints or DNA were found at the crime scene, the subject would readily be able to identify the false evidence as a lie. As noted by Stewart et al. (2016), the authors of the Reid Technique specifically address the possibility of the FEP backfiring in such a manner and caution practitioners who are considering its use.

- Losing credibility. The majority of the participants in my study identified that being caught in such a lie would be a tragic error on behalf of the interrogator because the interrogator would instantly lose all credibility and trust that he or she had tried so hard to establish with the subject during the course of the interrogation. Essentially, this is the photo negative argument to the need for trust while questioning a criminal subject. As previously discussed, the interrogative specialists whom I interviewed routinely noted how important it is for a subject to develop trust in the law enforcement officer who is questioning them. If trust is a critical ingredient in successfully eliciting a truthful confession, then getting caught in a lie about existing evidence can only serve to torpedo the interrogation.

- Destroying rapport. One participant advised that the FEP is a "fine line" because while it allows the interrogator to see how the subject will react when being presented with false evidence, the interrogator also runs the risk of destroying rapport if the subject is caught in a lie. One participant recalled a situation in which a detective lied to a subject by stating that they found the subject's DNA at the scene of the crime when, in reality, the subject burned the clothing that he was wearing at the time of the offense. The participant with whom I spoke was then called in, built his own rapport with the subject, and eventually elicited a true confession. The subject then explained to the participant that he did not confess to the initial detective because he had lied to the subject. In light of this experience, this particular participant suggested that the risks of lying to a subject about non-existent evidence far outweigh the potential benefits.

- Trying to trick me. Some participants also suggested that if the subject catches the interrogator in a lie, they will come to the conclusion that the interrogator is not actually an ally, but is rather one more law enforcement officer who is out to get them. This can be particularly problematic for those interrogative subjects who suffer any degree of paranoia or maintain a strong distrust of police based on their previous experiences with the criminal justice system.

- "You got nothing." Participants also stated that catching an interrogator in a lie while presenting false evidence can cause the subject to conclude that if the interrogator has to lie in such a manner, then the interrogator must not have any real evidence against them. This may then cause the subject to gain confidence that all they have to do is keep denying their crime because the interrogator does not have any facts or evidence linking them to the crime being investigated. This will embolden the subject and encourage them to continue their denials or simply cause a subject to shut down and terminate the interview. Either way, some of the interrogative specialists I interviewed noted that getting caught in this type of lie may drastically decrease the likelihood of a truthful confession.

In light of the concerns outlined above, one participant described the interrogator's use of the FEP technique as "playing a card that he doesn't have." As a result, many of the participants offered various reasons for why they are hesitant to employ the FEP technique. For example, one participant reported that he does his best not to lie to the subject about things in which the participant could be readily caught in a lie. Instead, the participant prefers to use "inferences" that may be suggestive of a subject's guilt. Similarly, another participant advised that while he has used the FEP technique previously, he does not like using it unless there is a good chance that the false evidence could likely be true. Yet another participant cautioned that it is very important for an interrogator to do their research before using this technique by reviewing evidence and case facts so that they do not use a lie that cannot be backed up. Multiple participants also noted that they would never use such false evidence as the only purported proof of the subject's guilt. Instead, the participants advised that they would only use this technique if additional case facts and evidence indicative of the subject's guilt were available.

The acceptability of the FEP technique was also reported to depend on the type of false evidence used and the manner in which it is presented. For example, one participant identified that it is illegal to create a false laboratory report because this piece of false evidence would have to be presented in court. This "looks shady to the public" and leads the jury to wonder what else the law enforcement officer has fabricated. In other words, law enforcement interrogators who employ the FEP technique run the risk of looking bad in front of judges and juries.

Other participants offered that the manner in which the false evidence is presented also plays a critical role. To clarify this position, one participant noted that there is a difference between telling a subject, "We found your semen inside of the victim," and asking a subject, "Is there any reason we will find your semen inside of the victim?" While in the first presentation the interrogator runs the risk of being caught in a lie and losing credibility, the second presentation merely encourages the subject to offer an explanation as to why the evidence might exist. It was therefore suggested that if an interrogator was going to present false evidence, they should avoid doing so in such an inarguable and accusatory manner. Instead, one participant advised that they would be more apt to tell a subject, "What if I was to tell you I found your fingerprints at the scene?" Instead of accusing the subject, this type of presentation was suggested to simply leave the subject wondering whether the interrogator actually had such evidence or not. In short, it does not commit the interrogator to a known lie.

Overall, the majority of the state and federal polygraph examiners I interviewed reported that the FEP technique is acceptable as it is legally permissible to lie to a criminal subject. The acceptability of the FEP method also relied on the belief that when presented with false evidence of their guilt, an innocent subject will remain confident in their innocence since: a) they are certain that they did not commit the crime; b) the police therefore could not possibly have the evidence that they are claiming; and c) they will immediately conclude that the interrogator is lying. Ultimately, it was suggested that these factors may combine to significantly decrease the likelihood of a false confession. Still, some of the participants in my study suggested that lying to a subject about evidence is "bad practice" and that better approaches are available to law enforcement interrogators. As noted by one participant, presenting false evidence to a subject feels like a law enforcement officer is sacrificing their own integrity while simultaneously imploring the subject to be truthful with the interrogator.

Some participants offered that outright claiming that the interrogator is in possession of evidence that conclusively proves the subject's guilt, such as DNA evidence or a false scientific report "crosses the line." This technique was also described by some participants as not only "unacceptable," but "unethical," and "not right." One participant stated that in his assigned jurisdiction, a confession obtained through the use of false evidence would invariably be suppressed by the court. Another participant noted that if she expects the subject to be truthful with her, then she should be truthful with the subject to a certain extent as well. Some participants also reported that it would be unacceptable if the FEP technique is used without supporting evidence or case facts. Whereas some of the participants identified that they try to only use this technique when they have a reasonable belief that the false evidence is likely true, one participant suggested that the FEP technique is unacceptable if an interrogator is simply making a "stab in the dark" by randomly lying about case evidence to a subject.

It is important to identify that some participants concluded that the FEP technique is also unacceptable based on the impact that this technique may have on the elicitation of a false confession. For example, a participant reported that it is possible that the FEP technique may psychologically force a subject to confess. Another participant suggested that the FEP technique, when combined with an aggressive interrogator and a subject of low intelligence, could potentially cause a false confession. Others stated that when an interrogator falsely provides a subject with scientific evidence (like DNA evidence) that is highly suggestive of guilt and then combines this false presentation with a promise of leniency, the likelihood of a false confession may be increased. In short, for those participants who believed that the FEP technique could potentially cause a false confession, it would have to be combined with an abusive or unethical interrogation and/or a high-risk subject. So, while many of the participants considered the FEP technique to be acceptable, the majority were disinclined to use it as it was risky to both the interrogation and the voluntariness of the confession.

The Bluff Technique

In questioning state and federal law enforcement polygraph examiners about the Bluff Technique, I again provided an example of what this technique may sound like. More specifically, I asked participants what they thought about the interrogator bluffing the subject by saying something similar to, "You know, we found fingerprints at the scene and it is only a matter of time before we know who did this." All 23 participants reported that they found this to be an acceptable interrogative technique, and many of the participants admitted that they have employed this interrogative technique in the past. Participants offered various reasons for why this technique is acceptable.

- Non-accusatorial. Unlike the FEP technique, many participants identified the Bluff Technique as non-accusatorial and more of an "innuendo" or "suggestion" as opposed to an outright accusation of guilt. Because this method does not cite specific evidence that directly accuses the subject of a crime like the FEP and merely presents the subject with the possibility that evidence of their guilt may be found, many participants suggested that this approach is acceptable and is relatively devoid of coercion.

- Protection of the interrogator's credibility. Participants also reported that since the Bluff Technique does not specifically accuse the subject of criminality through the direct presentation of false evidence, the Bluff Technique protects the interrogator from being caught in a lie. As noted by two participants, the benefit of this technique is that it keeps the interrogator's "credibility in check" because the interrogator is not actually putting their "word on the line." In short, since the interrogator is not outright telling the subject that his fingerprint was found at the scene of the crime, the bluff falls far short of accusing the subject and greatly minimizes the risk that the interrogator will be caught in an obvious lie.

- The bluff may be true. In addition to the lack of a direct accusation, several participants suggested that the Bluff Technique is an acceptable interrogative strategy because of its very plausibility. In essence, a bluff similar to a fingerprint being found at the scene of the crime and subsequently analyzed by forensic personnel is not only inherently feasible, but highly probable. Anyone who has ever watched a police drama has observed an evidence technician dusting for prints, swabbing a steering wheel for DNA, or using a pencil to pick up a discarded revolver by the trigger guard. Yet these investigatory actions are not simply relegated to the scripted behaviors of Hollywood extras. Even several of the participants in my study noted that a logical investigation is likely to involve such evidentiary techniques as analyzing fingerprints and DNA collected from the crime scene. For this reason, participants offered that an interrogator's decision to bluff a subject about physical evidence currently being analyzed by laboratory officials cannot automatically be construed as a deceptive statement. To the contrary, it is the very feasibility of the bluff that caused some interrogative specialists to identify the Bluff Technique as acceptable.

- It works on the guilty, but protects the innocent – In addition to its effectiveness in convincing the guilty to confess, many of the participants also found the Bluff Technique to be an acceptable practice based on its foreseeable protection of innocent subjects. These participants suggested that when the Bluff Technique is employed, the truly guilty person will come to the conclusion that once the evidence is analyzed, their guilt will be made clear to investigating officials, and they will "know that they are caught." Metaphorically, the guilty subject will know that their goose is cooked. However, these same participants also noted that the Bluff Technique will actually strengthen or bolster the innocent subject's denials of wrongdoing and cause them to "hunker down" during the interrogation because they will know that the analysis of the purported evidence will soon prove their innocence. This position is consistent with the fact that

75% of the innocent students in the study by Perillo and Kassin (2011) reported that they refused to falsely confess when bluffed as they knew that the evidence being analyzed would soon prove their innocence. As some participants suggested, the innocent subject will be "thankful" that exonerating evidence will soon become available. While some academic researchers absurdly put forth the notion that a truly innocent subject in a criminal investigation will confess to a crime now because they know that the evidence will prove their innocence later, participants in my study suggested that this news will lead to the exact opposite response. In fact, such a bluff may actually encourage the subject, regardless of their guilt, to end the interview prematurely. For example, an innocent subject, upon hearing that evidence is being analyzed and knowing that it will prove their innocence, may conclude that there is no reason to continue speaking with the interrogator since investigators will soon realize conclusively and without a doubt that they have the wrong person. It is also possible that a truly guilty subject who is either confident that they did not leave a fingerprint at the scene and/or who is anxious to leave the interrogation room may try to use the anticipated delay associated with the laboratory analysis as a means to escape current questioning. In short, both the innocent and guilty subjects may take an approach of, "Let me know when the results are in" and walk out of the interrogation room.

- Alternative wording – Despite the unanimous agreement that the Bluff Technique is an acceptable interrogative strategy, multiple participants advised that they would not necessarily word a bluff in the same manner that I did in my example. Instead, they suggested that they would be more inclined to ask the subject a question similar to: "Is there any reason that we're going to find your fingerprint on that door?" Another participant advised that they would say something similar to, "They found a fingerprint. Will it be yours once it's examined?" or "If it comes back as yours, will you be able to explain it?" Participants suggested that wording the bluff in this manner encourages the subject to provide an explanation in advance of the purported laboratory analysis that may contradict previous statements made by the subject. As such, the Bluff Technique may not be used solely as a means of persuading the subject to admit their involvement in the crime. Instead, it may be used to observe their behavioral and emotional responses subsequent to the bluff and gradually chip away at their denials by highlighting their inconsistent statements.

Summary

A review of false confession cases identified that the FEP technique was frequently used during interrogations in which false confessions were elicited (Drizin & Leo, 2004; Kassin, 2005; Leo & Ofshe, 1998). In their laboratory experiments with university students who engaged in a minor infraction, Kassin and Kiechel (1996) concluded that the presentation of false evidence increased the likelihood of a false confession. Henkel et al. (2008) suggested that the use of the FEP technique in law enforcement interrogations is commonplace, and Kassin et al. (2007) identified that 92% of the law enforcement officers that they surveyed reported using the FEP technique at least some of the time. However, the participants in my study were split as to whether they found the FEP technique to be an acceptable practice. Those who found it acceptable offered various explanations for this opinion to include: a) it is legally permissible for an interrogator to lie to a subject during an interrogation, b) it does not necessarily trap the subject in a box because they still have the options of admitting their crimes, offering an excuse as to why the evidence against them exists, or continue denying their criminal actions, and c) it only works on the guilty as the innocent subject will know that the false evidence is not plausible. Those participants who found the FEP technique unacceptable similarly offered explanations for their opinion to include: a) it is perceived as unethical, b) it can potentially cause a false confession when used by an overly aggressive interrogator or against a high-risk subject, and c) it could potentially backfire on the interrogator in a variety of ways.

The majority of the participants, even those who suggested that the FEP technique is acceptable, identified that it is very easy for this technique to backfire and can destroy any trust or rapport that may have been established during the course of the interrogation. In addition, participants reported that if the interrogator is caught in a lie, the subject will shut down, increase their denials, refuse to confess, and possibly even end the interrogation because they will know that the interrogator has no proof or evidence of their guilt if they are forced to lie during the interrogation. The participants' insights about the potential downside of being caught in a lie while employing the FEP technique are supported by the findings of Kebbell et al. (2006) who conducted a laboratory experiment with university students and concluded that when students were able to identify the evidence against them as a lie, they were less likely to confess. Based on this finding, Kebbell et al. concluded that it is critically important that law enforcement officers present accurate evidence to criminal subjects since inaccurate evidence will decrease the likelihood of a confession. Similarly, the Wisconsin Criminal Justice Commission (2007) suggested that: a) the FEP can cause the subject to catch the interrogator in a lie that will negatively impact their ability to obtain a confession; b) false evidence can cause the truly guilty subject to strengthen their denials because they now realize that the interrogator is lying; and c) a truly innocent subject will be bolstered in their claims of innocence because evidence of their guilt could not possibly exist since they were not involved in the crime. In light of these concerns, real-world interrogators should be mindful to only use the FEP technique if they are relatively certain that the false evidence they presented to the subject was true.

As noted in this chapter, because the FEP technique is so fraught with potential dangers, it may not be as frequently used as some false confession researchers claim. In addition, based on the experiences and insights of the participants in my study, it appears that the FEP technique alone may not be enough to convince an innocent subject to falsely confess. The reasons for this are twofold: a) an innocent person will know that they were not involved and evidence of their guilt could therefore not exist; and b) like the guilty subject who catches the interrogator in a lie, an innocent subject who identifies the evidence as false will come to realize that the interrogator has no idea about the crime and has simply been pushed to such levels of desperation that he/she has to tell lies.

Unlike the FEP technique which involves false evidence that conclusively links the subject to the crime, the Bluff Technique merely infers that the discovery of the truly guilty subject's identity is imminent. It is important to note that while some researchers have suggested that the Bluff Technique can cause false confessions, the participants in my study found it to be an acceptable interrogative practice. Various reasons were offered for this opinion to include: a) the Bluff Technique was not accusatorial, b) the interrogator's credibility remained intact because they could not be caught in a lie, c) there is a very real possibility that the techniques forming the basis of the bluff will actually be conducted as part of a logical investigation, and d) it protects the innocent subject by causing them to strengthen their denials knowing that the soon-to-be analyzed evidence will finally prove their innocence.

The information provided by the participants in the current study contradicts the findings of Perillo and Kassin (2011). More specifically, while Perillo and Kassin suggested that the Bluff Technique increases false confessions, the participants in my study, based on their knowledge and experience in criminal interrogation, suggested that the Bluff Technique actually disincentivizes a subject from falsely confessing. Participants reported that claiming that evidence will soon be analyzed that will conclusively identify the truly guilty party reinforces the fact that the subject will soon be exonerated. These diametrically opposed conclusions relating to the Bluff Technique exemplify the problem with unrealistic laboratory experiments that do not accurately reflect the stark realities of the criminal justice system. Perhaps the fact that so many students confess falsely in the laboratory has more to do with the insignificance of the offenses than the inherent coercion of the

Bluff Technique. This begs the question: Would these students be so ready to render a false confession on the pending analysis of the evidence if they stood accused of bank robbery, rape, or murder? Based on the insights of state and federal law enforcement polygraph examiners who specialize in the interrogation of criminal subjects suspected of violating serious criminal laws, this does not seem likely. In fact, the participants' opinions are supported by the additional findings of Perillo and Kassin which indicated that 75% of the innocent students in their study also cited the Bluff Technique as the reason why they refused to admit to an offense they did not commit. This finding, when combined with the information provided by the participants in my study, may suggest that the Bluff Technique is actually more likely to encourage innocent subjects to maintain their innocence than it is to cause them to falsely confess.

Based on the information outlined above, one thing is certain; it is highly inappropriate, and dare I say unethical, to assume that the laboratory conclusions relating to false evidence apply equally to the presentation of false evidence in the real world. Yes, college students may falsely confess in the laboratory when the FEP or the Bluff Technique are used. However, it is a tremendous leap of faith to assume that the same behavior takes place among criminal subjects in the actual criminal justice system. In the real world, would an innocent man confess to raping a young girl because the interrogator falsely claimed to have found the man's DNA inside the child? In the real world, would an innocent person admit to robbing a liquor store because there is doctored video evidence showing him doing so? In the real world, would an innocent person confess to stabbing his fiancé to death because he believes the evidence will prove him innocent later? These are the kind of questions we must ask and answer before we assume that the conclusions of artificial laboratory experiments automatically apply to the realities of the criminal justice system.

It is important to note that FEPs are generally considered legal and constitutional so long as they do not include the fabrication of physical evidence that can persist outside of the interrogation room or otherwise be excessively coercive (Woody & Forrest, 2009). This would include the creation of false lab reports, fabricated audiotapes of a law enforcement officer pretending to be an eyewitness, and so on. Moreover, despite their repeated claims that the presentation of false evidence leads to false confessions, it cannot be overlooked that even some academic researchers and expert witnesses must admit that this interrogative approach is effective in the elicitation of truthful confessions (Jayne & Buckley, 1999, Leo & Liu, 2009). In short, presenting false evidence has proven effective in getting guilty people to confess their crimes. In addition, there appears to be some disagreement about how influential false evidence can be. For example, Kassin and Gudjonsson (2004) believe that the presentation of false evidence on its own is enough to make an innocent person falsely confess. Conversely, Ofshe and Leo (1997) offer that an FEP alone may not be sufficient to cause a false confession. In essence, even the purported experts cannot agree on how powerful this type of interrogative technique may be. This becomes a problem for the academics and expert witnesses who continue to rail against law enforcement officers who choose to present subjects with false evidence.

Kebbell et al. (2006) also noted that if a law enforcement officer presents false evidence to a subject that the subject knows to be inaccurate, they may be less likely to confess because they can prove the evidence is false, and/or the jury may equally determine that the evidence is false. In other words, presenting false evidence can decrease the likelihood of a confession if the subject correctly identifies the evidence as false, thereby potentially making the FEP and the Bluff Technique a risky undertaking. All of this information suggests that the presentation of false evidence in and of itself is not the mother of all techniques. Yes, it is helpful in obtaining truthful confessions from truly guilty subjects. No, it does not automatically cause a false confession outside of laboratory experiments with university students. Yes, it is legally permissible within reason. No, it does not come without the risk of destroying rapport with the subject or bringing a hastened end to the interrogation if the subject catches the interrogator in a lie. To belabor an overused cliché in law enforcement, the False Evidence Ploy and the Bluff Technique are simply tools in the criminal interrogator's tool box. Like any tool or technique, there is a time and place for them to be used and, like any tool or technique, they can be overused or mishandled.

It is also misleading to suggest that the FEP or the Bluff Technique causes false confessions simply because they were employed during an interrogation that led to a proven false confession. Again, it is faulty logic to assume that since a subject falsely confessed, every technique that was used during his interrogation must be responsible for causing the false confession. This is particularly true in light of Drizin and Leo's (2004) observation that the average length of an interrogation leading to a false confession is 16.3 hours. If a criminal subject were to be interrogated for such an outrageously long period of time, it can only be assumed that interrogators threw in every possible interrogative technique they could think of. Is every technique that was employed responsible for the false confession? If so, why didn't the subject immediately confess falsely when they were given a particular technique? Why did it take 16.3 hours to falsely confess? If one particular technique is so overwhelmingly powerful, why wouldn't the interrogator just start off with that technique? If only one technique is responsible for the false confession, how do you select which of the many techniques employed had the biggest influence? These are all logical questions that must be conclusively answered before the FEP and Bluff Technique are impugned. Still one thing remains clear; it is a false assumption to assume that presenting false evidence to a criminal subject automatically causes false confessions.

CHAPTER 15

Is Law Enforcement Capable of Differentiating Between True and False Confessions?

As noted by Woestehoff and Meissner (2016), while jurors may be called upon to evaluate a confession rendered by a criminal subject, confessions are not always reliable. Unfortunately, many Americans automatically accept these confessions at face value (Leo & Davis, 2010). According to some academic researchers, the problem is exacerbated because many Americans believe that law enforcement officers automatically accept false confessions as true and prosecutors automatically use these false confessions to prosecute the subject (Lassiter, 2010; Leo & Davis, 2010). These assumptions stem in part from the belief of some academics, expert witnesses, and wrongful conviction advocates that law enforcement officers can't actually identify a false confession when they are presented with one (Kassin, 2012). Others have suggested that once a law enforcement officer obtains a confession, regardless of the truthfulness of the confession, the law enforcement officer immediately closes the case with no additional investigation (Kassin, 2012; Leo & Davis, 2010). Furthermore, it has been posited that laypeople fail to discount confessions even when they are later retracted by the subject and determined by a judge to have been obtained as a direct result of police coercion (Kassin, 2012). For these reasons, Lassiter (2010) concluded that false confessions virtually guarantee that the innocent person who falsely admits to a crime will ultimately be prosecuted and convicted for that crime. As such, Kassin (2005) noted how vitally important it is for law enforcement officers and prosecutors to accurately identify false confessions when they occur.

While it may be critically important to accurately differentiate between true and false confessions, some in academia maintain that law enforcement officers have a hard time doing so (Bradford & Goodman-Delahunty, 2008; Malloy et al., 2014). In fact, Redlich et al. (2011) point to various studies that suggest that true and false confessions are indistinguishable. One reason for this stems from the fact that in the real world of policing, many false confessions are highly accurate, detailed, and even offer motives for the crime and reports of specific emotions at the time that the offense was committed (Bradford & Goodman-Delahunty, 2008; Kassin, 2012; Perillo & Kassin, 2011). Based on the fact that some false confessions contain true details of the crime to which an innocent person would not be privy, some have suggested that law enforcement officers may inadvertently provide this information to the subject through leading questions, or officers may even outright feed this information to the subject as a means of bolstering the confession (Kassin, 2005; Kassin, 2012). As discussed in an earlier chapter, when the ability of human beings to accurately detect deception has been tested, it has been concluded that distinguishing truth from lies is not an easy undertaking (Levine et al., 2010). Similarly, it has been posited that because false confessions can be so highly believable and appear to lack an obvious motive for deception, they are extremely difficult to identify (Levine et al., 2010).

In an attempt to test the reported difficulty in distinguishing between true and false confessions, Levine et al. (2010) conducted three experiments, yet again with college students, to examine the extent to which truthful confessions and false confessions can be accurately identified. During the first two experiments, students reviewed 27 interviews containing true and false denials as well as true and false confessions. In the first experiment, students were only able to accurately identify a false confession 11.6% of the time. During the second experiment, students accepted false confessions as true 73.7% of the time. As if realizing the inherent weakness in using university students as judges of truthfulness, Levine et al. also sought to test the ability of law enforcement officers in identifying true and false confessions. After conducting a third experiment in which law enforcement officers with varying levels of experience were given a similar task, Levine et al. reported that police officers accurately identified false confessions only 23.4% of the time. Levine et al. therefore concluded that confessions, even false confessions, are more often believed than denials. Yet again, a laboratory experiment is utilized to lend credence to an academic assumption about criminal interrogation. In this case, the assumption is that law enforcement officers are inherently incapable of identifying a false confession when they are presented with one. Unfortunately, the research design left law enforcement officers to consider the truthfulness of a subject in an interrogation they did not personally conduct and for which they had very little, if any, investigative information. Still, it is interesting to note that in the aforementioned study, law enforcement officers were more than twice as likely to identify a false confession than college students. Not surprisingly, the results of the study were not presented through such a pro-law enforcement lens.

While many researchers cling to the belief that a false confession is nearly indiscernible from a true confession, others have noted that clear differences do exist. For example, Ali and Levine (2008) examined the differences in language usage during truthful and deceptive confessions as well as truthful and deceptive denials given by university students during a cheating experiment. Findings indicated that dishonest subjects exhibited fewer negative emotions, less discrepancy, fewer modal verbs, more modifiers, and tended to speak for a longer duration. In my career, I have certainly experienced this last point. For those in law enforcement experienced in interrogating criminal subjects, you may have found that guilty subjects are often difficult to get out of the interrogation room. If you were to directly confront an innocent person about their involvement in a crime, you may find that many times they will not sit and listen to your accusations for very long. At times they may be cordial with you and even express an appreciation for your efforts to solve the crime under investigation before they get up and walk out. Other times, they may accuse you of being full of human excrement before they storm out the door. Either way, practicing interrogators have likely experienced an innocent person's unwillingness to be questioned about a matter for which they were not involved.

To the contrary, experienced interrogators may also note the tendency of guilty subjects to remain in the interrogation room indefinitely. Especially when presented with subjects who have been involved with the criminal justice system on multiple occasions, you may find that they will continue to claim their innocence for hour after hour while exhibiting no overt interest in leaving. This may stem from an underlying belief that they have to convince you of their innocence if they are going to get out from under the current investigation. Similarly, the guilty subject's efforts may be accompanied by statements like, "Listen, if I was involved, I would tell you" or "Why would I lie about this?" In my experience, these tend to be the more experienced criminal subjects who have come to realize that if they appear cooperative and simply maintain their innocence, they will eventually convince you of the same. In these situations, you may find yourself standing up, opening the door, and stepping aside so that the subject can leave, only to have the subject remain seated and continue their denials. The same behavior is not typically observed in the innocent subject who has been wrongfully accused.

Building on the aforementioned research, Villar, Arciuli, and Paterson (2013) attempted to identify linguistic indicator differences between true and false confessions. Villar et al. anticipated that the formulation of a false confession would require the innocent subject to create a statement that includes specific details they may not be aware of such as facts related to the criminal act under investigation. Conversely, a truly guilty person who denies their wrongdoing must suppress their full knowledge of the crime details in feigning their ignorance. In short, while both the false confessor and guilty denier are required to lie, they must do so in different ways. As such, Villar et al. posited that the inherent differences in these two types of lies may impact the use of nouns, verbs, and adjectives. Therefore, they examined the linguistic differences in true and false confessions rendered by university students. The findings indicated that there are measurable linguistic differences between true and false confessions, especially as they relate to the use of adjectives. More specifically, when students provided a false confession, they tended to use fewer adjectives than when they provided a truthful confession (Villar et al., 2013).

Willen and Stromwall (2012) also noticed a difference between true and false admissions of guilt after analyzing the usefulness of the Supreme Court of Sweden's credibility assessment criteria for differentiating true and false confessions. In their study, Willen and Stromwall directed 30 criminal offenders to use their experience in committing a crime to develop a true confession and then manufacture details of a crime they did not commit to develop a false confession. At the conclusion of their study, Willen and Stromwall identified that truthful confessors were much more clear and vivid in their recounting of events than false confessors. Building on this type of research, Villar, Arciuli, and Paterson (2014) directed 85 female undergraduate students to provide a true confession relating to a social transgression that they had recently experienced and felt guilty about and a false confession regarding a social transgression that they were not actually involved in. These true and false confessions were given both orally and in writing. Upon analyzing the confessions, Villar et al. identified that when participants truthfully confessed (both orally and in writing), their confessions included a higher proportion of remorseful words. Moreover, it was identified through an acoustic analysis that participants' remorseful statements were considerably louder in their truthful confessions than in their false confessions. In short, this study suggests that truthful confessors may exhibit more and louder statements of remorse than a false confessor.

Studies like those outlined above are noteworthy as they support the premise that it may, in fact, be possible to actually identify when a confession is false. Still, some academics refuse to believe that law enforcement officers have any ability to identify a false confession when one arises. In fact, Kassin et al. (2005) conducted yet another laboratory experiment to compare university students and law enforcement officers in their ability to successfully differentiate between true and false confessions. In this experiment, Kassin et al. had college students and law enforcement officers watch a video or listen to an audio recording of 10 prison inmates who were asked to truthfully confess to the crime for which they were incarcerated and then falsely confess to a crime that they were provided by the researchers. It was then concluded that university students were more accurate in identifying the truthfulness of a confession than their law enforcement counterparts, partly because of law enforcement's inherent bias toward judging subjects as guilty. In other words, law enforcement officers were yet again disrespected by the incessant academic drumbeat that untrained and inexperienced college students are more skilled in the ways of law enforcement than those who do the job every day. Up until this writing, it appears that no one is willing or brave enough to highlight the very real probability that the problem lies in academia's unceasing reliance on laboratory experimentation with college students. Equally concerning is academia's willingness to so thoroughly trust convicted inmates to follow instructions in these types of studies. Afterall, only the inmates know if the confessions they gave were true or false. Yet, academic researchers have no problem trusting the integrity of people who have already proven that they are inherently untrustworthy.

As with other experiments, the study by Kassin et al. (2005) creates what, in essence, could be considered a game show guessing match as young college students and law enforcement professionals square off against one another to speculate which confession is false. Unfortunately, these types of experiments continue to leave out one key variable—the criminal investigation that necessitated the interview in the first place. Not only are officers in this study again presented with a brief video/audio recording of which they are precluded from asking questions or controlling the interview, but officers are also denied case facts, victim statements, evidence, or any corroborating details like they would have in a real investigation. Simply put, the officers participating in the study have no known truths on which to base the veracity of the confessions that are being given. As such, this study fails to reflect the critical realities of real-world criminal investigation and interrogation. Instead, this study and those like it, are simply identifying who is a better guesser, a college student or a cop? Still, it cannot be forgotten that Kassin et al. did not find either group particularly skilled at distinguishing between true and false confessions. Therefore, while this experiment may be interesting, it really only identified that college participants were slightly better guessers than those in law enforcement. This may not be surprising as college students, based on the very nature of their educational pursuits, are frequently called upon to make an educated guess on tests, homework assignments, or in response to an unexpected question from their professor. Criminal investigators, on the other hand, are asked to develop their investigative theories based on the existence of actual evidence and case facts. As a result, this study may simply be tapping into the guessing abilities of university students rather than accurately identifying the ability of law enforcement officers to recognize a false confession when they hear one.

Identifying a True and False Confession

As opposed to relying on the faulty conclusions of unrealistic laboratory experiments, I decided to ask state and federal law enforcement polygraph examiners who specialize in criminal interrogation if there are ways that they can distinguish between true and false confessions. In response, participants offered a number of ways in which they could differentiate these true confessions from false confessions. The following is a discussion of their responses.

False Confessions

The participants identified the following potential indicators which may suggest that a confession is not truthful.

Inconsistent Information. The participants in my study overwhelmingly reported that they would suspect a confession may be false if the information that the subject provides in the confession does not match existing case facts or evidence. Similarly, it was suggested that if the confession and the facts that comprise the admission of guilt cannot be verified through additional investigation, participants would have concerns about the truthfulness of the confession. As participants had also reported that they review a confession with the subject multiple times during the course of an interrogation, some noted that their concerns would become elevated if the facts provided by the subject appear to change with each reiteration of their story. Suppose for example, that an interrogation subject confesses to the abduction of a child and then states that he entered the home through the child's bedroom window. As the confession is reiterated or written down, the subject then states he jimmied the back door lock to gain entrance. The interrogative specialists whom I interviewed suggested that this change in detail may cause them to start questioning the veracity of the confession.

Insufficient and Unverifiable Details. An additional indicator of a potentially false confession reported by the participants in my study involves a lack of details in the subject's statement. More specifically, the participants identified that they would be suspicious of a confession if the subject was unable to provide details of the crime to include specifics relating to how the crime was committed, the location, the victim, and/or their motive for committing the crime. Not only does such information fill in the blanks for investigators, but it permits an independent verification of the confession. For example, if the aforementioned child abductor claims that he kidnapped, killed, and buried the child, yet is unable to take investigators to where the body is located, law enforcement may be unable to confirm the subject's claims. In essence, if a confession is truthful, the confessor should be able to provide concrete evidence of their involvement such as identifying the location of the victim, identifying the murder weapon, directing investigators to evidence, and so on. For some, proclaiming that, "I committed the crime" may be a great admission, but there should be more to substantiate such a claim. Multiple participants in my study also reported that they would question the veracity of a confession if, when pressed for specifics, the subject responded with comments like "I don't remember" or "I don't know."

Pleasing the Interrogator. Many participants advised that they would suspect that a confession may be false if the subject appeared to simply be agreeing with the interrogator or trying to please him or her as opposed to actually taking ownership for their criminal actions. Therefore, interrogators should be suspicious if the statements of the subject simply sound like the interrogator's own words echoing off the face of a canyon.

Questionable Statements. The participants in my study identified that an additional factor that may be suggestive of a false confession relates to questionable statements made by the subject. The participants clarified that questionable statements immediately before or after the confession may help to identify the confession as false. The following is a list of examples of questionable statements noted by participants that may come immediately *before* the confession:

- "Yeah, if that's why you say I did it . . ."
- "If I say I did it, can I go?"
- "If you want me to admit that I did it . . ."
- "What do you want me to say?"
- "Do you want me to just say this?"
- "You say I did it, so I'll just say, 'I did it.'"

Participants also provided the following list of questionable statements that may be given by the subject *after* the confession, which should also raise concerns:

- "Are you happy now?"
- "There, I said it."
- "Did I tell you what you wanted to hear?"

The kind of statements outlined above should suggest to an interrogator that the subject's confession had more to do with pleasing the interrogator or simply ending the interrogation rather than being a solemn acceptance of responsibility. As such, officers may be well-advised to view with skepticism any information provided immediately before or after such statements.

Ulterior Motives. Participants offered that they would also question the truthfulness of a confession if the subject appears to have ulterior motives for their confession. Such ulterior motives may include a desire for notoriety, the need to protect another person, or the hopes of being charged with a lesser crime. Participants also noted that if the subject appears to be confessing based solely on a motivation to end the interview/interrogation, participants would also be more suspicious of the confession's legitimacy.

Illogical Information. Participants identified that they might consider a confession to be untruthful if it contains inconsistencies and inherently does not seem to make sense. As noted by one participant, a false confession is a lie, and "a lie by its nature doesn't fit." It cannot be forgotten that a false confessor is a liar. As such, they are put in the position of having to fabricate information that will likely appear illogical. This may become increasingly more apparent as the interrogator drills down on specifics. To illustrate this point, I could easily inform a person that I have visited the White House in Washington, DC. While some may believe this statement initially, I would be at a loss if the recipient of my lie asked me to describe what my experience was like. If I were certain that my conversation partner had never been to the White House, then I could easily fabricate information about the check-in procedures I experienced, the route I took through the building, the artwork on the walls, and even the layout of the Oval Office. After all, *they* certainly can't prove me wrong. However, if I tried to feed the same cock and bull story to a member of the uniformed branch of the U.S. Secret Service working at the White House, my lies would quickly become apparent as they are not only incorrect, but highly implausible. Having never been in the White House, I am unable to even make up a semi-realistic lie about such a visit. This is why investigative case facts are so important when interrogating a criminal subject. Knowing the specifics of an event can help law enforcement easily spot inaccurate and implausible claims in a subject's false confession.

Quick Confessions. Some participants reported that in their experience the truth tends to come out a little at a time. As such, they would have concerns about the truthfulness of a confession if the admission of guilt came either too quickly or in one all-encompassing admission. Over the years, I have explained to criminal subjects that telling the truth is a bit like filling a lawn mower from a plastic gas can. For anyone who has engaged in such an act, they may recognize that while gas will pour out of the spout initially, the vacuum caused by the gas leaving the nozzle will eventually cause the initial stream to slow to a trickle. As if taking a breath, the gas can will then suck air into the container and allow another stronger stream of gas to begin again. When criminal subjects confess their crimes, the information tends to come in similar gasps. While they may have started the interrogation with the claim that they were not involved, they may later admit to being at the scene and witnessing the crime. Later on, they may admit to being at the scene and holding the gun, but not firing it. Soon, they may claim that the gun fired accidentally. Then, they may admit that they shot the victim because of her proven infidelity. In essence, confessions often come out bit by bit as the subject becomes more comfortable with each partial recognition of their guilt. Law enforcement interrogators may therefore want to question any confession that comes out too quickly or in one fell swoop.

Explanations and Emotions. Multiple participants explained that a confession is often an emotional and cathartic experience. As a result, they reported that they would be skeptical if they received a confession that did not have some emotional component to it. Similarly, it was offered that there should be some type of explanation for why the subject engaged in the criminal act. Therefore, some participants noted that they would have some reservations about accepting a confession in which the subject did not at least attempt to explain or rationalize their criminal actions. This may, however, depend on the person being interviewed. For example, if the interrogation subject is a psychopath with no feelings of remorse or an antisocial 'frequent flier,' who has been through the system countless times before and lacks any sense of guilt, the interrogator should not anticipate any meaningful degree of emotion. Still, even these types of subjects are likely to offer an explanation for their criminal behavior, even if the explanation is as incomprehensible as, "because I was bored" or "because she pissed me off." Conversely, the first-time criminals like the bank teller who steals from her till, the school teacher who engages in sexual activity with his or her minor student, or the exasperated caregiver who violently shakes the life from the child in their care may be more likely to experience strong emotions or a noticeable change in behavior at the time of their *mea culpa.* After all, this is their first interaction with the harsh realities of the criminal justice system and admitting to their criminal wrongdoing is likely to be accompanied by a flood of new and powerful emotions.

Surprise Confessors. The interrogative specialists interviewed in my study also cautioned about the surprise confessor who shows up at the station unannounced. Officers may want to analyze more deeply a confession from a walk-in who was never considered a subject in the case. This is particularly true if the case under investigation is well-publicized. An example of this phenomenon is reflected in the scores of individuals who reported to authorities that they were responsible for abducting the child of famed American aviator Charles Lindbergh. Such surprise confessors are consistent with the aforementioned possibility that some innocent people may falsely confess as a means of gaining notoriety or to punish themselves for earlier crimes for which they were never caught.

True Confessions

In addition to the reported indicators of a false confession outlined above, the participants in my study also identified the following indicators that would increase their confidence that the confession that they just elicited is true and accurate. While the majority of these true confession indicators are simply the obverse of the false confession indicators, they are nonetheless worthy of discussion.

Consistency with Existing Case Facts. When questioned about how they would go about identifying a truthful confession, the participants unanimously noted that the confession must match, and be consistent with, existing case facts that have not previously been publicized or fed to the subject by law enforcement personnel. This unanimous response not only indicates that these interrogative specialists are mindful of not feeding a subject case information, but it helps to demonstrate why the Kassin et al. (2005) study discussed earlier simply reflects a guessing game between cops and college students. Law enforcement officers in the real world have case facts and evidence on which to base the accuracy of these confessions.

Guilty Knowledge. Multiple participants noted that a truthful confession will likely contain information that only the truly guilty person would know. In providing this answer, multiple participants in my study again reiterated that the interrogator must be careful not to provide this type of knowledge to the subject either accidentally during questioning or deliberately to bolster the confession.

Sufficient and Consistent Detail. Participants in my study also reported that a truthful confession is likely to be detailed and address the "who, what, where, when, and why" of the crime in question. Participants added that these details should remain consistent between the oral, written, and recorded confessions. If sufficient and consistent details are offered, the participants noted that they would feel much more confident that the confession they obtained was truthful.

Subject Behavior and Emotions. Some of the interrogative specialists that I interviewed advised that they determine the truthfulness of a confession based on the subject's behavior. For example, one participant noted that truthful confessions tend to occur 'bit by bit' with the true details of the offense gradually being released by the subject. Other participants reported that they look to the subject's emotions and non-verbal behavior as a means of determining the veracity of the confession. Some participants explained that a subject rendering a truthful confession tends to have some type of physical release at the time of the confession such as a change in expression or posture that would indicate the subject's resignation that the truth of their guilt has finally been disclosed. One participant noted that this release may include the subject tearing up, looking the interrogator directly in the eye, and/or displaying some change in emotion. Another participant identified that he looks for emotion from subjects rendering a truthful confession as their confession will put them in a position in which they have to emotionally and mentally relive the crime as they recall the events surrounding their criminal actions. Other physical indicators suggestive of a truthful confession include the subject dropping their head, crying, and/or other observable indications that the subject is feeling the vulnerability associated with coming clean about their criminal wrongdoing. If these types of emotional and behavioral changes occur during the time of the confession, participants advised that they would have a much greater degree of confidence in the confession.

Testing Confessions. Many participants offered that they actually conduct personal tests to verify the accuracy of the subject's confession. Multiple participants reported that when reviewing the subject's confession, they will ask the subject questions or make statements that deliberately contain false information to see whether the subject corrects the participant or simply agrees with them. The participants do this as a means of testing the subject's veracity. Other participants offered that they deliberately withhold important case facts that only the truly guilty party would know. This is done to verify that the information provided in the confession is truthful. Still other participants advised that they will call upon the lead investigators to either observe the interrogation or enter the interrogation room once the confession is elicited to verify the accuracy and plausibility of the subject's confession. Participants clarified that the lead investigators are called upon in this manner as they have access to significantly more case facts than the participant does as a polygraph examiner.

Summary

As can be observed throughout the existing literature, academic research-ers, expert witnesses, and wrongful conviction advocates like to portray law enforcement officers as inept, bumbling, and unqualified characters who con-tinue to pale in comparison to the much smarter and highly-skilled university student. The supposed inability of law enforcement to differentiate between a true and false confession is yet another example of this belief system. However, when in-depth discussions are had with skilled law enforcement interrogators regarding their approaches to distinguishing between true and false confessions, it appears that there are numerous ways to differentiate fact from fiction. In short, unlike laboratory experimentation, real-world law enforcement officers do not have to simply guess whether the confession they just elicited is truthful. To the contrary, they ask the following questions when assessing the truthfulness of the confession:

- Is it consistent with existing case facts?
- Can the information in the confession be independently verified?
- Does it contain sufficient and consistent details?
- Is it prefaced or followed up by questionable statements that would suggest the subject just wants to leave the room?
- Did it come too quickly?
- Is it logical?
- Is it indicative of ulterior motives like trying to please the interroga-tor, covering up for the truly guilty party, or seeking notoriety?
- Is it accompanied by an emotional or behavioral change?
- Does it contain guilty knowledge that only the true offender would know?
- Does the subject correct the interrogator when they deliberately misrepresent things the subject has said?

In reviewing this list of considerations, it hardly appears that law enforce-ment officers, at least those who specialize in criminal interrogation, simply guess or assume that a confession is truthful. This list also helps to demonstrate just how illogical and unrepresentative the "game show" approach can be when studying false confessions in the laboratory.

Recommendations

Law enforcement officers may wish to ask themselves the aforementioned questions as a means of verifying the veracity of a subject's confession. As mentioned above, some of the participants in my study noted that they will actually test a subject's confession by deliberately misrepresenting or misreporting information that the subject provided. They do this to see if the subject will correct them on this inaccurate information. Such testing allows these participants to see whether the subject's information is consistent, or whether they are simply agreeing with what the interrogator has to say. This is a very important technique which should be employed by all criminal interrogators. As previously outlined, the defense attorney tasked with defending a client who has already confessed to law enforcement will have no other available option than to attack the voluntariness of the defendant's statement. As such, testing the subject's confession will help interrogators defend against the coercion argument if they can demonstrate examples of where the subject fought them on certain information, corrected the interrogator when necessary, and remained consistent when presenting their information.

It is important to note that some academic research actually recommends other ways of testing the truthfulness of the information elicited during a criminal interrogation. Hartwig, Granhag, Stromwall, and Vrij (2005) examined how the timing of the interrogator's disclosure of evidence to the criminal subject may assist in identifying deception exhibited by the subject. In an experiment in which university students engaged in mock criminal activity, Hartwig et al. concluded that when interrogators waited until later in the interrogation to disclose evidence of the subject's guilt, they were able to accurately identify a deceptivestatement 67.6% of the time. In other words, not only does evidence help an interrogator discern when the subject is lying, but strategically waiting until later in the interrogation to provide this evidence to the subject may increase this ability.

Noting that lying is a cognitively demanding activity, Vrij, Fisher, Mann, & Leal (2006) put forth a cognitive load approach to identifying deception in a criminal subject. This cognitive load approach specifies that individuals choosing to lie to investigators are required to engage in numerous extra tasks in an attempt to appear truthful. More specifically, lying subjects must make sure their story remains consistent; they have to correctly assume what the interrogator is actually asking; and they must anticipate future questions. Not only is this a difficult balancing act for the subject, but they must engage in this balancing act while controlling their behavior. Vrij et al. described these tasks as a "cognitive load" and noted that law enforcement officers can become much more adept at identifying deception if they pay attention to, and tax, a person's cognitive load. For example, interrogators may want to have the subject tell their story in reverse order. A lying subject may have only remembered their story in chronological order. Having the subject reverse this order may tax their already overburdened minds and cause them to make mistakes which may indicate deception. Similarly, interrogators may want to distract subjects as they give their statement. For example, the interrogator can interrupt them with clarifying questions or ask them to go back over a particular point. These distractions may also tax the subject's mind and highlight inconsistencies or deception in the subject's statement.

While these techniques were not presented in relation to a subject's actual confession, they can certainly be employed by law enforcement officers to help verify the truthfulness and consistency of a subject's confession. Again, if an officer can take the stand and explain to the judge and jury how they went about testing a subject's confession to verify the confession's accuracy, the officer may effectively take the wind out of the defense attorney's false confession sails. What became abundantly clear during the course of my qualitative interviews with state and federal law enforcement polygraph examiners is that some law enforcement officers, at least those who specialize in criminal interrogation, are capable of identifying numerous ways in which to differentiate between true and false confessions. To assume that law enforcement is completely incapable of distinguishing between the two is yet another example of a false assumption made by many academics studying the false confession phenomenon.

CHAPTER 16

Reassessing the Impact of Confessions on Criminal Subjects

As noted by Kassin (2005), confession evidence is very powerful and has a significant impact both during and after a criminal trial. For some in academia, the subject's decision to confess can lead to "aversive legal, social, or other personal consequences" (Davis & Leo, 2012, p. 678). Some false confession researchers have concluded that people who confess are treated differently and more harshly at every stage of the criminal justice process when compared to their counterparts who refuse to admit wrongdoing. These researchers claim that subjects who confess are more likely to be charged; are more likely to be charged with a greater number of crimes; are less likely to have their cases dismissed; are more likely to have their cases resolved through a plea bargain; are more likely to be found guilty of their crimes, and are more likely to receive harsher punishment once they are convicted (Kassin et al., 2007; Leo & Ofshe, 1998; Drizin & Leo, 2004). It has also been presumed that once a confession is obtained, police automatically accept it as true; they automatically close their case without further investigation; and prosecutors naturally prosecute the subject based on the confession regardless of its truthfulness (Lassiter, 2010; Leo & Davis, 2010). It has similarly been identified as problematic that even defense attorneys tend to give into a feeling of hopelessness when presented with a client who has already rendered a confession (Ofshe & Leo, 1997). Simply put, many in academia have posited that confessions, even truthful confessions, do nothing but harm those individuals who decide to admit to their criminal misdeeds, and they all but guarantee the subject's conviction.

It has not been uncommon in my career for people to confess their crimes to me and then thank me before leaving the room. On occasion, I have even received hugs from subjects at the conclusion of the interrogation as well as an occasional wave or nod as they sit at the defense table in the courtroom. These experiences left me questioning the position that confessions only hurt the subject. I have heard too many times from criminal subjects that the interrogation felt like therapy to believe that confessions are only a negative experience. My professional experiences often stand in direct contrast to the words of Leo (2007) as he spoke to University of Michigan law students during a symposium on false confessions. His views on criminal interrogation and the solely negative impact of criminal confessions are clear in his choice of words.

> Interrogation, psychologically, is a two-step process: convince somebody they're caught, their situation's hopeless, there's no way out, no one's going to believe they're innocent. Decimate their subjective self-confidence that they are going to get out of this without agreeing that they are guilty of something, or they did something, they did the act. And then when you've broken them and destroyed their resistance, convince them that - and this is the counterintuitive part that bedevils lawyers and law professors – that it's somehow in their self-interest, somehow in their self-interest to stop denying and start admitting (pp.715-716).

As a professional interrogator and polygraph examiner who is routinely called upon to question criminal subjects, I can personally attest that the bias dripping from these assertions is inconsistent with the successful elicitation of truthful confessions. I have also been in the company of too many fellow interrogative professionals to believe that I am alone in this realization. In fact, just days before writing this portion of the book, I discussed with a professional colleague and fellow examiner a snarky comment I observed a defense psychologist make during his clinical interview with a criminal subject who had already confessed to sexual contact with a child. Upon reiterating the psychologist's statement, my colleague laughed and remarked, "If they only knew how nice we were to people." I have been a law enforcement officer for too long; I have worked too many cases; and I have obtained too many confessions to unquestioningly accept the premise that confessions do nothing but harm a criminal subject. Similarly, in light of my experiences as a career law enforcement officer, I was left scratching my head at the academic assertion that the receipt of a confession effectively ends the investigative process and guarantees prosecution. As a result, I decided to question state and federal law enforcement polygraph examiners in my study about their opinions on whether confessions benefit or harm a criminal subject and what their experiences were with the legal process after a confession was received. The following is a discussion of their responses to these areas of inquiry.

Does a Confession Benefit or Harm the Subject?

I questioned participants, based on their experiences, as to whether a confession ultimately benefits or harms the subject within the state and federal criminal justice systems where they are employed. My review of their responses identified that there was nearly an equal split with five of the participants responding that a confession ultimately benefits a subject and four responding that a confession ultimately harms the subject. The largest number of respondents (14) responded that a confession both benefits and harms the subject. The following is a discussion of the explanations behind these conclusions.

Confessions Benefit the Subject

The state and federal law enforcement polygraph examiners in my study offered various explanations for why a confession ultimately benefits a subject. These reasons can be broken down into three main categories: a) legal benefits; b) attitudinal benefits; and c) psychological benefits.

Legal Benefits. Federal participants suggested that when a subject renders a confession within the federal criminal justice system, the Federal Sentencing Guidelines generally provide the subject with two points for their acceptance of criminal responsibility. These points ultimately translate into a decrease in the subject's sentence. In addition, participants reported that a confession further benefits a subject because it affords the federal prosecutor the option of charging a subject with a lesser offense which will also translate into a lesser sentence. Participants also noted that once a subject confesses, they are more likely to plead guilty which allows them to receive a better deal from the federal prosecutor. Yet again, this translates into a lesser sentence for those subjects who choose to confess. When taken in totality, the majority of federal law enforcement polygraph examiners questioned for this study suggested that a confession ultimately benefits a criminal subject because they are more likely to receive an overall decrease in their ultimate sentence.

Some federal participants also noted other legal/procedural benefits to confession. For example, one participant identified that when a subject decides to confess, they allow for the full and accurate documentation of what actually occurred. Put another way, the confession benefits the subject personally by affording him an opportunity to "get his story out." Instead of relying on the victim, witness, or prosecutor to outline what took place, a subject that confesses takes control of his own narrative. Similarly, a participant noted that on a limited basis, the subject may benefit by confessing to his actions as the subsequent investigation may identify that the actions taken by the subject were not actually criminal in nature. In other words, subjects who confess may sometimes learn that their actual actions in the matter under investigation may not even be worthy of prosecution based on the information that they provide.

Some of the state polygraph examiners I interviewed also reported that when a criminal subject confesses, it increases the likelihood that the prosecutor will work with the subject and offer them a deal. As noted by one participant, the confession demonstrates that the subject is both cooperative and remorseful. In response, state prosecutors tend to charge the subject with lesser or fewer crimes. As noted by one particular participant, a confession paves the road for the subject to "plead out so they don't get the book thrown at them." In short, 83% of state and federal law enforcement polygraph examiners interviewed for my study reported that in their professional experience as law enforcement officers and interrogators, a confession ultimately benefits the subject because it serves to decrease their eventual sentence. This stands in direct contrast to Drizin and Leo's (2004) proclamation that a confession brings more severe punishment to the criminal subject.

Attitudinal Benefits. Federal participants also identified that criminal subjects experience attitudinal benefits when they confess. Participants reported that the criminal justice system, being that it is comprised of human beings, takes into account a person's acceptance of responsibility. One participant noted that, "When you confess, most humans have a place in their heart for that." Moreover, when the subject's confession is then heard by others, "people want to believe that you are sincere and remorseful" for the criminal acts that you have committed and, "our (legal) system takes that into account." Participants in my study also suggested that while the criminal justice system as a whole may take a subject's acceptance of responsibility into account, the attitudes of those employed within the system are also positively influenced by a subject's confession. As a representative of the federal criminal justice system, one participant commented, "We respect the people who admit their mistakes and fully cooperate." In a similar vein, another participant offered that law enforcement officers and prosecutors like to see people cooperate which, in turn, causes these groups to feel more positively toward subjects who choose to confess. Participants also suggested that when a subject confesses and decides to cooperate, investigators and prosecutors similarly do their best to cooperate with the subject. In other words, we are more likely to cooperate with those who cooperate with us. In light of these attitudinal shifts experienced by criminal justice personnel subsequent to a criminal's confession, participants reported that criminal subjects who admit to, and take responsibility for, their criminal actions are more likely to experience a smoother and more cordial legal process.

Psychological Benefits. Multiple state participants offered that a confession ultimately benefits the subject because of the psychological effects brought about by their admission of wrongdoing. A variety of descriptions of these psychological benefits were given. For example, the participants reported that by confessing, a criminal subject can "take the weight off" and get the "monkey off their back." Moreover, the participants explained that for a criminal subject, "The truth will set you free" as the subject can experience "a (psychological) release" from their admission and feel confident that "the game is over with" and the subject can begin to "move on." One participant noted that a confession is akin to Alcoholics Anonymous (AA) in that criminal subjects can admit that they have a problem so that their healing can begin, and they can finally get the help they need such as drug/alcohol treatment, stress management, anger management, mental health treatment, and/or assistance with their financial problems.

Based on the information provided by these interrogative specialists, it becomes readily apparent that confessions may not solely harm criminal subjects as reported by many academic false confession researchers. To the contrary, those who actually work within the system reported various legal, attitudinal, and psychological benefits to the act of confession. While the overwhelming majority of these interrogative specialists clearly outline such benefits, it would be incorrect to assume that there are no negative repercussions when a criminal subject decides to confess.

Confessions Harm the Subject

While only four (17%) of the state and federal law enforcement polygraph examiners interviewed for my study reported that a confession does nothing but harm the subject; it cannot be overlooked that a total of 78% of the participants reported that some negatives are associated with the subject's confession. The following is a discussion of the harm that can be brought to bear on the criminal confessor.

Evidence Strength. The overwhelming majority of participants suggested that a confession harms the subject because of the strength of confession evidence. Participants reported that a subject's confession to a criminal act is a very strong piece of legal evidence that can be used against a subject at trial and which can prove incredibly difficult for the subject's attorney to defend against. Due to the potency of this type of evidence, many participants reported that a confession ultimately harms the subject because it increases the likelihood that the subject will be prosecuted and convicted. Several participants also noted that a confession is particularly harmful when the case involves very little physical evidence, and the subject may have gotten away with their criminal actions if they had simply remained silent. Another participant reported that in her experience, confessions are often sought when investigators do not have strong evidence against a subject. Both of these statements highlight the fact that it is not in the best interest of a criminal subject to confess when there is a strong possibility that the subject would have escaped any charges or punishment if they maintained their innocence.

Loss of Leverage. While most participants identified the potency of confession evidence as the primary harm brought upon a subject who confesses, one other participant reported that once a subject confesses, they have lost their "leverage" to bargain with federal prosecutors for a lesser charge or sentence. This was perceived as yet another way that confessions ultimately harm a criminal subject.

Are Confessors Treated Differently?

In light of their personal experiences, I questioned state and federal participants about their impressions as to whether criminal subjects are treated differently by the state and federal criminal justice systems when compared to those who choose to continue their denials. In total, 78% of the participants in my study reported that they have noticed a distinct difference in the treatment of criminal subjects who confess as compared to those who refuse to admit their wrongdoing. The following is a discussion of the noted differences in treatment of confessors and non-confessors as reported by the state and federal law enforcement polygraph examiners I interviewed.

Lesser Sentences. As previously mentioned, the majority of the federal participants I interviewed reported that criminal subjects who confess to their crimes tend to receive a lower sentence than those who do not. Again, participants noted that these lower sentences were generally a result of the prosecutor's tendency to charge a confessor with a lesser offense; their tendency to offer the subject a better deal or plea agreement; and their tendency to offer lower sentencing recommendations to the court. Federal participants also advised that the Federal Sentencing Guidelines provide confessors with two points for their acceptance of responsibility which lowers the calculations that ultimately determine their sentence. To the contrary, one participant noted that when a subject fails to admit their crimes and then loses at trial, they tend to have "the book thrown at them."

Similar to the observations of the aforementioned federal participants, most of the state participants reported that they too observed that subjects who confess tend to receive a lesser sentence than those who do not. Although one state participant reported occasionally observing situations in which confessors have gotten "screwed," most state participants noted that when a criminal subject confesses, they typically are permitted to plea to lesser charges, and state prosecutors are more inclined to work with the subject. As such, confessors tend to receive lesser sentences on the state level than their counterparts who continue to deny their criminal wrongdoing. This is particularly true with those confessors who confess and then go on to cooperate against their co-defendants. Still, it is important to note that a few state participants reported that, in their experience, subjects who confess tend to receive harsher sentences. While this supports the views put forth by many in academia, it cannot be overlooked that the vast majority of the state and federal law enforcement polygraph examiners I interviewed reported that confessing to your crime will likely result in a lesser sentence than what can be expected with continued denials.

Smoother Legal Process. In addition to their observations that confessors tend to receive a lesser sentence, federal participants also noted that confessors generally fare better in the criminal justice system process than their counterparts who continue their denials. Multiple participants reported that in their experience, it is typically easier for investigators and prosecutors to work with a subject who confesses their crimes. As one participant reported, "a good conversation" can begin between the investigators and the subject once the subject decides to confess. This generally tends to translate into a subject experiencing a legal process that is much "smoother," more "cordial," and significantly less adversarial.

Federal participants also frequently reported that when criminal subjects confess their crimes, they tend to receive more empathy from the investigators who come to appreciate the subject's willingness to accept responsibility for their actions. On the contrary, participants reported that the same appreciation and empathy is not shown toward those who deny their criminal actions. In fact, some participants reported that investigators tend to work harder against those individuals. One participant commented that from a philosophical position, it is ironic that people are ultimately penalized for using all of the constitutional rights that they are afforded by choosing not to cooperate with the governmental entities bringing a criminal case against them. However, the majority of the participants agreed that those who do confess tend to receive the best possible resolution whereas those who fail to confess and take their matter to trial generally receive the worst possible outcome.

Similar to their federal counterparts, state polygraph examiners in my study also noted that confessors generally receive better treatment as they progress throughout the state legal process. As noted by one state participant, law enforcement officers can actually take offense when a subject fails to confess. This can then cause the officer to become more motivated to work against the subject to prove their guilt and have them punished. Conversely, some state law enforcement polygraph examiners reported that when a subject does confess, they tend to receive more understanding and compassion from those in the criminal justice system. In summary, according to the experiences of most of the state and federal participants with whom I spoke, criminal subjects who confess receive better treatment from those in the criminal justice system than subjects who do not confess.

Are Cases Automatically Closed in Response to a Confession?

In light of the belief held by some academic researchers and expert witnesses that police automatically close their cases once a confession is obtained, I decided to ask state and federal law enforcement polygraph examiners whether they have found this to be true. All of the federal participants reported that cases are *not* automatically closed once a confession is obtained, and all but two of the state participants reported the same. Nearly all of the state and federal participants also noted that despite the elicitation of a confession in a state or federal case, further investigation must be conducted. Participants explained that this additional investigation is designed to "corroborate," "substantiate," "validate," or "verify" the confession rendered by the subject and to collect additional information. Participants also offered that a confession only gives context to the investigation and merely serves to corroborate existing case facts. As such, additional investigation would need to occur. One federal participant noted that the use of additional investigation to corroborate a subject's confession is particularly important to him as he "couldn't sleep at night" knowing that a subject was convicted based on a confession that he elicited and for which there were no supporting case facts. Participants also noted that additional investigation is required subsequent to a confession: a) to identify additional victims, subjects, and witnesses; b) to prove basic facts of the case; c) to collect information from co-conspirators; and d) to confirm that the subject is actually guilty of the crime to which he confessed.

Despite the need for additional investigation subsequent to the elicitation of a criminal confession, several participants suggested that the extent of the subsequent investigation may still be influenced by the receipt of a confession. More specifically, depending on the nature of the offense, it is possible that some investigative measures may not need to be conducted in light of a confession. For example, if the case involved a single offense conducted by a single actor, it would be unnecessary to interview co-conspirators or collect information from additional crime scene locations. Similarly, a confession may serve to focus any subsequent investigative efforts on specific aspects of the specified criminal offense. For example, if a criminal subject were to confess that he/she killed their child and placed them in a specific dumpster, investigators can focus their investigative efforts on the pickups and travels of that particular disposal method rather than organizing vast searches of unrelated areas.

It is important to remember that not all interrogations occur at the start of an investigation. Oftentimes, an interrogation may actually be the last step of an investigation after vast amounts of evidence have been collected. Still, numerous participants in my study noted that even in these situations, additional investigation may still be necessary to verify new and previously unknown information elicited during the course of the confession. Some participants also noted that additional investigation is mandatory as a confession alone is "never enough" to win at trial. Despite what some may believe, even if a person walks into a police station and states voluntarily, yet unequivocally, "I killed my wife," police do not automatically place the subject in handcuffs, and prosecutors do not blindly start typing an affidavit for an arrest warrant. Some degree of investigation is needed to prove the accuracy of this person's claims. As noted by many participants in my study, any confession that is not supported by case facts and evidence will immediately and understandably be challenged by defense attorneys. In fact, investigators and prosecutors can logically anticipate that any confession, regardless of the amount of supporting evidence, will reflexively be questioned by the defense, and motions will undoubtedly be made to have the damning statement suppressed. After all, what choice does the defense attorney have? They have no other option but to attack the voluntariness and validity of the admissions that all but guarantee their client's successful prosecution. Competent investigators and prosecutors therefore operate under the stark realization that the subject's confession "can be tossed at any time." If the confession is successfully suppressed by the court, the prosecution will then be left with only the evidence that was collected by investigators during the course of the investigation. This is why additional investigation and evidence collection is so critically important. Those false confession researchers and expert witnesses who claim that cases are automatically closed upon receipt of a criminal confession are suggesting that law enforcement officers and prosecutors make it a habit of placing all of their prosecutorial eggs into a single confessionary basket.

Do Prosecutors Automatically Prosecute a Subject Based on their Confession?

In light of the academic position that confessions are problematic because prosecutors automatically use them to prosecute criminal subjects, I also decided to ask state and federal law enforcement polygraph examiners for their experiences regarding this premise. Two participants reported that they were unsure whether the aforementioned premise was true because, as polygraph examiners, they were not often privy to the prosecutorial decisions made after they obtained a confession. One of these participants noted that while a subject is likely to be prosecuted more quickly based on their confession, federal prosecutors are inherently unlikely to prosecute a subject based on their confession alone. A third participant in my study advised that he generally agrees with the premise that prosecutors automatically prosecute subjects based on their confession.

All of the remaining state and federal participants (87%) identified that neither federal nor state prosecutors automatically prosecute a subject based solely on their confession. One participant who has served as a law enforcement officer on the local, state, and federal levels noted that in his experience, "no prosecutor on any level would ever consider prosecuting a subject based solely on a confession." Another participant reported that she has never conducted a polygraph examination in which she obtained a confession and the subject was subsequently prosecuted based solely on their confession. While some participants identified that a confession is a strong piece of evidence that is generally desired by prosecutors, the majority of the participants advised that even when a confession is obtained during the course of a polygraph examination, prosecutors still require additional investigation.

Participants went on to explain that additional post-confession investigation is designed to obtain evidence that will corroborate, verify, or support the subject's confession. One participant similarly suggested that the collection of corroborating evidence will help to prevent the veracity of the confession from later being called into question by defense attorneys. Participants also reported that evidence that supports a subject's confession strengthens a prosecutor's case and ensures that their case against the subject will be "airtight." As expressed by one participant, "confessions rarely stand alone." In regard to the overwhelming desire of federal prosecutors to obtain additional evidence beyond the confession, another federal participant expressed her frustration by stating that when it comes to federal prosecutors, regardless of what evidence you have, "It's never enough for them." Some state law enforcement polygraph examiners noted a similar situation on the state level. More specifically, some advised that while a confession on the state level may be enough to obtain a plea deal from a criminal subject, it would not be enough to convict them at trial. Instead, state prosecutors typically require additional details, additional evidence, and further corroboration of the confession in the event that the defense attorney tries to "punch holes" in the confession. In fact, one of the state participants advised that they have had individuals walk into their state police post and confess to a crime, at which time troopers would have to work backward to corroborate the confession; otherwise a prosecutor would not take the case.

Summary

As outlined at the beginning of the chapter, the academic literature often suggests that confessions rendered by criminal subjects can only be viewed from a negative standpoint as confessions:

- increase the likelihood that the subject will be charged.
- increase the number of crimes with which the subject will be charged.
- decrease the likelihood that their case will be dismissed.
- increase the likelihood that their case will be resolved via plea bargain.
- increase the likelihood of being found guilty.
- increase the harshness of the sentence that will ultimately be received by the subject.

(Kassin et al., 2007; Leo & Ofshe, 1998; Drizin & Leo, 2004).

Based on these perceptions, it is not difficult to see why some in academia assert that a confession can do nothing but harm a criminal subject. I posit that these perceptions lie somewhere on a continuum between a willful misunderstanding of the criminal justice system and an overarching bias against law enforcement officers and criminal prosecutors.

Admittedly, it is both impossible and illogical to argue that a false confession rendered by an innocent person does anything other than harm that subject. If an innocent person falsely admits to being responsible for a crime and is subsequently convicted in error, this is a profound tragedy for both the innocent subject and the criminal justice system. However, if a truly guilty subject were to honestly admit to criminal wrongdoing, and this confession was then utilized to assist in his prosecution, this would be a clear example of where the criminal justice system worked appropriately. The only way a person could argue with this second point would be if they have a fundamental disagreement with the belief that criminal actions are deserving of punishment. If there are academic researchers, expert witnesses, or advocates who think that no truly guilty person should ever be punished for their criminal misdeeds, then it would make sense that a criminal confession does nothing but hurt the subject. Yet, for those who believe that the innocent should be exonerated and the guilty punished, then the information provided to me by the interrogative specialists I interviewed identifies a palpable and inarguable benefit to the criminal confession.

Many in law enforcement may likely concur with the premise that a criminal confession does, in fact, increase the likelihood that the subject will be charged, that they will plead guilty, and that they will be found guilty in a court of law. In regard to these specific outcomes, the positions put forth in the academic literature are accurate. Still, these researchers and expert witnesses are inaccurate in their assumptions that confessions inherently increase: a) the number of charges brought against the subject; b) the severity of charges brought against the subject; and c) the severity of the eventual punishment. In fact, according to the interrogative specialists I interviewed, the exact opposite may be true.

While the majority of the state and federal participants in my study readily admit to the evidentiary power of the criminal confession, even more of the participants noted that confessions also benefit the subject. This benefit comes in the form of prosecutors charging subjects with lesser crimes, charging them with a fewer number of crimes, and offering them deals in the form of a plea agreement. All of these benefits ultimately result in a lesser sentence than if the subject had denied their criminal activity, proceeded to trial, and were found guilty by a judge or jury. This is the exact opposite of what some academic researchers, expert witnesses, and advocates claim. Again, this may ultimately be a reflection of their bias, their lack of familiarity with how the criminal justice system actually works, or a wrongheaded belief that if a truly guilty criminal subject simply refuses to confess, all further investigation or prosecution disappears, and they will effectively avoid any type of punishment.

It should also be noted that while some academic literature suggests that subjects who confess are treated differently at every stage of the criminal justice system, in reality the difference in treatment appears to actually benefit the subject. According to the state and federal law enforcement polygraph examiners in my study, criminal subjects who confess tend to receive a lower sentence than those who do not because of the tendency of prosecutors to charge them with a lesser offense, offer them a better deal through the plea agreement process, and recommend lower sentences to the court. Participants also reported that confessors tend to receive respect and appreciation from investigators and prosecutors who, in turn, do their best to cooperate with the subject. These differences in treatment ultimately lead to a legal process that is smoother, more cordial, and significantly less adversarial.

Similar antithetical findings were identified regarding the claims that: a) cases are reflexively closed; and b) prosecutors automatically prosecute once a confession is obtained. Again, the majority of the participants I interviewed explained that in their experiences, cases are *not* automatically closed. To the contrary, additional investigation is needed to validate and corroborate the information provided by the subject. This is consistent with the reports of other law enforcement officers who also noted that a simple confession, without corroboration, is insufficient to clear a case (Frantzen, 2010). Likewise, the participants in my study repeatedly stated that a confession is never enough to successfully prosecute a criminal subject and prosecutors always want more proof of guilt from investigators. The need for additional investigation and the desire for more evidence of guilt are the natural result of police and prosecutors being keenly aware that a confession can always be suppressed by the court. If the case is based solely on the subject's confession, investigators and prosecutors run the risk of having to dismiss their case if the confession is ruled to be inadmissible.

Over and over again, when the time is taken to actually consult with law enforcement practitioners, a drastically different picture is painted about how the American criminal justice system operates. Whether it is caused by the tendency of some academic researchers to hyper-focus on interrogations gone drastically wrong, the artificial and nonrepresentative nature of laboratory experiments with college students, or simply an underlying bias toward those who have dedicated themselves to enforcing the laws of our country, some in academia continue to put forth an unrealistic and inaccurate view of criminal interrogation.

As previously noted, Kassin and Gudjonsson (2004) identified that confession can be found in three key areas of human interaction: religion, psychotherapy, and the criminal justice system. They note that the confessions in religion and psychotherapy respectively help to cleanse one's soul and bring about therapeutic release and healing. However, it is maintained by many in the academic literature that the same is not true within the criminal justice system. While the other admissions of wrongdoing greatly help the religious observer and mental health patient, the criminal confession is unique in the fact that it is only equated with pain. Based on the experiences of those who specialize in the elicitation of truthful criminal confessions, it appears that this position is not only profoundly untrue, but highly distorted. In reality, interrogative specialists are able to excel in convincing the truly guilty to accept responsibility for their criminal actions because they know that a criminal confession, like a religious confession or therapeutic admission, has significant and tangible benefits. The simple fact is, criminal subjects who confess generally receive better deals, are charged with lesser and fewer offenses, and receive reduced punishments, all while traversing the legal process in a smoother and more cordial manner.

Upon analyzing the claims put forth by some academic researchers studying both true and false confessions, it becomes apparent that they may mistakenly be viewing criminal interrogation as a zero-sum game in formulating their positions. Just because a law enforcement officer obtains a confession does not mean that he/she wins and the subject loses. If such a juvenile approach to interrogation is being employed to formulate academic theory, then it is not difficult to see why some may believe that criminal confessions only hurt those who confess. Similarly, just because a criminal subject does not confess does not mean that he/she naturally gets off scot-free. If such a naïve interpretation of the criminal justice system is fueling the positions offered by false confession researchers and expert witnesses, then it is again understandable why some may think that confessions only harm the criminal subject. In the simplest of terms, truly guilty subjects of a criminal investigation are routinely prosecuted *without* a confession. In addition, truly guilty subjects frequently receive better deals when they do decide to confess. It is the inaccurate and misguided positions that: a) criminal subjects will never be convicted if they simply remain silent; and b) criminal subjects will receive a much harsher sentence if they decide to confess that have fostered the false assumption that confessions do nothing but harm the criminal offender.

CHAPTER 17

Would Law Enforcement Officers Truthfully Disclose Their False Confession Experiences?

After initially questioning federal law enforcement polygraph examiners about their experiences with false confessions, I presented my findings at a professional conference. Of particular note was the fact that none of the 13 federal participants in my initial study reported eliciting a known false confession. After my presentation, one of the attendees pulled me aside and expressed skepticism over whether a law enforcement officer would ever voluntarily tell me about their false confession experiences. This led to some additional conversation at which time it occurred to me how some may be misinterpreting how law enforcement officers view the elicitation of a false confession. As a career law enforcement officer and a long-time polygraph examiner, it is my experience that false confessions do not automatically reflect the misdeeds of the officer. In other words, eliciting a false confession is not akin to stealing drugs from the evidence room, planting evidence on an innocent subject, or accepting bribes in exchange for turning a blind eye toward the criminal activities of a citizen. While some may believe that eliciting a false confession from an innocent subject reflects ineptitude, and possibly even brutality on behalf of the interrogator, I did not perceive this in the same manner. Therefore, I did not believe that interrogative specialists would be unwilling to discuss these types of experiences.

The reason I felt comfortable in the fact that participants in my initial study would readily discuss their experiences with false confessions was because I have personally experienced a false confession and have no shame in discussing the matter. In my situation, I had been called upon to conduct a polygraph examination of a young man in his early twenties who was suspected of viewing child pornography. A search warrant was executed at his home to collect evidence relating to his suspected child pornography activity. During the course of the search warrant, the subject was interviewed, and he confessed to downloading sexually explicit images of children. The natural concern with a child pornography subject is whether he has ever acted upon his sexual interest in children by having sexual contact with a child. As such, the subject was asked whether he would be willing to be tested by means of the polygraph regarding whether he has ever had sexual contact with children. The subject readily agreed to such an examination and was brought to my office for a test.

After failing an examination relating to whether he has ever engaged in sexual activity or contact with a child, I began interrogating the subject. After approximately one hour, the subject began recounting a story in which, as a teenager, he became sexually attracted to a cognitively disabled toddler who lived next door to his family. He then went on to explain that he had sexually fondled the child behind a tree located between his house and the neighbor's house. After he had gone into additional detail about what transpired, I became suspicious of the claims that the subject had engaged in this type of activity in a public setting. I then asked the subject about where the toddler's mother was at the time that he fondled the child. He replied that the toddler's mother was talking with the subject's mother in the front yard.

As stated by the participants in my study and recounted in an earlier chapter, a false confession is, by definition, a lie. Therefore, a false confession may be inherently illogical or nonsensical when it is rendered by an innocent subject. For me, the likelihood of a teenager engaging in such reckless behavior with an intellectually disabled toddler behind a tree when both his mother and the mother of the child were in such close proximity seemed highly unlikely.

344

While he may have fantasized about engaging the child in such activity, the subject's story seemed implausible. I then asked the subject whether anything he had just told me was true. The subject then replied that he had made up this information. I asked the subject why he would make up such a story, and he explained that he is simply the type of person who makes up stories when he is accused of something he did not actually do. The subject then explained that he has always done this type of thing and noted a similar instance in elementary school when he was standing in the lunch line and was twisting back and forth with his cafeteria tray. He recalled accidentally hitting a student next to him with his tray, at which time the student told a teacher that the subject had deliberately struck him. The teacher then asked why the subject had chosen to hit his fellow student. Although he initially claimed that it was an accident, upon being questioned further, the subject falsely claimed that he deliberately struck the student with his tray because he was mad at him. The subject then reiterated for me that he is simply the type of person who takes responsibility for things he didn't do.

After obtaining this confession and then immediately confirming that it was not truthful, I exited the polygraph suite and informed the lead investigator of the subject's admission and my belief that the statement was not accurate. I later learned that the subject's confession was presented to the parents of the toddler who confirmed that there was no conceivable way for this interaction to have taken place. In essence, the confession was disproved by subsequent investigation. Similar to the experiences expressed by the participants in my study, I recognized that there was something wrong with the confession; I did not accept the confession; the confession was subsequently proven to be false by additional investigation; and the confession was not used against the subject in any future legal proceedings. While my aforementioned experience is nearly identical to the experiences shared by the interrogative specialists in my study, it appears to be profoundly inconsistent with the prevailing beliefs of some false confession researchers, expert witnesses, and advocates.

Like the participants in my study, I did not use any unusual interrogative practices with this particular subject, and I certainly did not abuse or mistreat him in any way. I simply used the same methods as I have always used and continue to use. As a result, and consistent with the subject's statement that he is just the kind of person who falsely accepts responsibility for acts he did not commit, the false confession I experienced had more to do with the subject's personality and behavior than it did with my interrogation techniques. Perhaps it would be a different story if I had beaten a confession out of the subject, prevented him from seeing an attorney, threatened him, promised him he could go home if he confessed, or fed him case facts. But, since none of this happened, and I did not engage in any form of unethical or inappropriate behavior, I have no problem disclosing the fact that I have obtained, and readily identified, a false confession in my many years of interrogating criminal subjects. I do not consider this a black mark on my career; nor do I see it as the natural consequence of abusing a subject behind closed interrogation room doors. Moreover, it was not until I had that discussion with a colleague at a forensic psychology conference that I realized that some may view the elicitation of a false confession as the interrogative equivalent of a 'scarlet letter,' bringing disgrace and dishonor to a law enforcement officer. In fact, even though none of the federal law enforcement polygraph examiners with whom I spoke identified an instance in which they knowingly elicited a false confession, they certainly seemed willing to talk about such an eventuality. Still, upon deciding to continue my research with state law enforcement polygraph examiners, I decided to ask these new interview subjects if they would be willing to disclose instances in which they may have elicited a false confession from an innocent person. The following is a discussion of what they had to say.

Would You Tell Me?

It is interesting to note that when I questioned state law enforcement polygraph examiners about their willingness to discuss their false confession experiences, all 10 of the examiners readily advised that they would have no problem discussing instances in which they elicited a false confession or the circumstances at the time that such a confession was obtained. Multiple state participants advised that they strive to be honest and transparent in their job so they would not be reluctant to discuss a false confession. Another participant offered that he has no problem admitting when he makes a mistake. Still another participant advised that as law enforcement officers, we should be interested in obtaining "ground truth," not simply taking a statement from someone. In other words, contrary to what some academics, expert witnesses, and advocates might believe, law enforcement is actually interested in obtaining the truth as opposed to mindlessly pushing for a confession so that they can put the current investigative matter to bed and close their case.

The majority of state law enforcement polygraph examiners responded that disclosing instances in which they may have obtained a false confession will help them to not only learn more about what went wrong in an interrogation, but will prevent it from occurring again. These responses help to demonstrate that, like countless other vocations and careers, law enforcement officers are conscientious professionals who care about the manner in which they conduct their job. Like many other occupations, law enforcement officers also strive to improve and master the knowledge, skills, and abilities associated with their chosen field.

It is of critical importance to highlight that the willingness of state law enforcement polygraph examiners to discuss their experiences with eliciting false confessions was not solely for their own benefit and knowledge. Multiple participants noted their altruistic concerns over getting the wrong answer during an interrogation and the harm that such an error can cause. As one participant noted, "The last thing I would ever want to do is to wrongfully convict someone." Another participant similarly responded by stating, "I don't want to see anybody go down for something they did not do. That's just not right." Lastly, one of the participants highlighted the simple fact that a false confession "benefits no one." Again, these statements directly contradict the protestations heralded by some academic researchers and expert witnesses that criminal interrogators care only about eliciting a confession and will never relent until the subject admits to some manner of wrongdoing.

After digesting the responses provided by the state law enforcement polygraph examiners interviewed for my follow-up study, it becomes clear that for at least some law enforcement interrogative specialists, a false confession does not appear to be the inexcusable and indefensible blemish on a criminal interrogator's career that some may think it is, especially if the interrogator did not engage in unethical behavior. It also does not appear to be an inherent source of shame for the interrogator. Unanimously, the state law enforcement polygraph examiners I interviewed expressed a willingness to openly and honestly discuss their experiences with false confessions. Their answers also illustrate that they not only have pride in their chosen vocation, but they desire to ethically and continually strengthen their unique craft. Lastly, as my own experience in eliciting a false confession demonstrates, the true problem with false confessions may not be the interrogative methods employed, but rather the unique qualities of the person being interrogated. If this is true, the academic attack on the interrogative techniques of law enforcement officers may be a misguided one. Regardless, it is a false assumption to believe that professional criminal interrogators would never openly admit to, or discuss, instances in which they had elicited a false confession.

CHAPTER 18

Is the University Laboratory a Good Place to Test the False Confession Phenomenon?

In studying the phenomenon of false confessions, a considerable portion of the research has involved laboratory experiments with university students (Forrest et al., 2012; Guyll et al., 2013; Hasel & Kassin, 2009; Kassin & Fong, 1999; Kassin & Kiechel, 1996; Kassin & McNall, 1991; Kassin et al., 2005; Kassin & Norwick, 2004; Kebbell et al., 2006; Klaver et al., 2008; Levine et al., 2010; Mastroberardino & Marucci, 2013; Narchet et al., 2011; Nash & Wade, 2009; Newring & O'Donohue, 2008; Perillo & Kassin, 2011; Pimentel et al., 2015; Russano et al., 2005; Swanner & Beike, 2010; Villar et al., 2013; Woody & Forrest, 2009). These researchers believe that the laboratory is the best means of investigating a complex issue like false confession. In fact, Kassin, Appleby, and Perillo (2010) stated:

> In order to create and systematically assess methods of interrogation that produce diagnostic outcomes – inducing perpetrators but not innocents to incriminate themselves – researchers must bring the phenomenon for testing into the laboratory (p. 45-46).

Still, some of these same researchers have also suggested that the results produced during laboratory experimentation may be difficult to extrapolate to the real world of law enforcement due to the artificiality of the laboratory setting, the ethical limitations that preclude a direct replication of the stressors associated with actual criminal interrogation within a laboratory setting, and the inherent differences between the university student and criminal offender populations (Kassin et al., 2010a, Narchet et al., 2011). This contradiction raises the very important question: Is the laboratory the best means of assessing the false confession phenomenon?

The problem for law enforcement officers and prosecutors is that they are inherently unfamiliar with research. Whereas some academics have chosen to ask questions about the world around them, formulate hypotheses, design experiments, analyze data, and draw conclusions, law enforcement officers and prosecutors have chosen a life on the front lines of the criminal justice system. Due to limited resources and large caseloads, their chosen professions do not generally allow them the time or freedom to explore the intricacies of the legal systems like those in academia. While this is not meant to be a criticism of either academia or law enforcement practitioners, it may simply serve to identify why investigators and prosecutors are unfamiliar with the academic literature, especially as it relates to false confessions. Unfortunately, people tend to be avoidant, or even afraid, of the things they don't understand. As a result, academic researchers and expert witnesses are left relatively unchallenged while on the witness stand as their "research" is afforded a certain level of reverence. In reality, this sanctity often stems from the fact that prosecutors may simply not know what to ask these individuals. As was observed during the COVID-19 Pandemic, 'experts' in both the medical and political realms often belabored the importance of "following the science." In many ways, this pervasive catchphrase was used as a bludgeon to immediately and decisively thwart any questioning of the policies that were subsequently proposed, oftentimes without actually presenting even a hint of research. In response, citizens simply went along with the knee-jerk, and often inconsistent, political mandates that were imposed because, after all, that's what the "science" is telling us to do. Not surprisingly, the same response is often received from prosecutors, investigators, and possibly judges and juries who are presented with an academic researcher or expert witness who claims to be in possession of false confession 'science.' This same bludgeon is designed to cast doubt in the minds of jurors while simultaneously portraying law enforcement interrogators as psychological torturers. For this reason, it is important to point out the inherent weaknesses in academic research, particularly the laboratory experimentation that is routinely employed to investigate the phenomenon of false confessions. The following is a discussion of the inherent flaws associated with the university laboratory.

Lack of Realism

As noted by Moston and Stephenson (1993), in the laboratory "it is difficult to recreate artificially anything like the circumstances in which a suspect in a criminal investigation might be questioned" (p. 101). Similarly, in discussing deception detection experiments in the laboratory, Kassin (2005) stated that performance in the laboratory is poor because participants are asked to identify both truth and deception in low-stake situations which can greatly weaken the cues people use to identify deception, thereby making it more difficult to make such judgments. In their laboratory experiment with college students regarding the interrogative techniques of maximization and minimization, even Kassin and McNall (1991) had to admit:

> Because our findings are based on inferences drawn by college students, relatively uninvolved but highly educated observers, it remains to be seen whether similar inferences are drawn by real crime suspects – that is, those who are the highly involved but often uneducated targets of these techniques (p. 249-250).

The simple fact is that the criminal justice system in general, and law enforcement investigators specifically, tend to deal with people on the worst days of their lives. Whether it be the victim of a violent crime or the offender who committed the crime, the real world of law enforcement comes with high emotions and immeasurable stressors. Due to the ethical constraints imposed upon those engaged in laboratory experimentation with human subjects, researchers simply cannot subject these participants to the same types

351

of trauma or strain experienced by victims and offenders. This is a good thing. However, it causes a natural decrease in realism. Leding (2012) documented this fact in her research on false memories by stating:

> Although it would be unethical to subject participants to the same pressure-filled interrogations that suspects are sometimes subjected to, attempts have been made to create experimental paradigms that mimic real-world interrogations. These experiments lack a certain amount of external validity (p. 263).

As statements like these demonstrate, academic researchers readily admit that due to ethical constraints, their laboratory experiments cannot fully approximate the harsh realities of criminal behavior, the seriousness of criminal interrogation, and the anticipated punishments resulting from a successful criminal prosecution. This is a point that law enforcement officers and prosecutors should be keenly aware of before they simply accept as gospel the research findings put forth by expert witnesses while on the stand. Moreover, it is of critical importance that prosecutors strive to make juries aware of this fact as well. In the Netflix series *The Innocence Files* (2020), Innocence Project attorney Chris Fabricant can be heard telling an audience during a public defender training session that, "Just because somebody is an expert witness doesn't mean they're right. They're as full as shit as anybody else." As Fabricant spent the remainder of this episode attacking the validity of forensic odontology, it can be assumed that this comment was directed toward forensic scientists. However, in light of the lack of realism associated with laboratory experimentation with university students, this comment can, and should, be equally applied to the false confession expert witness. This becomes clearer as we delve deeper into just how unrealistic these laboratory experiments can be.

Crime in the Laboratory

In the real world of criminal investigation, law enforcement officers are called upon to investigate some of the most heinous offenses that one human being can do to another. Rape, sexual abuse of a child, armed robbery, theft of a victim's life savings, and of course murder, are just a sample of the crimes for which a law enforcement interrogator may be called upon to question a criminal subject. Within the laboratory it would obviously be immoral and completely unethical to have one student physically or sexually assault another student just to bring a sense of realism to the experiment. As such, false confession researchers are left having to create experimental designs that do not bring either physical or psychological harm to a test subject. Although they have attempted to be somewhat creative in designing their research protocols, the criminal transgressions are, at best, unrealistic. In fact, at times these laboratory 'offenses' are downright comical. However, this profound lack of realism may not be known by law enforcement investigators and prosecutors and, as a result, they may be left blindly accepting the research findings touted by expert witnesses in court. Remember, their findings are based on 'research.' To get a better perspective on this issue, it helps to review what crime looks like in the laboratory as compared to the real world.

As previously discussed, perhaps the most impactful laboratory research relating to false confessions was the ALT Key experiment conducted by Kassin and Kiechel (1996). As a reminder, in this experiment, college students were called upon to participate in what they assumed was a computer-based study of reaction times. At the outset of the experiment, students were warned not to press the ALT key on the computer's keyboard as a glitch in the system would cause the computer to crash. If this were to occur, all data would be lost. Unbeknownst to the students, experimenters then deliberately crashed the computer and interrogated the innocent participants about pressing the forbidden ALT key. Half of the participants were presented with false eyewitness testimony that they had been observed pressing the ALT key. Based on the results, Kassin and Kiechel concluded that the presentation of false evidence, particularly false eyewitness testimony, increased the likelihood of a false confession. In short, the crime in this experiment was pressing a computer key that students were deliberately told not to press. The problem with this transgression is that pressing a computer key is not in and of itself criminal in nature. Furthermore, pressing the key, especially during a study purportedly designed to see how quickly participants can react by punching keys on a keyboard, could happen accidentally without the subject knowing they did so. Many of us have come to know this transgression as a "typo." Criminal acts like rape, robbery, and murder do not happen in this same way. In the simplest of terms, this misdeed in no way reflects the criminal behavior that law enforcement is tasked with investigating on a daily basis.

Despite the lack of realism in the Kassin and Kiechel (1996) experiment, Newring and O'Donohue (2008) borrowed the concept for their own experiment into the effects of the Reid Technique strategy of minimization on false confessions. The 'crime' in this case was again the pressing of the ALT key. Perillo and Kassin (2011) also utilized the ALT key paradigm to examine the effects of the Bluff Technique on false confessions. Swanner and Beike (2010) went on to conduct a study to test whether incentives would increase the likelihood that an informant would implicate another person. In this study, college students were asked to participate in a getting-to-know-you process in which they were set up in groups of two and directed to ask either a question designed to generate small talk or a question designed to generate personal disclosure. Unbeknownst to the participants, the person they were paired with was actually working on behalf of the researchers. As the student questioned this confederate, the confederate admitted to a misdeed the previous week. What misdeed did the confederate commit the previous week? Did they shoplift? Did they cheat on a test? Did they drink underage? Did they cheat on their significant other? No. The confederate was instructed to tell the student that they had participated in a study the previous week and hit the TAB key when they were specifically instructed not to. While the researchers can be given creativity points for changing the computer key from the ALT key to the TAB key, we are still left with an insignificant, and frankly comical transgression that has nothing to do with criminality.

While these purported 'crimes' are inherently ludicrous, researchers readily admit that the ethical limitations to which they are held when dealing with human subjects causes their designs to lack a certain degree of validity. As such, efforts continue to be made to make these experiments more realistic. For example, Klaver, Lee, and Rose (2008), sought to make their design more realistic in attempting to assess the impact of human compliance, interrogative suggestibility, self-esteem, and locus of control on false confessions and the internalization of false confessions. In particular, they realized that the ALT Key experiment lacked volition as the student participants could foreseeably have hit the ALT key accidentally without realizing they had done so. To combat this weakness, Klaver et al. designed an experiment which contained a 'crime' that was less likely to occur accidentally. As such, they decided to interrogate the subject about pressing the ESC key. Why? The ESC key is four inches farther away than the ALT key on the keyboard. In the field of laboratory experimentation, such a change is considered to be an increase in criminal purposefulness. Whether this alteration even remotely reflects the criminal intent of a husband who stabbed his wife to death during a jealous rage is obviously up for debate.

Russano, Meissner, Narchet, and Kassin (2005) correctly noted that pressing a forbidden computer key (as in the ALT Key paradigm) is neither a crime, nor necessarily a deliberate act. As such, they created a new paradigm with a more serious offense in order to test the effects of minimization techniques and offering subjects a deal in exchange for their confession. More specifically, Russano et al. paired university student participants with a confederate, and the two were instructed to solve logic problems. Some of these problems were to be solved jointly, and some were to be answered individually. In the experiment, the guilty condition involved the confederate asking the participant for help on a question that they were specifically instructed to answer individually. Kudos should again be given to these researchers for finally including at least an unethical, though not criminal, act. Still, it cannot be overlooked that these participants did not deliberately cheat to increase their grade in one of their classes. To the contrary, the students were actually tricked into helping someone else on a logic problem. Despite their efforts, this 'crime' is a far cry from buying a ski mask, walking into a bank with a shotgun, and ordering the tellers to empty their tills.

Other researchers have finally realized the value of adding actual criminality to their experiments, though the *mens rea* (or guilty mind) associated with these offenses is severely lacking. For example, in their experiment to test the biasing effects of confession evidence on eyewitness identifications, Hasel and Kassin (2009) developed a theft paradigm in which an adult walked into the laboratory, took a computer from the desk, and walked out, all in full view of approximately 30 students. Similarly, Nash and Wade (2009) sought to research the effects of doctored video evidence on false confessions. In their experiment, Nash and Wade instructed subjects to sit in front of a computer and answer questions. For each question they answered correctly, they were instructed to take fake money from a specific pile which the researchers identified as "the bank." For each incorrect answer, they were to take money from their own pile of fake money and put it into the bank pile. Researchers then doctored video evidence to make it appear as if the subject was taking money *from* the bank when they should have been putting their own money *into* the bank. The subjects were then interrogated for this 'crime.' While it is admirable that these researchers actually created something that even slightly approached a criminal act, it is difficult to compare an interrogation related to the taking of fake money from a pile at the wrong time to the interrogation of a criminal subject believed to be responsible for creating a fraudulent investment scheme and then using it to bilk elderly investors of their life savings. Because Nash and Wade's 'crime' could have occurred accidentally, it is much easier to sell a faked video than it would be in a real-world crime that actually required deliberate criminal intent.

The artificiality of these fake crimes can be observed in the instructions given to student participants in the experiment conducted by Kebbell, Hurren, and Roberts (2006). In this experiment, the researchers sought to investigate the effects of eyewitness evidence on confessions. More specifically, Kebbell et al. gave student participants in the guilty category the following instructions:

> You have been assigned to the theft condition. What you have
> to do is to go into the room marked experimental room. Once in
> the room you are to search for, and steal, a cell-phone. Once you
> have stolen the cell-phone leave the room and return to the wait-
> ing area where the experimenter will meet you. Try hard to act,
> and feel, as if you are really committing this crime (p. 479).

As these instructions indicate, it is difficult to consider the subject's actions a crime. When researchers have to stress that you must "try hard to act and feel" as if you are actually stealing something, you are far from committing a crime.

In seeking to understand why people waive their Miranda rights, Kassin and Norwick (2004) also directed students to steal, but this time they were instructed to walk into a room alone, open a drawer, take the $100 bill found inside, fold it in half, put it in their pocket, and walk out the door. In essence, within the confines of a laboratory, 'crimes' involve pressing a forbidden computer key (perhaps accidentally), being tricked into cheating, and pretending to steal. The reasons for this artificiality are a matter of research ethics. The conclusions drawn from this artificiality are a question of applicability. The simple fact is fake crimes have fake consequences. As such, even research-ers must admit that in the real world, the number of confessions are likely to decrease as stress levels and consequences grow (Pimentel et al., 2015; Russano et al., 2005).

The Laboratory Criminal

As false confession researchers create their experimental designs, it becomes necessary for them to create what could be considered 'cops and robbers.' In other words, they must identify people who will serve as the criminal and people who will serve as the interrogator. Consistently, both groups come from the pool of university students who agree to participate in these laboratory studies, often for college credit. It goes without say-ing that there is an inherent difference between college students and either criminals or law enforcement officers. Pimentel et al. (2015) cited various other researchers in noting that juvenile and adult criminal offenders tend to have low IQs and suffer from mental illness. This is a point that has been made by other researchers as well (Guyll et al., 2013). This makes this population inherently different from the college students who are called upon to pretend they are criminals within the university laboratory. It is also not uncommon for the majority of the students agreeing to participate in these laboratory experiments to be female (Forrest et al., 2012; Kebbell et al., 2006; Narchet et al., 2011). For those who interrogate criminal subjects for a living, you may want to consider what percentage of your interrogations involve female subjects? In addition to gender differences, Kassin and McNall (1991) also noted that in general, criminal subjects are far more involved in the criminal justice system and far less educated than university students volunteering to participate in laboratory studies. Simply put, even academic researchers have to admit that the inherent differences between college students and the real-world criminals and law enforcement officers they mimic in the laboratory can impact the ability to generalize their experimental conclusions to the real world (Bradford & Goodman-Delahunty, 2008; Hasel & Kassin, 2009; Kassin & Fong, 1999; Kassin & Norwick, 2004; Klaver et al., 2008; Newring & O'Donohue, 2008).

The Laboratory Punishments

It is highly likely that if you ask a person why people do not engage in criminal activity, you are likely to get a response relating to the anticipated punishments. Engaging in criminal activity is likely to lead to a myriad of undesirable repercussions. Depending on the seriousness of the offense committed, a criminal act can result in the death penalty, a lengthy prison sentence, a year in the county jail, probation, loss of one's family, loss of a job, loss of freedom, and so on. All of these punishments are severe and potentially life changing. Based on the severity of these repercussions and the ethical mandates of laboratory experimentation with human subjects, it is not possible to design experiments in which university students can anticipate being incarcerated for a number of years. As such, academic researchers must come up with their own negative consequences for the students who agree to participate in their studies. Although creative, these punishments are likely to cause a real-world law enforcement officer to laugh out loud. The following is a discussion of some of these laboratory penalties.

In an attempt to increase the stakes for student participants in their experiment, Kassin and Fong (1999) advised students that if they were judged to be deceptive during the course of the experiment, they would have to spend 5 minutes in the campus security office. While this ridiculous punishment was designed to approximate the fear of imprisonment, it is difficult to even entertain the premise that such an anticipated punishment reflects the realities of having to spend years incarcerated if convicted for the crime under investigation. Yet this is what law enforcement officers, prosecutors, judges, and juries are doing when they reflexively accept the conclusions of academic researchers and expert witnesses during court proceedings.

Because real-world criminals also lose their jobs, sources of income, and overall freedom when they are incarcerated, some researchers strove to create laboratory designs in which student participants felt what it is like to lose something. For example, Newring and O'Donohue (2008) informed the students in their study that if they confess during the course of the experiment, they would only receive $2 instead of the agreed upon $10 for participating in the study. While most college students may be consistently strapped for cash, it is a tall order to ask law enforcement officers, prosecutors, and triers of fact to assume some level of equivalency between the loss of eight bucks and the loss of one's freedom for an untold number of years in prison. Lastly, in their experiment, Russano et al. (2005) informed student participants that if they confess, the professor overseeing the experiment would have to be notified about the student's transgression. Like the other experiments, the "Ooh-I'm-telling!" punishment does not seem to hold the same weight as the real-world repercussions that can be anticipated if one decides to engage in criminal activity.

The Laboratory Interrogation

In testing the false confession phenomenon and related concepts in the laboratory, it naturally becomes necessary to actually interrogate the college student participating in the experiment. The length of these laboratory interrogations is where the problem arises. For example, in an attempt to examine how an officer's perceptions of guilt or innocence influenced their use of interrogation techniques, Narchet, Meissner, and Russano (2011) had college students who received some interrogation training question college students who either did or did not cheat in a specified task. The student interrogators were instructed on 15 different interrogative strategies and were informed that because of ethical constraints, they could only interrogate the student for up to 15 minutes. As anyone who has ever interrogated a criminal subject knows, this is a ridiculously brief period of time to interrogate a person. This is particularly true when you have 15 different interrogative methods to choose from.

Pimentel, Arndorfer, and Malloy (2015) looked at age and reciprocity and the extent to which these factors would impact the rendering of a false confession to protect someone else. In this study, the interrogations averaged approximately 10 minutes. In examining how well people can distinguish between true and false denials and the extent to which training in the detection of verbal and nonverbal cues can impact this ability, Kassin and Fong (1999) directed college students to interrogate other college students who may or may not have engaged in a mock crime. The interrogation sessions ranged from 3.5 to 6 minutes with the average interrogation lasting 4 minutes and 35 seconds. Again, this is an absolutely absurd length of time for an interrogation, even one done by students questioning other students about their involvement in a fake crime. In fact, in the real world of criminal interrogation, it would likely take this amount of time just to get through the Miranda waiver.

These studies involving brief interrogations are not unique or unusual. Newring and O'Donohue (2008) followed suit by evaluating the influence of the minimization technique on the production of false confessions and false witness statements. Yet again, these researchers employed the ALT Key experiment in which students were interrogated by other students about whether they pressed the ALT key on the computer keyboard, thereby causing the computer system to crash. In this experiment, Newring and O'Donohue had student interrogators engage in a 5-step interview/interrogation process in which: a) the student was asked what happened; b) the lead investigator entered the room and asked for a written statement; c) the student's verbal behavior was observed as they wrote out their statement; d) the student was asked to verbally review their statement; and e) the Reid Technique of minimizing the moral seriousness of the offense was employed. It is important to note that in this final portion of the 5-step process, student interrogators were told to say something similar to, "No real harm was caused;" "We just can't use the data;" "I just need some sort of explanation;" or "How do you explain what happened in there?" As noted by Newring and O'Donohue, the entire 5-step process, to include the subject writing out their statement, lasted between 5 and 7 minutes. As can be observed in the aforementioned experimental designs, the ethical and logistical constraints associated with the university laboratory leads to interrogations that are so unrepresentative of those conducted within the criminal justice system that we must become profoundly circumspect in applying the research findings to the real world of criminal investigation. In addition to these laboratory interrogations, the unrealistic nature of the laboratory environment can also be observed in how confessions are memorialized in these studies.

The Laboratory Confession

Within the laboratory setting, false confession researchers have an interesting way of identifying and documenting a confession. In the real world of criminal interrogation, a confession is considered a subject's acceptance of responsibility for a specified criminal act. At times this can be captured in a full recording, a summary recording, a written statement, and/or by reiterating the confession to another law enforcement officer. In fact, Beyer and Herndon

(2018) identified the often lengthy process in which federal law enforcement polygraph examiners go about documenting their confessions in a written statement. More specifically, real world interrogators identified that their documentation of a confession generally involves the following five steps:

1. Transition – This involves the interrogator encouraging the subject to memorialize their oral confession in written format. For example, the interrogator may explain to the subject that writing out their statement can prevent important information from being missed or overlooked. The interrogator may also suggest that a written statement may prevent any discrepancies about what the subject actually confessed to. The interrogator may also encourage the subject to write out their confession as a means of demonstrating that the confession was voluntary. Some interrogators may similarly explain that a written statement allows the subject to include personal factors such as expressions of their guilt, attestations of their regret, apologies to the victim, and so on.

2. Documentation – This involves the confession actually being committed to paper. Some participants identified that they have the subject write their own confession. Some participants identified that they will write the statement for the subject if the subject is overly emotional, has problems writing, if they are uneducated or low functioning, if they are embarrassed by their spelling or handwriting, et cetera. Participants noted that when they write the statement on behalf of the subject, the construction of the statement is done collaboratively. More specifically, the interrogator may write one sentence at a time as the subject dictates their confession, or the interrogator may ask the subject specific questions about their oral confession and then write/type the subject's answers. These officers reported that writing the statement for the subject can be a grueling process as they immediately read each sentence to the subject after it is documented to verify that it is true and accurate.

362

3. Review/Verification – This involves efforts to make sure that the statement is true by having the subject read the statement aloud or by having the interrogator read the statement back to the subject. It can involve verifying the accuracy of each sentence, each paragraph, the entire statement, or a combination of all of these.

4. Corrections and Additions – This involves efforts to rectify errors, mistakes, and/or illegible or confusing information in the subject's written statement. If corrections are needed, participants have the subject cross out and initial the mistake. This demonstrates that the corrections were made by the subject and not the interrogator. These officers also noted that they frequently have the subject review the statement again after the corrections are made as a means of further confirming the accuracy of the overall statement.

5. Execution – This involves having the subject sign the statement, thereby indicating that it is true and accurate. If the interrogator wrote the statement on behalf of the subject, the subject may be asked to add a sentence that says the statement was written on their behalf, but the subject reviewed the statement and confirms that it is true and accurate.

As outlined by Beyer and Herndon (2018), the aforementioned process is time consuming and involves a great deal of interaction between the subject and the interrogator. Yet this is not what is seen within the laboratory setting. In laboratory designs, the researcher typically asks university students accused of engaging in a mock crime or minor infraction to confess their wrongdoing by signing a pre-printed form that was drafted by the researcher before the experiment even started (Klaver et al., 2008; Narchet et al., 2011; Pimentel et al., 2015; Russano et al., 2005; Swanner & Beike, 2010). The following are examples of entire confession statements signed by student participants during laboratory experiments:

- "The other participant admitted to hitting the TAB key and causing the computer to crash." (Swanner & Beike, 2010).

- "I pressed the ALT key and caused the computer to crash. All data were lost." (Klaver et al., 2008).
- "I (participant's name) admit to having learned the answers to the test ahead of time." (Pimentel et al., 2015).

In the realm of academic laboratory experimentation, such pre-printed statements are placed in front of a college participant at which time they are instructed to sign the document. This act of signing a brief pre-printed form represents not only the decision to confess, but the actual documentation of the student's confession. For real world interrogative specialists, document-ing a confession involves a significantly longer and much more thorough process designed to obtain a truthful and voluntary written confession. More importantly, this prolonged process of documenting a confession in the real world affords the subject many more opportunities to correct, refute, or recant their confession (Beyer & Herndon, 2018). The same is not true for college students in the laboratory setting. In the laboratory, students posing as crimi-nals are often encouraged to sign a one- or two-sentence statement that is pre-written by the experimenters. This act of signing the statement is then considered not only the student's confession, but also the act of document-ing their 'criminal' wrongdoing. Based on this process, it is not surprising that 'false confessions' can happen so easily in the laboratory. This begs the question: If university participants were subjected to a longer and more detailed documentation process in which they were more personally involved in writing the statement and were given multiple opportunities to review the statement, would these 'confessions' occur so easily? Simply put, before law enforcement officers, prosecutors, judges, or juries readily accept the findings of false confession researchers and expert witnesses, perhaps they should be made aware of just how unrealistic the laboratory experiments and laboratory confessions are.

Summary

There is no way to get around the very real fact that what takes place in the laboratory is not even remotely close to what takes place in the real world of law enforcement. The false confession research taking place in university laboratories is not like the laboratory experiments in other areas of science. This primarily stems from the ethical constraints faced by social science researchers. While this is necessary to protect the well-being of human subjects, it also precludes the generalizability of laboratory findings to the criminal justice system. As clearly outlined throughout this chapter, the false confession and interrogation-related experiments are, at times, laughable when viewed through the lens of a law enforcement officer who experiences the harsh reality of criminal offenders, their heinous criminal actions, and the serious legal punishments they receive on a daily basis. Yet, this profound lack of realism does not stop academic researchers and expert witnesses from entering the courtroom, climbing the steps to the witness stand, and using these same laboratory experiments to incessantly attack the credibility of law enforcement interrogators and the confessions they elicit. In fact, the following is a small sampling of the claims put forth by academic researchers at the conclusion of their unrealistic experimental designs:

- False incriminating statements increase the likelihood of a false confession (Kassin & Kiechel, 1996).
- Investigator bias can lead to the increased use of minimization tactics which increases the likelihood of a false confession (Narchet et al., 2011).
- The Reid Technique "may not be effective—and, indeed, may be counterproductive—as a method of distinguishing truth and deception" (Kassin & Fong, 1999, p. 512).
- The Reid Technique may cause some to falsely confess and implicate others (Newring & O'Donohue, 2008).
- Offering incentives increases the likelihood that an informant will sign a secondary confession which implicates another person in a criminal act (Swanner & Beike, 2010).
- Confessions can corrupt eyewitness identification (Hasel & Kassin,

2009).

- Bluffing subjects during an interrogation increases false confessions because innocent participants see the bluff as a promise of future exoneration (Perillo & Kassin, 2011).

- Minimizing the moral seriousness of an offense and offering a deal in exchange for their confession increases the likelihood of a false confession (Russano et al., 2005).

- Minimization techniques can lead to false confessions, especially with individuals who are highly suggestible (Klaver et al., 2008).

- Being shown doctored video evidence of their guilt may increase false confessions and cause a subject to internalize the act more deeply (Nash & Wade, 2009).

As these conclusions demonstrate, academic researchers and false confession expert witnesses can attack various aspects of a law enforcement interrogation in an attempt to suggest to the judge and jury that the confession elicited by officers may be false. Based on the unrealistic and nonrepresentative nature of the laboratory experiments employed to arrive at these conclusions, we must ask ourselves whether these types of conclusions can be generalized to the real world of law enforcement and criminal interrogation. I contend that the answer to this question is a resounding "No." Law enforcement officers, prosecutors, judges, and juries should not automatically accept the conclusions put forth by false confession expert witnesses on the stand. As outlined above, these conclusions are based on incessant laboratory experimentation with college students (oftentimes with predominantly female college students) who pretend to be criminals or who are tricked into committing a misdeed. The acts they engage in have no meaningful repercussions and therefore no meaningful levels of stress. They are then interrogated by fellow students who have, at best, brief periods of training in interrogation techniques and zero law enforcement experience. Yet, too many actors in the criminal justice system bow at the feet of these expert witnesses and readily accept their testimony because, after all, it's based on 'research.' Why is this?

Innocence Project attorney Chris Fabricant made the following statement in the Netflix series *The Innocence Files* (2020):

> Most lawyers are terrified of science. So are judges. So are
> jurors. Part of my job is to highlight the areas where forensics
> really has never been established as valid and reliable evidence.

As a career law enforcement officer and a specialist in interrogating criminal subjects, I have to agree with Mr. Fabricant. While he may have been referring to forensic odontology and bite mark evidence when he made this statement, I now find it part of my job to highlight the areas where *social* science is not only invalid and unreliable, but completely inconsistent with the realities of criminal interrogation. As such, we must not continue to treat academic researchers and false confession expert witnesses with such deference, and we should no longer view their flawed conclusions as sacrosanct.

Innocence Project co-founder Peter Neufeld made a similar point in *The Innocence Files* (2020) when he stated, "It's really hard for jurors to set aside those preconceived notions. Somebody walks into a courtroom wearing a lab coat. They must be telling the truth." In the same vein, Fabricant went on to claim, "There has to be some pushback when you just get nonsense being spewed as scientific reality." With this, I couldn't agree more. The conclusions reached by academic researchers and testified to by false confession expert witnesses is often nonsensical and far from scientific reality. For this reason, law enforcement and prosecutors must make greater efforts at pushing back against this research which reflexively seeks to cast doubt on legitimate and ethically obtained confessions.

CHAPTER 19

Examining the Motivations of Academic Researchers, Expert Witnesses, and Advocates

E ven a cursory review of the academic literature involving the phenomenon of false confessions will reveal a consistent two-part recommendation. The first recommendation that is repeatedly put forth by researchers is that jurors need to be educated about the false confession phenomenon (Bull & Soukara, 2009; Davis & Leo, 2012; Forrest et al., 2012; Kassin, 2008; Kassin & Gudjonsson, 2004; Kassin & McNall, 1991; Leo & Liu, 2009; Woody & Forrest, 2009). The second recommendation is to record every interrogation in its entirety (Johnson & Drucker, 2009; Kassin, 2005; Kassin, 2008; Kassin et al., 2010; Kassin et al., 2010a). While there are a myriad of reasons for these recommendations which will be discussed below, it is important to note that hidden motivations may be fueling these proposals.

Educating Jurors About False Confessions

Forrest et al. (2012) cited various researchers in claiming that "most individuals do not believe that they or others like them would falsely confess in the absence of physical coercion" (p. 345). In other words, most Americans operate under the premise that unless they were physically tortured, they would never falsely confess to a crime they did not commit. This is a problem for false confession expert witnesses as research suggests that the majority of individuals selected to sit in the jury box may not be so quick to accept the false confession premise. In fact, it can be argued that the unwillingness of many Americans to buy the concept of a false confession led to the creation of the false confession expert witness. As noted by Kassin and Gudjonsson (2004), when there is a case involving a disputed confession, a preliminary hearing is held so that the trier of fact can rule on whether the confession was voluntary and can therefore be admitted in court. Within recent years, social scientists and psychologists with backgrounds in the clinical, personality, developmental, cognitive, and social specialties have stepped forward with their theories and research to help aid in this decision-making process. The ultimate goal of these defense expert witnesses during the preliminary hearing is to suppress the confession. If this undertaking proves to be unsuccessful and the judge allows the confession evidence to be presented at trial, the jury may then hear testimony from an expert witness acting on behalf of the defense (Woody & Forrest, 2009). When the expert witness testifies at trial, they have to overcome the belief held by many jurors that neither they, nor anyone else, would ever falsely confess to a crime they did not commit unless they were physically coerced into doing so (Leo, 2008). Woody and Forrest (2009) suggested that informing jurors that some people may falsely confess without actually being tortured is likely to introduce jurors to new information that they have not previously heard of or considered.

In an attempt to assess the impact of expert witness testimony on the decision-making of potential jurors, Woody and Forrest (2009) conducted an experiment with 387 university students in which the participants, acting as potential jurors, read trial materials to include interrogation transcripts. Some of these trial materials included an interrogation transcript in which a false evidence ploy was used, and some contained expert witness information relating to false evidence ploys. It was reported that the students who read interrogation transcripts containing a false evidence ploy found the interrogations to be more deceptive and coercive. The same was true for the students who read expert witness testimony relating to how false evidence ploys increase the likelihood of a false confession. Furthermore, these potential jurors were less likely to convict the subject after reading these materials. In short, Woody and Forrest (2009) concluded that "Expert testimony reduced convictions and increased interrogation deception and coercion ratings" (p. 333).

In light of this particular piece of research, it is not hard to see what is going on. Academic laboratory experiments are being conducted, and the conclusions are being presented in court by expert witnesses as a means of decreasing how frequently subjects who confessed to their crimes are convicted. It appears as if there has been a shift from trying to prevent the innocent from being wrongfully convicted to trying to prevent *anyone* from being convicted based on their self-incriminating statements. In essence, there is a movement underway to convince judges and juries that all confessions are suspicious, coerced, and false. In a similar study involving mock jurors and their perceptions of the False Evidence Ploy, Forrest et al. (2012) concluded that an expert witness who "educates potential jurors about the relationship between police deception and false confessions can change juror's evaluations of interrogation strategies and subsequent decisions in court" (p. 351). They go on to recommend that expert witnesses should be called upon to educate jurors about the FEP technique. Woody and Forrest (2009) noted that it cannot be overlooked that the FEP technique has generally remained legal so long as it does not involve the creation of physical evidence that could continue to exist outside of the interrogation room or prove to overly coerce the subject. As such, the expert witness's goal in this situation is not to counteract the results of an illegal and abusive interrogation, but rather to cast doubt in the minds of the jury that the confession that the police legally and ethically elicited may possibly be false. In short, some in academia are attempting to give hope to the defense attorney who receives a confession case and has no other option but to attack the voluntariness of the statement. To no great surprise, these false confession experts are ready, willing, and able (for a price) to ascend the steps of the witness stand, grab their research football, and sling a Hail Mary pass in the direction of the jury box hoping that jurors will believe that the subject's confession is actually false.

In calling on the need for false confession expert witnesses, Leo and Liu

(1999) looked to the conclusions of their own survey research in which they questioned college students about their knowledge of police interrogative methods and false confessions. They then reported:

> Experts may inform jurors that coercive interrogation techniques
> can lead to false confessions and how and why they may do so.
> If we cannot be sure that what potential jurors believe about false
> confessions is accurate, then we cannot be sure that real jurors
> will make an accurate determination of the reliability of confes-
> sion evidence without the additional assistance provided in the
> testimony of an expert witness (p. 3397).

What Leo and Liu (2009) are saying in this statement is that expert witnesses are needed to ensure that jurors understand the "truth" about false confessions and how law enforcement interrogative techniques cause those false confessions to occur. Unfortunately, we must remember that academia's idea of the truth is one that they themselves have created. It is a truth based on an underlying bias against both law enforcement and the criminal justice system, their reliance on flawed and unrealistic research with college students, and their tendency to focus on those interrogations that have gone horribly wrong. In short, the 'truth' that they want jurors to be educated about is a truth that fits their own unique and self-created worldview. Predictably, it is also a truth that serves almost solely the criminal defense attorney.

To prove the elemental motivation of some academic researchers and expert witnesses, we need only look to their own stated desires masquerading as implications for reform. For example, Davis and Leo (2012) recommend:

> Currently, the courts are most receptive to expert testimony on
> chronic mental disabilities that increase suggestibility, and tend
> to exclude or disregard testimony on acute suggestibility or the
> forces of the interrogation. Interrogation experts must argue
> more extensively and persistently for the relevance of broader
> psychological science to interrogation, as we have exemplified

here, rather than to defer to the tendencies of the courts to regard research not explicitly conducted with interrogation as irrelevant.

As has been discussed in previous chapters, and as can be observed in the statistics of the Innocence Project and the National Registry of Exonerations, mental illness and cognitive deficiencies play a huge role in an innocent subject's decision to confess falsely. The aforementioned statement by Davis and Leo (2012) acknowledges the court's awareness of this relationship and the willingness of the court to accept expert witness testimony relating to how such chronic mental disabilities may lead to the rendering of false confessions. However, this statement also acts as a 'call to arms' for academic researchers and expert witnesses to make judges increasingly more aware that they can discount the confessions legally elicited by law enforcement officers for other reasons as well. In simplest terms, these experts are creating their own industry undergirded by a promise of mutual benefit with defense attorneys which sounds like this: "Hire me at top dollar to testify about false confessions, and I will give you a fighting chance with your subject who has already confessed to police."

In perhaps one of the most self-serving research undertakings, Kassin, Redlich, Alceste, and Luke (2018) created their own research design to bolster the need for expert witness testimony. Their self-aggrandizing motivations become readily apparent in their summary of this study. In essence, Kassin et al. conducted online surveys with 87 'experts' in the psychology of confessions. They questioned these experts about their opinions on 30 propositions relating to deception detection, police interrogation, confessions, and related general principles of psychology. They then concluded that several of the propositions were reliable enough to be presented in court as expert testimony. Nearly all of those surveyed reported that their main goal in testifying as an expert was to educate juries so that jurors may be more competent in evaluating confession evidence. Kassin et al. then suggested that these findings should help judges and expert witnesses in identifying which areas of the false confession research can be considered generally acceptable and therefore suitable for presentation in a court of law.

Essentially, the survey conducted by Kassin et al. (2018) clearly illustrates that too many false confession expert witnesses are being prevented from testifying because of the fact that their findings are not found to be generally acceptable. Their answer to this problem was to ask themselves whether they believe their research findings enough to allow them to testify about these findings as expert witnesses. This is similar to asking Detroit Lions fans if they believe that the Lions' receiver actually caught a disputed last-minute, game-winning pass in the end zone or whether the pass was incomplete. Naturally, nearly all Lions' fans would say that the ball was caught and the Lions had won the game. Upon being questioned about their research in the study by Kassin et al., false confession experts similarly found their findings to be generally agreed upon and suitable for in-court testimony. In discussing the need for their survey, Kassin et. al stated that, "with increasing frequency, psychologists and other social scientists in the United States, Canada, and elsewhere have served as expert witnesses in trials that contain disputed confessions" (p. 66). It should be known that confessions are routinely disputed by the defense as they have no other option but to question the legality and truthfulness of the confession. While not every case involving a disputed confession proceeds to trial, the problem for these 'experts' is that they are too frequently being precluded from testifying, at times because "such testimony is not reliable and valid or is not generally accepted" (Kassin et al., 2018, p. 66). As further noted by Kassin et al., "U.S. courts have proved inconsistent in their willingness to admit expert testimony on the psychology of confessions" (p. 66). The survey research put forth by Kassin et al. was one attempt to try and fix this problem. Unfortunately for them, this research project was also fraught with issues.

From the outset of the Kassin et al. (2018) survey research, a clear bias existed. The nature of this bias stemmed from their operational definition of the term 'expert.' Their concept of 'expert' was defined as individuals with a "Ph.D. and who had published on confessions or had testified in court as a confession expert" (p. 67). It is interesting to highlight that the actual act of interrogating criminal subjects is not considered a prerequisite for being considered a confession 'expert.' One has to wonder in what other profession this may be considered reasonable. For example, if called upon to testify on the particulars of heart surgery, one would expect that the expert witness had actually conducted such a surgery in the past. Similarly, if called upon to testify about the failures of catalytic converter design, one would expect that the expert witness had actually designed catalytic converters at some point in their career. However, when it comes to expert witnesses in the field of criminal interrogation, all that is required for expertise according to Kassin et al. is a Ph.D., a published article, and/or testimony experience. According to this definition, those who actually conduct criminal interrogations for a living have a lesser degree of expertise than those who sit in the bleachers and protest that the athletes on the field are doing things incorrectly. Put another way, those who can, do. Those who can't, claim that they are the experts.

With such a profound level of academic arrogance, it is not difficult to guess the findings of this research. Upon asking a group of academics who study, publish, and/or testify about the phenomenon of true and false confessions whether they agree with statements about lie detection, Miranda warnings, sleep deprivation, minimization, and so on, Kassin et al. (2018) almost seemed surprised that the overwhelming majority of these individuals agree with the same positions. Let us not forget that the overwhelming majority of these individuals, by the very same inclusion criteria put forth by Kassin et al., come from the same background . . . academia. This is akin to asking Planned Parenthood employees whether they agree with a woman's right to choose, or asking attendees at the Conservative Political Action Conference (CPAC) whether they agree that the Second Amendment's right to bear arms should not be abridged. What *is* surprising is the fact that Kassin et al. seem surprised in the near unanimity of agreement among these self-described 'experts.' While it is posited that this level of agreement is suggestive of a requisite degree of scientific consensus, it can also be interpreted that what Kassin et al. have actually tapped into is the profound level of 'groupthink' among many academics. In fact, this latter interpretation is actually supported by the data offered by Kassin et al.

It cannot be ignored that in addition to having academic backgrounds, 3,399 of the 3,727 (or 91%) of the requests that these survey participants received to testify originated from defense attorneys. Similarly, 87% of those who agreed to testify in court did so on behalf of the defense. Kassin et al. attribute this monumental imbalance to the simple fact that most requests for false confession expert witness testimony come from defense attorneys. While this may be true, it cannot be overlooked that this is really the only product that these experts are selling. If a criminal confession is generally assumed to be true, then the only need for an expert witness would be to try to plant a seed of doubt in the minds of judges and juries on behalf of the defense. This is like expressing shock at learning that the overwhelming number of calls to an automotive body shop come from individuals who have experienced damage to their cars. The simple fact is that body shops exist to fix cars, and false confession expert witnesses exist to weaken the prosecution's confession evidence. This realization also helps to illustrate the homogeneity of the pool from which Kassin et al. recruited their survey participants.

It is also important to highlight the manner in which Kassin et al. (2018) assessed the beliefs of their so-called 'experts' on three questions relating to the relevance of expert witness testimony. In one of the questions, participants were asked, "In your opinion, are juries better equipped to evaluate confession evidence with or without the aid of a competent expert?" (p. 69). Again, let us all guess as to how the survey participants responded to this question. This question is similar to asking members of the U.S. Congress whether they feel that the lives of American citizens are better because of their efforts as congressmen and congresswomen. The aforementioned question posed by Kassin et al. is even more absurd when it is considered that the answer given by the expert will impact whether the expert can receive large sums of cash for their testimony in the future. In the simplest of terms, if asked whether a jury is better equipped to evaluate a confession with their help, a false confession expert really has no other option but to answer in the affirmative. Answering "No" to such a question would suggest that their professional pursuits have been irrelevant and inconsequential while simultaneously decreasing the likelihood of being handsomely compensated for their testimony in the future. Yet, this does not preclude Kassin et al. from heralding the naturally anticipated response to such a self-serving question as proof that false confession expert witness testimony is of critical importance.

The academic arrogance and self-serving methods associated with the Kassin et al. (2018) survey continues with statements like, "On propositions addressing lay perceptions of confessions, respondents exhibited little confidence in the notion that people can evaluate confession evidence" (p. 72). Similarly, Kassin et. al state, "In addition to indicating the degree to which jurors are purportedly aware or not aware of generally accepted propositions, our survey revealed a number of ways in which jurors may harbor erroneous beliefs and misconceptions" (p.74). What these statements suggest is that not only are law enforcement officers and prosecutors unabashedly ignorant as to the false confession phenomenon, so too is the average person. In other words, it is only this small group of academics who have never interrogated anyone and whose findings often run counter to commonsense that are smart enough to see what is really taking place in America's interrogation rooms. They believe that they alone hold the truth because they come from an academic background, because they read, review, support, and regurgitate one another's positions, and/or because they have received substantial consultation fees from defense attorneys in exchange for their expert testimony. This level of arrogance is astounding, yet pales in comparison to the belief held by Kassin et al. that this group of reported experts are considered a "diverse" sample (p. 75) on which to base their surveys.

Ethical Considerations

It is important to recognize that many false confession expert witnesses come from the halls of academia. As such, many expert witnesses take the witness stand to discuss the conclusions reached through the research they themselves have conducted. While this is not problematic in and of itself, it does begin to skirt the issue of ethicality when it comes to their unending calls for more expert witnesses to educate judges and jurors about the phenomenon of false confessions. Although not all expert witnesses are psychologists, it is important to keep in mind the Ethical Principles of Psychologists and Code of Conduct (APA, 2002). More specifically, Section 3.05 of the Ethics Code relates to the issue of Multiple Relationships and states that a psychologist should refrain from:

> Entering into a multiple relationship if the multiple relation-
> ship could reasonably be expected to impair the psychologist's
> objectivity, competence, or effectiveness in performing his or her
> functions as a psychologist (p. 6).

Similarly, Section 3.06 addresses the issue of Conflict of Interest. This section cautions that:

> Psychologists refrain from taking on a professional role when
> personal, scientific, professional, legal, financial, or other inter-
> ests or relationships could reasonably be expected to impair their
> objectivity, competence, or effectiveness in performing their
> functions as psychologists (p. 6).

In addition to the APA Ethics Code, forensic psychology practitioners must also adhere to the Specialty Guidelines for Forensic Psychology (APA, 2011). Of particular importance is Section 1.02 which relates to Impartiality and Fairness and states in part that:

> When conducting research, forensic practitioners seek to repre-
> sent results in a fair and impartial manner. Forensic practitioners
> strive to utilize research designs and scientific methods that
> adequately and fairly test the questions at hand, and they attempt
> to resist partisan pressures to develop designs or report results
> in ways that might be misleading or unfairly bias the results of a
> test, study, or evaluation (p. 3).

Furthermore, Section 1.03 discusses the need for Avoiding Conflicts of Interest. This section states in part that:

> Forensic practitioners refrain from taking on a professional role when personal, scientific, professional, legal, financial, or other interests or relationships could reasonably be expected to impair their impartiality, competence, or effectiveness (p. 3).

As mandated by these ethical guidelines, psychologists engaging in research or testifying before the court must not only prevent their bias from impacting their professional opinions and assessments, but they must also avoid entering into a dual relationship. For example, in the field of clinical psychology, it would be unethical to administer a psychological assessment to a client, conclude that the client requires therapeutic treatment, and then recommend your own services to provide that treatment. This would be problematic because the psychologist has a financial motivation to recommend treatment to the client. The same reasoning could be applied to academic researchers who conduct their studies and then continuously recommend that expert witnesses be used to inform juries about the very same issue they addressed in their research. Unfortunately, some within the academic research community are shameless in this regard, and their research conclusions sound strikingly similar to the following proposition: "Based on my research, I recommend that expert witnesses be hired by the defense to inform the jury about false confessions. By the way, I also provide expert witness services if you are looking for somebody." After a while, these studies and related recommendations begin to sound less like unbiased research and more like an infomercial for their false confession expert witness services.

The Need to Record Interrogations

In addition to the recommendation that expert witnesses be employed to inform jurors about the intricacies of false confessions, it is also routinely recommended that law enforcement interrogations be recorded in their entirety. In fact, these recommendations are frequently made together (Kassin, 2008). Academic researchers offer a variety of reasons for why interrogations should be recorded. For example, Kassin, Appleby, and Perillo (2010) offered that a key problem within the United States is that judges and juries are often only presented with the subject's written statement or a summary recording of their confession as opposed to being furnished a complete recording of the entire interrogation that produced the confession. The underlying assumption fostered by many defense attorneys is that something of critical importance must have happened during the interrogation process that the police do not want the jury to see. More specifically, defense attorneys often discreetly strive to leave jurors with the impression that officers must have engaged in unethical, immoral, and illegal interrogative tactics that forced the subject to confess; otherwise the police would have recorded the interrogation.

In an effort to encourage law enforcement agencies to record interrogations in their entirety, it has been suggested that such recordings will help to prevent frivolous lawsuits or combat unfounded defense claims that the officers engaged in overly coercive interrogative techniques. In short, some have posited that recording the entire interrogation will ultimately help to protect law enforcement interrogators. Academic researchers have also put forth the idea that recording criminal interrogations in their entirety will help to provide a more accurate representation of everything that transpired during the course of the interrogation, which can help judges in their efforts to determine the voluntariness of a subject's statement while simultaneously assisting juries in their efforts to determine the subject's guilt (Johnson & Drucker, 2009; Kassin, 2005; Kassin, Appleby, & Perillo, 2010; Kassin et al., 2010). Furthermore, it has been offered that recording the entire interrogation will not only encourage law enforcement officers to utilize ethical interrogative techniques (Kassin, Appleby, & Perillo, 2010), but it will also help to discourage law enforcement from engaging in inappropriate or overly coercive interrogative methods (Kassin, 2005; Kassin et al., 2010; Kassin, Appleby, & Perillo, 2010). This last assertion is particularly bothersome and can arguably reflect yet another underlying bias of some academic researchers. More precisely, it suggests that if not for the watchful eye of the video camera, law enforcement officers will naturally resort to abusive and unethical treatment in order to elicit confessions from criminal subjects. While serving in

380

the United States Army Infantry, we were taught the credo that "integrity is doing what's right when no one else is looking." Suggesting that police are more likely to behave appropriately in the interrogation room when a video recorder is running suggests that police default to unethical behavior unless observed by outside parties. The bias of such a position is unmistakable.

As scores of academic researchers lobby for the recording of all law enforcement interrogations, one has to wonder whether all academics would be so willing to have each and every one of *their* lectures or office hour meetings recorded? Before this question is answered, let's consider the words of Matthew Kay, an English teacher at the Science Leadership Academy, who tweeted on August 9, 2020 the following concerns stemming from the decision to transition children to online learning during the COVID-19 pandemic.

> So, this fall, virtual class discussion will have many potential spectators – parents, siblings, etc. – in the same room. We'll never be quite sure who is overhearing the discourse. What does this do for our equity/inclusion work? How much have students depended on the (somewhat) secure barriers of our physical classrooms to encourage vulnerability? How many of us have installed some version of 'what happens here stays here' to help this? While conversations about race are in my wheelhouse, and remain a concern in this no-walls environment – I am most intrigued by the damage that 'helicopter/snowplow' parents can do in the host conversations about gender/sexuality. And while 'conservative' parents are my chief concern – I know that the damage can come from the left too. If we are engaged in the messy work of destabilizing a kid's racism or homophobia or transphobia – how much do we want their classmates' parents piling on? (Manfredi, 2020).

While some may understandably question why some of these topical areas are being addressed by an educator tasked with teaching English to high school students, Kay's questions nonetheless highlight the underlying concerns associated with giving nonparticipants unfettered access to every word spoken during Kay's classroom instruction. If we are to strictly adhere to the theoretical foundations supporting academia's argument for the mandatory recording of all interrogations, then it must be assumed that Kay and all educators are engaged in inappropriate and potentially corrupting activities with students unless every portion of their classroom instruction is recorded. While it is clearly unreasonable and without merit to assume that every educator who expresses an unwillingness to be recorded in such a manner must be engaging in unethical or immoral behavior with their students, the same also holds true for criminal interrogators.

Let's also recall that USA Gymnastics national team doctor Larry Nassar was convicted for sexually abusing scores of young female athletes; Penn State football coach Jerry Sandusky was charged with sexually abusing 10 boys through his youth charity; untold numbers of Catholic priests have been accused of sexual abuse of children; and Jeffrey Epstein was charged with the sexual trafficking of dozens of minors before his apparent suicide in prison. Despite these egregious criminal acts, there is no similar clamor to record every doctor's office, sports locker room, church, or bedroom. If such mandatory recording was in place at the time, thousands of children in just these handful of cases could have been spared immense pain and suffering. It is likely that there is no movement to have mandatory recordings conducted in these venues because of an inherent realization that the crimes that took place in these locations were anomalies. As such, society may not be so ready to relinquish our collective rights to privacy in exchange for catching a few bad actors. Yet there exists an incessant call for every aspect of policing to be recorded. While body cameras are now ubiquitous, the same movement is now underway to have all interrogations recorded in their entirety. It is curious that this drumbeat for nonstop recording is directed at a profession that requires a certain degree of education, a clean police record, a background check, a psychological evaluation, a drug test, and even a polygraph examination before a person can even join their respective agency. As a society, we do not demand this level of scrutiny of our child care providers, our teachers, our medical staff, our clergy, and certainly not our politicians. Still, some academic researchers, expert witnesses, and advocacy groups have served to create an environment in which law enforcement officers, especially those tasked with questioning criminal suspects, are assumed to be acting unethically unless a video recording proves otherwise. This, by its very nature, is a bias that would not be tolerated in any other aspect of our society. Just as we cannot infer guilt if a subject chooses not to testify in court, we should also not infer wrongdoing by law enforcement if an interrogation is not recorded.

In reality, what the repeated recommendation to record every aspect of the interrogation process may actually be doing is setting up a system of job security for academic researchers and expert witnesses. Kassin (2008) stated that a benefit of recording the entire interrogation is that it ensures that "judges and juries can observe how the confessions are produced" (p. 252). Kassin et al. (2010) also stated that when entire interrogations are recorded, false confessions will be reduced as the resulting method of interrogation will involve "less egregious uses of the tactics that cause us great concern (e.g., the false evidence ploy and certain minimization tactics")" (p. 50). At first blush, this last sentence rings with a certain level of arrogance. More specifically, the use of the word "us" suggests that it is the academic researcher, not the courts or legal system, that will determine what interrogative techniques are concerning. When both of these statements are combined, it can be concluded that what is likely to occur with the recording of every interrogation is a steady stream of expert witnesses who are willing to testify about the interrogative methods that their flawed laboratory experiments and their repeated analysis of the very worst examples of criminal interrogation have led *them* to believe are problematic.

Based on my review of the literature, what I anticipate occurring as a result of the push to record every interrogation in its entirety is the following scenario. The false confession expert witness will take the stand, explain their educational and research background, and begin educating the jury about all of the things *they* believe contribute to a false confession. The defense attorney will then play snippets of the interrogation at which time the expert witness will interject and state, "Ladies and gentlemen of the jury, what you just observed was Detective Smith employing the Bluff Technique. According to the research, the Bluff Technique increases the likelihood of a false confession." The defense will then play the next snippet only to have the expert witness state, "What you can see here is that Detective Smith is attempting to reduce the moral seriousness of the offense. This is what is referred to as a minimization strategy which is taught in the Reid Technique. The research has shown that both the Reid Technique and minimization strategies can cause false confessions."

Simply put, while the academic research is purportedly fueled by altruism, some in academia have come to realize that lucrative expert witness fees await them if they can effectively sway the opinions of jurors and positively influence trial outcomes in favor of the defense. Woody and Forrest (2009) all but admit to this by stating, "if expert witnesses have even small effects on outcomes, defendants and attorneys may seek expert testimony to sway jurors" (p. 340). Moreover, they note that many expert witnesses outright advertise their willingness to testify regarding interrogation techniques and their impact on confessions (Woody & Forrest, 2009). I personally take no issue with those in academia who seek to study the false confession phenomenon or expert witnesses who testify on behalf of the defense. We should have educated people who study all issues impacting our society, and our legal system is founded on the premise that a subject who stands accused of a crime has the right to mount a meaningful defense. In fact, it is hard to ignore the need for experts in countless fields to testify for either the prosecution or the defense. However, we should all be concerned when academic researchers consistently recommend the very services they provide as a means of solving the problem that they themselves have defined.

Let's apply this concept to the local government structure. Suppose the mayor of a small town informed the community that he believes a problem exists with the landscaping at the local park. More specifically, after looking into the problem, the mayor has determined that the overgrown hedges around the playground prevent parents from adequately observing their children. As such, he recommends that the bushes be removed and replaced with flower beds containing small plants and bushes so as not to obstruct the view of watchful caretakers. He also recommends that this work be done professionally. Then, two months later, the city council hires the landscaping company owned by the mayor to do the work. In the realm of government, this would be considered corruption. Can the same not be said for academics who use their research to tout the need for expert witnesses while simultaneously providing expert witness services?

As mentioned at the outset of this text, there is an undeniable nobility in fighting to ensure that those who are wrongfully convicted are freed and that those who are innocent are never wrongfully convicted in the first place. Moreover, I am in no way suggesting that every law enforcement interrogation is conducted ethically and legally. Still, despite the nobility underlying the efforts of the wrongful conviction advocates, it cannot be assumed that they are all motivated by solely altruistic desires. This is particularly true of academic researchers and expert witnesses. In reality, the false confession movement has inarguably become an industry. In addition to the media productions related to this topic, there are also those who have enriched themselves through their academic exploration of the false confession phenomenon and their ready testimony as false confession expert witnesses for the defense. Unfortunately, these two ventures often go hand-in-hand. Clearly, not all researchers engage in these dual roles. However, it would be a false assumption to believe that every academic researcher cares only about preventing wrongful convictions when the highly lucrative false confession expert witness industry continues to thrive.

CHAPTER 20

The Problems Facing Academic Researchers, Expert Witnesses, and Advocates

Throughout this text, I have undoubtedly made comments and drawn conclusions that may be considered controversial and most certainly unpopular among those who have chosen to study the issue of false confessions. In the simplest of terms, the very basis of this book stands in stark contrast to many of the prevailing sentiments found within the existing false confession literature. I have sought to present countervailing arguments to the general positions repeatedly put forth by academic researchers, false confession expert witnesses, and wrongful conviction advocates. While I anticipate that many may quickly line up to disagree with these arguments, I have presented these positions because, as a law enforcement practitioner who specializes in the interrogation of criminal subjects, I wholeheartedly disagree with many of their assumptions. I disagree that false confessions happen routinely. I disagree that law enforcement is inept at identifying deception. I disagree that routine interrogative practices cause false confessions for the normal functioning adult subject. I disagree that the conclusions drawn from laboratory experiments with college students can be applied to the real world of law enforcement. I disagree that the Reid Technique causes false confessions, and I disagree that academic researchers have remained unbiased in their approach to the false confession phenomenon or their perception of law enforcement interrogators. Running the risk of sounding argumentative, I find many of the positions of academia to be equally controversial. Yet, I believe that two incontrovertible facts exist regarding this phenomenon: 1) confessions are an overwhelmingly powerful form of evidence that can greatly assist in convicting a truly guilty subject; and 2) innocent people sometimes falsely confess. While I am quite confident that many academics and expert witnesses will agree with these positions, I am also confident that they face inherent problems when it comes to offering their own conclusions. The following is a discussion of the issues that academia, expert witnesses, and advocates, despite their best efforts, simply cannot get around.

They Just Don't Know

Although academics and expert witnesses continue to claim that false confessions happen routinely (Kassin, Appleby, & Perillo, 2010; Klaver et al., 2008; Narchet, Meissner, & Russano, 2011), the truth remains that they simply do not know how often they actually occur (Davis & Leo, 2012; Kassin et al., 2010a; Kassin & Fong, 1999; Malloy et al., 2014; Schatz, 2016; Trocino, 2016; Villar, Arciuli, & Paterson, 2013; Wrightsman & Kassin, 1993). In fact, some have suggested that an adequate method to calculate their frequency does not exist (Kassin, 2005; Kassin & Fong, 1999; Kassin & Gudjonsson, 2004; Pimentel et al., 2015). So, while Redlich et al. (2010) maintain that, "it is difficult, if not impossible, to obtain accurate objective rates of false admissions" (p. 80), this does not stop some in academia from professing their belief that the true number of false confessions is far greater that what is currently known (Bradford & Goodman-Delahunty, 2008; Davis & Leo, 2012; Kassin, Appleby, & Perillo, 2010; Leo, 2007). Villar et al. (2013) attempted to put a number on the frequency of false confessions by citing the work of Gudjonsson. In doing so, Villar et al. (2003) claimed that the existing data may indicate that 7-12% of subjects in the United States may have provided a false confession to law enforcement. While this may cause some to become alarmed, the statistic is falsely reported and completely inaccurate. More specifically, the numbers from the study of Gudjonsson et al. (2007)

and referenced by Villar et al. (2013) actually related to survey research with 1,896 Icelandic college students about the number of times that they may have falsely confessed to Icelandic police. In short, the statistic offered by Villar et al. (2013) is not only based on self-report, but it has absolutely nothing to do with false confessions occurring in the United States. Such misinterpretations help to exemplify how the largest conundrum for academic researchers and expert witnesses is that they simply have no ability to accurately identify how frequently false confessions occur. It is therefore a blind leap of faith for these reported experts to claim that the number of observable false confessions represent the tip of a much vaster, yet unknowable, iceberg.

Based on the dated nature of the Innocence Project and National Registry of Exonerations cases, it is equally plausible that the continuous professionalization of the law enforcement profession within the United States may mean that false confessions now occur to a far lesser degree than they did fifty or sixty years ago. If academia has to grudgingly admit that law enforcement has done away with the 'third degree' approach to criminal interrogation, then it only makes logical sense that the frequency of false confessions has similarly fallen by the wayside. To believe otherwise would be to overlook just how many false confessions were actually caused by beatings, suffocations, electric shocks to the genitals of criminal subjects, and other unspeakable acts of interrogative torture that occurred decades earlier. Simply put, if the reported experts cannot accurately identify how many false confessions occur, then it is also possible that false confessions are largely a thing of the past. "We don't know how many there are, but we know that it's a lot" is not an acceptable or well-reasoned conclusion.

False Confessions are Rare

Despite their admitted uncertainty, some in academia seem to rely on faith when it comes to false confessions. As noted by Schatz (2018), "People falsely confess. It is a fact of the criminal justice system proved time and again" (p. 645). Similarly, Gudjonsson (2010) states, "false confessions to serious crimes do happen more commonly than previously thought.

Anecdotal cases and numerous DNA exonerations provide strong evidence for this" (p. 44). Relying on 'anecdotal' cases or pointing to proven cases of false confession when they represent such an infinitesimal fraction of the overall number of violent crimes committed provides an insufficient basis on which to make such claims. From a statistical standpoint, it appears that false confessions occur to a far lesser degree than what academia may believe, or more importantly, what they would like others to believe. For starters, we must look at how frequently subjects confess generally. Cassell and Hayman (as cited by Moston & Engelberg, 2011) have suggested that 42% of criminal subjects render a confession after being interrogated by law enforcement. Leo (as cited by Moston & Engelberg, 2011) reported that 64% of subjects offer confessions/admissions. In referencing the work of various others conducting research in England and the United States, Davis and Leo (2012) reported an overall confession rate of between 42% and 76%. The ridiculous range of these statistics makes this information unusable as it suggests that either the majority of criminal subjects *do* confess or the majority of criminal subjects *do not* confess. Put another way, this statistical inconsistency demonstrates that not only does academia not know how frequently *false* confessions occur, they cannot even accurately identify how frequently *true* confessions occur. One thing is for certain however. Regardless of how you view the flawed statistics outlined above, a sizable portion of interrogation subjects refuse to confess to a crime they either did or did not commit. This cuts into the very premise that routine interrogation techniques are highly coercive. If these methods of questioning are so coercive, how can so many guilty and innocent subjects resist them? Similarly, if the overall rate of confessions can be as low as 42%, then proportionally, false confessions may actually be far lower than academics and expert witnesses would like us all to believe.

In their surveys with 631 law enforcement officers in the United States and Canada, Kassin et al. (2007) identified that survey respondents reported that only 4.78% of confessions are false. As previously outlined, we must remember that only .97% of those confessions are full confessions. What is not discussed in this statistic is how many of those .97% of full false confessions were elicited from subjects who were mentally ill, cognitively deficient, abused by their interrogators, or who falsely confessed to protect someone else, to gain notoriety, to obtain consistent shelter and meals, or were voluntarily given for some other reason. As documented in the chapter reevaluating the Innocence Project data, when these same factors were deducted from the false confession data presented by the Innocence Project and the National Registry of Exonerations, the number of proven false confession cases leading to a wrongful conviction was extremely low. Moreover, the number was infinitesimal when compared to the overall number of violent crimes occurring within the United States during the same time period. Lastly, in conducting qualitative interviews with 23 state and federal law enforcement polygraph examiners who specialize in criminal interrogation, only 2 participants reported ever eliciting a false confession that wasn't given to protect the truly guilty subject. Even then, neither of these two false confessions were accepted by the interrogator.

This information indicates that contrary to the popular belief of some academic researchers and expert witnesses, it does not appear that false confessions happen routinely. Furthermore, the number of false confessions that occur as a direct result of police interrogative techniques, as opposed to the dispositional risk factors unique to the subject, is even smaller still. So, if the exact number of false confessions cannot be known, then it is equally plausible that the reported 'tip of the iceberg' metaphor is actually an exaggeration of a relatively infrequently occurring phenomenon. Those in our legal system must therefore resist the temptation to accept the baseless assumption that false confessions occur frequently and that there exists a much larger, yet unknown, number of false confessions out there. The existing numbers and research simply don't support this premise, and the repeated recitation of this claim does not make it so. Still, some academic researchers, expert witnesses, and advocates desperately long for this to be true as it can help to cast doubt on every lawfully-obtained confession.

Some people may choose to hide behind the intellectually lazy argument that even one wrongful conviction caused by a false confession is one too many. While such platitudes make for a cliched bumper sticker, T-shirt, or tote bag, those serving within the criminal justice system must resist the temptation to fall for this short-sighted argument. The fear of making a rare mistake cannot serve as the basis for eradicating all legally permissible interrogative techniques. As previously discussed, for some academics, expert witnesses, and advocates, the true and ultimate motivation behind their efforts is to prevent *all* interrogations. The rationale for this anti-interrogation philosophy is quite simple and tacitly understood; law enforcement interrogations work. Criminal confessions routinely assist in the successful prosecution of truly guilty criminal subjects. This should be considered a good thing. Unfortunately, some refuse to concede that the concept of 'justice' not only means the exoneration of the innocent, but also the prosecution and conviction of the guilty. Some of the individuals holding this view grace the halls of academia and/or routinely testify on behalf of the defense attorneys who pay their hefty sums. However, law enforcement practitioners and career prosecutors must resist the pressure to discard lawful interrogative strategies and the true justice they help to bring about. Similarly, we as a society must ensure that the baby is not thrown out with the bathwater because of the misleading and highly inaccurate mantra that false confessions happen routinely.

Most Confessions are True and Interrogative Techniques Work

Another problem that continues to plague those academics targeting the interrogative methods of law enforcement is the fact that the majority of confessions elicited by police officers are true. Many academic researchers concede to this fact. For example, Leo and Ofshe (as cited by Klaver et al., 2008) stated, "In real-life criminal settings, most suspects who confess during police interrogations are guilty and most confessions are corroborated" (p 72). Similarly, Moston and Engelberg (2011) noted that, "most confessions are (in all probability) true confessions" (p 518). Other researchers have also acknowledged this fact (Davis & Leo, 2012; Levine et al., 2010). This is a problem for academics, expert witnesses, and advocates as it becomes difficult to blame the routine and legal interrogative practices of law enforcement officers when most confessions are true admissions of criminal wrongdoing. The question therefore arises: If most confessions are true, why should law enforcement divest itself of the techniques that elicited them?

Another stumbling block for these 'anti-interrogationists' stems from their acknowledgement that the same interrogative techniques that researchers believe cause false confession also lead to the elicitation of truthful confessions (Conti, 1999; Gaines, 2018; Janda, 2015; Kassin, 2005; Kassin, 2008; Perillo & Kassin, 2011; Russano et al., 2005). For example, Leding (2012) stated, "It is important to point out that the techniques used in interrogations are extremely effective and typically used for the purpose of eliciting a confession from a criminal" (p. 263). In other words, the interrogative methods used by police, yet maligned by some in academia, actually work. In fact, despite the incessant criticism, even the Reid Technique has been reported to be successful. As reported by Johnson and Drucker (2009), "The Inbau-Reid modern psychological interrogation approach can be effective in securing 'confessions' from suspects" (p. 68). Again, for those who actively lobby against the use of interrogations in general, the target placed upon routine interrogative techniques may have more to do with their frequent success than their occasional contributions to the relatively rare false confession.

The fact that routine interrogative practices are effective in eliciting truthful confessions, as well as the fact that most confessions elicited by police are true, presents a problem for expert witnesses and advocates. More specifically, it is inherently illogical to put forth the idea that the same interrogative techniques that cause guilty subjects to truthfully confess also cause innocent people to falsely confess. This is particularly true in light of the fact that many *guilty* people are able to withstand police interrogative methods and refuse to *truthfully* confess, and the overwhelming majority of *innocent* people are able to withstand police interrogative methods and refuse to *falsely* confess. A good way to conceptualize this is through the following analogy.

In suggesting that routine interrogative practices cause both true and false confessions, some academics are essentially suggesting that a recipe for chocolate chip cookies can both create perfect, golden-brown cookies while also causing the cookies to burn. How can this be? Routine interrogative practices are, in essence, a recipe for how to ethically interrogate a criminal subject to increase the likelihood that a guilty subject will truthfully confess while an innocent person will avoid falsely confessing. Cookie recipes are written down because they allow bakers to repeatedly and consistently create delicious baked goods. Similarly, the reason routine interrogative techniques are taught to law enforcement officers is because they have been shown to be successful at eliciting truthful confessions. Cookies are burned when the chef does not follow the recipe. False confessions are elicited when law enforcement officers deviate too far from the routine interrogative techniques they were taught. An incompetent baker who misreads the recipe or decides to tinker with the ingredients is asking for trouble. The same holds true for an unethical law enforcement officer who deviates from the commonly accepted methods of interrogation. Proof of this can be seen in the wrongful conviction vignettes provided on the Innocence Project website. Beating a subject with a flashlight, holding a gun to their head, or suffocating them until they confess is not taught in any legitimate interrogative manual. As such, it is not the approved recipe that leads to a false confession, but rather an unethical and out-of-control interrogative chef.

In light of the aforementioned analogy, some may quickly suggest that ethical interrogative techniques applied to a subject with profound risk factors like mental illness, cognitive deficiencies, or adolescence can also lead to false confessions. While this argument has merit, it can still be argued that in these particular situations, it is not the interrogative technique, but rather the subject's unique dispositional risk factors, that cause the false confession. In short, unless the defense attorney can demonstrate either: a) the interrogator acted in an unethical manner that was inconsistent with normal interrogative techniques; or b) the subject was a juvenile, mentally ill, or severely cognitively impaired, then it is illogical to blame an otherwise ethical interrogative technique for causing a false confession. In reality, the claim that a false confession was caused by a routine interrogative technique is a convenient, yet flawed, point for expert witnesses to rely upon. Judges and juries should therefore avoid accepting this one-size-fits-all defense strategy.

Now some could argue that there is a flaw in this analogy, namely that while the recipe may work in getting the guilty subject to confess, this recipe is specifically designed to use only on the guilty. It would therefore be problematic to use a chocolate chip cookie recipe on banana bread ingredients. Put another way, it would be inappropriate to use interrogative techniques designed for the guilty on innocent people. While there is also some merit to this argument, it ultimately depends upon how the concept of 'success' is defined. I contend that a successful interrogation on a truly guilty subject involves the elicitation of a truthful confession. Conversely, a successful interrogation on an innocent subject means that the innocent subject *does not* confess. It can therefore be logically argued that the recipe analogy works for the interrogation of both guilty and innocent subjects in light of the fact that academia has conceded that: a) interrogative methods are effective in eliciting truthful confessions, and b) most confessions are true. If a guilty subject fails to confess, either the interrogator was ineffective, or the subject had personality traits that precluded their confession. If an innocent subject confesses, either the interrogator was too abusive and heavy-handed, or the subject had personal characteristics that caused him to do so. For these reasons, law enforcement officers, prosecutors, judges, and juries must again resist efforts to blame the recipe because the recipe works when the directions are followed and the cookies are not burned.

They Don't Know What Causes False Confessions

As has been discussed throughout this text, some academic researchers, expert witnesses, and advocates believe that the interrogative techniques employed by law enforcement officers routinely cause innocent people to falsely confess. However, it cannot be overlooked that they simply have no proof of this position. In fact, in discussing the use of minimization techniques, Kassin and McNall (1991) admit, "It is difficult to determine the frequency with which these interrogation techniques are used, or their effects on guilty and innocent crime suspects" (p. 235). This lack of knowledge has often prevented false confession expert witnesses from testifying before the court. For example, in the case of *United States v. Deuman*, 892 F. Supp. 2d 881 (W.D. Mich. 2012), a false confession expert witness was called upon by the defense. This expert was expected to testify that Deuman, who stood accused of causing the death of his infant daughter and made incriminating comments to law enforcement officers about this matter, made statements that could be false and conditions may have existed during his interrogation that could cause an innocent person to make false statements. The following is part of the reasoning behind the court's decision to exclude this expert's testimony. I removed legal citations to make this information more readable.

> As Dr. ****** forthrightly admits, despite extensive research and review of false confession cases, his methodology cannot accurately predict the frequency and causes of false confessions... His theories cannot discern whether a certain interrogation technique, used on a person with certain traits or characteristics, results in a predictable rate of false confessions. In addition, he has formulated no theory or methodology that can be tested. While the Court is aware that some laboratory studies, such as the ALT key study by Professors Kassin and Perillo, suggest that coercive interrogation tactics produce a significant rate of false confessions, such studies shed no light on real-world interrogation practices and results because they "were not conducted by law enforcement, were not part of a criminal investigation, did not involve actual suspects, and did not present the students with a serious penalty." ...Moreover, as Dr. ****** testified at the *Daubert* hearing, there is no way of knowing how frequently false confessions occur in the real world.

As noted by the court in this particular case, academic researchers and false confession expert witnesses have some very real problems when it comes to the reliability of their studies, the relevance of their conclusions, and the applicability of their beliefs to the real world of criminal interrogation.

For this reason, law enforcement interrogators, prosecutors, judges, and juries should remember that these types of expert witnesses, as well as the academic research on which they base their conclusions, cannot accurately predict how often false confessions occur or what specifically causes them. Similarly, they cannot predict whether a certain interrogative technique, when used on a specific type of person, will result in a false confession. Furthermore, their theories are typically not able to be tested, and their research offers no meaningful insight into actual criminal interrogations occurring outside of the laboratory setting. Claims to the contrary are simply an attempt to sneak one past the judicial goalie in hopes of bringing a win for the defense.

False Confessions Are Counterintuitive

A final problem facing academic researchers, expert witnesses, and advocates relates to the fact that, for most people, false confessions just don't make sense. Trocino (2016) states:

> It seems to defy logic that a person would confess to a crime,
> especially a rape or a murder, that he did not commit. It is
> difficult to believe that someone could be so fooled, cajoled
> or coerced into falsely admitting to a crime that carries a life
> sentence or even the death penalty. The first reaction is that this
> must be wrong (p.85).

Lackey (2020) similarly reports that:

> Most of us find it very difficult to imagine ourselves confessing
> to something we didn't do and so we conclude that the suspect
> must be guilty. This is especially compelling when a violent
> crime is at issue, such as murder (p. 65).

Forrest et al. (2012) noted that "most individuals do not believe that they or others like them would falsely confess in the absence of physical coercion" (p. 345). Various other researchers have reported arriving at the same conclusion (Henkel et al., 2008; Leo, 2008; Woody & Forrest, 2009). Moreover, Leo (as cited by Schatz, 2018), identified that even law enforcement officers and prosecutors find it difficult to believe that an innocent person would falsely confess to a crime for which they are innocent. The counterintuitive nature of the false confession remains a significant issue for academia. The tendency of most human beings to believe that they would never falsely confess to a crime unless tortured into doing so means that academics and expert witnesses are forced to fight an uphill battle against common logic in trying to convince judges and jurors that false confessions happen routinely. The realization of this fact may explain why so many academic researchers recommend the need for expert witnesses to educate judges and juries about false confessions and their assumptions about what causes them. Still, despite this battle cry, it is extremely difficult to convince the average person that a normal-functioning adult would confess to a crime they did not commit. Simply put, this places academia in the unenviable position of having to argue against what many take to be common sense.

CHAPTER 21

Final Thoughts

False confessions occur. Despite the arguments raised throughout this text, it cannot be forgotten that false confessions *do* occur. While they are obviously problematic for the innocent person who is wrongfully convicted for a crime they did not commit, these innocent subjects are not the only victims. If the wrong person is convicted of a crime, that means that the truly guilty subject is left on the street to continue their raping, pillaging, and plundering of our communities. This means that other potential victims of future crimes exist. If the wrong person is convicted, then the law enforcement agency and municipality from which the false confession emanated is at risk of potential legal actions. This obviously harms the department and the municipality. When an innocent person is wrongfully convicted, the law enforcement officer who elicited the confession may experience costly lawsuits and profound damage to their reputation. Lastly, with each wrongful conviction, society loses faith in the justice system as a whole. In short, wrongful convictions impact countless individuals and our society in general. For this reason, the efforts of groups like the Innocence Project are of critical importance in serving as the last check and balance on a system comprised of fallible human beings. Still, it must be remembered that not all wrongful convictions are caused by false confessions. Furthermore, not all false confessions lead to a wrongful conviction. So yes, false confessions do occur, but as discussed in the preceding chapters, they do not appear to occur frequently and certainly not to the extent that some would have you believe. In addition, those that do occur do not appear to be automatically accepted by investigators or prosecutors.

Despite my repeated disagreements with many academics dedicated to the study of false confessions, there are some areas where interrogative specialists and academic researchers seem to agree. For example, young people, the mentally ill, those with serious cognitive impairments, and those who have a strong desire to please the interrogator are at an increased risk for falsely confessing. However, this area of agreement should not be misconstrued as inherently identifiable causes of false confessions. In other words, just because an interrogation subject was 16 years of age at the time of the interrogation does not mean that the confession they rendered is therefore false. The same holds true for a subject with a low IQ or a diagnosis of bipolar disorder. For those law enforcement officers reading this text, you must be careful when interrogating individuals with these risk factors, and you must be aware of the potential ease with which you may be able to influence their behavior. In addition to these risk factors, there appears to be a level of agreement between academia and interrogative specialists regarding interrogative behaviors that can increase the likelihood of a false confession. More specifically, egregiously lengthy interrogations, overly coercive interrogations, and overt threats or promises to a criminal subject can increase the likelihood of a false confession. As such, those in law enforcement who conduct criminal interrogations must strive to avoid such interrogative behaviors to decrease the likelihood of eliciting a false confession. Again, because these concepts are inherently subjective, it should not automatically be concluded that the subject's confession was false simply because one of these behaviors was present at the time of the questioning. As previously stated, presence does not mean causation.

Outside of these areas of agreement, I have thoroughly explained throughout this text why I disagree so frequently with many academic researchers, false confession expert witnesses, and advocates. At present, there is a very strong anti-law law enforcement base within this country. Shouts of, "Defund the Police" and "All Cops are Bastards" make it difficult to ignore where some stand when it comes to the profession of law enforcement. However, these feelings are not relegated solely to police patrols and arrest techniques; nor are they espoused solely by protestors. As I have indicated in earlier chapters, a similar anti-law enforcement bias is also held by many in academia to include some who have chosen to study the false confession phenomenon. This unique worldview has not only colored the way in which some academics view police, but it has also served as an accelerant in the undeniable and ongoing movement to attack the law enforcement investigatory process of criminal interrogation. For some, the war against criminal interrogation stems from the fact that the criminal confession is an overwhelmingly powerful form of evidence that is inherently difficult for defense attorneys to counteract. In fact, a criminal confession is like giving the prosecutor's team a 48-point lead in the game before the opening kickoff even commences. As such, defense attorneys are left with no other option but to attack the voluntariness of the subject's confession. The best option they have comes in the form of the false confession expert witness who will then sit before the jury, educate them about the false confession phenomenon (as they see it), suggest that the subject has certain dispositional risk factors that make him/her more susceptible to falsely confessing, and then point out interrogative techniques that were employed which, according to their own research, increases the likelihood of a false confession.

Because the vast majority of these 'experts' have never actually interrogated a criminal subject; their 'expertise' originates from their own analysis of the problem. This analysis often relies on the study of the most egregious examples of criminal interrogation or never-ending laboratory experimentation with university students anxious for extra college credit. Such inherently flawed and biasing sources of information then allow the expert witness to speak with authority as they pocket their handsome fees and offer the defense a fighting chance at a 'not guilty' verdict. It is a symbiotic relationship that hinges on a solitary, yet crucial, undertaking. The expert witness must effectively raise doubt in the minds of the jury that the defendant may have falsely confessed to police. To the false confession expert witness and the defense attorney who retains their services, besmirching the reputation of the law enforcement officer who elicited the confession or impugning the efficacy of an interrogative method or technique is immaterial. They are merely roadblocks to their ultimate destination—cultivating doubt in the minds of the jury. This is where my primary concern lies.

Untold scores of law enforcement officers have dedicated their lives to the law enforcement profession. Unlike many other occupations, they are routinely called upon to work long and odd hours. They are routinely asked to miss holidays, birthdays, ball games, and recitals. They are routinely called upon to run toward danger while others run in the opposite direction. And, unlike the majority of other professions, they are subjected to the worst aspects of society like murder, suicide, car accidents, child abuse, and sexual assault, while all the time being reminded that they are to remain professional, unemotional, and unbiased. Unlike almost every other job category, before they can even begin this work, they are drug tested, polygraphed, psychologically evaluated, medically assessed, physically tested, and every aspect of their background is reviewed. Then, when they are called upon to engage in the very acts that protect citizens and maintain order, they are second-guessed, criticized, and critiqued by countless individuals who would likely be found unsuitable to even hold the same position.

I once heard that golf is a game in which every shot makes somebody unhappy. A good shot makes the competition unhappy while a bad shot makes the individual swinging the club unhappy. The same holds true for the law enforcement officers of this country. For every crime, there is typically a victim and an offender. While the victim may be glad to see the police, the offender is likely anything but. Instead, the offender chooses from a variety of responses to the officer's actions. These may include filing a formal complaint against the officer, initiating a lawsuit against the department for a violation of their rights, assaulting the officer verbally and/or physically, and even attempting to take the officer's life. These responses often occur regardless of the subject's guilt or innocence.

It is important to remember that justice is a two-sided coin. On one side, those who are innocent of a crime should be identified as such and cleared of any wrongdoing. It is hard to conceive of any citizen not agreeing with this aspect of justice. Despite what some might think, it is equally hard to conceive of a law enforcement officer who consciously chose to raise their hand and swear an oath to support and defend the Constitution of the United States while simultaneously maintaining a desire to put innocent subjects behind bars. The flip side of the justice coin mandates that those who are guilty of a crime should be identified and punished for their wrongdoing. For some, this second side is a tough pill to swallow. Simply put, some in our society, including some in academia, study the false confession phenomenon and do not believe in the value of this aspect of justice. It is not difficult to project the likely result of a child who is never corrected or punished for their misdeeds. It is even more terrible to consider the likely result of a society in which criminal misdeeds are ignored. Yet, this is exactly what is happening currently in many of America's cities under a misguided interpretation of criminal justice reform. As a career law enforcement officer, I believe in both tenets of justice. The guilty should be punished. The innocent should not. I am quite confident that I am not alone as either a law enforcement officer or as a citizen of the United States regarding the need to have both. The question arises, however: Would every false confession academic researcher, expert witness, and advocate agree with the need for the guilty to be identified, arrested, prosecuted, convicted, and sentenced? Unfortunately, since 91% of the requests for false confession expert witness testimony come from defense attorneys (Kassin et al., 2018), the answer to this question cannot automatically be assumed.

I propose that a staunch belief in the need to protect the innocent while simultaneously disavowing the righteous need to punish the guilty renders a person's overall belief in justice questionable. As many parents would likely attest, though critically important, punishment is not an enjoyable part of parenthood. A just society operates in much the same manner. Punishment for criminal wrongdoing is not an enjoyable part of our societal makeup. After 25 years in law enforcement, I know that I would gladly and readily live in a civilization in which no one violates the laws of the community and both victimization and the need for punishment disappear. Sadly, due to the inherent nature of human beings and the free will with which we are blessed, no such society appears anywhere on the horizon. As such, we are left with the stark realization that those who engage in criminal behavior must experience a significant enough punishment to ensure that not only do they avoid such behaviors in the future, but others in the community will observe these consequences and follow suit. With this in mind, it is the law enforcement officer, by the very nature of their title, who is called upon to enforce the laws of the community. While many may not like it, this is the mechanism of our criminal justice system.

Unlike the firefighter or EMT who bring the promise of rescue, the arrival of the police is not always welcomed with open arms, especially for those who have chosen to engage in criminal wrongdoing. The nature of their profession therefore causes law enforcement officers to frequently receive the brunt of society's ire, regardless of how professional the officer may act in discharging their duties. Too often, law enforcement officers serve as a reminder of that necessary, yet distasteful, part of our societal contract. As a result, pockets of our society will always hate the law enforcement officer for what they represent. For these individuals, the benefit of the doubt will always slant in the direction of the criminal actor and away from the individuals who have dedicated their lives to serving and protecting their communities, often at great costs to their families and their own well-being. This tendency is further fueled by the media which repeatedly jumps to anti-law enforcement conclusions before all facts are uncovered, as well as Hollywood, which has consistently come to glorify the criminal in productions like *The Sopranos*, *Dexter*, *Breaking Bad*, and shockingly a series entitled *Lucifer*. What is left is the knee-jerk response of many to blame law enforcement first, not only in instances of police use of force and police shootings, but also in the realm of criminal interrogation.

404

Like most occupations, law enforcement has become increasingly more professionalized as time has gone by. This is certainly true in the realm of criminal interrogation. Long gone are the days of the 'third degree' in which confessions were beaten out of criminal subjects. Even a cursory review of the Innocence Project vignettes will reveal the dated nature of their wrongful conviction cases. No longer do police point guns at the heads of subjects. No longer do police obtain confessions through the application of a nightstick to a subject's genitals. No longer do police elicit incriminating statements by suffocating subjects with plastic typewriter covers. These types of behaviors may make for exciting television, but they do not accurately represent the techniques of today's law enforcement interrogator. While this fact should be heralded by those in academia who study the false confession phenomenon, some have simply moved the goal post while simultaneously continuing to heap criticism upon interrogators. Instead of praising police for professionalizing their means of questioning, those like Ofshe and Leo (1997) or Trocino (2016) allege that interrogators have simply replaced their physical implements of torture with psychological abuses that conveniently avoid leaving scars on the subject. In other words, some in academia believe that law enforcement continues to torture interrogation subjects, but they now do so psychologically rather than physically. It is hard to interpret such claims as anything more than a pervasive worldview that law enforcement is, and always will be, wrong.

Are there bad police? Absolutely. Do some criminal interrogators go too far in their questioning of criminal subjects? Certainly. Still, despite the claims made by some academic researchers, expert witnesses, and advocates, this problem is not systemic. I have recently observed a billboard while driving on the interstate which read that medical mistakes are the third leading cause of death in the United States. If true, this is an obvious problem. Should this claim serve as a basis to begin removing doctors or banning medical procedures? I highly doubt that anyone is trumpeting such an idea. In fact, I am guessing that the billboard was probably created by an attorney looking to drum up clients for their medical malpractice business. The same form of advertising is likely true for many academics who conduct research into the false confession phenomenon and then repeatedly testify as expert witnesses on behalf of the defense. While I don't fault these individuals for attempting to make a living, I do criticize them for doing so by maligning the character of honorable law enforcement interrogators and the ethical and effective interrogative techniques they employ. Too many investigations have been solved, and too many guilty people have been removed from the streets to abandon the practice of criminal interrogation. If an interrogator has acted unethically, then attention should be drawn to that particular round of questioning. However, it is intellectually lazy, factually inaccurate, and conveniently and financially beneficial to false confession expert witnesses to blame an interrogative technique for causing false confessions. Have no doubt, this approach of some false confession expert witnesses is designed for no other reason than to cast doubt in the minds of the jury and to aid defense attorneys trying to overcome the damning confession of their client.

For too long, academia has controlled the false confession narrative. Law enforcement officers and prosecutors have unfortunately been too preoccupied by their efforts to bring justice to both victims and offenders to mount a meaningful defense against the unrelenting attack on criminal interrogation waged by some academics. It is my great hope that this book will start to balance the current one-sided argument and blaze a path for law enforcement interrogators, the *real* experts on criminal interrogation, to finally present their side of the story, a side of the story that is not based on theory and conjecture, but rather real-world experience and practical application. Still, this will not be an easy endeavor. The points made in this book will undoubtedly lead to temper tantrums within the academic community. In fact, I received a small, yet hyperventilating, sample of the anticipated academic response when this book was submitted for academic peer review. As noted by one academic peer reviewer, my positions against the existing false confession literature are like "arguing against the existence of climate change" or "arguing the earth is flat." As such, this reviewer cautioned that the book "should never see the light of publication." In light of such an emotional response and the apparent fear that seems to emanate from it, it is clear that some in academia have no interest in hearing a countervailing viewpoint, and certainly not from a career law enforcement officer. However, this does not mean that the conversation should not take place. A balance in the research is drastically overdue.

As parity is finally permitted in the false confession debate, it will readily become apparent that academia is replete with false assumptions about the problem of false confessions. For a great many of those in academia who have arrived at these false assumptions, it is important that you know that your research designs are flawed; your opinions about law enforcement are biased; and the conclusions you have reached about how law enforcement officers interrogate and effectively obtain confessions are largely inaccurate. It is long overdue that those employed within the American criminal justice system be made aware of these points and that prosecutors and law enforcement officers learn to push back against the flawed research and conclusions that have created the false confession expert witness industry.

REFERENCES

Ainsworth, P. B. (2002). *Psychology and policing.* Portland, OR: Willan Publishing.

Ali, M., & Levine, T. (2008). The language of truthful and deceptive denials and confessions. *Communication Reports, 21*(2), 82-91. doi:10.1080 /08934210802381862

American Psychiatric Association. (2020). *What is intellectual disability?* https://www.psychiatry.org/patients-families/intellectual-disability/ what-is-intellectual-disability

Aviv, R. (2017, June). Remembering the murder you didn't commit. *The New Yorker, 6(19)*, 1-16.

Baldwin, J. (1993). Police interview techniques: Establishing truth or proof? *British Journal of Criminology, 33,* 325-352.

Baseball Reference. (2020). *Career leaders & records for batting average.* Retrieve from: https://www.baseball-reference.com/leaders/batting_avg_career.shtml

Bering, J. M., & Shackleford, T. K. (2005). Evolutionary psychology and false confession. *American Psychologist, 60*(9), 1037-1038. doi:10.1037/0003-066X.60.9.1037

Bernhard, P. A., & Miller, R. S. (2018). Juror perceptions of false confessions versus witness recantations. *Psychiatry, Psychology and Law, 25*(4), 539-549. doi :10.1080/13218719.2018.1463874.

Bond, C. F., & DePaulo, B. M. (2006). Accuracy of deception judgments. *Personality and Social Psychology Review, 10*(3), 214-234. doi:10.1207/ s15327957pspr1003 _2

Bordens, K. S., & Abbott, B. B. (2008). *Research design and methods: A process approach* (7th ed.). New York, NY: McGraw Hill.

Bradford, D., & Goodman-Delahunty, J. (2008). Detecting deception in police investigations: Implications for false confessions. *Psychiatry, Psychology, and Law, 15,* 105-118. doi:10.1080/13218710701873932

Brady v. United States, 397 U.S. 742 (1970).

Bram v. United States, 168 U.S. 532 (1897).

Brandl, S. G. (2014). *Criminal investigation.* Thousand Oaks, CA: Sage.

Brown v. Mississippi, 297 U.S. 278 (1936).

Bull, R., & Soukara, S. (2009). Four studies of what really happens in police interviews. In G. D. Lassiter & C. Meissner (Eds.), *Police interrogations and confessions: Current research, practice and policy recommendations* (pp. 249-263). Washington, DC: American Psychological Association.

Chambers v. Florida, 309 U.S. 227 (1940).

Chapman, F. E. (2013). Coerced internalized false confessions and police interrogations: The power of coercion. *Law and Psychology Review, 37*, 159-209. doi:org/10 .2139/ssrn.2467049

Cole, T., Bruno Teboul, J. C., Zulawski, D. E., Wicklander, D. E., & Sturman, S. G. (2013). False confessions and the use of incriminating evidence. *Linguistic Evidence in Security, Law and Intelligence, 1*(1), 67-75. doi:10.5195/lesli.2013.4

Colorado v. Connelly, 479 U.S. 157 (1986).

Conti, R. P. (1999). The psychology of false confessions. *The Journal of Credibility Assessment and Witness Psychology, 2*(1), 14-36.

Creswell, J. W. (2013). *Qualitative inquiry and research design: Choosing among five approaches* (3rd ed.). Thousand Oaks, CA: Sage Publications.

Culombe v. Connecticut, 367 U.S. 568 (1961).

Davis, D., & Leo, R. A. (2012). Interrogation-related regulatory decline: Ego depletion, failures of self-regulation, and the decision to confess. *Psychology, Public Policy, and Law, 18*(4), 673-704.

Davis, D., & O'Donohue, W. T. (2004). The road to perdition: Extreme influence tactics in the interrogation room. In W.T. O'Donohue, P. R. Laws, & C. Hollins (Eds.), *Handbook of forensic psychology* (pp. 897-996). New York: Basic Books.

Department of Defense. (2016). *National Center for Credibility Assessment: About the PDD program*. Retrieved from http://www.ncca.mil/pdd_program_about.htm

Disastercenter.com. (2019). *United States Crime Rates 1960-2018*. Retrieved from http://www.disastercenter.com/crime/uscrime.htm

Drizin, S., & Colgan, B. (2004). Tales from the juvenile confession front: A guide to how standard police interrogation tactics can produce coerced and false confessions from juvenile suspects. In G. D. Lassiter (Ed.), *Interrogations, confessions, and entrapment*. New York: Kluwer Academic/Plenum Publishers.

Drizin, S. A., & Leo, R. A. (2004). The problem of false confession in the post-DNA world. *North Carolina Law Review, 82*, 891-1007.

Escobedo v. Illinois, 378 U.S. 478 (1964).

Evans, J. R., Schreber, S., Compo, N., & Russano, M. B. (2009). Intoxicated witnesses and suspects: Procedures and prevalence according to law enforcement. *Psychology, Public Policy, and Law, 15*, 194–221. doi:10.1037/a0016837

Federal Bureau of Investigation. (2016). Uniform crime reports. Retrieved from http://www.ucrdatatool.gov/search/crime/state/runcrimetrendsinonevar.cfm.

Forrest, K. D., Wadkins, T. A., & Larson, B. A. (2006). Suspect personality, police interrogations, and false confessions: Maybe it is not just the situation. *Personality and Individual Differences, 40,* 621-628. doi:10.1016/j.paid.2005 .09.002

Forrest, K. D., Wadkins, T. A., & Miller, R. L. (2002). The role of pre-existing stress on false confessions: An empirical study. *Journal of Credibility Assessment and Witness Psychology, 3,* 23-45 doi:10.1016/j.paid.2005.09.002

Forrest, K. D., Woody, W. D., Brady, S. E., Batterman, K. C., Stastny, B. J., & Bruns, J. A. (2012). False-evidence ploys and interrogations: Mock jurors' perceptions of false-evidence ploy type, deception, coercion, and justification. *Behavioral Sciences and the Law, 30,* 342-264. doi:10.1002/bsl.1999

Frankfort-Nachmias, C., & Nachmias, D. (2008). *Research methods in the social sciences* (7th ed.). New York, NY: Worth.

Frantzen, D. (2010). Interrogation strategies, evidence, and the need for Miranda: A study of police ideologies. *Police Practice and Research, 11*(3), 227-239. doi:10.1080/156142 60902830005

Frantzen, D., & Can, S. H. (2012). Police confidence in lie detection: An assessment of crime types, Miranda and interview techniques. *Journal of Criminal Psychology, 2*(1), 26-37. doi:10.1108/20093821211210477

Frazier v. Cupp, 394 U.S. 731 (1969).

Frenda, S. J., Berkowitz, S. R., Loftus, E. F., & Fenn, K. M. (2016). Sleep deprivation and false confessions. *PNAS, 113*(8) 2047-2050. doi:10.1073/ pnas.1521518113

Gaines, P. (2018). Discourse processes and topic management in false confession contamination by police investigators. *The International Journal of Speech, Language and the Law, 1,* 175-204. doi:10.1558//ijsll.34951

Garbus, L., Gibney, A., & Williams, R. R. (Executive Producers). (April 15, 2020). *The Innocence Files* [TV series]. Netflix.

Garrido, E., Masip, J., & Herrero, C. (2004). Police officers' credibility judgments: Accuracy and estimated ability. *International Journal of Psychology, 39,* 254-275. doi:10.1080 /00207590344000411

Gudjonsson, G. H. (1989). The psychology of false confessions. *The Medico-Legal Journal, 57,* 93-110. doi:10.1037/12085-002

Gudjonsson, G. H. (2010). The psychology of false confessions: A review of the current evidence. In G. D. Lassiter & C. A. Meissner (Eds.). *Police interrogations and false confessions: Current research, practice, and policy recommendations* (pp. 31-47). American Psychological Association.

Gudjonsson, G. H., Sigurdsson, J. F., Asgeirsdottir, B. B., & Sigfusdottir, I. D. (2006). Custodial interrogation, false confession and individual differences: A national study among Icelandic youth. *Personality and Individual Differences, 41,* 49-59. doi:10.1016/j.paid.2005.12.012

Gudjonsson, G. H., Sigurdsson, J. F., Asgeirsdottir, B. B., & Sigfusdottir, I. D. (2007). Custodial interrogation: What are the background factors associated with claims of false confession to police? *Journal of Forensic Psychiatry & Psychology, 18*(2), 266-275. doi:10.1080/ 14789940701284312

Gudjonsson, G. H., Sigurdsson, J. F., Bragason, O. O., Einarsson, E., & Valdimarsdottir, E. B. (2004). Confessions and denials and the relation-ship with personality. Legal and Criminological Psychology, 9, 121-133. doi:10.1348/135532504322776898

Gudjonsson, G. H., Sigurdsson, J. F., Bragason, O. O., Newton, A. K., & Einarsson, E. (2008). Interrogative suggestibility, compliance and false confessions among prisoners and their relationship with attention deficit hyperactivity disorder (ADHD) symptoms. *Psychological Medicine, 38*(7), 1037-1044. doi: http:// dx.doi.org/10.1017/ S0033291708002882

Gudjonsson, G. H., Sigurdsson, J. F., Sigurdardottir, A. S., Steinthorsson, H., & Sigurdardottir, V. M. (2014). The role of memory distrust in cases of internalised false confession. *Applied Cognitive Psychology, Applied Cognitive Psychology, 28,* 336-348. doi:10.1002/acp.3002

Gudjonsson, G. H., Sigurdsson, J. F., & Sigfusdottir, I. D. (2010). Interrogation and false confessions among adolescents: Differences between bullies and victims. *Journal of Psychiatry & Law, 38,* 57-76. doi:10.1177/009318531003800104

Gudjonsson, G. H., Sigurdsson, J. F., Sigfusdottir, I. D., Asgeirsdottir, B. B., Gonzalez, R. A., & Young, S. (2016). A national epidemiological study investi-gating risk factors for police interrogation and false confession among juveniles and young persons. *Social Psychiatry and Psychiatric Epidemiology, 51,* 359-367. doi:10.1007/s00127-015-1145-8

Gudjonsson, G. H., Sigurdsson, J. F., Young, S., Newton, A. K., & Peersen, M. (2009). Attention deficit hyperactivity disorder (ADHD). How do symptoms relate to personality among prisoners? *Personality & Individual Differences, 47,* 64-68.

Guest, G., Bunce, A., & Johnson, L. (2006). How many interviews are enough? An experiment with data saturation and variability. *Field Methods, 18*(1), 59-82.

Guyll, M., Madon, S., Yang, Y., Lannin, D. G., Scherr, K., & Greathouse, S. (2013). Innocence and resisting confession during interrogation: Effects on physiologic activity. *Law and Human Behavior, 37*(5), 366-375. doi:org/10.1037/lhb0000044

Haney-Caron, E., Goldstein, N. E. S., & Mesiarik, C. (2018). Self-perceived likelihood of false confession: A comparison of justice-involved juveniles and adults. *Criminal Justice and Behavior, 45*(12), 1955-1976. doi:10.1177/0093854818799806

Hartwig, M., Granhag, P. A., Stromwall, L. A., & Vrij, A. (2005). Detecting deception via strategic disclosure of evidence. *Law and Human Behavior, 29,* 469-484. doi:org/10.1007 /s10979-005-5521-x

Hasel, L. E. & Kassin, S. M. (2009). On the presumption of evidentiary independence: Can confessions corrupt eyewitness identification? *Psychological Science, 20,* 122-126. doi: 10.1111/j.1467-9280.2008.02262.x

Haynes v. Washington, 373 U.S. 503 (1963).

Henkel, L. A., Coffman, K. A. J., & Dailey, E. M. (2008). A survey of people's attitudes and beliefs about false confessions. *Behavioral Sciences and the Law, 26,* 555-584. doi:10.1002/bsl.826

Hilgendorf, E. L., & Irving, M. (1981). A decision-making model of confessions. In M. Lloyd-Bostock (Ed.), *Psychology in legal contexts: Applications and limitations* (pp. 67-84). London, MacMillan.

Hill, J. A., & Moston, S. (2011). Police perceptions of investigative interviewing: Training needs and operational practices in Australia. *British Journal of Forensic Practice, 13*(2), 72-83. doi:10.1108/14636641111134314

Horselenberg, R., Merckelbach, H., & Josephs, S. (2003). Individual differences and false confessions: A conceptual replication of Kassin and Kiechel (1996). *Psychology, Crime, and Law, 9,* 1-8. doi:10.1080/10683160308141

Inbau, F. E., Reid, J. E., Buckley, J. P., & Jayne, B. C. (2001). *Criminal interrogation and confessions* (4th d.). Gaithersburg, MD: Aspen.

Innocence Project. (2016). *The causes of wrongful conviction.* Retrieved from http://www.innocenceproject.org/causes-wrongful-conviction

Janda, S. (2015). Decision-making during interrogation: Towards a new approach for determining the propensity of deceptive police techniques to produce false confessions. *Lincoln Law Review, 43,* 79-110.

John Reid & Associates. (2015). Interviewing vs. interrogation. Retrieved from http://policetraining.net/blog/2012/04/18/interviewing-interrogation/

Johnson, M. B., & Drucker, J. (2009). Two recently confirmed false confessions: Byron A. Halsey and Jeffrey M. Deskovic. *Journal of Psychiatry and Law, 37,* 51-72. doi: 10.1002/bsl.2063

Joselow, M. (2019). Promise-induced false confessions: Lessons from promises in another context. *Boston College Law Review, 60*, 1641-1687.

Juvoren, J., Graham, S., & Schuster, M. A. (2003). Bullying among young adolescents: The strong, the weak, and the troubled. *Pediatrics, 112,* 1231-1237.

Kassin, S. M. (1997). The psychology of confession evidence. *American Psychologist, 52,* 221-233.

Kassin, S. M. (2005). On the psychology of confession: Does innocence put innocents at risk? *American Psychologist, 60,* 215-228.

Kassin, S. M. (2008). False confessions: Causes, consequences, and implications for reform. *Current Directions in Psychological Science, 17*(4), 249-253. doi: 10.1177/ 2372732214548678

Kassin, S. M. (2012). Why confessions trump innocence. *American Psychologist, 67*(6), 431-445. doi:10.1037/a0028212

Kassin, S. M., Appleby, S. C., & Torkildson Perillo, J. (2010). Interviewing suspects: Practice, science, and future directions. *Legal and Criminological Psychology, 15,* 39-55. doi:10.1348/135532509X449361

Kassin, S. M., Drizin, S. A., Grisso, T., Gudjonsson, G. H., Leo, R. A., & Redlich, A. D. (2010). Police-induced confessions: Risk factors and recommendations. *Law and Human Behavior, 34,* 3-38. doi:10.1007/s10979-009-9188-6

Kassin, S. M., & Fong, C. T. (1999). "I'm innocent!": Effects of training on judgments of truth and deception in the interrogation room. *Law and Human Behavior, 23*(5), 499-516. doi:0147-7307/99/1000-0499

Kassin, S. M., Goldstein, C. C., & Savitsky, K. (2003). Behavioral confirmation in the interrogation room: On the dangers of presuming guilt. *Law and Human Behavior, 27,* 187-203.

Kassin, S. M., & Gudjonsson, G. H. (2004). The psychology of confessions: A review of the literature and issues. *Psychological Science in the Public Interest, 5*(2), 33-67. doi: 10.1111/j.1529-1006.2004.00016.x

Kassin, S. M., & Kiechel, K. L. (1996). The social psychology of false confessions: Compliance, internalization, and confabulation. *Psychological Science, 7,* 125-128. doi: 10.1111/j. 1467-9280.1996.tb00344.x

Kassin, S. M., Leo, R. A., Meissner, C. A., Richman, K. D., Colwell, L. H., Leach, A-M., & LaFon, D. (2007). Police interviewing and interrogation: A self-report survey of police practices and beliefs. *Law & Human Behavior, 31,* 381–400. doi:10.1007/s10979-006-9073-5

Kassin, S. M., & McNall, K. (1991). Police interrogations and confessions: Communicating promises and threats by pragmatic implication. *Law and Human Behavior, 15,* 233-251. doi:0147-7307/91/0600-0233$06.50/0

REFERENCES

Kassin, S. M., Meissner, C. A., & Norwick, R. J. (2005). "I'd know a false confession if I saw one": A comparative study of college students and police investigators. *Law and Human Behavior, 29,* 211-227.

Kassin, S. M., & Norwick, R. J. (2004). Why people waive their Miranda rights: The power of innocence. *Law and Human Behavior, 28,* 211-221.

Kassin, S. M., Redlich, A. D., Alceste, F., & Luke, T. J. (2018). On the general acceptance of confessions research: Opinions of the scientific community. *American Psychologist, 73,* 63-80. doi:10.1037llamp0000141

Kassin, S. M., & Wrightsman, L. S. (1985). Confession evidence. In S. M. Kassin & L. S. Wrightsman (Eds.), *The psychology of evidence and trial procedure* (pp. 67-94). Beverly Hills, CA: Sage.

Kebbell, M. R., Hurren, E. J., & Roberts, S. (2006). Mock-suspects' decisions to confess: The accuracy of eyewitness evidence is critical. *Applied Cognitive Psychology, 20,* 477-486. doi:10.1002/acp.1197

Klaver, J. R., Lee, Z., & Rose, V. G. (2008). Effects of personality, interrogation techniques and plausibility in an experimental false confession paradigm. *Legal and Criminological Psychology, 13,* 71-88.

Kostelnik, J. O., & Reppucci, N. D. (2009). Reid training and sensitivity to developmental maturity in interrogation: Results from a national survey of police. Behavioral Sciences and the Law, 27, 361-379. www.interscience.wiley.com/doi:10.1002/bsl.871

Lackey, J. (2020). False confessions and testimonial injustice. *Journal of Criminal Law & Criminology, 110*(1), 43-68. doi:0091-4169/20/11001-0043

Lassiter, G. D. (2010). Psychological science and sound public policy: Video recording of custodial interrogations. *American Psychologist, November,* 768-779. doi:10.1037/0003-066X.65.8.768

Lassiter, G. D., & Meissner, C. A. (Eds.). (2010). *Police interrogations and false confessions: Current research, practice, and policy recommendations.* Washington, DC: American Psychological Association.

Leding, J. K. (2012). False memories and persuasion strategies. *Review of General Psychology, 16*(3), 256-268. doi:10.1037/a0027700

Lewis-Beck, M. S., Bryman, A., & Liao, T. F. (2004). Interrater reliability. In M. S. Lewis-Beck, A. Bryman, & T. F. Liao (eds.), *The SAGE Encyclopedia of Social Science Research Methods* (2, 513-514). SAGE.

Leo, R. A. (1996). Inside the interrogation room. *Journal of Criminal Law and Criminology, 86,* 266-303.

Leo, R. A. (2007). Police interrogation, false confessions, and alleged child abuse cases. *University of Michigan Journal of Law Reform, 50,* 693-721.

Leo, R. A., & Davis, D. (2010). From false confession to wrongful conviction: Seven psychological processes. *Journal of Psychiatry & Law, 38*, 9-56.

Leo, R. A., & Drizin, S. A. (2010). The three errors: Pathways to false confession and wrongful conviction. In G. D. Lassiter & C. Meissner (Eds.). *Police interrogations and false confessions: Current research, practice, and policy recommendations.* Washington, DC: American Psychological Association.

Leo, R. A., & Liu, B. (2009). What do potential jurors know about police interrogation techniques and false confessions? *Behavioral Sciences and the Law, 27*(3), 381-399. doi:10.1002/bsl.872

Leo, R. A., & Ofshe, R. J. (1997). The social psychology of police interrogations: The theory and classification of true and false confessions. *Studies in Law, Politics, & Society, 16*, 189-251.

Levine, T. R., Kim, R. K., & Blair, J. P. (2010). (In)accuracy at detecting true and false confessions and denials: An initial test of a projected motive model of veracity judgments. *Human Communication Research, 36*, 82-102.

Luteran Church in America. (1978). *Lutheran book of worship.* Minneapolis, MN: Augsburg Publishing House.

Malloy, L. C., Shulman, E. P., & Cauffman, E. (2014). Interrogations, confessions, and guilty pleas among serious adolescent offenders. *Law and Human Behavior, 38*(2), 181-193. DOI: 10.1037/lhb0000065

Manfredi, L. (2020, August 10). Philadelphia public school teacher worries about 'conservative' parents listening in on virtual classes. *Fox News.com.* https://www. foxnes.com/us/ Philadelphia-public-school-teacher-worries-about-conservative-parents-listening-in-on-virtual-classes

Mastroberardino, S., & Marucci, F. S. (2013). Interrogative suggestibility: Was it just compliance or a genuine false memory? *Legal Criminological Psychology, 18*, 274-286. DOI: 10.1111/j.2044-8333.2012.02048.x

Meissner, C. A., & Kassin, S. M. (2002). "He's guilty!: Investigator bias in judgments of truth and deception. *Law and Human Behavior, 26*, 469-480. doi: 0147-7307/02/1000-0469/1

Miranda v. Arizona, 384 U.S. 336 (1966).

Moston, S., & Engelberg, T. (2011). The effects of evidence on the outcome of interviews with criminal suspects. *Police Practice and Research, 12*(6), 518-526. doi:10/1080/ 15614263.2011.563963

Moston, S., Stephenson, G. M., & Williamson, T. M. (1992). The effects of case characteristics on suspect behavior during police questioning. *British Journal of Criminology, 32*, 23-40.

Munsterbeg, H. (1908). *On the witness stand.* Garden City, NY: Doubleday.

Najdowski, C. J. (2011). Stereotype threat in criminal interrogations: Why innocent black suspects are at risk for confessing falsely. *Psychology, Public Policy, and Law, 17*(4), 562-591. doi:10.1037/a0023741

Narchet, F. M., Meissner, C. A., & Russano, M. B. (2011). Modeling the influence of investigator bias on the elicitation of true and false confessions. Law and Human Behavior, 35, 452-465. doi: 10.1007/s10979-010-9257-x

Nash, R. A., & Wade, K. A. (2009). Innocent but proven guilty: Eliciting internalized false confessions using doctored-video evidence. *Applied Cognitive Psychology, 23*, 624-637. doi: 10.1002/acp.1500

National Center for Education Statistics. (2020). *Undergraduate retention and graduation rates.* Retrieved from: https://nces.ed.gov/programs/coe/indicator_ctr. asp#:~:text=The%206%2Dyear%20graduation%20rate%20was%2061%20 percent%20at%20public,at%20both%20public%20(64%20vs.

National Geographic. (2016). Shark Facts: Attack stats, record swims, more. Retrieved from http://news.nationalgeographic.com/ news/2005/06/0613_050613_sharkfacts.html

National Oceanographic and Atmospheric Administration. (2016). U.S. lightning fatalities since the 1940s. Retrieved from http://www.nws.noaa.gov/om/hazstats/ resources/ weather_fatalities.pdf

Neff, J. (2018, April 7). They did 30 years for someone else's crime. Then paid for it. *The New York Times.* https://nyti.ms/2EoFb9L

Newring, K. A. B., & O'Donohue, W. (2008). False confessions and influenced witnesses. *Applied Psychology in Criminal Justice, 4*(1), 81-107.

Nichols, M. P., & Zax, M. (1977). *Catharsis in psychotherapy.* New York, NY: Gardner Press.

North Carolina Coalition for Alternatives to the Death Penalty. (2020, May 2). *Henry McCollum & Leon Brown.* https://nccadp.org/ henry-mccollum-leon-brown/

Nurmoja, M., & Bachmann, T. (2008). On the role of trait-related characteristics in interrogative suggestibility: An example from Estonia. *Trames, 12*(62/57), 371-381. doi:10.3176/ tr.2008.4.01

Ofshe, R. J., & Leo, R. A. (1997). The decision to confess falsely: Rational choice and irrational action. *Denver University Law Review, 74,* 979-1122

O'Sullivan, M., Frank, M. G., Hurley, C. M., & Tiwana, J. (2009). Police lie detection: The effect of the lie scenario. *Law and Human Behavior,33*(6):542-3. doi: 10.1007/s10979-008-9166-4

Owen-Kostelnik, J., Reppucci, N. D., & Meyer, J. R. (2006). Testimony and interrogation of minors: Assumptions about maturity and morality. *American Psychologist, 61*(4), 286-304. doi:10.1037/00003-066X.61.4.286

Patton, M. Q. (2002). *Qualitative research and evaluation methods* (3rd ed.). Thousand Oaks, CA: Sage Publications.

Pearse, J., & Gudjonsson, G. H. (1996). Police interviewing techniques at two South London police stations. *Psychology, Crime and Law, 3,* 63-74. doi:10.1080/10683169608409795

Pennebaker, J. W. (1989). Confession, inhibition, and disease. *Advances in Experimental Social Psychology, 22,* 211-244. doi:10.101016/S0065-2601(08)60309-3

Perillo, J. T., & Kassin, S. M. (2011). Inside interrogation: The lie, the bluff, and false confessions. *Law and Human Behavior, 35,* 327-337. doi:10.1007/s10979-010-9244-2

Pimentel, P. S., Arndorfer, A., & Malloy, L. C. (2015). Taking the blame for someone else's wrongdoing: The effects of age and reciprocity. *Law and Human Behavior, 39*(3), 219-231. doi:10.1037/lhb0000132

Redlich, A. D. (2004). Law & Psychiatry: Mental illness, police interrogations, and the potential for false confession. *Psychiatric Services, 55*(1), 19-21. doi:10.1176/appi.ps.55.1.19

Redlich, A. D., & Goodman, G. S. (2003). Taking responsibility for an act not committed: The influence of age and suggestibility. *Law and Human Behavior, 27,* 141-156. doi:0147.73007/03104

Redlich, A. D., Kulish, R., & Steadman, H. J. (2011). Comparing true and false confessions among persons with serious mental illness. *Psychology, Public Policy, and Law, 17*(3), 394-418. doi:10.1037/a0022918

Redlich, A. D., Summers, A., & Hoover, S. (2010). Self-reported false confessions and guilty pleas among offenders with mental illness. *Law and Human Behavior, 34,* 79-90. doi:10.1007/s10979-009-9194-8

Russano, M. B., Meissner, C. A., Narchet, F. M., & Kassin, S. M. (2005). Investigating true and false confessions within a novel experimental paradigm. *Psychological Science, 16,* 481-486.

Schatz, S. J. (2018). Interrogated with intellectual disabilities: The risks of false confession. *Stanford Law Review, 70,* 643-690.

Schmid, P., & Betsch, C. (2019). Effective strategies for rebutting science denialism in public discussions. *Nature Human Behavior, 3,* 931-939. https://doi.org/10.1038/s41562-019-0632-4

REFERENCES

Shenton, A. K. (2004). Strategies for ensuring trustworthiness in qualitative research projects. *Education for Information, 22,* 63-75.

Sigurdsson, J. F., & Gudjonsson, G. H. (2001). False confessions: The relative importance of psychological, criminological and substance abuse variables. *Psychology, crime, and Law, 7,* 275-289.

Statista. (2020). *Share of electoral college and popular votes from each winning candidate, in all United States presidential elections from 1789 to 2016.* Retrieved from https://www.statista.com/statistics/1034688/share-electoral-popular-votes-each-president-since-1789/

Stewart, J. M., Woody, W. D., & Pulos, S. (2016). The prevalence of false confessions in experimental laboratory simulations: A meta-analysis. *Behavioral Science and Law, 36,* 12-31. doi:10.1002/bsl.2327

Swanner, J. K., & Beike, D. R. (2010). Incentives increase the rate of false but not true secondary confessions from informants with an allegiance to a suspect. *Law and Human Behavior, 34,* 418-428. DOI 10.1007/s10979-009-9212-x

Trocino, C. J. (2016). You can't handle the truth: A primer on false confessions. *University of Miami Race & Social Justice Law Review, 16*(1), 85-100.

United States v. Deuman, 892 F. Supp. 2d 881 (2012)

Villar, G., Arciuli, J., & Paterson, H. (2013). Linguistic indicators of a false confession. *Psychiatry, Psychology and Law, 4,* 504-518. doi:10.1080/13218719.2012.712834

Villar, G., Arciuli, J., & Paterson, H. (2014). Remorse in oral and handwritten false confessions. *Legal and Criminological Psychology, 19,* 255-269. doi:10.1111/lcrp.12012

Vrij, A., Fisher, R., Mann, S., & Leal, S. (2006). Detecting deception by manipulating cognitive load. *Trends in Cognitive Sciences, 10,* 141-142. doi:10.1016/j.tics.2006.02.003

Walsh, D., & Bull, R. (2010). What really is effective in interviews with suspects? A study comparing interviewing skills against interviewing outcomes. *Legal and Criminological Psychology, 15,* 305-321. doi:10.1348/135532509X463356

Walsh, D., & Bull, R. (2012). How do interviewers attempt to overcome suspects' denials? *Psychiatry, Psychology and Law, 19*(2), 151-168. doi:10.1080/13218719.2010.543756

Waxman, S. P. (2020). Innocent juvenile confessions. *The Journal of Criminal Law & Criminology, 110*(1), 1-8. doi:0091-4169/20/11001-0001

Whitbourne, S. K. (2011, October 22). *The essential guide to defense mechanisms. Can you spot your favorite form of self-deception?* Psychology Today. Retrieved from https://www.psychologytoday.com/us/blog/fulfillment-any-age/201110/the-essential-guide-defense-mechanisms

Wilford, M. M., & Wells, G. L. (2018). Bluffed by the dealer: Distinguishing false pleas from false confessions. *Psychology, Public Policy, and Law, 24*(2), 158-170. doi:10.1037/law0000165

Willen, R. M., & Stromwall, L. A. (2012a). Offenders' lies and truths: An evaluation of the supreme court of Sweden's criteria for credibility assessment. *Psychology, Crime & Law, 18,* 745-758. doi:10.1080/1068316X.2010.548815.

Willen, R. M., & Stromwall, L. A. (2012). Offenders' uncoerced false confessions: A new application of statement analysis. *Legal and Criminological Psychology, 17,* 346-359. doi: 10.11111/j.2044-8333.2011.02018x

Wisconsin Criminal Justice Study Commission. (2007). *Position paper of false confessions.* Madison, WI: Author.

Woestehoff, S. A., & Meissner, C. A. Juror sensitivity to false confession risk factors: Dispositional vs. situational attributions for a confession. *Law and Human Behavior, 40*(5), p. 564-579. doi: 10.1037/lhb00000201

Woody, W. D., & Forrest, K. D. (2009). Effects of false-evidence ploys and expert testimony on jurors' verdicts, recommended sentences, and perceptions of confession evidence. *Behavioral Sciences & the Law, 27,* 333-360. doi:10.1002/bsl.865

Woody, W. D., Stewart, J. M., Forrest, K. D., Camacho, L. J., Woestehoff, S. A., Provenza, K. P., Walker, A. T., & Powner, S. J. (2018). Effects of false-evidence ploys and expert testimony on jurors, juries, and judges. *Cogent Psychology, 5,* 1-22. doi:10.1080/23311908.2018.1528744

Zuckerman, M., DePaulo, B. M., & Rosenthal, R. (1981). Verbal and nonverbal communication of deception. In L. Berkowitz (Ed.), *Advances in experimental social psychology* (Vol. 14, pp. 1–59). New York: Academic Press.